The History of the Restoration Movement in Illinois in the 19th Century

James L. McMillan
Thomas H. Olbricht

SULIS
ACADEMIC
PRESS

An Imprint of Sulis International Press
Los Angeles I London

THE HISTORY OF THE RESTORATION MOVEMENT IN ILLINOIS IN THE
19th CENTURY
Copyright ©2019 by James L. McMillan and Thomas H. Olbricht
First Edition

Published by Sulis Academic Press
An imprint of Sulis International
Los Angeles and London
www.sulisinternational.com

Cover design by Sulis International Pressa
Photographs: top row, left to right: Clara Babcock, Barton W. Stone, Daniel Sommer.
Bottom row, left to right: John S. Sweeney, Walter S. Russell, D.P. Henderson.

Library of Congress Control Number: 9781946849564
ISBN (print): 978-1-946849-56-4
ISBN (eBook): 978-1-946849-57-1

Contents

McMillan and Olbricht have compiled an extremely valuable account of the complex formation and diversification of the Stone-Campbell Restoration movement in Illinois during its first century of existence. Though drawing extensively from earlier studies, the authors expand, contextualize and at times correct those treatments in useful ways. Charts spread among the chapters and in four appendices chronicle the history of Illinois congregations, key leaders and institutions. McMillan and Olbricht give readers glimpses into very human stories that illustrate how congregations served and fought. They also provide a fertile field for further investigation and interpretive work on numerous themes such as the history of African American churches in the state.

The authors have produced an indispensable reference for anyone wishing to examine Stone-Campbell history in Illinois, and how the state both shaped and was shaped by larger social and religious trends in the nation.

Douglas A. Foster, University Scholar in Residence
Abilene Christian University

McMillan and Olbricht provide an exhaustive history that will serve as an essential reference for Stone-Campbell history in Illinois for a long time, but it also functions as a microcosm of Stone-Campbell history in the United States because the book covers national themes and developments—the Second Great Awakening revivals and accompanying "exercises," the role of women, religious periodicals, colleges, instrumental music, African American history, theological liberalism, seeds of the Modernist-Fundamentalist controversy, and early calls for division from the "innovators." Moreover, the book is a treasure trove of primary and secondary sources on its topic.

James Gorman, Associate Professor of Church History
Johnson University

Acknowledgements

The authors express their appreciation to the following people for their assistance with our research:

The following people and their institutions provided access to Stone-Campbell items in their collections:

- Dan Boudreau, American Antiquarian Society.

- Shelley Jacobs and Rick Lowery, Disciples of Christ Historical Society.

- Mac Ice and Carisse Mickey Berryhill, Abilene Christian University.

- Scott Seay, Christian Theological Seminary.

- Nancy Olson and Mike Reid[1], Lincoln Christian University.

- Michael Bain, Point University.

- Bob Turner and Don Meredith, Harding School of Theology.

- Barry Jones and Tom Childers, for their ministry of providing digitized versions of Stone-Campbell works, especially periodicals.

- Richard H. Taylor, for sharing his unpublished materials on Christian Denomination conferences and congregations in Illinois.

Besides the authors, the Illinois Study Group included Bradley Cobb, David Kenney, Jan Staggs, Jim Kilson, Ken Christensen, Michael Moss, Nathan Soice, P. D. Odum and Steve Wolfgang. Ken Christensen and Jan Staggs were especially helpful throughout the project, asking questions and offering insights.

Last, but not least, we thank Markus McDowell, publisher, Sulis International Press, for his willingness to publish this volume.

---

[1] Mike passed away on November 8, 2016.

We dedicate this volume to our wives who have supported our research interests for many decades:

Barbara Guillory McMillan
Dorothy Kiel Olbricht

Table of Abbreviations for Sources[1]

ACR	American Christian Review
AT	Apostolic Times
BA	Bible Advocate (Illinois)
Barrett	*Centennial of Religious Journalism* (Christian Connexion)
BAT	Bible Advocate (edited by John R. Howard, in Tennessee and Missouri)
Boring	Eugene Boring, *Disciples and the Bible*
CA	Christian Age
CB	Christian Baptist
CE	Christian Evangelist (Iowa)
C-E	Christian-Evangelist (St. Louis)
CH	Christian Herald (Foster; Christian Connexion)
CHI	Christian Herald (Illinois)
CL	Christian Luminary (Christian Connexion)
CLead	Christian Leader
CM	Christian Messenger
CP	Christian Pioneer
CPall	Christian Palladium (Christian Connexion)
CR	Christian Record
CS	Christian Standard
CSent	Christian Sentinel (Illinois)
Cummins	D. Dwight Cummins, *Disciples Colleges*
D	Discipliana
E	Evangelist (Walter Scott)
EI	Evangelist (Iowa)
ESCM	Foster, et al., *Encyclopedia of the Stone-Campbell Movement*
FF	Firm Foundation
GA	Gospel Advocate
GE	Gospel Echo
GH	Williams, et al., *The Stone-Campbell Movement: A Global History*
Haynes	N. S. Haynes, *History of the Disciples of Christ in Illinois*
HGL	Herald of Gospel Liberty (Christian Connexion)
Humphreys	E. W. Humphreys, *Memoirs of Deceased Christian Ministers*
MH	Millennial Harbinger
NWCM	North-Western Christian Magazine
OR	Octographic Review
RQ	Restoration Quarterly
SCM	Stone-Campbell Movement
WE	Western Evangelist (Iowa)

---

[1] This list includes sources frequently cited but is not an exhaustive list of periodicals or books cited.

The History of the Restoration Movement In Illinois

Introduction

Illinois is ideal for a statewide study of the history of the American Restoration Movement. People with restorationist goals moved to and worked in the state even as early as Illinois became a territory in 1809, They arrived in increasingly larger numbers after Illinois gained statehood in 1818 but with an ever accelerating influx after 1825 with the opening of the Erie Canal, the National Road, which terminated in Vandalia, Illinois, and then railroads. Restorationists in the state have multiplied consistently from these early years to achieve noteworthy numbers.

Restorationists moved to Illinois from the four major trajectories, the (1) New England Jones/Smith Movement, (2) the Kentucky/Ohio Stone Movement, (3) the Pennsylvania/Kentucky/Ohio Campbell Reformers and (4) the O'Kelly movement from Virginia. The majority of the early Illinois migrants were from the Jones/Smith and the Stone Movements, but increasingly over the years from the Campbell Reformers. As far as is known migration from the O'Kelly movement was minimal. Through the decades to the present, whenever rifts appeared in the movement Illinois has hosted significant numbers of all the major divisions, that is, (1) the Disciples of Christ, (2) the Churches of Christ and (3) the Christian Church/Churches of Christ. Illinois has served as the home base for Restorationist colleges and religious journals. Nevertheless, the state has neither hosted the principle centers of influence for any of the groups from the earliest to the present nor has it produced the most influential leaders. Powerful leaders from all the groups have visited the state and Barton W. Stone lived in Jacksonville from 1834 until his death in 1844.

The study of Illinois is desirable and feasible because of the many extant sources of information. These include journals of the various groupings, historical lists of the various contingences, biographies and autobiographies, congregational and regions of Illinois histories, city and county histories and newspapers. Many of the needed resources are now

1

available on-line or have been digitized for this project, a substantial improvement over the past that required travel to the places where the sources were located. Furthermore, we have uncovered a coterie of history buffs intensely focused on the Restoration Movement in the state.

The Restorationist Trajectories

Before we set forth reflections regarding the multiple restorationists who arrived in Illinois it is crucial to attain a common perspective on the four foundational trajectories. The roots of the Restoration Movement extend backward to the period after the Revolutionary War in which several Americans with religious interests grew restless over autocratic structures, European control and theology, and denominational boundaries. These pressures revamped the mainline churches, but also resulted in independent constituencies springing up in various regions.[1]

The O'Kelly Movement

In Virginia in the 1780s, a group of Methodist ministers led by James O'Kelly (1757-1826) sought freedom from supervision so that Methodist circuit riders could determine their own itinerancy. For a time it seemed they would succeed, but the outcome was that preaching assignments were placed in the hands of the Bishop. Those who favored self-determination broke away, founding the Republican Methodist Church. In 1794 they changed the name of the body to the Christian Church. O'Kelly emphasized the authority of Scripture over creeds and the headship of Christ.

---

[1] The below items constitute a basic bibliography for the Restoration Movement. *The Encyclopedia of the Stone-Campbell Movement*, eds. Douglas A. Foster, Paul M. Blowers, Anthony L. Dunnavant and D. Newell Williams (Grand Rapids: William B. Eerdmans Publishing, 2004) 212-220. *The Stone-Campbell Movement: A Global History*, eds. D. Newell Williams, Douglas A. Foster, Paul M. Blowers (St. Louis: Chalice Press, 2013). David Edwin Harrell, *Quest For A Christian America: The Disciples Of Christ And American Society To 1866* (Nashville: Disciples of Christ Historical Society, 1966) and *The Social Sources of Division in the Disciples of Christ 1865 to 1900* (Atlanta: Publishing Systems, 1973); Leroy Garrett, *The Stone-Campbell Movement: An Anecdotal History of Three Churches* Joplin, Mo.: College Press Publishing Co., 1981, rev. 1994). See also the accurate and fair assessment of the movement written by a Roman Catholic: Richard M. Tristano, *The Origins of the Restoration Movement: An Intellectual History* (Atlanta: Glenmary Research Center, 1988).

"All may see what I am at, I wish the divine Saviour to be the only head and governor of the Church, her law and center of union. I wish all the faithful followers of our Lord to love one another with a pure heart fervently. Let them break down the middle wall of partition; and all break bread together."[2]

Before the turn of the century, preachers from this movement were traveling into the Carolinas and making their way through the Cumberland Gap into Kentucky and Tennessee. They also went west to the Ohio River and migrated into Ohio and Indiana.

The Jones/Smith Movement

In New England, especially in the newly developing regions of New Hampshire and Vermont, persons of Baptist heritage, chiefly Abner Jones (1772-1841) and Elias Smith (1769-1846) formed new churches. Smith founded the significant journal the *Herald of Gospel Liberty* (1808-1922). The congregations went by the name Christian, or Christian Connexion. They championed defeat of tax support for establishment ministers (Congregational), and rejected Calvinistic or Puritan theology in regard to election and predestination. The Bible was heralded, especially the New Testament, as the only source of authority and faith. These New England leaders contended that Christians should cut adrift from historical encrustations so as to create the New Testament church in its first-century purity. Members commenced migrating into upper New York after 1810, where they became especially strong, then Ohio, Indiana, Illinois and Michigan.[3]

Second generation preachers from New York now moved to the forefront including David Millard (1794-1873), Joseph Badger (1792-1852) both who lived in central New York and Simon Clough (1793-1844) of

---

[2] W. E. MacClenny, *The Life of Rev. James O'Kelly and the Early History of the Christian Church in the South*, (Raleigh, Va.: Edwards and Broughton Printing Company, 1910), 250.

[3] A. Jones, *Memoirs of the Life and Experience, Travels and Preaching of Abner Jones* (1807); A. D. Jones, *Memoirs of Elder Abner Jones* (1842). Thomas H. Olbricht, "Christian Connexion and Unitarian Relationships 1800-1844) RQ (1966) 160-186. Milo True Morrill, *A History of the Christian Denomination in America* (1911), Michael G. Kenny, *The Perfect Law of Liberty: Elias Smith and the Providential History of America* (1994), Elias Smith, *The Life, Conversion, Preaching, Travel, and Sufferings of Elias Smith* (Portsmouth: Beck & Foster, 1816).

Boston all of whom battled Trinitarianism. Because of their views on the Trinity they had contacts with the Unitarians, and were declared partners in the operation of Meadville Theological Seminary, but their contribution was negligible. They also founded new journals: the *Gospel Luminary* (1825-32) and the *Christian Palladium* (1832-1860).

The two most important tributaries for the larger Stone-Campbell-Scott Movement resulted from the work of Barton W. Stone (1772-1844), the two Campbells, Thomas (1763-1854) and Alexander (1788-1866), father and son and Walter Scott (1796-1861).

The Stone Movement

We will first consider Barton W. Stone. At the turn of the century the second great awakening titillated the Kentucky and Ohio frontiers. Camp meetings sprang up throughout the region, the largest extravaganza being the 1801 Cane Ridge, Kentucky, northeast of Lexington. Denominational barriers crumbled and the call to struggle followed by conversion, diluted traditional election theology. As the weeks extended into months, some of the preachers, especially among the Presbyterians, favored the ecumenical atmosphere created as they worked with other groups in the revivals. They thereupon formed an independent presbytery in which Barton W. Stone was a participant. Not too long after, carrying these interests to their logical conclusion, they dissolved the Springfield Presbytery in order to "sink into union with the body of Christ at large." These leaders found many frontiersmen ready to embrace their sentiments and rapid growth ensued.

Barton W. Stone, a Presbyterian minister at Cane Ridge and Concord, Kentucky, sent out the invitation for the great camp meeting at Cane Ridge. Stone was born in Maryland, and then lived in North Carolina before migrating to Kentucky. By 1810 he had emerged as the chief spokesman for those who had embraced the dissolving of the Springfield Presbytery. The five ministers of the Presbytery published "The Last Will and Testament of the Springfield Presbytery" in 1804. Those who did so, at the suggestion of Rice Haggard who had prior to this convinced the O'Kelly group to call their churches "Christian," designated their congregations Christian Churches.[4] These three trajectories of Christians high lighted Holy Spirit conversion, the mourners bench, conferences of

---

[4] D. Newell Williams, *Barton Stone: A Spiritual Biography* (St. Louis: Chalice Press, 2000), "Autobiography of Barton W. Stone (1847)" *Voices from Cane Ridge*, ed. Rhodes Thompson (St Louis: Bethany Press, 1954).

preachers, quarterly celebration of the Lord's Supper, and anti-trinitarianism thereby frequently conflicting with Campbell-Scott-Scott commitments.

A subset of the Stone Christians was known as the Mulkeyites. Phillip Mulkey, a son of the restorationist patriarch John Mulkey (1773-1844), founded Mulkeytown, Illinois, in 1836 in south central Franklin County, and evangelized in the region. The Mulkeys were Baptists from South Carolina, moved to Tennessee and then to Kentucky. Several of the Mulkeys were preachers. They commenced questioning predestination and eternal security, became separated from the Baptists, and later associated with the Stoneites. They decided in 1809 to go by the Bible alone and designated their congregation The Old Mulkey Christian Church.[5]

The Campbell-Scott Movement

In 1807 Thomas Campbell, born in North Ireland of Scottish descent, arrived in Pennsylvania, settling in Washington County. Long a Presbyterian minister, he exerted considerable energy in the land of his nativity in promoting evangelism and missions and afterward got caught up in a struggle to unify dissident Presbyterian groups. His efforts at similar rapprochement in Pennsylvania resulted in litigation to oust him from the Presbytery. Seeing the handwriting on the wall, he resigned and with others of like-mind, formed the Christian Association of Washington, Pennsylvania. The foundational document of this group which Campbell authored was *The Declaration and Address*, 1809. In this document Campbell set forth his vision for a restored church.

> Our desire, therefore, for ourselves and our brethren would
> be, that, rejecting human opinions and the inventions of
> men as of any authority, or as having any place in the
> Church of God, we might forever cease from further con-
> tentions about such things; returning to and holding fast by
> the original standard; taking the Divine word alone for our
> rule; the Holy Spirit for our teacher and guide, to lead us
> into all truth; and Christ alone, as exhibited in the word, for
> our salvation; that, by so doing, we may be at peace among

---

[5] *ESCM*, 547-48.

ourselves, follow peace with all men, and holiness, without which no man shall see the Lord.[6]

In 1809, his gifted son Alexander arrived with the rest of Thomas' family after a stint at the University of Glasgow. Out of the Campbells' efforts, churches were formed in the region around Pittsburgh. After 1816, the Campbells joined with Baptist ministers of the Redstone and a decade later the Mahoning Associations, winning several Ohio and Kentucky Baptist churches to their outlooks. The Campbells envisioned a mass exodus of believers from sectarian Protestantism so as to become one body—one New Testament church.

Early in the 1830s the churches from the Stone and Campbell-Scott groups commenced merging in Kentucky. The amalgamation expanded to churches in Pennsylvania, Ohio, Virginia, Tennessee, Indiana, Illinois, Arkansas and Missouri. Several churches from the New England Jones-Smith, and Virginia O'Kelly movement in these mid-west regions also became a part of the Stone-Campbell-Scott merger. After the Civil War the Christian Connexion churches that did not merge established headquarters in Dayton, Ohio. In 1931 they merged with the Congregational Church, then with the Evangelical and Reformed Church, to form in 1957 the United Church of Christ.

By 1850 Alexander Campbell, because of his journal editing, book publishing, debating, lecturing, and founding of Bethany College, in West Virginia, became the best known leader of the movement. His outlooks left a permanent stamp on all his descendants regardless of location on the theological spectrum. Thomas and Alexander Campbell were highly influenced by the Scottish Enlightenment that emphasized reason as opposed to enthusiasm. The Campbells highlighted exterior constructs in regard to the church, as opposed to inner feeling. They modified their reform views, that is, the heritage of John Calvin (1509-1564) accordingly, though remaining far more Reformed than they themselves recognized.[7]

Alexander set forth what he declared to be the focus of the restoration churches in his "Prefatory Remarks" to the 1850 Millennial Harbinger. In

---

[6] *Declaration and Address* reprinted in: Charles Young, *Historical Documents Advocating Christian Union* (Chicago: The Christian Century Company, 1904) 73-74.

[7] Robert Richardson, *Memoirs of Alexander Campbell* (Cincinnati: Standard Publishing, 1913), Lester G. McAllister, *Thomas Campbell: Man of the Book* (St. Louis: Bethany Press, 1954). For the British years of Thomas Campbell, see: James L. Gorman, *Among the Early Evangelicals: The Transatlantic Origins of the Stone-Campbell Movement* (Abilene, TX: ACU Press, 2017)

looking back over twenty-eight years of editing, Campbell was expansive as he surveyed the advance of restorationism through most of the English speaking world.

> "...the earth has been almost girdled with advocates, calling upon their contemporaries to enquire for the old paths, and beseeching them to walk in them."[8]

Campbell was at that time sixty-two years old and in a reflective mood. He proceeded to set fourth the fundamental platform of the movement in five topics: (1) "The Bible, the whole Bible, and nothing but the Bible," (2) "Jesus Christ himself being the chief corner stone," (3) "on this rock I will build my church," (4) the voice of the "Messiah and his Apostles" that is, the New Testament, and (5) "organized effort" that is, churches working together on cooperative projects.

Walter Scott (1796-1861) directed the Stone-Campbell-Scott Movement into an approach to evangelism that procured many new converts. Scott was born in Moffatt, Dumfriesshire, Scotland. He studied at the University of Edinburgh from 1812 to 1818. Upon completion of his studies he migrated to the United States seeking employment as a teacher. After teaching on Long Island he moved westward and accepted a position at a school founded by George Forrester in Pittsburgh, Pennsylvania. It was there he met and was impressed by Alexander Campbell in 1819. After Forrester died Scott took over the school. But soon he turned to preaching and left Pittsburgh for eastern Ohio.[9]

A turning point came in Scott's career in 1827 when he attended the annual meeting of the Mahoning, Ohio, Baptist Association to which Thomas and Alexander Campbell belonged. The Association bemoaned the small number of its acquisitions and voted to appoint Walter Scott as evangelist for the Association. Whereas in 1826 less than 100 new members were added, Walter Scott baptized over 1000 in his first year of preaching. Scott believed his chief contribution to the fledgling Restoration Movement was his clarity in presenting the "Ancient Gospel." This gospel was defined by the gospel plan of salvation, something Scott also designated as "the first principles of the Gospel." What was required was not a Holy Spirit conversion, but a hearing of the Gospel preached and obedience to the requirements found in Scriptures. According to Scott the Gospel plan of salvation consists of duties and privileges.

---

[8] MH. 1850, p. 3.

[9] *Walter Scott: A Nineteenth-Century Evangelical*, ed. Mark G. Toulouse (St. Louis: Chalice Press, 1999).

Duties
1. Faith. 2. Repentance. 3. Baptism

Privileges
1. Remission of Sins. 2. The Holy Spirit. 3. Eternal Life

Over the next few years all the preachers of the Stone-Campbell-Scott movement pleaded with auditors to accept these terms of the Gospel and thus be received by God. Scott's proclamation was the mode of evangelism the Stone-Campbell-Scott brought into Illinois.

Scott set forth in his book *The Gospel Restored* what he considered the accomplishments of the Restoration Movement.

> The present century, then, is characterized by these three successive steps, which the lovers of our Lord Jesus have been enabled to make, in their return to the original institution. First, the Bible was adopted as sole authority in our assemblies, to the exclusion of all other books. Next the Apostolic order was proposed. Finally the True Gospel was restored.[10]

The true Gospel focuses upon Jesus.

> JESUS—First, the grand fundamental proposition, "Is Jesus the Christ." He who would be master of assemblies must discuss this, times and ways without number: then his natural character as Son of God: then his official character, as prophet, priest, and king; the principles of the Ancient Gospel, beginning with faith; the Ancient Order, beginning with the article of worship, & birth, life, ministry, poverty, zeal, obedience, humiliation, transfiguration, trial, confession, condemnation, death, burial, and resurrection, ascension, glorification in heaven, the prophecies, miracles, with the external and internal evidences of our religion.[11]

---

[10] Walter Scott, *The Gospel Restored: A Discourse of the True Gospel of Jesus Christ, in which the Facts, Principles, Duties, and Privileges of Christianity are Arranged, Defined, and Discussed, and the Gospel in its various Parts Shown to be Adapted to the Nature and Necessities of Man in his Present Condition* (Cincinnati: Ormsby H. Donogh, 1836), v. vi.

[11] Scott, *The Evangelist* (2 April 1832), 104.

It is important to keep these multifaceted backgrounds in mind as we proceed to set out the beginnings of the Restoration Movement in Illinois. These varied groups embraced the authority of the New Testament, non-creedalism, the death of Christ for the sins of the world, evangelism, the importance of immersion, and congregational independence. These beliefs were central to their preaching, teaching, and worshiping in Illinois in the nineteenth century.

N. S. Haynes as Historian

Any work on the Stone-Campbell Movement in Illinois in the nineteenth century must begin with and rely heavily upon Nathaniel Smith Haynes 1915 history.[12] The reader will quickly see that we quote extensively from Haynes. Our work, however, is not a "second edition" of Haynes. We have these advantages over him:

1. Electronic, full text access to his book enabled us to search word for word for key expressions. We have been able to pull together data in ways he did not, with the goal of making what we hope are helpful observations.[13]

2. The major Illinois, regional and national periodicals of the Stone-Campbell and related movements are digitized and priced reasonably. From our research of these materials, we were able to provide details that Haynes did not know[14] or chose not to provide.[15]

3. The digitization of the periodicals has provided easy access to the thousands of obituaries published therein. Biographical information in online databases such as Find A Grave, Ancestry and scores of genealogical web sites as well as in the hundreds of online county histories means that the lives (and deaths) of our forebears can be chronicled. Regarding biographical information, Haynes (11) regretted:

---

[12] Nathaniel S. Haynes, *History of the Disciples of Christ in Illinois 1819 – 1914* (Cincinnati: The Standard Publishing Company, 1915) 670 pages; numerous portraits of individuals and photographs of buildings.

[13] https://Archive.org has five copies of the book, with more than 10,000 views spread between the copies.

[14] The *Christian Freeman* periodical, for example. See Chapter 8.

[15] Illinois conservative congregations and preachers. See Appendix 4.

The preparation of the biographies has been no less difficult. It is painfully deficient both in the subjects and in their
fair proportions of treatment. Without doubt the names of
some who are not mentioned should appear, while some of
those who do appear should have received less and others
larger notice. Many deserving younger men have been
crowded out.

Claude Spencer records that chronologically Haynes's Illinois history is
the sixth state history published by SCM historians, preceded by histories
of the Western Reserve (1875), Kansas (1883), Missouri (1888), and Virginia (1905).[16] Of these histories, in our opinion, Haynes is the better
organized and most comprehensive, reflecting the effort he made to collect the information. We wholeheartedly concur with Haynes' belief in
his Foreword about his efforts:

It is believed that this volume will be a source of valuable
information and joyful inspiration to many multitudes.[17]

For additional bibliography see: William E. Tucker and Lester G. McAllister, *Journey
in Faith* (St. Louis: Bethany Press, 1975) the standard history for the Disciples of
Christ. Mark G. Toulouse, *Joined in Discipleship:The Shaping of Contemporary Disciples
Identify*, 1997. *Yearbook and Diretory of the Disciples Christ.* (Annual) For the Christian
Churches/Churches of Christ (NACC) the references are James DeForest Murch,
Christians Only (Cincinnati: Standard Publishing Co., 1962) and James B. North,
Union in Truth: An Interpretive History of the Restoration Movement (Cincinnati: Standard
Publishing, 1994). Henry E. Webb, *In Search of Christian Unity: A History of the
Restoration Movement*, 2003, Zella McLean, ed. *Directory of the Ministry: A Yearbook of
Christian Churches and Churches of Christ*, published annually. The books available
concerning the Churches of Christ, include, Earl West, *Search for the Ancient Order*
(Vol. I, Nashville: The Gospel Advocate Co., 1949; Vol. II, Indianapolis: Religious
Book Service, 1950; Vol. III, Indianapolis: Religious Book Service, 1979; Vol. IV,
1988); Robert E. Hooper, *A Distinct People: A History of Churches of Christ in the
Twentieth Century* (Nashville: The Gospel Advocate Company, 1993); Richard T.

16 Claude E. Spencer, "[Review of] *Florida Christians" Discipliana* 1.4 (December 1941)
35.
17 Haynes, 11.

Hughes, *Reviving the Ancient Faith: The Story of Churches of Christ in America* (Grand Rapids: William B. Eerdmans, 1996). For the demographics of the membership of the Churches of Christ in the United States, see Carl H. Royster, compiler, *Churches of Christ in the United States Inclusive of Her Commonwealth and Territories 2006 Edition* (Nashville: 21st Century Christian, 2012).

1. Beginnings in Illinois

We will begin our narrative with observations on the peopling of Illinois by persons of European ancestry. We will first consider dates, travel modes, and regions of origin. We will next focus on the early arrival of the various Christian groups that gained a toe hold in early Illinois history.

Immigration to Illinois

The territory of Illinois was established in 1809 and statehood in 1818. The population of Illinois in 1810 was 12,282 and in 1820 had grown more than fourfold to 55,211. By 1830 the state had acquired 157,485 residents. Indians were still a threat in 1830, but the Blackhawk War of 1832 along the Illinois River in the north essentially ended the hostilities.[1] A number of immigrants arriving in Illinois came from the Northeast, the middle colonies and Ohio and Kentucky and they brought with them their Christian Connexion perspectives and planted churches. These were the people from the Jones/Smith and Stone movements described in the introduction. We will discuss at greater length their settlement as well as that of those from the Campbell-Scott reformers in Chapter 2.

The earliest settlers in Illinois were French Canadian fur trappers. They traveled the northern waterway through the Great Lakes beginning at Lake Ontario and ending in Lake Michigan. They gave French names to several Illinois cities, including Joliet, Des Plaines, LaSalle, and East St. Louis. Congregationalists and Presbyterians from the Northeast in the United States likewise traveled the St. Lawrence Waterway and through the Great Lakes. Some of the Christians from the Jones-Smith movement followed the identical route.

Those from farther south including the Methodists, Baptists and adherents of the O'Kelly and Stone movements came by rivers that emp-

---

[1] https://en.wikipedia.org/wiki/History_of_Illinois; Douglas K. Meyer, *Making the Heartland Quilt: a Geographical History of Settlement and Migration in Early-Nineteenth Century Illinois* (Carbondale: Southern Illinois Press, 2000).

tied into the Ohio. Not long after they passed Evansville, IN, on the Ohio River between there and Paducah, KY they arrived at the mouth of the Wabash River flowing down from Terre Haute, IN. The Wabash from Terre Haute to the Ohio River formed the boundary between Indiana and Illinois. Several persons who moved to Illinois employed barges on the Ohio then took packet boats up the Wabash to the Illinois counties that adjoined the Wabash. Rivers running through Kentucky emptied into the Ohio including the Kentucky River that entered above Louisville and the Tennessee River just east of Paducah. Those who lived in central Tennessee traveled down the Cumberland River. The Cumberland joined the Tennessee River not far south of the Ohio.

Steam boats entered the mix of available river transportation in these early years. Robert's Fulton's steamboat ran a service on the Hudson River between New York and Albany in 1807. Henry Shreve, after whom Shreveport, Louisiana, was named, started building small steamboats in Brownsville, Pennsylvania, in 1813. Shreve took his steamboat the Enterprise from Pittsburgh to New Orleans and back. By 1819 thirty-one steamboats were plying the rivers, many between Pittsburgh and New Orleans but even on up the Mississippi and the Arkansas and Missouri Rivers.[2] The Midwest became accessible by regularly scheduled boats to those who could pay the fare.

Most of the people in Wabash County, where the earliest churches were founded, came by the rivers. Haynes, who published the earliest comprehensive history on the Disciples of Christ in Illinois, reported, "Joseph Wood came to the settlement [Barney's Prairie] about 1815. Ira Keen and others came from Ohio, New York, Virginia and Kentucky all by the rivers."[3]William Barney who helped found one of the earliest congregations in Illinois at Barney's Prairie took the river route.

> William Barney, with his family, left the banks of the Genesee River, in New York, in 1808. They came by raft down the Ohio River to the mouth of the Wabash. There the raft was sold and a keel-boat bought. In this they pushed upstream to Ramsey's Rapids, afterward the site of Bedell's Mill. This was eight miles up-river from the site of Mt. Carmel. His family consisted of

---

[2] Paul Schneider, *Old Man River: The Mississippi River in North American History* (New York: Henry Holt and Company, 2013) 246-250. Louis A. Garavaglia, *To the Wide Missouri: Traveling in America during the first Decades of Westward Expansion* (Yardley, PA: Westholme, 2011).

[3] Haynes, 417

Mr. Barney, his wife and his twelve children and three sons-in-law. The male members of the family struck out through the forest to find a place on which to build their cabins. They reached a beautiful stretch of land, covered with grass ten feet high, and afterward known as Barney's Prairie. Shortly afterward came Mr. Barney's three sons-in-law. They were Ranson Higgins, Philo Ingram and William Aldridge.[4]

Most of the people who settled along the Wabash and inland came from Kentucky, Ohio and Indiana, but a few came from Tennessee. A Restorationist congregation in Johnson County near the southern tip of Illinois, Bethlehem (Vienna) founded in 1847 was made up predominantly of Tennesseans.

This is thought to be the oldest church of Christ in the county. Many of the people of the neighborhood came from Middle Tennessee, as did Minister Wooten also. The first meetings were held in a brush arbor. Then a log house was built. In later years this gave way to a comfortable frame building.[5]

About this time several persons moved into Illinois from Tennessee because of their opposition to slavery.

Railroads

Somewhat later the railroads helped transport newcomers to the "Prairie State." It was only after the 1840s that they made a significant contribution to the arrival of migrants and the development of the state. As early as 1832 the Lieutenant-Governor Alexander M. Jenkins proposed a railway through central Illinois from Cairo to the Illinois and Michigan Canal. A charter was granted by the Illinois Legislatures in 1836 under the name Wabash and Mississippi Railroad the forerunner of the Illinois Central Railroad, with Governor Jenkins as President of the Company. The company gave up the charter the next year and the state undertook construction but without completing any section of the line. In 1843 the line was incorporated as the "Great Western Railway company but little was constructed and the charter was repealed in 1845. It wasn't until 1850 that Senator Douglas introduced a bill in the United States Senate giving land along a railroad from Cairo to Duluth that became the basis of the

---

[4] Ibid., 415.
[5] Ibid., 238.

Illinois Central Railroad. The earliest section was opened in the Chicago area in 1852. The entire road (705.5 miles) was finally completed, Sept. 27, 1856.[6]

It seems that the first railroad was the Galena and Chicago Union that began operation in 1849. Several other short lines soon followed. The Chicago, Burlington and Quincy railroad became operational in the early 1850s going through Aurora, Mendota, Galesburg and on to Quincy. By the end of the nineteenth century railroads traversed most of the state of Illinois.

The earliest settlers established their homesteads near wooded streams. The trees provided logs for houses and shade in the heat of the summer. They also sheltered birds and wild turkeys as well as fur animals and deer. Some coal was discovered along river banks but it wasn't until the 1840s that it was mined beneath the surface in the East St. Louis area.

> The first discovery of coal in North America was in Illinois by Marquette and Joliet. In 1673, they observed and recorded coal outcrops along the Illinois River. However, it wasn't until the 1800's that the settlers first mined outcropped coal for black-smithing and other domestic uses. It took underground mining a few more years to get started, but by 1848, Belleville became home to the first underground mining operation.[7]

For the earliest settlers fire wood was the fuel of choice and therefore living out on the open prairie had little appeal.

Log church buildings likewise were often the meeting houses normally built by the early migrants to Illinois. A church was established at Hallsville (Formerly Old Union) in DeWitt County in 1832. It started out under trees and eventually moved into a log-cabin building and finally a wooded frame building was constructed.

> Under the spreading branches of a large white-oak tree, he constituted this congregation on October 13 the second Sunday of the month with seventeen charter members. It was composed mainly of the Bowles and Hall families. A part, and probably all, of these first members were turned to the Lord at Caneridge,

---

6 Kim Torp, "Illinois Railroads in 1901 (Including Chicago-based)" *Historical Encyclopedia of Illinois*, 1901. http://genealogytrails.com/ill/cook/railroads.html; Simon Cordery, *The Iron Road in the Prairie State: the Story of Illinois Railroading* (Bloomington: Indiana University Press, 2016).
7 http://www.imsif.com/about-mine-subsidence/history-of-mining-in-illinois

Kentucky…The first meetings were held in the log-cabin homes of the people and in groves…The first chapel was built of logs in 1838. It was used jointly by the Disciples, Baptists and Methodists. This fact gave the word "Union" to this place of public worship. As the years passed, "Old" was added. In 1864 a frame building, with a seating capacity of six hundred and costing $3,000, was erected. This was owned and used by the church of Christ only.[8]

The various places of meeting are also reported at the Table Grove congregation in Fulton County founded in 1851.

After years of meetings in residences, barns, schoolhouses and groves, the chapel was completed in 1868 and dedicated by John S. Sweeney. Later this was replaced by a modern building.[9]

Clearly the trees provided an important context for living and worshipping.

Prior Religious Denominations

In order to appreciate the religious climate in which the early Restorationists found themselves, it is important to give some attention to the earliest beginnings of other church groups in Illinois.

Roman Catholics

The earliest settlers of European descent in Illinois were French Canadians who traveled the St. Lawrence Seaway through the Great Lakes then down the Illinois River. The French Roman Catholic explorers commenced founding parishes in Illinois in the late seventeenth century. Jacques Marquette, a priest, established a church at Kaskaskia on the Mississippi River south of St. Louis in 1675. A later mission point, Guardian Angel, was founded near Chicago in 1676. In 1699 a more permanent congregation was planted at Cahokia just south of East St. Louis. The numbers of Catholics continued to increase until statehood in 1818 but especially later in the nineteenth century with the migration of Irish, Ital-

---

[8] Haynes, 176, 177.
[9] Ibid., 210.

ians and Poles.[10] The Roman Catholics immigrants to Illinois formed the earliest Christian churches in Illinois. These were soon followed by the Methodists, Baptists and Presbyterians.

Methodists

The earliest Methodists came in the late 1700's. They mostly came through Kentucky though born in Virginia, Scotland, and Georgia. The first was likely Joseph Ogle, who, though born in Virginia, came from Kentucky in 1787. [11] He had settled in St. Clair County near St. Louis in 1785. The first preacher who was a Methodist when he arrived was Joseph Lillard who came from Kentucky in 1793. In 1798 John Clark, born in Inverness, Scotland, but then living in South Carolina, made his way to Illinois. He had spent time with John Wesley and left South Carolina because he despised slavery. In 1811 he became a Baptist. Hosea Rigg was said to be the first local Methodist preacher in Illinois. He had moved to St. Clair County in 1797. William Scott was born in Virginia but had moved to Kentucky, then to Illinois in 1797. Benjamin Young who was born in Virginia then moved to Illinois had contact with about two hundred fifty Methodists in the state according to his letter of 1804.

A letter from him, in possession of Rev. Dr. De Hass, gives us some insight into his labors and sufferings during his year on the Illinois mission. It is dated "Indiana Territory, Randolph County, June 1, 1804." In it he says,

> I am and have been very sickly since I have been here, but I hope I'm on the mend. As for the state of religion, it is bad. I have formed a circuit and five classes of fifty members. In some places there is a revival. About twenty have professed to be converted since I came, but the bulk of the people are given up to wickedness of every kind. Of all places, it is the worst for stealing, fighting, and lying. My soul, come not into their secret

---

[10] https://books.google.com/books?
id=0bGbAAAAQBAJ&pg=PA17&lpg=PA17&dq=Earliest+Roman+Catholic+mi
ssionaries+in+Illinois&source=bl&ots=06-
wcGxRvG&sig=NTsQXWz3bR8MxcERVNv1vM8XTnA&hl=en&sa=X&ved=0a
hUKEwjz_PWlnbfOAhXGuRoKHXJBDq0Q6AEIQTAG#v=onepage&q=Earlie
st%20Roman%20Catholic%20missionaries%20in%20Illinois&f=false
[11] James Leaton, *History of Methodism in Illinois from 1793-1832* (Cincinnati: Walden and Stowe, 1883) 28-37.

places! I met with great difficulties in coming to this country. I lost my horse in the wilderness, fifty miles from any settlement, and had to walk in and hire a horse to go and find mine. The Kickapoo Indians had stolen him and Mr. Reed's, who was with me, but we got them with cost and trouble. When I got to Kaskaskia I preached there, but they made me pay two dollars for the room, and twenty shillings for two days' board. I am out of money and had to sell my books. At last the people began to help me, but I thank God I can make out, though I have suffered with cold. Last winter my clothes were thin and worn out, and I had no money to buy new. But I trust I am in the way to heaven, and I know my heart is engaged in the work of God.[12]

Baptists

Baptists started working in Illinois about the same time as the Methodists and were fairly well established by the time persons who were Restorationists arrived in Illinois. The first Baptist congregations were along the Mississippi south of St. Louis. Some of these Baptist churches later became Restorationists.

The Baptists were the first Protestant Christians to enter this region. The conquest of the county by General George Rogers Clark, in 1778, and the organization of a civil government by Virginia, opened the way for American emigration, and by 1786, a number of families had settled on the American Bottom, and in the hill country of what is now called Monroe County. [South of East St. Louis] They came chiefly from Western Virginia, and Kentucky. In 1787, Elder James Smith, a Baptist minister, whose name is found on the first table for Kentucky, made them a visit, and preached the gospel with good effect. A few families from their first settlement had been in the habit of keeping the sabbath, governing their children, and holding meetings for religious purposes. At that period there were none who had been members of churches. Their methods of observing the Sabbath was to meet, sing hymns, and one would read a chapter from the Scriptures, or a sermon from some author. No public prayer was made till after the visit of Smith and some

[12] Ibid., 36.

had professed to be converted. It deserves to be noted that
the descendants of these families are now exceedingly numerous, that a very large proportion are professors of religion, that they are marked for industry, sobriety and good
order in their families, that there is not an immoral person
among all their descendants, and that of one family are five
brothers who are ministers of the gospel. James Smith visited the settlements in Illinois three times. The Indians made
frequent depredations, and on one occasion they captured
Smith, and conveyed him prisoner to their town on the
Wabash. The people of Illinois, though extremely poor,
raised $170 for his ransom. . . Early in 1796, Elder David
Badgley removed his family from Virginia, to this land of
promise, and on the 28th of May the same year, constituted
the New Design church of 28 members. Mr. Badgley had
preached to the people for several weeks previously, in a revival, aided by Joseph Chance, an exhorter, and had baptized
15 converts. An association called the *Illinois Union* was organized in 1807, consisting of five churches, New Design,
Mississippi Bottom, Richland, Wood River and Silver Creek;
four ministers, David Badgley, William Jones, Robert Brazil,
and Joseph Chance, and 62 members. In 1809, difficulties
arose on the question of a correspondence with the Associations in Kentucky, where slaves were held. Those who declined correspondence adopted the appendage, "Friends of
Humanity," to the term Baptists, which they still retain. In
other respects they accord with the Baptists generally. The
South District, North District, Saline, Vandalia, and Colored
Associations in Illinois, and the Missouri District, a small
body in Missouri, are of this class. Correspondence, co-operation and fellowship exist between these Associations and
other Associations and the Convention in Illinois, though by
tacit consent it does not extend beyond that State. The pecu-
liarities of the Friends of Humanity have been presented in
our notes on Kentucky.

The "United Baptists," re-organized themselves by a subsequent meeting into the "Illinois United Baptist Association,"
which, in 1812, included 8 churches, 4 in Illinois and 4 in
Missouri, and 4 ordained and 2 licensed preachers. A third
party grew out of the division, of two or three small church-

es which still claimed to be the "Illinois Union," but which in 1819 merged in the Illinois Associations, which at that period numbered 10 churches, 8 ministers, and 194 members. The Friends of Humanity in 1821, reported 4 churches, 9 ordained ministers and 186 members. The subject of both Foreign and Domestic missions, was introduced into the Illinois Association in 1818, and met with approbation, and a social organization for mission and education purposes was recommended to be formed in conjunction with the Bethel and Missouri Associations west of the Mississippi, the same autumn…. Two churches, Little Wabash and Lamotte, were gathered on the eastern side of the Illinois Territory in 1815, which appear on the minutes of the Wabash District Association of that year. Thomas Kennedy was a licensed preacher and a member of the latter church. In 1820 the churches of Lamotte, Little Village, Grand Prairie, Little Wabash and Glady Fork existed in the settlements near the Wabash River, and were connected with the Wabash District Association. They numbered jointly 130 members. The same year (1820) the Muddy River Baptist Association, consisting of six churches, four preachers, and 150 members, was formed in the south-eastern part of the State. Some of the churches had been in existence several years and connected with an association in Kentucky.

In 1818, the eccentric Daniel Parker, removed from Tennessee to Crawford County, Ill., of whose doctrine some notice has been given under Indiana…His efforts against missions produced divisions in the Associations in Illinois, so that the Illinois Association declared a virtual non-fellowship with missionary operations in 1824, and similar declarations were made by other associations at subsequent periods. For several years very few revivals of religion were enjoyed and the principle additions to the churches were from immigration.[13]

Reflecting on the inroads of Campbellism into these early Baptist Churches in Illinois E. P. Brand wrote:

---

[13] http://baptisthistoryhomepage.com/illinois.bap.hist.html.

For a few years, from 1827 onward, this teaching spread among Baptists like a forest fire, on a line west and south of west from Pennsylvania. In the northern, southern and eastern states it never made much headway. In 1827 the Pennsylvania Baptists Association that fellowshipped Mr. Campbell's church, announced a disfellowship. The example was followed by other surrounding Baptist Associations. From that time the movement was a separate sect. They were known as Reformers, then as Christians, then as Disciples, etc., all unobjectionable; only they cannot be distinctive names for there are other disciples and other Christians. Many Baptist churches were divided, and some went entirely over. But this generally happened through the manipulation of the pastor.

In 1830 the Sycamore Street Baptist church, Cincinnati, under the personal influence of Mr. Campbell accepted his teachings and changed their name to the "First Christian Baptist Church" of Cincinnati. After a time the "Baptist" was dropped and all that was left was the plain christian; and yet one might question whether it was christian or not. In 1832 the pastor of the Shelbyville Illinois Baptist church became "Campbellite," and succeeded in having "Baptist" stricken from the name of the church, and "christian" substituted. It was many years before there was another Baptist church in Shelbyville. Decatur, two years afterwards, had a similar experience. The church was organized as the "Christian Baptist church," and when the suitable time had come the "Baptist" was stricken off. The Friendship Baptist church, Perry County, three miles from Tamaroa, as late as 1869 went the same road. Missouri Baptists suffered most, Indiana next, Illinois came third. Butler University, Ind., was the gift of one of the Baptist families that lapsed to Campbell in those days.[14]

Haynes mentioned at least seven church changes from Baptist to Restorationist. These include Atlanta in Logan County, Mt. Moriah in Marion County, Pleasant Plains in Mason County, Sweet Water in Menard County, West Crow in Moultrie County, Cantrall in Sangamon County, and Shelbyville in Shelby County.

---

[14] E. P. Brand, *Illinois Baptists: A History* (Bloomington: Pantagraph Printing & Sta. Co., 1930) 112, 13.

Presbyterians

Presbyterians came somewhat later, the largest numbers in the same area along the Wabash as the Restorationists.

> So far as I am aware the first Presbyterian minister who visited the Illinois country was John Evans Findley. He was from Chester county, Pennsylvania. After descending the Ohio with some companions in a keel boat and ascending the Mississippi, he landed at Kaskaskia in 1797. Rev.

> Thomas Lippincott tells us his design was to labor in the Spanish colonies on the Mississippi, mainly perhaps with a view to the Indians.... He preached and catechised, also baptized several of the Red Men...The next Presbyterian ministers — they were licentiates — who set foot on Illinois territory, were John F. Schermerhorn and Samuel J. Mills. They were sent to the great Southwest by the Massachusetts and Connecticut Missionary Societies and by local Bible Societies, They commenced their tour early in the fall of 1812, passing through Pennsylvania, Western Virginia, Ohio, Kentucky and Tennessee. Their observations of the religious condition of the regions through which they passed were thorough, and their reports deeply interesting. Of Illinois territory they say, 'In the Illinois territory, containing more than 12.000 people, there is no Presbyterian, or Congregational minister. There are a number of good people in the territory who are anxious to have such ministers amongst them.

In a letter containing a general summing up of their observations, and which was dated on the Mississippi, below New Madrid, January 20, 1S15, they say:

> The Illinois Territory contains about 15,000 inhabitants. Until last summer titles of land could not be obtained in this Territory. Now land offices are opened. The principal settlements, at present, are situated on the Wabash, the Ohio, the Mississippi and the Kaskaskia. The eastern settlements extend thirty miles up the Wabash, and forty down the Ohio...We are thus brought forward to the year 1815. Illinois Territory had then about 15,000 inhabitants exclusive of Indians. One ordained Pres-

byterian minister had landed at Kaskaskia ; another, James Mc-
Gready, had preached a few times in White county. Three licentiates had pressed their feet upon its soil. Two of the three had
made the trip from Shawneetown to Kaskaskia and St. Louis and
back. That was all. No Presbyterian minister or church in the
territory. The next year, 1816, was to witness a change.

The church of Sharon, in what is now White county, is the
oldest Presbyterian church in Illinois. It was organized by Rev.
James McGready, of Henderson, Ky., in 1816, probably in the
month of September. The first book of its records is lost but
the following synopsis of the history of the church is found in
the present volume. The first three ruling elders were Peter
Miller, James Mayes and James Rutledge, all of Ohio had emi-
grated from Henderson, Ky. The members of the church were
from the Carolinas, Georgia, Tennessee and Kentucky. Rev.
James

McGready had preached for them occasionally for two or
three years, coming over from Kentucky where he resided,"
Doubtless numbers of them had been his parishioners in Kentucky and the Carolinas...His principal field of labor in Kentucky was in Logan county, where from 1796 to 1814 he was
pastor of Gasper River, Red River and Muddy River congregations.[15]

James McCready was a significant personage in the background of Barton Warren Stone.[16] Some of Stone's earliest struggles in regard to a religious commitment resulted from listening to McCready as he evangelized
at the Caldwell Academy in Guilford County, North Carolina. After
Stone became a Presbyterian minister at Cane Ridge and Concord in
Kentucky he traveled to Logan County, Kentucky, where McCready was
involved in a significant religious revival. Some designate this revival as
the launching pad for the Second Great Awakening. Stone returned from
Logan County to his Kentucky parish and extended an invitation to all
comers to attend a communion service at Cane Ridge. The result was the
now famous Cane Ridge Camp Meeting. McGready, as we have seen, also
left his impact on religion in Illinois.

15 A. T. Norton, *History of the Presbyterian Church in the State of Illinois* (St. Louis: W. S.
Bryan, Publisher, 1879) 11, 12; 16; 19; 22.
16 *ESCM*, 706 - 708.

In Summary

The below data regarding religion in Illinois spanning the years sums up the significance of the various groups and their relative importance from the beginning.[17]

Before 1830, little religion of any sort was practiced on the Illinois frontier. Energetic Protestant missionaries set out to evangelize this un-Christian population and they largely succeeded. By 1890, 36% of the adults in Illinois were affiliated with evangelical denominations—chiefly Methodist, Disciples of Christ, Baptist, Congregationalist, and Presbyterian—while 35%, mostly immigrants, belonged to liturgical denominations (chiefly Roman Catholic, Lutheran, and Episcopal). The remaining adults acknowledged no particular denomination.

Illinois has had episodes of religious bigotry: at Carthage in 1844 the Mormon founder Joseph Smith was killed by a mob; strong but brief waves of anti-Catholicism developed in the 1850s (the "Know-Nothing" movement) and 1920s (the Ku Klux Klan). Robert Green Ingersoll, a self-proclaimed agnostic, was appointed attorney general of Illinois in 1867–69, but his identity as an agnostic prevented him from ever being elected into politics. Nevertheless, tolerance of religious diversity has been the norm for most of the state's history.

In 2000, the largest religious institution in Illinois was the Roman Catholic Church, with 3,874,933 adherents in 1,225 congregations. The largest Protestant denomination was the United Methodist Church, with 365,182 adherents, followed by the Southern Baptist Convention with 305,838 adherents. Other major Protestant groups include the Evangelical Lutheran Church in America with 279,724 adherents and the Lutheran Church—Missouri Synod with 278,008 adherents. The Jewish population was estimated at 270,000 in 2000 and the Muslim community had about 125,203 adherents. There are over 11,000 Mennonites throughout the state. The Churches of Christ report 29,295 adherents, the Christian Churches/Churches of Christ 108,472, and the Disciples of Christ 47,099. About 44.7% of the population of almost 13,000,000 did not claim membership in any religious organization.

---

[17] http://www.city-data.com/states/Illinois-Religions.html

2. The Founding of Restoration Churches in Illinois

The earliest Restorationist to preach in Illinois was likely Joseph Taylor in 1813. At that time Illinois had a population of about 16,000, but in another twenty years there were above 160,000 inhabitants. The incoming Restorationists added to these significant growth totals. Churches of various denominations already dotted the landscape as we have seen, but still, because of the large numbers of recent arrivals, many were unchurched. Joseph Taylor was probably from a Jones-Smith background since he sent his 1813 report to the *Herald of Gospel Liberty*,

> Illinois Territory, Nov. 21, 1813.
> Dear Sir,
> There appears to be a great inquiry after truth among the people in this part of the country. Truly the harvest is great, and the labourers [sic] few...I have a circuit of about two hundred and fifty miles, which I have constantly attended to for some time when health & strength would admit...I am your unworthy friend, Joseph Taylor."[1]

The outcome of evangelization did not always include the organizing of congregations in the O'Kelly, and Jones/Smith movements. Mark Fernald of Kittery, Maine, who started going on evangelistic tours in 1808 made this clear when he wrote:

> It will be observed that much of my labor was among the Free-will Baptists. In most of the places I visited, there were no churches of the "Christian connection;" and I cared not where I labored, if the people were benefitted, and souls saved. The Free-will Baptists received me kindly and with open heartedness; made no objection to my doctrine or practice. Hence I assisted

---

[1] Joseph Taylor, "Extract of a Letter from Joseph Taylor, to the Editor, dated Illinois Territory, Nov. 21, 1813," *HGL*, 6.15 (March 4, 1814) 574.

them in church labors, had revivals among them, and baptized for them, until some of their preachers got in the doctrine called Trinity.[2]

The regions of Illinois where the Restorationists planted Congregations

The main areas where Restorations planted congregations before Illinois statehood in 1818 were in mid-eastern Illinois along the Indiana border. The people who settled in that region may have been mostly Stoneites though there are obviously some preachers from the Jones/Smith Movement. Two other regions were settled next, first in the central Illinois counties in the areas around Bloomington, Champaign, Springfield and Decatur. The major influence here may have been those coming from the Jones/Smith Movement though Stoneites also had considerable impact. In the late 1810s churches were also started in western Illinois near the Mississippi River from Galesburg south to Alton and in the Spoon River region. These churches often had help from major preachers across the Mississippi in Missouri, including Jacob Creath, Jr., and Winthrop H. Hopson.[3] After the early 1830s many of the Illinois Restorationist preachers were from a Stone-Campbell-Scott background.

In his book on the *History of the Disciples in Illinois* Haynes identifies 69 churches that were founded before 1840 in 34 Illinois counties out of 102. In these 34 counties both before and after 1840, these churches are by majority located in a belt of six counties up and down in the middle of Illinois across the state from east to west. They are about four counties deep to the west from the Wabash River border starting with congregations that are three counties above the tip in the south.[4] Churches in "Little Egypt"—the southern region of Illinois—were planted later.

Haynes indicates where the churches were located in 1914 on the county map below. Each county has one or two numbers: the number of churches in 1914 and, in thirty-four counties, a circled number for the number of churches founded before 1840.

---

2 Mark Fernald, *Elder Mark Fernald* (Newburyport, MA: Geo. Moore Payne and D. P. Pike, 1852) 55.

3 Craig Churchill, "Jacob Creath, Jr." *ESCM*, 250, 251 on. On Hopson, see: W. T. Moore (editor), *Living Pulpit of the Christian Church* (Cincinnati: R. W. Carroll & Co., Publishers, 1871) 277, 278.

4 Data compiled by Thomas H. Olbricht, from Haynes, passim.

Note: Haynes reported 755 congregations in Illinois.

Of the churches Haynes reported that were founded before 1840, some were Christian Connexion, that is, O'Kelly, Jones/Smith and Stone congregations that did not go in with the Stone-Campbell-Scott merger of 1832. But he does not report all of these, so other data is needed to provide a list of these congregations in Illinois. We have some data, but we think it likely not conclusive. After 1906, when the Churches of Christ reported separately to the Federal Religious Census, Haynes includes some Churches of Christ in his 1915 book as conservative congregations, but not all. But this information must await a history of twentieth century Restorationists. At this point we will set out what we know about the early Christian Connexion congregations in Illinois which combined the three streams (O'Kelly, Jones-Smith, Stone) noted above. Later we will present data from a study by Richard Taylor listing the Christian Connexion Associations in Illinois.[5]

To clarify the Haynes terminology we will note his usage. Haynes employs the names Church of Christ, Christian Church and Disciples of Christ to refer to Stone-Campbell congregations. These congregations according to his vocabulary are Restorationist churches. He employs the terms "New Light" or Christian Denomination to depict churches from the Jones/Smith, O'Kelly, Stone movement that did not go with the 1832 and afterwards merger to form the Stone-Campbell movement. The term applied by others later, which Haynes does not employ, is the Christian Connexion. Haynes rejects the Christian Denomination congregations as part of the Restoration Movement. He writes about the two groups:

> It may be properly noted here that the Disciples of Christ absorbed the larger part of the Christian Denomination, not only in Illinois, but elsewhere. However, the latter body still lives. The appeal of both parties was to the Bible as the only recognized authority in religion, and in this way many of the latter concluded that the Disciples were nearer the divine standard than themselves.[6]

---

[5] On the Christian Connexion see: Millo True Morrill, *A History of the Christian Denomination in America* (Dayton: The Christian Publishing Association, 1912). Thomas H. Olbricht, "Christian Connexion and Unitarian Relations 1800-1844," *Restoration Quarterly*, 9.3 (1966) 160-186. For the history of Christian Denomination congregations in Illinois: Matthew Spinka, *A History of Illinois Congregational and Christian Churches* (Chicago: The Congregational and Christian Conference of Illinois, 1944). For the New Lights: Colby D. Hall, *The "New Light Christians," Initiators of the Nineteenth Century Reformation* (Fort Worth: Stafford-Lowdon Co., 1959).

[6] Haynes, 30.

Haynes uses the term Christian Church as the same as church of Christ in writing about the Sidell congregation in Vermilion County:

> In 1884, Evangelist W. F. Black conducted a meeting of days there, when most of the congregation became Christians only. These he then organized into the Antioch Christian Church. In about ten years this congregation was absorbed by others, and the chapel was sold and turned into a barn. Evangelist Creighton held a meeting in Sidell in the Baptist chapel in 1895 and organized a church of Christ of about one hundred members. Among them were members from Antioch, a goodly number of Baptists and converts to the Lord.[7]

One of the earliest congregations in Illinois was found at Allison in Lawrence County. About this congregation Haynes wrote:

> Allison (Vincennes, Ind.).
> Organized 1815-28; present membership, 170; value of property, $5,500; Bible School began 1874; present enrollment, 102. This society was first formed by members of the Christian Denomination. A reorganization took place in 1828, at which time it is probable that the membership came nearer the position of the Disciples.[8]

Haynes also employs the term church of Christ as equivalent with Disciples as he writes about the Pontiac Congregation in Livingston County.

> During his pastorate an agreement was made between the Disciples and the Christian Denomination to erect a union house of worship. It was a brick building without any claims to architectural beauty. However, it was honored by the presence of Abraham Lincoln, who delivered an address therein. After five years the legal title was passed to the church of Christ exclusively, and later to Mr. Powell.[9]

Haynes' terminology may be seen in this comment on the Sweet Water congregation in Menard County founded in 1825.

---

[7] Ibid., 413.
[8] Ibid., 252.
[9] Ibid., 263.

Sweet Water
Organized 1825; present membership, 115; value of property,
$4,000; Bible-school enrollment, 100. Menard County was a part
of Sangamon until the meeting of the General Assembly in
1838-39. The first name of this locality was Sugar Grove, which
was applied to it because of the large grove of these trees that
grew there. The congregation was first organized as a Baptist
church; next it affiliated with the "New Lights," or Christian Denomination; later it became a part of the Restoration
movement.[10]

Haynes uses the word "Christian Denomination" twenty times, ten of
the times referring to specific congregations of the "Denomination."
These were Little Prairie (Ellery) in Edwards County, Newton in Jasper
County, Allison, Lawrenceville and Mt. Erie (Sumner) in Lawrence County, Pontiac in Livingston County, Sweet Water in Menard County, Barney's Prairie and Lick Prairie in Wabash County and Seven Mile in White
County. All of these were in southeast Illinois not far from the Wabash
except for Livingston near Chicago and Menard in central Illinois. They
were all founded before 1840 except for those in Jasper and Livingston
Counties. The total number of congregations for which Hayes presents
some data totals above 755. Haynes employs "New Light" twice when
speaking about specific congregations. He explains his usage.

A goodly number of the earliest churches of Christ in the State
grew out of a reformatory movement that preceded our own.
These people were widely known as "New Lights." But, since
they now disclaim this name, they are throughout this work referred to as the "Christian Denomination" their accepted
name.[11]

It is clear that Haynes did not include a number of the early "Christian
Denomination" churches as he called them since he did not list the
churches of this background except for the most part those in the
Southern Indiana/Southern Illinois Wabash Conference founded in
1817. He does not, with possibly two exceptions, mention churches in
four other early Christian Denomination conferences. The four with
founding dates, where known, are: 1833 South Western Illinois Confer-

[10] Ibid., 327.
[11] Ibid., 9, 10.

ence, 1840 Spoon River Conference, 1840 Northern Illinois and Wisconsin Conference, and 1841 Christian Union, Pike County Conference.[12]

Disciples or Christian Connexion Congregations

A pressing question when commenting on the nineteenth century Restoration in Illinois is whether a congregation is from a Jones/Smith, Stone, or Campbell-Scott background. In some cases the origins of the churches in this regard are clear and in various cases not. For example, Haynes mentions persons coming from Cleveland who established congregations in Lake County north of Chicago. These settlers were most likely from a Jones/Smith Background but they changed at least in Haynes' judgment to become a Disciple congregation.

> In the thirties, Darius Gage and two of his brothers, with Benedict Stevens and Emmons Shepard, came from near Cleveland, O., and settled on lands in the northern part of Lake County. A village, located about three miles northeast of Fox Lake and one mile south of the Wisconsin line, was laid out, to which the name of Gageville was given. Some years afterward the name was changed to Antioch, by which it is still known. In this community a church after the primitive order was constituted Aug. 7, 1841 with twenty members, by Min. William Davenport, then of Walnut Grove. It was the first church of Christ in the northern tier of counties in the State.[13]

We will try to approach the history with as much clarity as to these distinctions as possible. But even at the end of the nineteenth century fluidity persisted with people transferring from one group to another. Various leaders expressed their frustrations that fragmenting lingered. The sentiments S. M. Fowler expressed to the readers of *The Christian-Evangelist* in 1901 makes clear these conundrums.[14]

> S. M. Fowler, "The Old Christians and Disciples of Christ"
> It is a pitiable weakness that this distinction ever obtained among
> a people moved by the same divine impulse, the love of Christ,

---

[12] Richard H. Taylor, *Christian Conferences in Illinois* (Unpublished Document). Taylor has also documented Illinois Christian Denomination congregations. We will refer to his data on congregations below.

[13] *Haynes*, 246.

[14] *C-E* (September 5, 1901) 1129.

with the same goal in view, the restored unity of his broken body, on such superficialities as have in the past so estranged them from each other. 'Tis 66 years since I entered the ways of higher life. For 66 years I have been a reader of the *Christian Palladium* and *Herald of Gospel Liberty*. For a part of this time the *Christian-Evangelist* has made me its weekly visits. I read "Christianity Restored," by Mr. A. Campbell, in the early forties, and his debates with Owen on Infidelity, and Adolphos Skinner on the merits of Universalism.

I have always admired Mr. Campbell as a debater and scholar—a Christian and, as a whole, a theologian, but I do not think he swung out so free from the apostasy, and so fully into the clear, simple, yet sublime teaching of Christ as did B. W. Stone. He paraded some of the Babylonian garments, while Stone stood forth in the seamless vesture of Jesus. Admitting that "born of water" refers to John's baptism, he seems to attach the same importance to the flesh being "born of water," as to the Spirit being born from above. Nicodemus, with others, was expecting the kingdom of God immediately to appear and had doubtless submitted to John's baptism. Jesus gave him to understand that that, like John, was only pointing to the higher, the divine— the Holy Spirit and fire, truth and love, — that would drive out the false and consume the evil. The first was temporal and temporary, the second spiritual and eternal.

I have even felt that Mr. Campbell placed an undue emphasis upon the word, especially in regard to ordinances, and not enough upon the presence and help of God by the Spirit "who works all in all." I also have a corresponding impression that the Christians felt or fancied themselves to be entirely under the guidance of the Holy Spirit, trusting in it to teach them what they should have learned and believed in or from the Bible.

These were two extremes on the two wings of the two movements, more than the central sober thought that pervaded both alike. Had they known each other better, had they stuck more closely to the wise motto of which both alike approve, "speak where and as the Bible speaks, and be silent (or at least modest) where it is silent, and obey where it commands," they never could have fallen apart. In this I might include the Free Baptists, the Baptists, and in fact all Protestant sects.

The editor James H. Garrison[15] appended a note:

We are glad to give this venerable brother space to state his view concerning the defects of the two religious bodies to which he refers. As he reads the literature of both bodies, he has a better right to be heard on this subject than those who only read one side. We are sure our readers will agree with him in the position that the two movements pleading for Christian union should be one. Are we not justified in expressing the belief that had our old Christian brethren followed the example of Barton W. Stone, whom our brother so highly commends, they would have been one body? At any rate, we should not cease to study the things that make for peace and unity.—Editor.

Congregations and Conferences of the Christian Connexion in Illinois

Congregational historian Richard H. Taylor has collected information on Illinois congregations affiliated with the Jones/Smith, Stone/O'Kelly background (later designated Christian Connexion or the Christian Denomination), arranging them alphabetically by county, and alphabetically within each county, similar to Haynes' arrangement, although Taylor does not provide as much detail as Haynes.[16] The particular congregations in his listings of interest are those that chose not to affiliate with the Stone-Campbell "merger" in 1832.

Taylor has a total of 552 congregations in Illinois on the list. Of this number he was able to place 467 of the congregations in a county. He was not able to locate the county of 85 congregations.

The counties with more than fifteen congregations are: Champaign, Crawford, Fulton, Jackson, Jasper, Piatt, and Vermilion. Vermilion, with 35 congregations had the largest number.

Most of these congregations are at the Indiana border in the middle of the state. The region running west from Vermilion County through Champaign and Piatt Counties has the most congregations. Crawford westward including Jasper County has a number of congregations. Other pockets are in Jackson County around Carbondale, and in Fulton County on the Illinois River southwest of Peoria. No congregations are listed for

---

[15] *ESCM*, 350, 351.

[16] Richard H. Taylor (Unpublished twenty-one pages of data on *Illinois Christian [Denomination] Churches*, 2016).

Cook County. The County near Cook with a larger number is Kendall County with 11 congregations.

Sixteen congregations are identified as starting before 1829. Several of these congregations are also listed by Haynes in his Illinois Disciples history. Such congregations according to Taylor are Barneys Prairie in Wabash County, founded in 1816 and the Albion Congregation in Lawrence County founded in 1815 are among those so listed. The 16 congregations are founded in Crawford, Edgar, Franklin, Lawrence, McLean, Menard, Vermilion and Wabash Counties. All these countries are on the Indiana border except for McLean and Menard north of Springfield, and Franklin in the south in the midway between the Wabash and the Mississippi.

While the later pockets of congregational density differ from those of the Disciples of Christ, the early pockets are much the same.

It is however, beyond the scope of this volume to document all of the Illinois Christian Denomination congregations. Two examples will illustrate the complexity of determining if a congregation was purely a Disciples congregation when started or if loyalties to the Christian Connexion lay dormant in a Disciples congregation, only to arise at an opportunity to start a Christian Connexion congregation.

Little Grove, Edgar County

Haynes' (187) insistence that the Little Grove congregation "was always a church of Christ; it was never in any way connected with the Christian Denomination" indicates there actually might have been some Christian Denomination influence. The founding minister of Little Grove was Samuel McGee, about whom, and a "Rev. Mr. Ward," we learn:

> Rev. Samuel McGee is one of the first preachers remembered in
> Stratton Township. He was from Tennessee, and came to the
> settlement as early as 1825. Rev. Mr. Ward came a few years later.
> They first preached the New Light doctrine, but is what is now
> the Christian Church belief. The Little Grove Church was built
> under the administration of Rev. Mr. McGee, and was one of
> the first church edifices built in the county. The society was orig-
> inally formed in a schoolhouse at Sassafras Grove, about 1832 –
> 33, and the first church built in 1834 – 35. It was a frame build-

ing, 36 x 40 feet, and in this edifice they worshiped until 1864, a new house was built, 30 x 40, at a cost of $800.[17]

Although there are differences in the details between the two sources about building dates, it is evident that McGee and Ward had some New Light background or the source for the Edgar County history conflated New Light and Disciple teaching. As the century progressed, the distinctions between the two groups became clearer.

Jacksonville, Morgan County

Another observation is individuals with Christian Denomination backgrounds felt comfortable in Disciple congregations but did not necessarily abandon their older loyalties.

In Chapter 10 we discuss in greater detail the Walter Scott Russell controversy involving the Jacksonville Christian Church. Charles E. Russell, Walter's father, had an affinity for the Christian Denomination that surfaced in the mid-1860s when the congregation weighed its options about its future relationship to the Stone-Campbell Movement.

In June 1864, the group loyal to W. S. Russell, still in possession of the original building, but marginalized in the SCM because of their loyalty to the Russell faction, considered what group of churches it should establish relationships with. W. W. Happy suggested the congregation "cooperate with the churches of the Springfield Baptist Association." In the ensuing discussion, we read:

> Bro. Russell [C. E. Russell, Eds.] was opposed to the resolution principally because of the close communion principles of said Baptist Denomination. He thought we could do better; was in favor of uniting with the 'old Christian Brethren.'

Neither Happy's nor Russell's suggestion prevailed. The congregation decided to pursue reconciliation with their estranged fellow Christians in Jacksonville. The process concluded several months later when the two congregations reunited, with the calling of Enos Campbell as their minister.[18]

---

[17] *The History of Edgar County, Illinois* (Chicago: Wm. Le Baron, Jr. & Co., 1879) 481.
[18] James L. McMillan, *Transcription of the Minutes of Jacksonville Christian Church* (Unpublished Manuscript of the Congregation's Papers housed at the Disciples of Christ Historical Society).

This development did not sit well with elders C. E. Russell and Hiram Smedley. Rather than staying with the Disciple congregation, both were part of the twelve person nucleus that established a Christian Denomination congregation in 1866:

> Another "Christian" church was organized in the old Court House, in 1866, by twelve persons, adherents of that denomination. Among them were Workman Cully, L. B. Ross, Charles E Russell and Hiram Smedley and their families. Rev. J. E. Wright was the pastor, and continued to serve them until 1869 or 1870. They occupied the Court House until the completion of their house of worship, on South Main Street, in 1868. The pastors succeeding Rev. Wright were Revs. J. J. Summerbell, C. W. Garoutte and P. W. Sinks.[19]

Conferences and their Characteristics

One manner of distinguishing Christian Connexion congregations from the Stone-Campbell-Scott churches may be that the latter did not employ the term "conference" for a gathering of preachers and representatives from churches. The Campbells were accustomed to the use of "association" for a larger gathering, for example the Redstone Baptist Association and the Mahoning Baptist Association. The three groups that comprised the Christian Connexion rather employed the term "conference" which was also used by Congregationalists, Free Will Baptists and other groups. The above five Illinois conferences were all of Christian Connexion congregations. When the Stone-Campbell groups about 1840 started having larger gatherings they called them state cooperative meetings or evangelization societies.[20]

Since conferences became important to the Christian Connexion we need to make a few observations about them. After forming the Spring-

---

[19] Charles M. Eames, *Historic Morgan and Classic Jacksonville* (Jacksonville, Illinois: Daily Journal Steam Job Printing Office, 1855) 173. Richard Taylor documents a Jacksonville Conference that was established at that time. J. J. Summerbell, son of Nicholas Summerbell, graduated from the Christian Connexion institution, Merom College, Indiana, in 1864.

[20] George L. Peters, *The Disciples of Christ in Missouri Celebrating One Hundred Years of Co-operative Work* (The Centennial Commission, 1837) 29; http://www.therestorationmovement.com/_states/tennessee/fanning,tolbert.htm, look at entries for 1842 and 1852.

field (Ohio-Kentucky) Presbytery Barton W. Stone and five other ministers decided to dissolve this more formal structure so as to associate freely with whomever they wished and thereupon published a document known as "The Last Will and Testament of the Springfield Presbytery." [21] They stated:

> *Imprimis.* We *will,* that this body die, be dissolved, and sink into union with the Body of Christ at large; for there is but one body, and one spirit, even as we are called in one hope of our calling.
>
> Item. We will, that our power of making laws for the government of the church, and executing them by delegated authority, forever cease; that, the people may have free course to the Bible, and adopt the law of the spirit of life *in Christ Jesus.*
>
> Item. We will, that the people henceforth take the Bible as the only sure guide to heaven; and as many as are offended with other books, which stand in competition with it, may cast them into the fire if they choose: for it is better to enter into life having one book, than having many to be cast into hell.

Because of the dismantling of the Springfield Presbytery, early on, no official conferences were created though informal gatherings occurred over such topics as baptism. Sometime in the early 1810s conferences were created. By the time Stone founded *The Christian Messenger,* in 1826, however, conferences were called with some frequency. The first volume of Stone's journal contains an essay on Conferences. It is in the form of a letter written by Philip. The letter opens,

> Brother Stone:
>
> As the subject of Conference is considerably agitated at present, in the religious community, on the propriety of which there is (as upon almost every other subject) a variety of opinions; and as it certainly is a matter of no small importance, I beg leave to invite your attention to the subject, with a single view of eliciting information, and ascertaining, if possible, what is propriety.[22]

---

[21] "The Last Will and Testament of the Springfield Presbytery," in Charles Alexander Young, *Historical Documents Advocating Christian Union* (Chicago: The Century Company, 1904) 19-26. See also D. Newell Williams, "Last Will and Testament of Springfield Presbytery," *ESCM,* 353-355.

[22] *CM,* 1.3 (January, 1827) 49.

He goes on to point out that an annual conference occurs among "the brethren of the Christian connexion" but that hostility toward it arises from some quarters. He says that many assume that the Christians associate for the purpose of legislation, but that cannot be the case since there is only "one law-giver," that is, the head of the church. He further declares,

> I do most sincerely, and I hope ever shall, contend for the absolute independency of each church, as the complete transaction of its own business; and for its want of responsibility to any human tribunal whatever. I know and acknowledge no higher tribunal that "*the church*," and every member is alone responsible and answerable to the particular church where his membership may be.[23]

He then goes on to describe the purpose of the conference as he understands it.

> It may then be enquired, what propriety is there in your Conference or annual meeting? I answer, simply to worship together and strengthen the bonds of union, to receive and obtain information from the different churches, either from their letters or messengers, and attend to their suggestions, and as far as in our power comply with their requests; attend to ordination, if thought proper, when required by the brethren; to arrange our appointments so as to supply the destitute churches with preaching; and imitate the primitive church by making such *requests* only as may be proper to *set things in order*. The brethren, who meet the elders as messengers, we do not recognize as representatives. Let that principle be established, and a foundation is at once laid for the final annihilation of Christian liberty. I would therefore oppose any convocation, the object of which is to take from the churches any of their sovereign rights and prerogatives, or to legislate in any manner whatever for them, or that will maintain or upon the doctrine, that any man or order of men are not *alone* answerable to the particular church where they may have membership. But I am nevertheless constrained to believe that our Conferences, as they are termed, with our present views of Christian liberty are highly beneficial. It enables the brethren to ascertain the situation of each other, and each church; to learn

---

[23] Ibid., 50.

the prosperity of God's cause; to meet and worship together; and to obtain a variety of information, important to be known. Surely then, none will oppose meetings, the object of which is alone information and edification, and not legislation.[24]

Both David Purviance and William Kinkade, the latter who moved to Illinois, believed that conferences should ordain preachers and resolve controversial matters for the churches.

David Millard (1794-1873) of the Jones/Smith movement in central New York State was more explicit about the work of the conferences. He wrote in 1848:

> In the Christian Connexion, churches are independent bodies, authorized to govern themselves and transact their own affairs. They have a large number of associations called Conferences. Each conference meets annually, sometimes oftener, and is composed of ministers and messengers from churches within its bounds. At such conferences candidates for the ministry are examined, received and commended. Once a year, in conference, the character and standing of each minister is examined, that purity in the ministry may be carefully maintained. Such other subjects are discussed and measures adopted, as have a direct bearing on the welfare of the body at large.[25]

Mark Fernald (1784-1851) of the Jones/Smith movement living in Kittery, Maine, described a conference he attended in 1816. From early years the Jones-Smith Christians were ambivalent about conferences that were characteristic of the Congregational, Baptist, Presbyterian and Methodist Churches around them.[26] Fernald, when younger, objected to decision making conferences but he attended regularly those of the church groups listed above. As conferences became accepted among the Christians in the second decade of the nineteenth century he became actively involved. Early in his ministry he met with other Jones-Smith preachers sometimes in large numbers and including the most important proclaimers in New England. One such gathering was in Windham, CT in 1816.[27] It is clear at

---

[24] Ibid., 50, 51.

[25] David Millard, "History of the Christians, or Christian Connexion" *History of all the Religious Denominations in the United States,* John Winebrenner, ed. (Harrisburg, PA: John Winebrenner, 1848) 167.

[26] Mark Fernald, *Elder Mark Fernald,* 46, 59, 172-73, 299, 301.

[27] Fernald 85-86. Others, 66, 171

this gathering that the participants were concerned to set out the purpose on parameters of such gatherings.

This conference was to aid each other in understanding the Bible, our Rule. It was not an Ecclesiastical court, but a Christian school, to get all the light and truth each other possessed. Various subjects were discussed.

> First, shall we have a moderator? The New Testament was silent on this, yet we considered it our duty to conduct orderly.
>
> Second, shall we have a clerk or scribe? We found no direct proof in the New Testament, but agreed it was best to keep records.
>
> Third, enquired for an example for holding a conference. Believed that Acts xv: 6, and other Scriptures justified the practice. At evening, Elder B. Taylor preached excellently. On the 12th, the conference met at 8, A. M. After prayer, the question, Is the right hand of fellowship any part of ordination was examined. All agreed that it had no connection with ordination, but applied (Gal. ii: 9) to Elders that are ordained elsewhere, when they come to such Elders as are considered pillars; such may thereby approbate them. To the question, What the ground of fellowship among God's children? the reply was, The new birth, regeneration or Christ in us, the hope or evidence of glory.
>
> In the evening, E. Smith preached. There was good attention.[28]

The five conferences set forth by Richard Taylor in his study reported on previously have more affinity with the Christian Connexion than with the Stone-Campbell-Scott Reformers. Evidence suggests that conferences in new regions tended to have 6 to ten preachers and perhaps as many churches. If we take ten as an average by 1841 there were about fifty Christian Connexion congregations in Illinois.

State Co-operative Meetings of the Stone-Campbell Movement

The earliest congregations in Illinois are described by Haynes. He includes both congregations from a Christian Connexion background mostly because they are the earliest and then lists congregations that were

---

[28] For additional reservations on conferences in New England see Olbricht, "Christian Connexion and Unitarian Relationships," fn 92, 93 and *CPall*, 2.2 (May 12, 1838) 17, 18.

planted by the Stone-Campbell Movement after the merger in Kentucky in 1832.[29] He does not often, however, clearly distinguish the two, nor highlight congregations that move from one group to the other. He does not distinguish Conferences from State Meetings, the first the vocabulary of the Christian Connexion, and the second the language used by those in the Stone-Campbell Movement. Williams' paper utilizes Haynes's history without much digging on his own so he does not help with distinguishing these two movements.[30]

Both Haynes and Williams identify the beginning of Illinois Co-operative meetings or later labeled Illinois State Meetings, but they do not specify that the Christian Connexion people still employ the word Conference for their gatherings. This means that the Stone-Campbell churches started organizing in 1834 in Springfield. The first major meeting was held in Jacksonville the same year.[31] Regularly schedule meetings soon follow. We can also point out that the Allison Prairie congregation embraced the Campbell Reformers views by 1828.[32]

Early Unity

Before the nineteenth century was over it is clear that the Christian Connexion and the Stone-Campbell trajectories formed essentially two distinctive groups. In some cases the separations went back to the 1830s and accelerated after the Civil War. But in earlier times and places the churches worked together as one and leaders from all the wings freely circulated in all the groups.

The work of Erma Jean Loveland on George Alkire which appears in Chapter 5: The Alkires Arrive in Illinois, indicates preachers from the Connexion and the Stone-Campbell Movement still met in gatherings at least into the 1840s. Loveland discusses some of the leaders from each group. While the vocabulary of Conferences as opposed to state meetings was not absolute, it provides some insight into the churches of the Connexion as compared with those of the Stone-Campbell Movement.

---

[29] Haynes, "Chapter II, Beginnings in Illinois," 20 - 32.
[30] Lowell Williams, "Beginning of the Church in Illinois," Unpublished Paper, Abilene Christian College, 1958.
[31] Ibid., 15; Haynes 88 - 90.
[32] http://lawrencelore.blogspot.com/2013/01/allison-prairie-christian-church-1815.html

The Alkire family came from O'Kelly country and made it to Kentucky by Cane Ridge days (1801).[33] They became acquainted with Stone even before the "Last Will and Testament" (1804). In Illinois, after 1836, George Alkire continued to be involved with all the wings of the movement.

To illustrate this we quote relevant excerpts from Chapter 5: The Alkires Arrive in Illinois:

> Barton W. Stone came to Williamsport, Ohio, where George Alkire and his brother, Michael, lived and held meetings in George's house in 1803. Stone returned in 1804 and organized a church there. The charter members included: Isaac Cade and wife; John Teverbaugh and wife; George Alkire and wife Catharine Rush; brothers Isaac W. and Simon Hornback and their wives. Simon Hornback was married to George Alkire's sister, Sarah. Until the first meeting house was built of hewed logs in 1810, the group met in each other's homes.
>
> This congregation had already been organized for three years when Thomas Campbell came to the United States in 1807. ....The Williamsport church, the oldest church in the Deer Creek township hosted several well-known preachers, including these noted editors: Barton W. Stone with *The Christian Messenger*, Joseph Badger with *The Christian Palladium*, and Isaac N. Walter with *Gospel Herald*. Joseph Thomas, a nephew of the White Pilgrim Joseph Thomas, was a good friend and traveling companion of George Alkire.

Williamsport is near Columbus, Ohio and the church had visitors from all the wings.

> Other preachers mentioned included George Zimmerman, William Kincade, James Hays, Matthew Gardner, James Marom, George Alkire, James Burbridge, S. Bradford, Daniel Long, John L. Green, Isaac Cade, Benjamin Seevers, John L. Perkins, Enoch Harvey, Thomas Hand, N. Dawson, C. A. Morse, T. A. Brandon, Peter McCullough, William Overterf, B. H. Chrisman, Josel Osgood, A. C. Hanger, and E. W. Humphreys. Humphreys was later instrumental in establishing the Union Christian College in Merom, Sullivan County, Indiana. When he wrote *The Memoirs of*

---

[33] D. Newell Williams, "Cane Ridge Revival," *ESCM*, 164-166.

Deceased Christian Ministers, he was well acquainted with the Alkires and Williamsport.

Alkire seemed especially to relate to the Jones/Smith second generation. In Joseph Badger's report of a trip he made to Williamsport, Ohio in 1925, he spoke in "respectful terms" of George Alkire. The next year, Badger noted in his journal: "In Elder Alkire's vicinity the churches have received large additions of late."

Gospel Luminary carried the proceedings from the 1826 yearly meeting and conference at Williamsport. The listing of elders present included: George Alkire, James Burbridge , Samuel Wilson, Enoch Harvey, Alexander Owen, Isaac N. Walter, Martin Baker, Joseph Thomas, Joseph Baker, George Limmerman, Samuel Rogers, Benjamin Breton, Matthew Gardner, George A. Patterson, James Baker, Isaac Cade. Unordained preachers were: Zarah Curtiss, William Dickinson, and Isaac Hornback.

George Alkire moved to Illinois in 1836. He was ill for a time but when he started preaching it involves all the groups. In January 27, 1841, George writes from Pittsfield, Illinois to the church at Jamestown, Ohio. The epistle was a travel log of his journey from Ohio to Illinois. Alkire preached regularly and set in order the things that were wanting on his "long but pleasant" journey. He visited overnight with Brother Stone in Jacksonville. He had been preaching in Pike County at the Highland, Pittsfield, Barre, and Perry congregations. Most of the congregations in the West have seemed in general union, with only a few exceptions where lines of distinction had been drawn between "the Reformers" (Campbellites) and the Old Christians. Once again Elder Alkire made the plea for unity and closed with "Finally, Brethren, farewell; be perfect, live in love and the God of love and peace shall be with you...."

The Christian Messenger carried minutes by B. F. Van Dooser of the Christian conference at Highland, Pike County, Illinois, April 9, 1841. Present were: George Alkire, B. W. Stone, J. Burbridge, D. Roberts, Wm. Strong, Wm. Gale, D. Henry, C. Bolin, J. Sweet, J. Green Jr., Wm. Gilliam. Elder G. Alkire gave the opening address. Wm. Gilliam was asked to chair the conference and B. F. Van Dooser to be secretary. A committee of five, including Alkire, was chosen to arrange the business that was to come before the meeting. Notice that Alkire sought unity of all the groups and noted that only in a few cases were lines drawn between the old Christians and the Campbell reformers.

Notice again:

He preached four times near Covington to divided congregations, part Reformers and part Old Christians. Some objections

were made by the Reformers to Alkire's sermons; however, all
came to give him "the right hand of fellowship" at the close of
the meeting.

and this statement,

> He met his good friend, Joseph Thomas, whom Alkire had
> wished for in one of his letters from Illinois, and Dr. Winans
> Borgman. The three men preached that night and "closed in all
> good feeling." Most of these preachers were of the Christian
> Connexion. Alkire seemed to travel freely among the Christian
> Connexion and the Stone people; he very much wanted a union
> of these believers.

We seldom see pointed out that three Stone preachers showed up at the
Mahoning Baptist Association in Ohio in 1827 when Scott was appointed
evangelist. It was rather common for preachers of various stripes to attend conferences close to where they lived even if the conference was
affiliated with a different faith community. One of the three was John
Secrist or Secrest who also later shows up preaching in Michigan and Illinois. He helped establish a congregation in Cuba, Fulton County in 1832.

> Min. John Secrist, of Ohio, held a meeting in the settlement, and
> in February, 1832, baptized eighteen persons and organized a
> church with Charles Rigdon and Morgan Hartford.[34]

Secrest prior to this time had preached also in Michigan and Indiana.

> Nathan J. Mitchell and Elder John Secrest left Belmont County,
> Ohio and preached in several places in southwestern Michigan in
> the spring of 1831. Secrest wrote Walter Scott, "I have been en-
> gaged in a tour on the frontiers of Michigan, Indiana and Illi-
> nois; preaching once or twice per day, except when in the
> wilderness where no inhabitants were, save the Indians. I im-
> mersed a number and formed them into Churches on the re-
> vealed plan."[35]

---

[34] Haynes, 205.

[35] Nathan J. Mitchell, *Reminiscences and Incidents in the Life and Travels of a Pioneer
Preacher of the "Ancient" Gospel* (Cincinnati: Chase & Hall, Publishers,1877) 89-90,
and *The Evangelist*, 1.10 (Oct 1832) 238.

Conclusion

We conclude, therefore, that in the first four decades of the Restorationist congregations in Illinois, the various strands of Restorationist churches persisted with considerable flexibility. People and congregations moved relatively freely from one group to another. By the 1860s, however, lines of distinction had become rigid with the state meetings of the Disciples (the Stone-Campbell Movement) separate from the conferences of the O'Kelly, Jones-Smith and Stone remnant, by then more likely known as the Christian Denomination.

3. Earliest Campbell Congregations in Illinois

The first Restorationist congregations in Illinois were from the O'Kelly, Jones/Smith, and Stone trajectories. Those influenced by Alexander Campbell followed shortly thereafter. We know that the Campbells and their congregations belonged to the Redstone Baptist Association in Pennsylvania and western Virginia prior to 1816 when Alexander Campbell was invited to present his often discussed "Sermon on the Law."[1] Those congregations influenced by the Campbells and later Scott became known as Reformed Baptists. When forced out of the Redstone Association the Campbells founded a congregation in Wellsburg, Virginia, now West Virginia, and joined the Ohio Mahoning Baptist Association.[2] Soon persons influenced by the Scott/Campbell thinking began to be pushed out of other Baptist Associations especially in Kentucky in the early 1820s.[3] Did some of these people make their way to Illinois at this stage and found congregations? We will return to that question after we show how Campbell's periodicals gained followers in Illinois.

Illinois in the Christian Baptist and Millennial Harbinger

Alexander Campbell edited and published the *Christian Baptist* from July 1823 until July, 1830. Although late with the first issue, he began the Millennial Harbinger with the January 1830 issue; both journals were published simultaneously until July 1830, when the twelfth issue of the *Christian Baptist* (Volume Seven) was published. As evidence of Campbell's growing influence in Illinois, we note the following:

• Agents or Subscribers to the *Christian Baptist*

---

[1] *ESCM* 680.

[2] Ibid., 501-02.

[3] Ibid., 119-122, Also Richard T. Hughes, *Reviving the Ancient Faith*, 10-18.

- Dr. Benjamin Edwards, Edwardsville, (Madison County) is a new agent, the first in Illinois.[4]

- James Fisher, Dillons, (Tazewell County); Francis Dickerson, Mt. Carmel (Washington County); and Abraham Berger (Sangamon County) are new agents.[5]

- M. R. Tremble (Sangamon County) paid for Volumes 6 and 7 of the Christian Baptist for himself, W. Morgan, A. Berger, and R. Cownover.[6]

- In December 1829, an unknown person, writing from Bluffdale (Greene County) Illinois, is impressed with the *Christian Baptist* and has read Campbell's *New Testament*. His incisive, appreciative remarks about Campbell's growing influence in Illinois merit repeating:

My opinion is not of sufficient importance to render any one vain, but such as it is, it is warmly in favor of the Christian Baptist. I know of no work in our country so well conducted, and, what will be far more gratifying to your feelings, none that is doing half the good in this state that it is. "Campbellism," and "Campbellites," have become very common terms in Illinois, and they are not unfrequently pronounced with a bitterness that reminds me of the "Christian Dog" of the Turks. Is hostility to pure, undefiled religion found no where except among Infidels? It is not; nor is persecution confined to the walls of the inquisition. Public opinion on the subject of religion is, however, rapidly undergoing a change: inquiry is abroad, and the time has gone by when religious sentiments are to be adopted merely because they are *prescribed* by men of high sounding titles. In bringing about this revolution, the fearless numbers of the Christian Baptist have been chiefly instrumental, and I deeply regret that you have felt so much of the persecuting spirit of the middle ages

---

[4] *CB* 4.11 (June 1827) 264. It is highly probable this Dr. Edwards is the brother of Illinois Governor Ninian Edwards. "When Governor Edwards was stricken down with cholera in July, 1833, and rapidly sinking, a messenger was sought among the terrified villagers to go at once to Edwardsville, twenty-five miles distant, for the Governor's brother, Dr. Benjamin Edwards." Newton Bateman, et al., *Historical Encyclopedia of Illinois and History of St. Clair County* (Chicago: Munsell Publishing Company, Publishers, 1907) Volume II, 971.

[5] *CB* 7.2 (September 1829) 43

[6] *CB* 7.10 (May 1830) 244.

assailing you from almost every section where your work circulates:—but go on; and may you not desist till primitive religion is every where restored.

- At the close of the letter, the writer shared his thoughts on how to translate John 2:4, referencing Campbell's *New Testament*:

> I have seen but one copy of your Testament. I set up a large portion of the night in examining it. I think it much truer to the spirit of the original than any other version that I have seen. I have not the presumption to criticise, but you will pardon me for thinking that a passage in John (Evangelist) is not conformable to the Greek of the common copy. Perhaps I shall only display my own ignorance. In John, chap. ii. ver. 4. *Ti emoi kai soi gunai;* I should have translated, *"Woman, what is that to you and me?"*[7]

Illinois in the Millennial Harbinger

The Illinois entries in the *Millennial Harbinger*, founded in 1830, accelerate. David McWhirter's invaluable index of the *Millennial Harbinger* has more than 260 entries for "Illinois" and many additional scores of entries for Illinois individuals and congregations.[8] Williams used several of these reports as the basis for the earliest conservative Illinois congregations.[9]

Dates for the 19th Century

The below chart of dates is helpful as we turn the reader's attention to the beginning of individual congregations. The chart also alludes to the topics we will take up in later chapters of this book.

---

[7] *CB* 7.7 (February 1830) 147, 148. The writer is familiar with higher education developments in Illinois and sarcastically remarks on political developments. He refers to "Mr. Ellis" (the Presbyterian John M. Ellis) and the eastern fund raising efforts that led to the founding of Illinois College at Jacksonville. We are almost certain the correspondent is the Baptist Dr. John Russell, "the noted pioneer scholar, of Bluffdale, Greene county." See, George Washington Smith, *A History of Southern Illinois: A Narrative Account of Its Historical Progress, Its People, and Its Principal Interests* (Chicago and New York: The Lewis Publishing Company, 1912) Vol. 1, 382, 383 for more on Russell, John M. Peck and Rock Spring Seminary.

[8] David I. McWhirter, *An Index to the Millennial Harbinger* (Joplin, Missouri: College Press Publishing Company, 1981).

[9] Williams, *History*, 14-20.

Date	Event	Notes
1818	Illinois Statehood	
1818	William Kinkade (1783-1832) moved to Lawrence County, IL, near Vincennes, IN	Knew David Purviance (1766-1847) in Ohio
1823	*Christian Baptist* started.	
1824	Andrew Scott and Theophilus Sweet preach near Berlin. Spring Creek/Mt. Zion/ Berlin Christian Church established. Claims to be second congregation in Sangamon County, fourth in Illinois.	
1826	Stone's *Christian Messenger* started.	
1827	Elijah Goodwin (1807-1879) preached in IN and IL, Early influenced by Stone, Later merged group	West and north of Evansville,IN
1832 -40	Conferences of churches that didn't merge with the Campbell reformers established in Illinois, Central and Spoon River area.	
1830	Illinois Population 157,485	
1830	*Millennial Harbinger* started. *Christian Baptist* ceased.	
1832	Black Hawk War	
1834	Barton W. Stone (1772-1844) moved to Jacksonville	Freed wife's slaves
1834 -36	Family of David Lipscomb (1831-1917) in Springfield area	In order to free slaves, but did so in Indiana
1838	Alexander Graham publishes the *Berean* at Springfield	
1839	Nauvoo, Illinois, founded. Eleven Christian Churches in Sangamon County.	

1840	First Annual State Meeting held in Springfield. Stone and 8 others call for the meeting.	
1844	Stone dies at Hannibal, Missouri. Joseph Smith killed at Carthage.	Sidney Rigdon (1793-1876) hoped to take over from Smith. Rigdon was in the Campbell movement earlier.
1845	Alexander Campbell (1788-1866) visits Winchester and nearby Jacksonville.	
1845	*Christian Messenger* ceases.	
1847	Alfred Padon publishes the *Christian*	
1850	Daniel Bates starts *Western Evangelist* in Iowa; later titles are *Christian Evangelist* and *Evangelist*, which ceases in 1865	Numerous articles about Illinois
1850	First Chicago SCM congregation started.	
1852	At Illinois Annual Meeting, an Education Task Force is started and tasked with guiding efforts to establish schools and support existing schools.	
1853	Alexander Campbell tours Illinois and Missouri.	
1853	*Christian Sentinel* started at Springfield in Sept.	
1855	Eureka, Abingdon and Berean Colleges founded; all are co-educational.	
1855	*Gospel Advocate* started in Nashville	
1856	Benjamin Franklin (1812-1878) starts *American Christian Review* in Cincinnati.	Many Illinois subscribers

1857	Walter Scott Russell (1832—1863). Moved to Jacksonville to be minister at Jacksonville congregation and president of Berean College	Died of disease as the result of contacts with sick soldiers in Civil War.
1857	Toward end of Illinois and Iowa tour, Alexander Campbell visits Chicago; is disappointed by lack of significant SCM congregation there. Also visits Paris, IL.	
1858	E. L. Craig and John S. Sweeney buy out the *Christian Sentinel* and start *Bible Advocate*	
1859	Founding of Union Christian College, Merom, IN The college closed down in 1924 South of Terre Haute on Wabash across from Crawford County, IL	A Christian Connexion College. Summerbells from Jones/Smith movement there
1860	Illinois Population 1,711,981 Berean College closed for lack of funding. Benjamin Franklin visits Jacksonville	
1860	*Christian Freeman* started at Jacksonville by W. S. Russell	
1862	Alexander Campbell visits Illinois	
1863	*Gospel Echo* started at Carrollton by E. L. Craig. *Bible Advocate* ceased.	
1861 -65	Civil War, 250,000 IL men served	
1864	Benjamin Franklin moves *American Christian Review* to Anderson, IN	Many Illinois subscribers
1865	Downs and Karr start *Christian Herald* at Wapella. Iowa brethren start *Evangelist*.	
1868	James Harvey Garrison (1842-1931), first as associate editor of *Gospel Echo* at Macomb, then Quincy	To Abingdon College; it later merged with Eureka

1869	*Christian Herald* ceases.	
1882	Garrison issued the *Christian-Evangelist*, merging other journals, representing more than ten predecessors	Moved to St. Louis
1886	Daniel Sommer (1850 – 1940) buys *American Christian Review*. New name, *Octographic Review*.	Significant influence in Illinois conservative congregations.
1889	Daniel Sommer and Sand Creek "Address and Declaration"	
1890	Founding of the University of Chicago	William Rainey Harper, President 1891
1894	Disciples Divinity House at University of Chicago	
1895	Edward Scribner Ames (1870-1958) Ph.D. U. Chicago, philosophy and theology	1900-1940 Hyde Park Minister
1896	Herbert L. Willett (1864-1944) Ph.D. U. of Chicago	Old Testament
1897	Winfred Ernest Garrison (1874-1969) Ph.D. U. of Chicago in church history.	Dissertation: The Theology of Alexander Campbell

Campbell Background Congregations in Illinois

We get some hint in various sources of congregations with a Campbell background planted before 1830. The first congregation may have been one at Keensburg in Wabash County according to Haynes:

> Keensburg.
> Organized 1819… on Saturday before the fifth Sabbath in August, 1819, a church of Christ was constituted consisting of seven members…This congregation has from its beginning, in 1819, always been a church of Christ; it was never of the Christian Denomination. Such is the united testimony of the oldest residents of the community, the original records of the congregation and the history of Wabash County.[10]

---

[10] Haynes, 419.

The church in Cantrall in Sanamon County organized in 1820 may have been the second congregation to have had Campbell influence according to Haynes's statement.

> Cantrall.
> Organized 1820, by Stephen England...In 1819 a band of pioneers made the first settlement north of the Sangamon River, a few miles northwest of Springfield. Stephen England was the leader. He was born in Virginia in 1773. When quite young he was taken to Bath County, Ky. There he married Anna Harper. They became the parents of twelve children. The family moved to Madison County, O., in 1813, and in the fall of 1818 to Madison County, IL. Mr. England was a Baptist preacher in Kentucky, but was never known as such in Sangamon County. In June, 1819, he first preached to his neighbors who assembled in his home. The next year (May15) he formed a church...The church has always been missionary. It was never affiliated with the Christian Denomination.[11]

Six years later a congregation was planted in Edgar County. The Little Grove congregation according to Haynes apparently had Campbell-Scott influence since he reserves the term Restoration Movement for either Campell or Stone-Campbell backgrounds.

> Little Grove (Vermilion).
> Organized 1826, by Samuel McGee...The church was formed through the efforts chiefly of Mrs. Mary Morrison and her sister. Mrs. Anna Fitzgerald. These women, with others in this settlement, had come to Edgar County from Kentucky, where they had come to some knowledge of the Restoration movement. The Little Grove congregation was always a church of Christ; it was never in any way connected with the Christian Denomination.[12]

We learn of people in Illinois who had direct contact with the Campbells. "Mrs. Margaret Carl was one of the charter members. She was baptized by Thomas Campbell in 1826, and at the age of ninety-five years passed to her reward." She was a member of the Wapello church in Dewitt

---

[11] Ibid., 373, 374
[12] Ibid., 186, 187.

County.[13] People knowing the Campbells settled in Hancock County sometime later.

> Mt. Pleasant (Plymouth), Hancock County
>   Organized 1833, by Gilmore Callison… Mt. Pleasant Church is located midway between Carthage and Plymouth… in 1833… Robert, John, James, George and Elizabeth Stark united with the church some years after its formation. The Starks, Pattens, Drawns and others were firm friends of Alexander Campbell in Scotland. Margaret Patten was one of his friends who ministered to him in prison. He called her and her girl companion his "ministering angels." Robert Stark, when he first came from Scotland, and probably James Stark also, made their residence at Mr. Campbell's home in Virginia.[14]

Early Preachers

As far as we can tell the earliest preachers from the Jones/Smith and Stone Connexion congregations came to the counties just west of the Wabash River, that is, also the Indiana line, in Wabash and Lawrence Counties half the way from Chicago to Cairo. We will set out details and insights into some of the important early preachers.

William Kinkade
One of the earliest preachers of note was William Kinkade (1783-1832). Kinkade (sometimes spelled Kincaid) was born in Pennsylvania but when he was three his family moved to a backwoods region of Kentucky. Kinkade was raised a Presbyterian. According to his account in the preface to his book *Bible Doctrine* 1829, his conversion took place a year after the great Cane Ridge Camp meeting:

> "I was brought under still deeper conviction for my sins, and my trouble of mind increased till the 26th day of September 1802, and then at a large camp-meeting, God converted my soul; he removed the burden of guilt from my mind, shed abroad his

---

[13] Ibid., 179.
[14] Ibid., 218.

love in my heart, and filled me with joy unspeakable and full of glory."[15]

Kinkade preached for a time then studied with a Dr. Stubs in Newport, Kentucky, across the Ohio River from Cincinnati. Later in the preface of his book, he wrote, "I disown all party names. I do not profess to belong to any sect of Christians. I fellowship all good people of every name without regard to how much they may differ from me in doctrines. I have written this book as the sentiments of no sect, nor denomination of people. It is a sketch of my own views. If you are a Christian, or a sincere seeker of religion, I remain your brother, in the patience, tribulation, and hope of the kingdom of Jesus Christ." These remarks are similar to those made by Abner Jones and Barton W. Stone.

Kinkade came to know David Purviance a chief leader among the Stoneites who did not go with the Stone-Campbell merger. In 1816 Kinkade bought a small acreage in Lawrence County, Illinois. He was a member of the state convention 1822-24 that drew up the state's consti-tution. He was influential in speaking against slavery in Illinois and pro-viding regulations for the freeing of slaves in the state. Because of his wife's health he moved to Ohio in 1826. He was buried in a cemetery at Burlington, Hamilton County, Ohio.

Kinkade along with B. McCorkle were among the first Stoneite Chris-tians to preach in Lawrence County. They preached in groves or in hous-es of the recent settlers. They also preached at the Barney's Prairie founded in 1816, the first Christian Church in Wabash County on the east bank of Crawfish Creek and perhaps in Illinois. Kinkade along with James Poole organized this congregation. Kinkade was the first to preach at the Spring Hill Church, established in 1820 and he continued to preach there along with Daniel Travis. The Spring Hill building was in located in Lawrence County southwest of Bridgeport which was about fifteen miles west of Vincennes, Indiana. The building was also used for a school and was available to other religious groups.[16] Samuel Rogers (1789-1877), a well known Kentucky and Ohio preacher, who later traveled through Illi-nois, visited Kinkade about 1825. Rogers mentioned that Kinkade along with John and Gabriel Scott were preachers in the congregation, but

---

[15] Levi Purviance, *The Biography of David Purviance, with His Memoirs* (Dayton, Ohio: B. F. and G. W. Ellis, 1848) 274.

[16] http://wc.rootsweb.ancestry.com/cgi-bin/igm.cgi? op=GET&db=adgedge&id=140787

Rogers felt that these men were not as dedicated to declaring the Gospel as they should have been.[17]

Elijah Shaw on Early Churches

These Wabash area churches were visited by traveling preachers a decade later. Elijah Shaw, who achieved fame as an Indiana preacher in succeeding years, stopped in at Barney's Prairie soon after he commenced preaching in 1826.

In the Summer of 1826, he [Shaw] received a letter from some friends in Illinois, near the mouth of Illinois river, [North of St. Louis, perhaps Pike and Calhoun Counties] requesting him to come out and hold a few meetings in that region. This he resolved to do, taking the Conference in his route. This body met that year at some point in Owen county [Indiana]. After its adjournment he set out on horseback for his Illinois appointments, having just twenty-five cents in his pocket.

There was at that time a flourishing church on Allison Prairie [See below], some ten miles west of Vincennes. He resolved to proceed by way of this church, to spend a night with the brethren there, and preach for them. He reached *Christian settlement* before night, and called on a brother Daniel Travis, to whom he made known the object of his coming. The brother, who looked upon the outward appearance, asked him several questions as to his age, the length of time he had been preaching, etc., and finally agreed to circulate the appointment. Quite a congregation assembled, to whom he discoursed in a manner that fully met their expectations.

Next morning he started at early dawn in hope of reaching the house of a brother by noon. It was necessary for him to keep within the brotherhood as much as possible, for his purse was light and he received little or nothing for his labor in the Lord. Some preached vehemently against receiving

---

[17] John I. Rogers, ed., *Autobiography of Elder Samuel Rogers*, (Cincinnati: Standard Publishing Company, 1880) 62.

any remuneration, but "he had not so learned Christ." Moreover it seemed to him that, if none were receiving more than he, there was no need of warning the brethren against paying the preachers! Previous to starting, his friend Travis asked him how far he was going. "Some hundred and fifty miles," was the reply. "How much money have you for the trip?" continued the questioner. "*Twenty-five cents*," said the preacher. The good brother then gave him an additional quarter—a liberal contribution in that day—and he went on his way rejoicing.

He reached the brother's by the way-side after the sun had crossed the meridian. But dinner was soon prepared, which proved to be the last meal he enjoyed until he reached the end of his journey. Remembering that "a righteous man regardeth the life of his beast," he spent his money for food for his horse, while he himself fasted *for two whole days*...

Having preached a week or two for his Illinois friends, he set out on his return, intending to reach a camp-meeting on Barney's Prairie, Wabash county, by Saturday night. But at the close of that day he found himself twenty miles from the camp-ground, the road to which ran through a thinly settled region, and was not much traveled. Nevertheless about nine o'clock, P. M. he left the old Vincennes and St. Louis road and set out afresh for the camp-meeting, resolved once more to travel all night rather than fail in his undertaking. Of him this determination to carry out his purposes is characteristic.[18]

Allison Prairie

A claim is also made for the early founding of a Restorationist congregation at Allison Prairie in 1815. We also learn from this history when the church came into the Campbell orbit in 1828 and a name change made in 1845.[19]

---

[18] http://www.therestorationmovement.com/_states/ohio/goodwin.htm
[19] http://lawrencelore.blogspot.com/2013/01/allison-prairie-christian-church-1815.html.

Allison Prairie Christian Church 1815-1942

The following article was written by Philip L. Young, and traces the early history of the Christian churches in Lawrence county, starting with the original Stoneite Christian Church (1815), evolving into the Church of Christ at Center School (1845) and finally being known as Allison Prairie Christian Church, which served the community for a total of 127 years before disbanding in 1942. From this first church, six other Christian churches began: Spring Hill, Lawrenceville, Pleasant Ridge (aka Little Ambraw Church of Christ), Pleasant Hill (aka White House), Russellville, and Rising Sun.

Illinois Christian History Series No.1

The Allison Prairie church and school – established 1815

"An act of the Illinois territorial legislature forming Crawford County was passed at the session of 1816 – 1817. The
legal description outlined the County as being 60 miles wide,
beginning at the mouth of the Embarras River and extending as far west as present–day Fayette County, and running
Northwest to the Canadian border. The cities of Cham-
pagne, Danville, Joliet, Chicago, Rockford, Milwaukee, and
Green Bay, all stand on ground once embraced by this grand
County.

But even previous to this time, in the summer of 1815, a
wagon train carrying about 100 settlers from Kentucky and
Tennessee, arrived on the open prairie about 8 miles northwest of Vincennes, Indiana. Within a year they had put in
land claims and built log cabins to house their large families.
They had also built a combination meeting house and
schoolhouse which served the church there for more than 30
years. This primitive double log house is thought to have
been the first building designed for religious and educational
purpose ever erected by American settlers in the state of
Illinois. The pioneers who built it were followers of Barton
W. Stone of Kentucky and were insisting the Bible was the
only sufficient rule of faith, and that the name 'Christian'
was the only appropriate for a believer to wear. Therefore
the newly established church was called the Christian Church

on the Allison Prairie, both at the time of its organization in 1815 and at its reorganization in February, 1828.

The members of this little church were very influential. The first two schoolmasters in Lawrence County (it was then the South part of Crawford County) were Eli Harris and John Martin. Both were members of Allison Prairie. So was Scott Riggs, the first blacksmith in the area. Riggs was also a preacher and later a member of the first state legislature held in 1818. Richard B. McCorkle, William Travis, and Robert Turner were citizens of repute. McCorkle's daughter married John Johnson of Tazewell County, Illinois. All three of their sons became noted preachers of the gospel. One of them B. W. Johnson was the editor of the widely used *People's New Testament with Notes,* and the author of the commentary on Revelation entitled *A Vision of the Ages.*

13 years after the first settlement a new group of families came to join the original colony. Unlike the first group many of these were acquainted with the reformers Thomas and Alexander Campbell, and their famous disciple, Raccoon John Smith. Following their arrival, therefore, a reorganization of the church took place on Sunday, February 10, 1828. The chartering statement reads in part, 'taking the Scriptures alone as their only system of faith and practice, and the name Christian as their only active ecclesiastical name'. 48 names were signed to this agreement initially and 51 more during the next few years. In this period weekly communion and immersion for their remission of sins was adopted and by 1845 the name was changed to the Church of Christ and Center School House.

The old log building having served its purpose, a new frame building was erected in 1850, a separate school house was constructed nearby, and a thriving general store began operating in the community. In 1873 the Allison post office was established about 1/2 mile east of the church location. The village came to be known as Centerville. By the end of the century the church had a membership of 170 and in attendance in excess of 100 per Lord Day's. In 1896 an even larger meeting place became necessary and was built by the prospering congregation, but soon after this a period of decline set in that gradually lessened the influence of the pioneer church. Although H. L. Hayes (afterward the longtime minister at Charleston) had a successful ministry here in the 1920s, the years following were lean. During the more than a century that Allison Prairie had been in existence it had colonized at least six other New Testament churches: Spring Hill (southwest of present-day Bridgeport), Lawrenceville, Pleasant Ridge (Little Embarras Church of Christ), Pleasant Hill (White House), Russellville, and Rising Sun. Weakened by these departures the church faced an uncertain future.

In 1942 the federal government chose the broad flat Allison Prairie as a site of a military installation, an Air Force training camp to be known as George Field. The emergency situation created by World War II allowed the government to confiscate many farms, the property of the old church, and all other holdings in the area. The houses were moved off, barracks, landing strips, and hangars were built in their place. The Christians now few in number, decided to disband and scatter into neighboring congregations of the same faith. The old Christian church (Stoneite), Church of Christ at Center School, or Allison Prairie Christian Church (as it was known at the last) was now gone after hundred and 27 years of faithful service. .."

Seth Gard

Another man of importance who was likewise involved in local and state government was Seth Gard (1775-1845). He was born near Morristown, Ky. In 1788 his family moved to Ohio west of Cincinnati. In 1808 he became a member of the Stoneite Christians and soon began preaching. He moved with his wife and family to Illinois in 1814 and bought a small farm near Mt. Carmel in Wabash County in the Barney's Prairie settlement. In 1816, he was elected to a Wabash County judgeship. Not long after he was appointed a delegate to the state legislature and in 1818 elected a member of he convention to form a state constitution. It was there along with Kinkade and others that he opposed slavery in Illinois.[20]

---

[20] Humphreys, 137f.

According to Nathaniel Haynes, Gard came to Barney's Prairie settlement in 1813. Haynes identified him as the first elder of the Barney's Prairie congregation. Haynes declared that Gard "…with Min. James Pool, Joseph Wood and others, is due the honor of starting that church on the apostolic basis. Haynes further stated that, "He was a member of the third Territorial Legislature, and was also a member of the convention that framed the State Constitution in 1818."[21]

David McGahe(y)

In 1815 David McGahey moved to Crawford County, Illinois, to the region around Palestine on the Wabash River north of Vincennes, Indiana. He labored faithfully as a preacher but much as Kinkade and Gard served in the Illinois legislature. According to Humphries, "Not only did he preach a free salvation, but he wrote much, never hesitating to do what duty demanded. He was twice elected to the legislature, and served several years as receiver at the Land Office in Palestine.[22] Humphreys further remarked, "William Kinkade, Seth Gard, and himself, of the Christian, and Daniel Parker, of the Baptist Church, were four of the most active men in keeping slavery out of the constitution of Illinois."[23]

While serving in the legislature and elsewhere, several of the early restoration preachers in Illinois were involved in seeing to it that the state of Illinois declared itself a non-slave state. While Illinois clearly by legislative decision opposed slavery, the status of African Americans in the state was much more problematic. A case in point is the 1834 move of Granville Lipscomb, the father of the later famous Tennessee preacher editor David Lipscomb, from Tennessee to Sangamon County, Illinois, in expectation that he could free his slaves. He discovered, however, that he would have to pay a thousand dollar bond for the release of each slave and even then the right of the slaves in Illinois would be uncertain. The result was that he arranged to free the slaves in Indiana and then moved back to Tennessee.[24] Middleton explained the muddled state of Illinois laws and intentions regarding blacks:

---

[21] Haynes, 516.

[22] Humphreys, 227.

[23] Ibid., 228,

[24] Robert E. Hooper, *Crying in the Wilderness: a Biography of David Lipscomb* (Nashville: Lipscomb University, 1979) 21 – 23.

Illinois adopted its first comprehensive slave code—black laws —in 1819. Through the codes, Illinois discouraged the immigration of free blacks by compelling them to produce a certificate of freedom and to register with a county clerk. Refugees without a certificate would not have legal residence; consequently, they were ineligible for employment, subject to removal, or could be sold as runaway slaves. Illinois did not welcome blacks; it welcomed slave holders who brought along blacks as laborers.

Illinois also restrained masters who considered the free North the place to release worn-out slaves. Some people argued that the state's immigration law was necessary to prevent Illinois from becoming a dumping ground for slave holders. Stephen Douglas argued that Illinois would not become "an asylum for all the old and decrepit and broken-down Negroes that may emigrate or be sent to it." Whites threatened to resort to violence if the legislature of Illinois did not restrict black immigration. One anti-black spokesman threatened that whites "would take the matter into their hands, and commence a war of extermination."

A visiting master could legally free a slave in Illinois by paying $1,000 bond for each per on released in the state. This policy was mainly a prohibitive measure; Illinois, one of the most proslavery free states in the Union, did not want an extensive black population. Illinois might have faced an immigration crisis had it granted refuge to southern blacks. Its denunciation of black people, however, did not emanate from its migration problem; rather, from strong racial prejudice among whites in the state against people of color.[25]

We learn more details on the "Christian Settlement" in Lawrence County. Samuel Lemon, with four children, George, Thomas, Polly and Susan, came from North Carolina, about 1818, and settled on the N. E. i of sec. 26. He was a farmer and shoemaker, and resided permanently where he first settled. The family were members of the Christian Church.[26] The book has detailed information on where the families who settled in Christian Settlement were from:

---

[25] Stephen Middleton, *Black Laws in the Old Northwest: A Documentary History* (Westport, CT: Greenwood Press, 1993), 273.

[26] http://www.adkinshorton.net/histories/ combinedhistoryof%20edwardsawrenceandwabashcountiesIL-1883.pdf

In this year Scott Riggs settled on the N. W. quarter of section 26, T. 4 j E. 11. He brought to the settlement a family of four children, viz : Sally, Polly, Cynthia, and Harriet. He was a blacksmith by trade, and a minister of the gospel He subsequently moved to Scott county, where he died.

On Riggs and the Connection Haynes wrote:

His grandfather, Scott Riggs, came to Illinois in 1815 and settled on Allison Prairie, in Lawrence County, which was then a part of Crawford. He was a blacksmith, farmer and preacher. He served as a member of the first Legislature of the State in 1818. He was active in uniting the Christians and Disciples in that part of the State. He moved to Scott County in 1825, and was a member of the church at Exeter at the time of his death [Five miles west of Jacksonville].[27]

A few congregations were founded early in Logan County in the Lincoln region. A church was planted in Armington in 1828 by a mixture of people from different states.

Hittle's Grove and the prairies round about it were as pleasing as any upon which human eyes ever rested. Into that locality, eighty-five years ago, the following named families began to settle: the Hittles and Judys from Ohio; the Albrights from Tennessee; the Burts, Quisenberrys, Hainlines, Dills and Millers from Kentucky, and the Hieronymuses from Virginia.[28]

Tennessee preachers also came early to nearby McLean and Tazewell Counties.

Reuben Carlock was a native of Overton County, Tenn. [North of Cookville] came to Illinois in 1827 and on October 10 settled in Dry Grove, five miles southwest of the present site of Carlock. Carlock's family was the fifth to settle in Dry Grove. That was then a part of Tazewell County. In that year the county-seat was located at Mackinaw town. There were then five families in Twin Grove, seven families in Stout's Grove, three families in Brown's Grove, thirteen families in Keg's or Blooming Grove,

---

[27] Haynes, 590.
[28] Ibid., 285.

two families in Funk's Grove and one family in Three Miles Grove. All of the first settlers made their homes along the timber. Indians were then many in this section. Old Town was one of their camps. It was a strip of timber some two miles wide thirteen miles east of Bloomington. The country was full of deer, wild turkeys, prairie chickens and pigeons. These settlers traded at Springfield and Pekin.

William Brown was a Christian preacher who came from Tennessee to Dry Grove, IL, in 1828. He was a friend of Reuben Carlock. In August of that year, Mr. Carlock hitched up his ox team, and, accompanied by some members of his own family and his guest, Preacher Brown, drove to the cabin of Ebenezer Rhodes, in Blooming Grove, for a three days' meeting. It was during this meeting that the Rhodes and Carlock families were united in one church.[29]

While we don't know that these families came by the rivers to central Illinois, they could have left Tennessee on the Cumberland River, into the Tennessee River then the Ohio, the Mississippi and up the Illinois River almost to their destination.

We already mentioned that some moved from Kentucky and Tennessee during the Civil War because they favored the cause of the north. Sometimes several of those who came moved back from where they came after the war was over. Numbers moved away from the Metropolis congregation in Massac County which bordered on the Ohio River at the southern tip of Illinois

> Metropolis. Organized 1864, by Joseph Brown…the church was at first made up largely of refugees who had come from Kentucky and Tennessee during the Civil War. After its close many of them moved away. The organization was made in the courthouse. [30]

The same situation developed at Vienna in Johnson County near the southern tip of Illinois.

> During the Civil War, John Lemon and his son Josephus came as refugees from the South to Johnson County. They at once formed a church of Christ at Gum Spring, in 1863, four miles

---

[29] Ibid., 281, 282.
[30] Ibid., 323.

west of Vienna. Its members were also mostly refugees. The house used at Gum Spring was a union chapel. A Baptist church had been first organized there. After the close of the war, many returned to their homes in the South; thus the congregation ceased to be.[31]

The War also impacted congregations in central Illinois, for example, the Athens congregation in Menard County. "During the earlier years of the Civil War the congregation again went to pieces. But it was renewed again in 1864 by the return and faithful ministry of Clayborne Hall." The war also troubled the Centralia congregation in Marion County. "During the Civil War and for years following, the church sustained serious injury from the bitter political feeling that then existed.[32]

Some of those who came were from Tennessee and Kentucky of the Mulkey background. Philip Mulkey moved to Illinois in 1836 and founded Mulkeytown along with others of the Mulkey background. The congregation they founded may be the longest existing Restorationist church in Illinois.

> The original congregation began to meet in the home of John Kirkpatrick in the year 1818 with the formalized "Church" being organized in 1823. Thus, the Mulkeytown Christian Church is the oldest continuous congregation of the Christian Church in the State of Illinois.[33]

T. K. Means reported,

> The first settlers of this part of the country called themselves Baptists and met at the house of John Kirkpatrick, who settled here in 1818. But these people had been baptized in Kentucky and Tennessee by John Mulkey and his brother Philip, who were Baptist preachers, but went into the Reformation with B. W. Stone early in the last century. It is a fact that John Mulkey was tried for heresy in 1809 in Kentucky. No one now knows when these people left off the name "Baptist" and adopted the name "Christian," for there was no Baptist church and people who held to the usages of that church in this whole settlement...I once heard D. C. Mulkey say that when he came to Illinois in

---

[31] Ibid., 239.
[32] Ibid., 310.
[33] https://en.wikipedia.org/wiki/Mulkeytown_Christian_Church

1832, his elder brothers, John M. and Jonathan H. Mulkey, were then living here and that they were devoted church-members at that time. Then we must infer there was a church organization at that time.[34]

Early these churches may have been Christian Connexion, but if so they merged into the Stone-Campbell-Scott movement.

Many of those migrating to Illinois came down the Ohio to the Mississippi, then up the Mississippi to the Illinois to the region around Springfield. By 1836 a canal was chartered by the state to be constructed from Beardstown to Springfield on the Sangamon River making it possible to go by boat even farther inland. In the 1820s those coming from Virginia and North Carolina often traveled through Charleston, later West Virginia, and on west down the Kanawha River to the Ohio. This was the route of the forebears of George Alkire who moved to Illinois in 1836.[35] The Federal Land Grant Law of 1851 transferred 2.5 million acres to the Illinois Central Railroad. The land bordered on the 700 mile rail line running from Chicago to Cairo.[36] This land was sold to the many persons from the east and southeast moving into Illinois.

In some cases the origins of the churches as to Restorationist background are clear and in various cases not. For example Haynes mentions persons coming from Cleveland who established congregations in Lake County north of Chicago. These settlers were most likely from a Jones/Smith Background but they changed at least in Haynes' judgment to become a Disciple congregation.

> In the thirties, Darius Gage and two of his brothers, with Benedict Stevens and Emmons Shepard, came from near Cleveland, O., and settled on lands in the northern part of Lake County. A village, located about three miles northeast of Fox Lake and one mile south of the Wisconsin line, was laid out, to which the name of Gageville was given. Some years afterward the name was changed to Antioch, by which it is still known. In this community a church after the primitive order was constituted Aug. 7, 1841 with twenty members, by Min. William Davenport, then of

---

[34] Haynes, 24, 25.

[35] See Chapter 5: The Alkires Arrive in Illinois.

[36] http://www.icrrhistorical.org/history.html. See also Richard Lyle Power, *Planting Corn Belt Culture; The Impress of the Upland Southerner and Yankee in the Old Northwest* (Indianapolis: Indiana Historical Society, 1953).

Walnut Grove. It was the first church of Christ in the northern tier of counties in the State.[37]

Conclusion

Through this information about the founding of the congregations and the people involved we have attained a perspective on the beginnings of the Restoration Movement in Illinois. While we now have a clearer picture of the role of the various Restorationist groups in the early years, we still must accept the prospect that our insights are imprecise because of the various strains of Restorationism involved.

---

[37] Ibid., 246.

4. Bodily Exercises and Healing in Illinois

Various churches in Illinois were established by persons influenced by the Second Great Awakening. The Second Great Awakening got underway in Logan County and Cane Ridge, Kentucky. The influence of the Awakening became widespread throughout the United States in the early nineteenth century, and manifested itself in various ways from the great camp meetings of the frontier to the city evangelism of Charles Grandison Finney in Ohio, New York, and the east. In some of the extreme manifestations, tongue speaking, bodily exercises, and healings broke out in religious gatherings. Since those who planted the congregations in Illinois came from the regions where these activities occurred we are interested in the extent to which they were involved in the early Illinois years. These occurred in Methodist, Baptist and Presbyterian settings and later in the century in various Pentecostal congregations.[1] We are, of course, especially interested in these phenomena among the Restorationists. We will therefore set out the Kentucky, Ohio background of the Awakening before discussing especially healing as a feature of Restorationist churches in Illinois.

At Cane Ridge in 1801 bodily exercises were a common outcome of evangelism. William Kinkade, who moved to Illinois in 1818, encouraged these exercises and also believed that some contemporary Christian leaders had healing power.

Barton W. Stone reported on the outcroppings at Cane Ridge,

> The bodily agitations or exercises, attending the excitement
> in the beginning of this century, were various, and called by
> various names; — as, the falling exercise — the jerks — the
> dancing exercise — the barking exercise — the laughing and
> singing exercise, &c. — The falling exercise was very com-
> mon among all classes, the saints and sinners of every age
> and of every grade, from the philosopher to the clown. The

---

[1] See Grant Wacker, *Heaven Below: Early Pentecostals and American Culture.* (Cambridge: Harvard University Press, 2003).

subject of this exercise would, generally, with a piercing scream, fall like a log on the floor, earth, or mud, and appear as dead. Of thousands of similar cases, I will mention one. At a meeting, two gay young ladies, sisters, were standing together attending to the exercises and preaching at the time. Instantly they both fell, with a shriek of distress, and lay for more than an hour apparently in a lifeless state. Their mother, a pious Baptist, was in great distress, fearing they would not revive. At length they began to exhibit symptoms of life, by crying fervently for mercy, and then relapsed into the same death-like state, with an awful gloom on their countenances. After awhile, the gloom on the face of one was succeeded by a heavenly smile, and she cried out, precious Jesus, and rose up and spoke of the love of God — the preciousness of Jesus, and of the glory of the gospel, to the surrounding crowd, in language almost superhuman, and pathetically exhorted all to repentance. In a little while after, the other sister was similarly exercised. From that time they became remarkably pious members of the church.

The jerks cannot be so easily described. Sometimes the subject of the jerks would be affected in some one member of the body, and sometimes in the whole system. When the head alone was affected, it would be jerked backward and forward, or from side to side, so quickly that the features of the face could not be distinguished. When the whole system was affected, I have seen the person stand in one place, and jerk backward and forward in quick succession, their head nearly touching the floor behind and before...

The dancing exercise. This generally began with the jerks, and was peculiar to professors of religion. The subject, after jerking awhile, began to dance, and then the jerks would cease. Such dancing was indeed heavenly to the spectators; there was nothing in it like levity, nor calculated to excite levity in the beholders. The smile of heaven shone on the countenance of the subject, and assimilated to angels appeared the whole person. Sometimes the motion was quick and sometimes slow. Thus they continued to move forward and t backward in the same track or alley till nature seemed exhausted, and they would fall prostrate on the floor or earth, unless caught by those standing by. While thus

72

exercised, I have heard their solemn praises and prayers ascending to God.

The barking exercise, (as opposers contemptuously called it,) was nothing but the jerks. A person affected with the jerks, especially in his head, would often make a grunt, or bark, if you please, from the suddenness of the jerk. This name of barking seems to have had its origin from an old Presbyterian preacher of East Tennessee. He had gone into the woods for private devotion, and was seized with the jerks. Standing near a sapling, he caught hold of it, to prevent his falling, and as his head jerked back, he uttered a grunt or kind of noise similar to a bark, his face being turned upwards. Some wag discovered him in this position, and reported that he found him barking up a tree.

The laughing exercise was frequent, confined solely with the religious. It was a loud, hearty laughter, but one sui generis; it excited laughter in none else. The subject appeared rapturously solemn, and his laughter excited solemnity in saints and sinners. It is truly indescribable...[2]

Some of these exercises were reported in Christian Churches in Pike County, Illinois, in the 1820s.

The inhabitants were pre-imminently religious. Shouting was very common and the "jerks" had not ceased to afflict the religious fanatic. Preaching and prayer meetings were held at private houses until better accommodations could be had. The Christian Church prevailed at that time, and an organization was effected prior to 1828. There were five resident ministers; four of the Christian and one of the Baptist faith. The present Christian Church has been perpetuated since 1834."[3]

Kinkade also argued for the significance of these exercises and favored them but his outlook ran counter to that of his colleagues and resulted in the exercises dying out in the Christian Connexion churches. Kinkade wrote,

Many leaders in the Christian Connexion, however, disapproved the exercises. In the northeast by 1830 the exercises

---

[2] "Autobiography of Barton W. Stone," Voices from Cane Ridge edited by Rhodes Thompson (St. Louis: Bethany Press, 1954) 64 – 72.
[3] History of Pike County, Illinois (Chicago: C. Chapman & Co., 1880) 446.

were no longer obvious in the assemblies. Mark Fernald in Maine bemoaned their disappearance. He is not explicit about the gifts to which he referred, but even if these are the bodily exercises, they have disappeared.

In 1831 Fernald reflected on changes that had happened among the New England Christians since his early years.

> I had time for reflection, and looked back on the rise and progress of the Christian Connection, when myself and others commenced, and went forth in the name of the Lord, poor and illiterate, knowing no master but Christ, no rule but the New Testament, and in every meeting waiting for a spiritual manifestation of present duty. We had progressed until we numbered hundreds of preachers and thousands of members, with a host of churches in almost every state of the Union. But in my reflections I had some trouble,—the suppression of the gifts in the church had in public meetings, which we at first encouraged, and knew God approved,—the introduction of instrumental music, which we at first opposed as contrary to the New Testament. I feared that while we had enlarged our borders we had lost sight of some of the *landmarks.*[4]

The gifts to which Fernald referred may have been the Holy Spirit at work in the emotional response to the preaching rather than to the Cane Ridge bodily exercises. More likely he was depicting congregation response much like that to the preaching of James Davenport (1716-1757) in Connecticut.

> Divers women were terrified and cried out exceedingly. When Mr. Davenport had dismissed the congregation some went out and others stayed; he then went into the broad alley [aisle] which was much crowded, and there he screamed out, "Come to Christ! come to Christ! come away!" Then he went into the third pew on the women's side, and kept there, sometimes singing, sometimes praying; he and his companions all taking their turns, and the women fainting and in hysterics. This confusion contin-

---

[4] Mark Fernald, *Elder Mark Fernald* (Newburyport, MA: Geo. Moore Payne and D. P. Pike, 1852) 256.

ued till ten o'clock at night. And then he went off singing through the streets.[5]

The goal of the preaching was the emotional arousal of those gathered. This accelerating fervor could be gauged by weeping and vocal outbursts. "Our meetings however, were, in almost every instance, powerful, weeping seasons, with new cases of deep conviction, and crying openly for pardon."[6] In one case he observed solemnity. "The revival was very solemn; but little noise, save what I made, and sinners weeping and crying to Heaven.[7] As the outcome it was expected that a highly emotive period would ensue to be followed by the declaration of conversion and baptism." Regarding his conversion Fernald reported, "The cry went through the people as though the day-of-judgment had come indeed. After meeting I retired, wept, and promised the Lord to do the best I could to be a Christian and serve him. That evening I went to meeting, bowed the knee in public and cried vocally for salvation."[8] The improving of gifts in the Christian Connexion and other evangelicals of the time was often a manner of depicting the gift of effective preaching, which was believed to be Holy Spirit induced, rather than some bodily response by the audience of the sort described by Barton W. Stone.

These Jones/Smith preachers rejected both the reading of manuscript sermons, common among the Congregationalist and some Baptists, and the use of notes while preaching. They believed that the Spirit provided the preacher such a message as needed for the time and place:

> Moreover, that it is not according to the New Testament, that *instrumental* music be introduced into our meetings of worship, either by the unconverted, or by professed christians [sic]. Then adjourned for one hour and met accordingly. Agreed that preaching by *note* is not according to, nor warranted by the New Testament.[9]

Even earlier, George Alkire, who was influenced by Cane Ridge, in 1826 reported a much more subdued approach to the gatherings. Erma Jean

---

[5] *Diary of Joshua Hempstead of New London, Connecticut* (New London, 1901) 379 as reported in C. C. Goen, *Revivalism and Separatism in New England, 1740-1800: Strict Congregationalists and Separate Baptists in the Great Awakening* (Middletown: Wesleyan University Press, 1987) 21.

[6] Fernald, 45.

[7] Ibid., 44.

[8] Ibid., 24.

[9] Robert Foster, editor. *CH*, 10.5 (July 1827) 82.

Loveland reflected on his report found in the *"Gospel Luminary,* which carried the proceedings from the 1826 yearly meeting and conference at Williamsport, [Ohio, near Columbus].

> The listing of elders present included: George Alkire…After the conference was concluded, a church meeting was held. Outdoor stands in four different places were attended by "respectable and well behaved" folks. By noon Sunday, thousands were on the ground; however, a rainstorm drove the crowds for shelter. The meeting house soon overflowed and many from the crowd went away. A large collection was taken for the visiting preachers. "The most perfect decorum was observed" George Patterson, clerk of the conference, wrote and "all appeared solemn as that eternity which had been preached to them." This was a direct contrast to what had happened 25 years earlier at Cane Ridge.[10]

The Gift of Healing

Furthermore, unlike most of his fellow preachers, Kinkade believed that some preachers in the movement had the gift of healing though he did not explicitly make that claim for himself.

> Besides all this, there have been in the bounds of my acquaintance many miraculous cures performed in answer to prayer. I have been acquainted with several of the people who were healed, conversed on the subject with the persons who were present at the time: and some of these cures I have seen myself I as firmly believe that Elder David Haggard had the gift of healing, as that the apostles had. He has fallen asleep, but there are many alive who saw him perform cures, and what I saw myself puts the matter beyond doubt with me. I state these facts in honor to God, who, in every age of the world, has shown a willingness to bless his creatures in proportion to their faith and obedience. Those who oppose an apostolical ministry, frequently challenge us to confirm our special call by miracles. —To this I answer, that every sermon and exhortation delivered in the power of the spirit is itself a miracle, because it is superhuman; the man could not have done it of himself; besides, these discourses

---

[10] George A. Patterson, "Yearly Meeting and Conference at Williamsport Ohio," *GL* 2 (1826) 234-236.

frequently have miraculous effects: they are often the means of making those do good who had been long accustomed to do evil, which is as hard as for an Ethiopian to change his skin, or the leopard his spots. Jer. xiii. 23.[11]

David Haggard was the brother of the better known Rice Haggard, the later who proposed to the O'Kelly Methodists that they employ the title Christian Church, then after moving to Kentucky proposed the same to the Stoneites.[12]

These claims about healing are unusual in the Christian Connexion. Stone does not mention healing as one of the Cane Ridge accomplishments nor do others involved in the camp meeting, including the Methodists. A well known Illinois Methodist evangelist Peter Cartwright (1785-1872) was present at Cane Ridge in 1801. Cartwright moved to Illinois in 1824 because he hated slavery. He eventually settled near Jacksonville, Illinois, to which Barton W. Stone moved in 1834. In his autobiography Cartwright described the various bodily exercises but did not mention healing. Early in his ministry when he had to make a decision he came out against Christians after the first century possessing healing powers. He denounced all who so professed and mentioned by name Mormons and Shakers.

This was the most troublesome delusion of all the ability to heal; it made such an appeal to the ignorance, superstition, and credulity of the people, even saint as well as sinner. I watched this matter with a vigilant eye. If I opposed it, I would have to meet the clamor of the multitude; and if any one opposed it, these very visionists would single him out, and denounce the dreadful judgments of God against him. They would even set the very day that God was to burn the world, like the self-deceived modern Millerites. They would prophesy that if any one did oppose them, God would send fire down from heaven and consume him, like the blasphemous Shakers. They would proclaim that they could heal all manner of diseases, and raise the dead, just like the diabolical Mormons. They professed to have converse with spirits of the dead in heaven and hell, like the modern spirit-rappers. Such a state of things I never saw before, and I hope in God I shall never see again.

---

[11] Kinkade, *The Bible Doctrine*, 342.
[12] *ESCM*, 377.

I pondered well the whole matter in view of my responsibilities, searched the Bible for the true fulfillment of promise and prophecy, prayed to God for light and Divine aid, and proclaimed open war against these delusions. In the midst of them along came the Shakers, and Mr. Rankin, one of the Presbyterian revival preachers, joined them; Mr. G. Wall, a visionary local preacher among the Methodists, joined them; all the country was in commotion. I made public appointments and drew multitudes together, and openly showed from the Scriptures that these delusions were false. Some of these visionary men and women prophesied that God would kill me. The Shakers soon pretended to seal my damnation. But, nothing daunted, for I knew Him in whom I had believed, I threw my appointments in the midst of them, and proclaimed to listening thousands the more sure word of prophecy. This mode of attack threw a damper on these visionary, self-deluded, false prophets, sobered some, reclaimed others, and staid the fearful tide of delusion that was sweeping over the country.[13]

Another preacher known to claim healing powers in the Stone movement was William H. Ashley (1786-1875) who was born in Cenango County New York, but moved to Ohio. About him E. W. Humphreys wrote:

Elder Ashley's power consisted mainly in deep piety, strong faith and great earnestness as a speaker. He was a Reformer in every sense of the term, was opposed to slavery, whisky, and secret societies, and was a strong believer in the Christian power of healing the sick—yet he was no fanatic. Without agreeing with our deceased brother as to the continuance of the healing art in the churches of to-day, yet there were many instances of healing--more than five hundred--recorded by Elder Ashley, that are difficult to account for on any other principle.[14]

Later on Walter Scott Russell (1832 - 1863) believed the miraculous gifts should still be available. His opinion led to formal disapproval by major leaders in the Stone-Campbell-Scott Movement. Alexander Campbell's assessment of Russell is instructive:

---

[13] *The Autobiography Peter Cartwright the Backwoods Preacher*, ed. By W.P. Strictland (Cincinnati: L Swormstedt, A. Foe, 1859) 53

[14] E. W. Humphreys, *Memoirs of Deceased Christian Ministers* (Dayton: Christian Publishing Association, 1880), 27.

We do not wonder that some of the readers of the speculations of Bro. Russell have come to the conclusion that he maintains that true believers may yet work miracles, and that this power is still needed and may be yet expected. I have not seen this in these identical words, yet I confess that my fears have been, and yet are, that his progress is in that direction. His positive and dogmatic confidence in his own intuitions, and his philosophy of spiritual influence, are evidently in that direction, and that he is not one of us, is too manifest to be doubted by any discriminating and attentive reader of the outpourings of his dogmata. He has turned aside into vain janglings, and cannot legitimately be regarded as one of us. He is evidently now a schismatic, and as such, cannot be esteemed and regarded as a brother in communion with us.[15]

Conclusion

Based upon the evidence we present in this chapter, we conclude that at least by the 1830s both the "bodily exercises" and the claims to healing became very unusual in all wings of the Restoration Movement in Illinois.

---

[15] Alexander Campbell, "Philosophy, Dogmatism, Schism," *MH* 1860: 17, 18. See Chapter 10: The Walter Scott Russell Defection in Illinois for more information on Russell's beliefs.

5. The Alkires Arrive in Illinois

The Alkires made major contributions to the Restorationist churches in Illinois, but probably not superseding several other key leaders. We include this information about the Alkires therefore as representative of key persons. We offer it too because the lengthy essay on George Alkire was already prepared by the late Erma Jean Loveland who was one of his descendants. Mrs. Loveland was a Restoration archivist at the Brown Library, Abilene Christian University.

George Alkire: Bearing the Testimony Faithfully
by Erma Jean Loveland
Special Services Librarian
Brown Library, Abilene Christian University

"Religion and The Founding of the American Republic" was a 1998 exhibition at the Library of Congress in Washington, D. C. The exhibition essay contends, "The religion of the new American republic was evangelicalism which between 1800 and the Civil War was the grand absorbing theme" of American religious life. This evangelicalism found expression in revivals. The Great Revival in Kentucky spawned by the Baptists, the Methodists and the Presbyterians, was used to illustrate this thinking.

The Virginia Alkires were one family who was a part of this Great Revival. They moved westward from Moorefield, (West) Virginia to Kentucky, then to Ohio within one generation. Later

81

generations scattered into Indiana, Illinois, and then across the Great Plains and the Rocky Mountains into Oregon.

The early American records indicate Harmonus Alkire, married Mary Cramer near Northfield, Virginia in 1720.[1] Where they came from is still left to guesswork; but as German immigrants, likely, they landed in the settled colonies and then flowed down the valleys between the mountain ridges from Pennsylvania to Virginia.

Harmonus Alkire II, was born in Moorefield, Hampshire County, Virginia in 1730. Moorefield still exists as a village built on a grassy meadow near the joining of the Moorefield and South Branch of the Potomac Rivers. The mountain ridges parallel one another, running north and south, with the rich flood plain below. Grain fields were producing in the 1740s and the mills were already grinding meal. One of Harmonus' civic duties was to view, mark, and keep in repair the road from his place up to Peter Reed's mill on the South Fork.[2] At this time, valid titles to the land had not been given to anyone.

Harmonus II was 17 when James Genn, a Virginia certified surveyor, surveyed the 55,000 acres of the South Branch Manor for the Right Honorable Lord Thomas Fairfax, Baron of Cameron in Scotland.[3] George Washington, 16, was in the survey party. He recorded in his diary on Monday, March 23 [1748] that a great company of Dutch [German] people who lived along the South Branch River accompanied the surveyors while they worked.[4]

Between 1747 and 1748, at least three missionaries made their way into this "back" country of Hampshire County. Leonhard Schnell and Vitus Handrup wrote in their diaries, "the people are so forsaken that they haven't been to the Lord's Supper for four years." Mathias Gottlieb Gottschalk, another Moravian missionary, found "teaching of the Saviour very dear to them."[5] The people asked him to send someone to teach the truth of the Gospel to the old as well as the young. These pioneers expected their churches to follow them wherever they traveled.

---

[1] Wilmer L. Kerns, *Historical Records of Old Frederick and Hampshire Counties, Virginia* (Bowie, Maryland: Heritage Books, 1992) 103.

[2] Lyman Chalkley, *Chronicles of the Scotch-Irish Settlement in Virginia: extracted from the original court records of Augusta County, 1745-1800* (Baltimore: Genealogical Publishing, 1980) vol. 2: 55, 361.

[3] Commander Alvin Edward Moore, *History of Hardy County of the Borderland* (Parsons, West Virginia: McClain Printing Company, 1963) 15.

[4] Ibid., 18.

[5] William J. Hinke and Charles E. Kemper, eds., "Moravian Diaries through Virginia," *Virginia Magazine of History and Biography*, XII (June, 1905) 57.

The Alkires had German neighbors who were Lutherans, Mennonites, Dutch Reformed Church members, with a few Dunkers and Presbyterians.[6] The only record of the Alkire beliefs now to be found is in the E. W. Humphreys record where John Alkire was reported as a Deist.[7]

Harmonus II, 21, married Lydia Patten, 12, in 1751 at Moorefield. All of their children were [West] Virginians: William, Adam, Catherine, Margaret, Elizabeth, John, Dolly, Deborah, Michael, George, Sarah, Lydia and Harmonus.[8]

Lord Fairfax, Proprietor of the Northern Neck of Virginia, granted the Title to Lots 16 and 17 to Maunis Alkier on May 6, 1765.[9] Maunis made his mark, a backwards "N," for acceptance. "Maunis" was one of the many ways Harmonus' name was spelled.

In 1774-1775, Harmonus was listed on Captain James Parson's roll as a first lieutenant in the colonial army of Virginia. He served under Lord Dunmore in the Indian battles with Cornstalk in the Ohio country.[10] The treaty was made at Camp Charlotte in the Scioto Valley, Ohio.[11] [12] [13] In the 154 days that Lt. Alkire served, he had seen the westward side of his mountains. He carried the visions of lush growth and opportunity to the folks back home. In 1788, Harmonus' sons: William (and his wife, Elizabeth Moore) and John (and his wife, Susan Nave (Naef)) were settled in Bourbon County, Kentucky.[14]

Over 7,000 people populated Moorefield by 1800, including 454 slaves.[15] Harmonus II and Lydia Alkire started selling their Virginia land

---

[6] Moore, 60.

[7] Humphreys, 15.

[8] Daughters of American Revolution record number 445811 proven by Esther Muriel Hurst Haines.

[9] West Virginia State Archives, *Lord Thomas Fairfax Land Grant to Maunis Alkier* (Charlotte, West Virginia, 6 May 1765) 243.

[10] James R. Glacking, "Alkire Family," *Illinois State Genealogical Society Quarterly* XIV:11 (Summer, 1982) 77.

[11] Virginia. *Executive Department Romney Payroll* (Richmond, Virginia: Virginia State Library) 4-5.

[12] Daughters of the American Revolution, DAR Patriot Index. (Washington, D. C., 1966) 8.

[13] John H. Gwathmey, *Historical Register of Virginians in the Revolution* (Richmond, Virginia: The Diety Press, 1938) 8.

[14] Glacking, 80.

[15] E. L. Judy, *History of Grant and Hardy Counties, West Virginia* (Charleston, West Virginia: Charleston Printing Company, 1951).

in 1789[16] and purchased 20 acres for 41 pounds on the waters of Huston's Fork, Bourbon County, Kentucky.[17]

After the sales of their Virginia lands, Harmonus II and his family drove loaded pack-horses to the Kanawha River, built a keel boat and floated down the Ohio River to the mouth of the Slate River and thence to Harrod's Station, Kentucky.[18] [19] Harmonus I died there in 1796 at the reported age of 96 years.

Harmonus II purchased another 250 acres on the waters of the Huston's Fork of the Licking River, close to downtown Paris, Kentucky. An early historian of Bourbon County described these early pioneers as hardy, fearless, and self-reliant people where a man was esteemed for his merit, not his money.[20]

In 1800, Harmonus Alkire II, died at the age of 70. His will names his six sons: William, John, Adam, Michael, Monis, George and six daughters: Catty, Elizabeth, Deborah, Margaret, Sally, and Liddy. Most of them signed an "X" to legal land documents; reading and writing were not common achievements on the westward side of the Appalachians Mountains.[21]

Several of the Alkire families were in Bourbon County on August 6, 1801, when the Cane Ridge revival meeting occurred. No doubt, the Alkires were aware of the meeting, if not actually in attendance. John Alkire, as recorded in Humphreys, "was converted at Cane Ridge, by hearing the young converts in that great revival speak of the goodness of God." He began preaching shortly thereafter. Elder Long, one of his converts, said John "had a loud, strong voice... great reformations followed his preaching wherever he went."[22] Later public records indicate that ordained ministers, John and George Alkire, officiated at weddings and funerals.

---

[16] West Virginia, Hardy County, Deed Book 2, (Moorefield, West Virginia, 1789-92) 36-37.

[17] Kentucky, Bourbon County, Deed Book D (Paris, Kentucky) 424.

[18] Judge James M. Carter, *The Carter, Alkire, Kennedy, Williams, and Related Families* (Salt Lake City, Utah: Genealogical Department, Church of Jesus Christ of Latter Day Saints, n.d.) 430.

[19] Esther Muriel Hurst Haines letter (Boca Raton, Florida, 5 May 1971). Copy in my possession. Mrs. Haines was the granddaughter of Sarah who was the daughter of Michael Alkire.

[20] William Henry Perrin, ed., *History of Bourbon, Scott, Harrison and Nicholas Counties, Kentucky* (Cincinnati, Ohio: Art Guild Reprints, 1882) 39.

[21] Kentucky, Bourbon County, Will Book B (Paris, Kentucky) 82-83.

[22] Humphreys, 15.

Shaw, in *Buckeye Disciples*,[23] notes that many religions were experiencing "awakening" during those days. Dr. Abner Jones, a Baptist, organized a church in 1802 in Lyndon, Vermont. Elias Smith joined him shortly. James O'Kelley and Rice Haggard in Virginia were Methodist; and Barton W. Stone was Presbyterian. Barton W. Stone came to Williamsport, Ohio, where George Alkire and his brother, Michael, lived and held meetings in George's house in 1803. Stone returned in 1804 and organized a church there. The charter members included: Isaac Cade [24] and wife; John Teverbaugh and wife; George Alkire and wife Catharine Rush; brothers Isaac W. and Simon Hornback and their wives. Simon Hornback was married to George Alkire's sister, Sarah. Until the first meeting house was built of hewed logs in 1810, the group met in each other's homes.[25]

This congregation had already been organized for three years when Thomas Campbell came to the United States in 1807.

Humphreys described George Alkire as "tall and slim in person; his peculiar forte, as a preacher, was his earnestness as a reasoner. He was plain and somewhat old-fashioned in his appearance....He had an independent mind, a good heart, and a self-sacrificing disposition....Elder Alkire was an honest man, somewhat inclined to speculation, and when an idea struck him favorably he embraced it. He was so free from sectarianism, that it might properly be said of him, that he was partially a member of all churches, and of none, as to entire union of faith."[26]

The Williamsport, Ohio church, the oldest church in the Deer Creek township[27] hosted several well-known preachers, including these noted editors: Barton W. Stone with *The Christian Messenger*, Joseph Badger with *The Christian Palladium*,[28] and Isaac N. Walter with *Gospel Herald*. Joseph Thomas, a nephew of the White Pilgrim Joseph Thomas, was a good friend and traveling companion of George Alkire.[29]

---

[23] Henry K. Shaw, *Buckeye Disciples: A History of the Disciples of Christ in Ohio* (St. Louis: Christian Board of Publication, 1952) 11.

[24] Humphreys, 76.

[25] E. M. T. "Peek at the Past," Williamsport [Ohio] News, 23 March 1978.

[26] Humphreys, 16, 17.

[27] Aaron R. Van Cleaf, *History of Pickaway County, Ohio, and Representative Citizens* (Chicago: Biographical Publishing Co., 1906) 113.

[28] Humphreys, 33.

[29] Ibid., 363.

Other preachers mentioned included George Zimmerman,[30] William Kincade, James Hays,[31] Matthew Gardner,[32] James Marom, George Alkire, James Burbridge,[33] S. Bradford,[34] Daniel Long,[35] John L. Green, Isaac Cade,[36] Benjamin Seevers, John L. Perkins, Enoch Harvey,[37] Thomas Hand, N. Dawson, C. A. Morse, T. A. Brandon, Peter McCullough, William Overterf, B. H. Chrisman, Josel Osgood, A. C. Hanger, and E. W. Humphreys.[38] Humphreys was later instrumental in establishing the Union Christian College in Merom, Sullivan County, Indiana. When he wrote *The Memoirs of Deceased Christian Ministers*, he was well acquainted with the Alkires and Williamsport.

This listing of names indicated a variety of leaders, some educated by self-teaching and others by schooling. The ministers in the list were from the Christian Connexion, the O'Kelly, or the Stone movements.

The White Pilgrim, Joseph Thomas, was baptized by James O'Kelley in 1807. He wore white apparel both summer and winter with his long hair combed down on his shoulders.[39] He described Deer Creek country in his writings: "The grass is now on a level half leg high, spear-grass, clover, and what is called prairie grass covers the earth and makes it the best summer range for cattle and horses in the known world." Thomas was delighted with the beauty, fertility and natural grandeur of the country.

---

[30] Ibid., 402.

[31] Ibid., 165. Hayes was a writer for early volumes of *Gospel Herald*.

[32] Ibid., 138-141.

[33] Ibid., 71. Burbridge was a companion of George Alkire in Ohio and later in Pike County, Illinois. He wrote for early periodicals.

[34] Ibid., 64-65. Bradford, born in New York, was the minister of Williamsport and Mt. Sterling churches and wrote for the *CPal*.

[35] Ibid., 207-209. Long, born in Maryland, was a prominent figure in Central Ohio and Deer Creek Conferences.

[36] Ibid., 76.

[37] Ibid., 157, 158. Harvey, a physically massive-sized man, was a prominent minister of the Deer Creek Conferences.

[38] Robert A. Brown. "Historical Minutes of the Proceedings of the Peru Convention, the Executive Committee and the Board of Trustees of Union Christian College," *Story of Union Christian College Merom (Sullivan County) Indiana 1859-1924*, (Owensboro, Kentucky: McDowell Publications, 1981)10-14.

[39] Joseph Thomas.*The Life of the Pilgrim Joseph Thomas containing an accurate account of his Trials, Travels and Gospel Labours up to the Present date* (Winchester, Pennsylvania: J. Foster, Printer, 1817) 181.

The White Pilgrim noted that the people were working hard in corn planting season while he was there; however, he was chagrined that the women would not "trouble themselves to walk 6 or 7 miles to meeting."

Sat. 4th, [May 4, 1811] "I came to Alkier's [sic] meeting house (as it is called). This was a cold day for it snowed a little.

Sun. 5th. "A large congregation attended at this place. There is a large society of members here, and one preacher. They appear to be in a prosperous state. The most of them have been baptized.... The Christian church was established here before any other denomination; no other has succeeded here since....The inhabitants are generally industrious, hard working people, much given to farming what may distinguish the people is their plainnes [sic].... One thinks himself no higher than the other and the other no lower than he. They may be said to be rough and somewhat uncouth to people of polish manners and refinements but appear to be easily pleased, seem to have a happy turn to be agreeable to each other....They are not given to such extravagancies in gambling, fighting, stealling [sic], etc...; but this maybe chiefly owing to their being men of age and families....I suppose the most of them are republicans, for they detest slavery and bondage from every point of view."[40]

Humphreys reported that John Alkire[41] and Forgus Graham[42] were both converted at the Cane Ridge revival. Farmers and ministers by 1812, Alkire and Graham held camp-meetings near their homes and fed their own beef to the great crowds who came to hear them. Forgus came to Madison County, Ohio, in 1807 and organized the first Christian society in Pleasant township on June 30, 1812.[43]

Abner Jones, O'Kelley, and Stone movements were meeting in a General Conference by 1820.

John Alkire's son, Leonard, bought his first land in Sangamon County, Illinois, from the government in 1824, a practice which he continued un-

---

[40] Ibid., 183-190.
[41] Humphreys, 15.
[42] Ibid., 145.
[43] Shaw, 18.

til 1854.[44] His parents, John and Susan, joined him in Sangamon County in 1824, and began to purchase land by 1825.

David Millard, an influential spokesperson for the Jones-Smith movement from New York, established *The Gospel Luminary* in 1825. In June, 1826, a report of the Christian Conference held at Deer Creek, Pickaway County, Ohio, and signed by George Alkire and Enoch Harvey, Elders, was published on the front page of the Millard paper.[45]

The conference discussed church government and support of the ministry. Many preachers traveled among the brethren without support, in hazardous conditions, leaving their own families to fend for themselves at home. "Their funds are nearly exhausted...scarcely ever is there a collection made of money to bear their expenses." Many church people believed that was the way that it should be. No doubt, George Alkire could understand this problem since he had been an itinerant preacher for more than 20 years by this time.

Church government was a major concern of George Alkire. He had made his own observations of what happened to church groups who were left to flounder and/or disappear after the visiting preacher traveled on. He believed the new converts would continue to meet and worship if they were organized with a fledgling leadership.

In Joseph Badger's report of a trip he made to Williamsport, Ohio in 1925, he spoke in "respectful terms" of George Alkire.[46] The next year, Badger noted in his journal: "In Elder Alkire's vicinity the churches have received large additions of late."[47]

Gospel Luminary[48] carried the proceedings from the 1826 yearly meeting and conference at Williamsport. The listing of elders present included: George Alkire, James Burbridge , Samuel Wilson, Enoch Harvey, Alexander Owen, Isaac N. Walter,[49] Martin Baker, Joseph Thomas,

---

44 Illinois Public Domain Land Tract Sales http://www.sos.state.il.us/depts/ archives/data_lan.html.

45 George Alkire and Enoch Harvey, "Address of a Christian Conference, held at Deer Creek, Pickaway County, Ohio, to churches within that Conference and to the saints scattered abroad," *Gospel Luminary* 2.6 (June, 1826) 125-132.

46 E. G. Holland, *Memoir of Rev. Joseph Badger*, 281.

47 Ibid., 290.

48 George A. Patterson, "Yearly Meeting and Conference at Williamsport Ohio," · *GL*, 2 (1826) 234-236.

49 Humphreys, 376-378. Walter, born in Ohio, preached in New York City and baptized 2,343 persons. He was an editor of *Gospel Herald*.

Joseph Baker,[50] George Limmerman,[51] Samuel Rogers, Benjamin Breton, Matthew Gardner, George A. Patterson, James Baker, Isaac Cade. Unordained preachers were: Zarah Curtiss,[52] William Dickinson, and Isaac Hornback.[53]

After the conference was concluded, a church meeting was held. Outdoor stands in four different places were attended by "respectable and well behaved" folks. By noon Sunday, thousands were on the ground; however, a rainstorm drove the crowds for shelter. The meeting house soon overflowed and many from the crowd went away. A large collection was taken for the visiting preachers. "The most perfect decorum was observed" George Patterson, clerk of the conference, wrote and "all appeared solemn as that eternity which had been preached to them." This was a direct contrast to what had happened 25 years earlier at Cane Ridge.

Gospel Luminary had an editorial about the April 12 meeting at Deer Creek, "it will be seen that active exertions are being made by 'our brethren' [The Christian Connexion was recognizing Deer Creek as **our** brothers] at the west to set the things in order that are wanting among them." The editors continue, "We solicit a correspondence with Elders Stone, Smith, Purviance, McCoy, Adams, Gardner, and others whom though unseen we love." This was a listing of Stone people with which the *Gospel Luminary*, a Christian Connexion paper, wanted to correspond.[54]

Barton W. Stone's paper, *Christian Messenger*, was first published in 1826 in Georgetown, Kentucky.

Still showing a concern about the shouting, barking and such like in the worship service, Alkire wrote to the *Christian Messenger*[55] "God in a gracious and powerful manner, has once more visited us on Deer Creek....The converts come out firm and solid, with less noise than I ever saw in a revival."

---

[50] Ibid., 37-39.

[51] Ibid., 402. Zimmerman is likely the correct spelling.

[52] Ibid., 103, 104. Curtiss, born in Plymouth, Conn., was a military man of the staff of General Howe.

[53] Ibid., 173. Hornback was ordained by George Alkire.

[54] David Millard, ed., "The Christian Brethren at the West," *GL*, (June 1826) 140-141.

[55] George Alkire, "Letter to Brother Stone," *CM*, 4 (1829) 119-120.

In an April, 1832 article in the *Luminary*,[56] Alkire stated he was almost 50, had been a minister for 25 years and had been ordained when he was 20 years old. The eight-page article, started on the front page of the *Luminary*, was an essay about the quality of church leadership needed. Alkire bemoaned that he had planted many churches that were prospering when he left them only to return to find not a trace nor a mark of that church. "I am confident for want of a proper administration of the government and in this state of confusion the greater part of the labours of the travelling [sic] preacher is lost."

Barton W. Stone and "Raccoon John" Smith, as a representative of Alexander Campbell, shook hands on an agreement of unity between the two groups in 1832 at the Hill Street Christian Church in Lexington, Kentucky. Shortly thereafter, in 1834, Stone moved on westward to Jacksonville, Illinois, taking *The Christian Messenger* with him. He had started purchasing Illinois Government Land in October, 1830.[57]

The *Christian Palladium*[58] reported that the Ohio Central and Deer Creek Conferences met in Hebron, Ohio, on December 26, 1834. Derostus F. Ladley was elected president,[59] William B. Harding was secretary. Others present included: George Alkire, James Hayes, Harry Ashley.[60]

Thomas Cotterill, George Alkire, and D. F. Ladley were to draft a circular letter about church government, support of the ministry, and Christian Sunday School. D. F. Ladley wrote that at the public worship after the conference closed, Elders Alkire and Long delivered two very interesting and impressive discourses.

According to Illinois Land Records, George Alkire purchased lands from the federal government in Illinois on May 11 and August 1, 1836.[61]

Ohio Deer Creek Conference was held in Palestine August 18, 1838, and was reported in the *Christian Palladium*.[62] Elder David Roberts was elected chair and John G. Green as assistant clerk. Elders present:

---

[56] George Alkire, "Ohio Church Government," *GL*, 5:7 (April 1832) 205-213.

[57] Illinois Public Domain Land Tract Sales.

[58] Derostus F. Ladley and William B. Harding, "Ohio Central Conference," *CPall*, 3 (1834-5) 318.

[59] Humphreys, 197. Ladley, born in Chester County Pennsylvania, came to Ohio in 1832. He was ordained by Elders Walter, Currier, and Badger. As a man of taste, precision and order, Ladley acquired a library of well-selected books. He preached and wrote for the *CPall*.

[60] Humphreys, 28, 29.

[61] Illinois Public Domain Land Tract Sales.

[62] David Roberts and James Smith, "Ohio Deer Creek Conference," *CPall*, 7 (1838-39) 200.

George Alkire, David Roberts, Henry S. Bradford,[63] Samuel R. Dawson,[64] James Green. Licentiates: Cyrus Gordy, John R. Green. Representatives from Williamsport included: Cyrus Gordy, Ebenezer Davis, and Abraham Halstead,[65] Williams Francis, and John Hornback.

Christian Palladium carried a report from Christian Union Conference meeting at Williamsport, September 6, 1838. A newly organized conference, Anglaise (Ohio), presented its letter to petition for admission into this conference and was accepted. George Alkire, Enoch Harvey, and James Smith were appointed to send a letter to unrepresented conferences, asking for their views on how to achieve "a more perfect union as well as how to plant and organize churches."[66]

Deer Creek Christian Conference of Ohio, Mt. Sterling, April 17, 1840, charged George Alkire, William B. Hand, John N. Perkins, and James Smith to write a letter to the periodicals asking the conferences to consider the following four points and to publish their findings: church government, the operation of the Spirit, a proper name for the church (whether that be Christian church, Church of Christ, or Disciples), and the design and objective of baptism.[67]

An invitation was extended to all conferences to join in a general convention with a delegation of "holy men" from each congregation. The time and place suggested were Cincinnati in October, 1840.

Christian Palladium reported the minutes of Ohio Central Christian Conference that met in Mt. Liberty, August 18, 1840. Elder Zarah Curtiss, which had been unlicensed at the 1826 conference, chaired the meeting.

The subject of a general convention to reconcile certain differences existing in the churches was discussed at length by George Alkire, D.

---

[63] Humphreys, 64, 65. Bradford, born in 1809 in New York, moved to Ohio in 1832; and by 1839, he was the minister in charge of the church at Williamsport.

[64] Ibid., 107. Dawson, a colonel in the militia, married Dorothy Abigail Alkire, daughter of Adam Alkire, George's brother, and his wife, Margaret Hornbeck.

[65] Ibid., 405. Halstead was ordained by George Alkire, Isaac Cade, and George Zimmerman in 1806. Two of Halstead's children married children of George's brother, Michael Alkire. Hannah Halstead m. Benjamin Alkire and Albartis Halstead m. Ruanna Alkire.

[66] Enoch Harvey, "Ohio Union Conference," *CPall*, 8 (1838-9) 199-200.

[67] George Alkire, Wm. B. Hand, John N. Perkins, James Smith, "Letters," *CPall*, 8 (1839-40) 45.

Long, D. F. Ladley, J. W. Marvin, A. Stevens,[68] John Hayes, J. O. Harris, J. Plumb, O. True.[69]

After the speeches were over, the Ohio Central Christian Conference passed a resolution "that this conference do [sic] not as yet see the storm our brethren are so fearful of, nor do they think it expedient to meet in such a convention." There were 124 members at the conference, 36 Elders, 25 licentiates, 2 female laborers, 61 delegates representing 1,484 communicants which showed an increase of 718 over the last year's number.[70]

From Pittsfield, Illinois, December 19, 1840, G. Alkire writes to Stone that he is thankful he can again preach even though he cannot see his audience because of his failing eyesight. Depressed, he writes that the sun of his life will set soon; but even in this state of health, he reported travels in Ohio, Indiana, and Illinois.[71]

In January 27, 1841, George writes from Pittsfield, Illinois to the church at Jamestown, Ohio. The epistle was a travel log of his journey from Ohio to Illinois. Alkire preached regularly and set in order the things that were wanting on his "long but pleasant" journey. He visited overnight with Brother Stone in Jacksonville. He had been preaching in Pike County at the Highland, Pittsfield, Barre, and Perry congregations. Most of the congregations in the West have seemed in general union, with only a few exceptions where lines of distinction had been drawn between "the Reformers" (Campbellites) and the Old Christians. Once again Elder Alkire made the plea for unity and closed with "Finally, Brethren, farewell; be perfect, live in love and the God of love and peace shall be with you..."[72]

The Christian Messenger carried minutes by B. F. Van Dooser[73] of the Christian conference at Highland, Pike County, Illinois, April 9, 1841. Present were: George Alkire, B. W. Stone, J. Burbridge, D. Roberts, Wm. Strong, Wm. Gale, D. Henry, C. Bolin, J. Sweet, J. Green Jr., Wm. Gilliam.

[68] Humphreys, 343, 344. Stevens, born in Vermont, compiled and published *Union Hymn Book* in Vermont, joined the Central Conference in 1839 and became the conference president in 1842.

[69] Ibid., 367. True, born in Connecticut, was a theologian and wrote for papers.

[70] Isaac N. Walter, "Conference Minutes," *CPall*, 9 (1840-41) 156-57.

[71] George Alkire, "Letter to Brother Stone," *CM*, 11 (1840) 178, 179.

[72] George Alkire, "To the Church at Jamestown, O., with the Elders and Deacons," *CPall*, 8 (1839-40) 366, 367.

[73] Humphreys, 94. Van Dooser was born in New York. He wrote frequently for the *CPall*.

Elder G. Alkire gave the opening address. Wm. Gilliam was asked to chair the conference and B. F. Van Dooser to be secretary. A committee of five, including Alkire, was chosen to arrange the business that was to come before the meeting.

1. The agenda of issues and resolutions was printed:
   What qualifies a person to become a member of the church? Conference decision: faith, repentance and obedience to the Gospel.

2. How is a church organized? Conference decision: humble, obedient believers do by giving themselves first to the Lord and then to one another. The group becomes fully organized when they appoint and ordain elders and deacons.

3. Who are proper officers of the church and their duties? Conference decision: Elders should attend to the spiritual concerns of the church; deacons are to care for its temporal matters.

4. By what name shall the church be called? Conference decision: church of God or of Christ.

5. Does God give his spirit to his children? If so, how? Conference decision: Yes, by faith and obedience.

6. Shall we send out and support one or more evangelists? Conference decision: send out D. Roberts and Wm. Gale and plan to support them.

7. What cooperation should exist between the preacher and those to whom they preach? Conference decision: The congregations should contribute to the preachers' temporal wants and encourge them in their work.

Reportedly, the conference experienced a great unity of mind and spirit, as rarely seen before.

Chair William Gilliam requested the *Christian Palladium* (Christian Connexion) and the *Christian Messenger* (Stone) to publish these minutes.[74]

In the *Christian Palladium*, Alkire wrote to Brother Marsh that during the last year he had traveled 2,300 miles in poor health as well as poor

---

[74] Wm. Gilliam, "Minutes of a Christian Conference at Highland, Pike County, Illinois, April 9th, 1841, *CM*, 7 (June, 1841) 342, 343.

eyesight. Elder Alkire had been confined to his home for four years before 1841.

Alkire detailed some of his travels during the last month. He visited with Brother Riggs in Scott County; Riggs had served in the Illinois State Legislature in 1818 and later in the 48th and 49th United States Congress.[75] Alkire journeyed on to Jacksonville to meet with Elders Stone, Jones, Henderson, Vandozer. Alkire writes, "the church in this place seems to be spiritual and intelligent, manifesting the spirit of union and friendship." At Island Grove, he attended a meeting at Brother Wm. Grant's where he met Elder Scott.

Traveling on, G. Alkire crossed the Sangamon River at Elder Marsh's, the publisher's brother. Elder Marsh did not charge George for crossing the river even though Marsh was a rigid Reformer [Campbellite]. George held a meeting at his nephew's house, Wm. B. Cautrell, where he again met Brother Bandozer.[76] After leaving relatives and brethren, he traveled to Fountain County, Ia.[77] He preached four times near Covington to divided congregations, part Reformers and part Old Christians. Some objections were made by the Reformers to Alkire's sermons; however, all came to give him "the right hand of fellowship" at the close of the meeting.

He stayed with Judge Burbridge in Crawfordsville. While crossing the stream at Alexander's crossing, water ran into his carriage. This reminded him of an earlier accident crossing the Big Vermillion in eastern Illinois. "My papers and books were spoiled and clothing much injured."

In New Paris, Ohio, he met with Elders Purviance and Adams; Alkire said he preached to large, attentive, intelligent crowds here. Purviance with a classical education had represented both Kentucky and Ohio in state legislatures. Purviance and Stone were long-time friends, both coming from the Presbyterian movement to sign "The Last Will and Testament of the Springfield Presbytery."

Traveling on to Eaton in Preble County, he preached, by candlelight at the home of Judge Munfort. Brother Hathaway, a nephew of Levi Hathaway, closed the meeting. In Dayton, Alkire stopped to see Dr. Bowen, in Enon to see Elder Ladley with whom he had worked at Deer Creek, and then to Ebenezer to spend the night with Elder Briney. He met his good friend, Joseph Thomas, whom Alkire had wished for in one of his letters

---

[75] Haynes, 590.

[76] Likely B. F. Van Doozer from New York.

[77] Fountain County, Indiana, which lies between Illinois and Ohio. The normal abbreviation for Indiana at that time was "Ia."

from Illinois, and Dr. Winans Borgman. The three men preached that night and "closed in all good feeling." Most of these preachers were of the Christian Connexion. Alkire seemed to travel freely among the Christian Connexion and the Stone people; he very much wanted a union of these believers.[78] [79]

Christian Palladium reported Deer Creek Church Conference, at Mt. Sterling August 12, 1841. Elder Joseph Thomas was chair and Henry S. Bradford, Clerk. George Alkire, J. N. Perkins, E. Harvey and others discussed a religious periodical and a hymn book for the churches in the state of Ohio. Delegates to the Union Christian Conference in Ohio were to present the necessity of a paper and a hymn book to this gathering. The delegates were C. Gordy, J. N. Perkins, J. Thomas, Geo. Alkire, Bradford. Also, the conference agreed to give Elder George Alkire a letter of commendation to take with him to Illinois.[80]

George, Catharine and four of their children (Mary, Rebecca, Barton W., and Abner) migrated to Hadley Township, settling on section 31. The other four children joined them in the next year: Wesley J., Lydia, Gideon, and Josiah. The sons took care of the farming of the land.[81]

Christian Palladium reported that the Illinois Union Conference met at the Baptist Church in Barry, Pike County, Illinois, on November 19, 1841. William Gilliam was the chair and Job Sweet the secretary. Elder G. Alkire gave the opening address and served on the meeting agenda committee.

Alkire was an active participant in debating the issues to form a new conference. The resolutions included: Efforts would be made by elders and brethren to preach for the destitute.

The brethren were to contribute to sustain those who were preaching. Pike County would be the territory for the conference to be called Christian Union Conference. Membership would include elders, deacons, delegates, and brethren. The conference would patronize the *Christian Palladium*, the *Christian Messenger*, as well as other not named papers. Elder David Roberts would be the book agent.

---

[78] George Alkire, "Letter to Br. Marsh," *CPall*, 9 (25 My 1841) 78, 79.

[79] G. Alkire, "Letter to Br. Marsh," *CPall*, 10 (1 October 1841) 170.

[80] Joseph Thomas, "Ohio Deer Creek Conference," *CPall* (Dec. 1841) 239.

[81] Barton W. Alkire, *History of Pike County Illinois; Together with sketches of its cities, villages, and townships, educational, religious, civil, military, and political history; Portraits of Prominent Persons and biographies of Representative Citizens.* (Chicago: Chas. C. Chapman and Co., 1880) 741.

At the conclusion of the report, it was noted that Elder G. Alkire had been received as a member of the conference upon the presentation of his letter of commendation from the Deer Creek Conference. He was in a leadership position before the letter was presented.[82]

In the *Christian Messenger*, the Winchester, Illinois meeting report was given with the following preachers present: Barton W. Stone; Barton W. Stone Jr., George Alkire, James Burbridge, William Gale, David Roberts.[83]

A few weeks later, Stone died in Hannibal, Missouri, in November, 1844. He was buried for three years in Jacksonville, Illinois, and then removed to Cane Ridge, Kentucky. Alkire's relationship with Stone continued from 1803, if not before, until Stone's death in 1844. Alkire and Stone had attended the State Meeting in Winchester, Illinois together, Stone's last one. One of Alkire's sons was named Barton W. Alkire, no doubt, because of George's fondness of Stone. In Alkire's prospectus for his autobiography, he promised to related "many interesting incidents - not before published - connected with the life and public services of Elder Barton W. Stone."[84]

George's son, Barton W., joined the California Gold Rush in 1849-50 and returned to Illinois the next year a richer man able to support his parents and unwed sisters.

As far as known, George Alkire's brothers did not publish any writings. However, the family was interested in education. The proceeds from Elder Alkire's book were to go to Christian University, Canton, Missouri, and North-Western Christian University at Indianapolis.

John Alkire's daughter, Sarah, married Joseph Powell.[85] Three of their sons, John Alkire Powell, Noah Powell and Alfred Powell led the large group of Christians migrating to Oregon in 1851. Jerry Rushford's *Christians on the Oregon Trail*, Chapter 10, describes this generation of Alkire grandchildren in the Restoration Movement. John A. Powell was on the Board of Trustees of Christian College, just as his son, Franklin Smith Powell was.[86]

---

[82] Wm. Gilliam, "Illinois Union Conference," *CPall*, 10 (15 March 1842) 351.

[83] D. P. Henderson, "State Meeting," *CM* (October, 1844) 183-186.

[84] D. Bates, ed., "Eld. Alkire's Life," *CR* (February 1854) 61, 62.

[85] James R. Glacking, "Alkire Descendants," *Illinois State Genealogical Society Quarterly*, XV.1 (Spring, 1983) 39.

[86] Jerry Rushford, "Three Brothers for Oregon 1851," *Christians on the Oregon Trail* (Joplin, Missouri: College Press Publishing Co., 1997) 129-143.

This generation also produced J. N. Halstead, son of Nancy A. Alkire and Elliot Halstead. Nancy was the daughter of George's brother, Michael. Dr. J. N. Halstead moved to Merom, Sullivan County, Indiana and invited his Williamsport, Ohio, minister, E. W. Humphreys, to preach at his house near the Wabash River in Indiana. Merom had recently lost the county seat status to Sullivan, leaving a lovely courthouse empty. E. W. Humphreys, with the support of J. N. Halstead, acted as the General Agent to convince the Christian Church Conference to locate the Union Christian College at Merom, where it stayed from 1860 to 1924.[87]

In 1854, an announcement of a prospectus for the life of Elder George Alkire was published in the *Christian Evangelist*, Ft. Madison, Iowa. The volume was to include the journal of Alkire's life. Later, the *Christian Record* reported Elders Henderson and Shannon had taken the Alkire journal in hand and would bring it out soon. At the time of this writing, a copy of the journal has not been located.

Also, in 1854, a book written by Elder George Alkire, *The World That is and That is to Come or a treatise on the primitive condition of man* was published by Sentinel in Springfield, Illinois. Likely, *The World That Is* ... was the outcome of the prospectus. Alkire, in his writing over the years, had been concerned with church government and church unity.[88] G. Alkire's writings had reflected peace, love and unity. *The World That Is* ... is a renouncement of Roman Catholicism. It would seem this book might have reflected more the thinking of the editors, Elder Henderson[89] and Shannon, rather than Alkire.

Elder Alkire's last printed article to be located was in 1854 on Church Government.[90] He seems to have not published after 1854, even though he lived until 1868. *The Palladium*, *The Christian Messenger*, the *Luminary* were no longer publishing; the editors he had worked with were no more.

Where he obtained his education is a mystery. George Washington reported in his journals the existence of a school at Old Fields, near Moorefield in Virginia, and likely there were other schools in Kentucky; but most of George's siblings signed the deeds selling their father's estate

---

[87] E. W. Humphreys, "The Rise of Union Christian College," *Our Work* I (May, 1876).

[88] Elder George Alkire, *The World That Is and That Is To Come or a treatise on the primitive condition of man* (Springfield, Illinois: Sentinel Book and Job Office, 1854).

[89] Henderson was an editor of the *Christian Messenger*, a clerk of the court in Jacksonville and a long-standing minister.

[90] George Alkire, "Church Government--No. 1," *CE*, 5.4 (April 1854) 132-136.

with an "X." Yet George wrote clearly, developed his themes logically, and had a command of grammar and writing.

He mourned when his books became wet when he tried to cross a stream in his carriage. He mentioned these authors without titles in his writings: Mosheim, Adam Clark of England, Chronology of Usher, Clinton, and Dr. John Cuming of London. Whether by self-education or schooling, he used the tools of education.

The thunderstorm passed leaving only the droplets of water falling off the tree leaves onto the tombstone of George Alkire in Barry, Hadley township, Pike County, Illinois. The inscription reads:

George Alkire
b. 1781 d. July 21, 1868

Here lies a man that has died at his post aged 87 years.
Having embraced the Christian religion in Kentucky at the age of 17 years.
Bearing the testimony faithfully until the day of his death.

6. Restorationist Churches in the Nineteenth Century in Illinois

In this chapter we first present histories of six nineteenth century congregations or a group of congregations in an area in Illinois: Berlin in Sangamon County; Antioch at Cantrall in Sangamon County; Lytleville in McLean County; Bloomington in McLean County; congregations in the Danville area in Vermilion County; and the early history of congregations in Chicago, Cook County.

We close this chapter with data on sixteen existing Churches of Christ who report a founding date before 1900 and a compilation of the more than 750 congregations Haynes documented as in existence in 1914 when he published his history.

Essays on Nineteenth Century Restorationist Congregations in Illinois
Berlin Christian Church 1824[1]

> "In the beginning was the Word, and the Word was with God, and the Word was God." (John 1:1)

Our Beginning: The Word came to Island Grove Township with the arrival of Andrew Scott in 1824. He moved here, with his wife and seven children, from Richland Creek (also in Sangamon County) where he had settled in 1818, coming there from Indiana. He was born in North Carolina on November 21, 1786, the first child of John Wilson Scott, a Revolutionary War soldier. His grandfather, also named Andrew, was born in Scotland and came to Pennsylvania in 1725. Our Andrew married Anna Longest May 28, 1808, in Jackson County, Tennessee, where their first

---

[1] Judy (Robertson) Fitch, the great, great granddaughter of Andrew Scott wrote this essay. The Berlin Christian Church is the second oldest SCM congregation in Sangamon County and the fourth oldest SCM congregation in Illinois.

child was born. Six more children were born to them before they arrived at Island Grove, and four more after arriving in Berlin.

Andrew Scott was the first resident minister in this township. Upon his arrival he started preaching and holding meetings in his home. It was here he performed the first marriage in the township. He also held meetings in the log cabins of other early settlers. His aim was to teach and preach the true faith and the pure gospel, thus becoming part of the early restoration movement in Illinois. This movement protested against creeds and dogmas of fallible men. These reformers appealed to the Bible alone, using only God's word as their guide for teaching and preaching. They were known as "Christians only." Three of Andrew's brothers were also ministers of the Christian Church. All three of them settled in what is now DeWitt County, Illinois.

As this group of believers grew they began holding services in the log school house close to where Andrew Scott lived. This was about 1 ½ miles northwest of Berlin. At this time the church was called the "Mt. Zion Christian Church." They met here from 1830 to 1840. A log church building was erected on the Scott farm in 1840. Here services were held until the congregation moved to Berlin in 1859.

Seeing the need for a larger building and to be where more of the people lived, in 1857 a new facility was started in the village of Berlin. This building was dedicated in 1859. The cost of this structure was $2500. It was at this time that the name was changed to the "Berlin Christian Church," and the congregation began to associate with a fellowship of churches known as the "Christian Churches and Churches of Christ."

In this time period there were four churches in the village of Berlin. Only the Christian Church still remains.

The Antioch Christian Church is Born[2]

On May 15, 1820, at the home of Stephen and Anna (Harper) England. [Cantrall is north of Springfield] the following persons, all professing Christians meeting together, did sign the following agreement: Stephen England and his Wife, Anna (Harper) England Jechoniah Langston and his wife, Nancy (Dodson) Langston Levi Cantrall and his Wife, Fannie (England) Cantrall Mrs. Adelphia Wood Mrs. Sarah Cantrall, the wife of Wyatt Cantrall Mrs. Lucy (Scott), daughter of Stephen England, and afterwards Mrs. (John) Cline. Jr., the members of the Church of Jesus

2 "The Antioch Christian Church of Cantrall, Illinois, organized May 15, 1820," written by Stephen English.

Christ, being Providentially moved from our former place of residence from distant parts, and being baptized on profession of our faith, and met at the house of brother Stephen England, on a branch of Higgins' creek, in order to form a constitution, having first given ourselves to the Lord, and then to one another, agree that our constitution shall be on the Holy Scriptures of the Old and New Testament, believing them to be the only rule of faith and practice." Thus was born The Antioch Christian Church of Cantrall, Illinois.

The History of the Christian Church in Lytleville, Randolph Township, McLean County, IL[3]

Rev. Ebenezer Rhodes (1780-1842) moved with his family from Ohio to Blooming Grove in 1823 and became the first pioneer preacher in McLean County. Upon moving to Illinois his affiliation was with the Regular Baptists (ordained in 1819), but he soon became an adherent to the Christian Church or Restoration Movement (founded by Alexander Campbell and Barton W. Stone).[4] He organized the first Christian Church in McLean County, Blooming Grove Christian Church, in 1824.[5]

Rev. Rhodes was instrumental in the establishment of many rural pioneer churches in McLean County, including the Christian Church at Lytleville, Randolph Township, in the mid 1830s. The church was very active and strong in its Restoration practices during the first 40 years of life, but in the 1870s, membership began to dwindle and eventually the church was reorganized under the auspices of the Christian Union Church, an inter-denominational group (established in 1864) based out of Ohio with increasing numbers in the Midwest.[6]

An 1877 article in The Pantagraph reports of the Illinois State Council of the Christian Union meeting at the Christian Union Church in Lytleville.[7] The details surrounding the church's transition of affiliation are unknown.

[3] This article is by cohort member Nathan L. Soice, Associate Minister of Worship & Pastoral Care, Atlanta Christian Church, Atlanta, Illinois.

[4] Dr. E. Duis, *The Good Old Times in McLean County* (Bloomington, IL: The Leader Publishing and Printing House, 1874), 2.

[5] Haynes, 281, 282.

[6] Frank S. Mead, *Handbook of Denominations in the United States, Second Revised Edition* (New York: Abingdon Press, 1956), 69.

[7] The Bloomington Pantagraph, August 31, 1877.

It is highly likely that the Lytleville church transitioned out of the Restoration Movement around 1871. Michael W. Powell (1833-1923), an active member of the Christian Church at Lytleville, organized and led the music (without the aid of a musical instrument) at the revival services that led to the organization of the Christian Church in nearby Heyworth, IL in late 1871. Mr. Powell transferred his membership to Heyworth as a charter member of that congregation (likely out of disagreement with the Lytleville church transitioning to Christian Union leadership).[8] As farmers became well-to-do and moved to town, the rural Christian Churches at Grassy Ridge, Lytleville, Long Point, and Fairview contributed to the growth and strength of the Heyworth church.[9]

It is not known when Lytleville Christian Church's first house of worship was built, but we know the exact location based upon several Randolph Township maps. A McLean County atlas from 1874 (which spells Lytleville incorrectly) shows the Christian Union Church building located on the southeast section of Lytleville, just across State Street from the Methodist Church (which was built in 1874) on the 30.5 acre tract of land owned by William Rust (1792-1879).[10] Very little is known of the design of the church building, other than Clark E. Stewart reporting that as a small boy he remembered every church on South State Street in Lytleville having spires.[11]

In June of 1880 a Sabbath School multi-denominational meeting was held at the Christian Union Church. One of the many speakers was Rev. Sylvester Peasley of the Baptist Church.[12] In March of 1881, a 19-year-old George A. Stringfield, a student at Sparta School, delivered a lecture on temperance at the Christian Union Church.[13]

A major shift in church affiliation came once again to the Christian Union Church in Lytleville in 1881. The Christian Union Church, like the Christian Church before it, had become very weak, dormant, and was near the end of its life. The Disciples of Christ (Christian Church) county evangelist for McLean County, Rev. John S. Stagner (1828-1887), who organized the Christian Church in Heyworth in 1871, began a series of revival meetings at the church in Lytleville in hopes to revitalize the mis-

---

[8] Eva Quinn, compiler, Through the Ages: History of the Christian Church of Heyworth 1871-2005 (Heyworth, IL: Heyworth Christian Church, 2005), 11, 12.

[9] Haynes, 292.

[10] [Atlas of] McLean County, Randolph Township (Warner and Beers, 1874).

[11] Clark E. Stewart, On Randolph Hills (Heyworth, IL: Heyworth Star, 1943), 11.

[12] The Bloomington Pantagraph, June 22, 1880.

[13] The Bloomington Pantagraph, March 29, 1881.

sion. After Stagner's lengthy work with the congregation, the Christian Church was reorganized and revived for a promising future.[14] Reporting on the outcome of Stagner's revival, the Bloomington Pantagraph printed that twelve vile sinners have laid down their burdens of iniquity at the Christian Church at Lytleville during the present revival, and the thirteenth is on the anxious seat, with favorable symptoms."[15]

Grassy Ridge Christian Church, a country church south of Bloomington on Morris Avenue, was established in 1853 and disbanded in 1886. Some of the Grassy Ridge congregation united with the Christian Church in Lytleville in 1886.[16] In 1887, it was reported that Rev. Sylvester Peasley's second wife, Susan Crosby, was a member of the Christian Church in Lytleville.[17] In an 1888 newspaper wedding announcement, F.M. Phillips is cited as the pastor of the Christian Church in Lytleville.[18]

An 1895 map of Randolph Township shows the church building listed as the "Christian Church" once again in the same location. However, on this map, compared to the 1874 map, the Methodist Church building is now labeled as a school. The 1895 map now shows the church building sitting on a tract of land owned by D. Hougham.[19]

An 1897 article reports a quarrel between two sets of church trustees (one elected by a majority on the congregation, and one elected by only nine members) over access to the church building and the changing of the lock by one group without the other group's knowledge. At the time of this event, the congregation numbered 60 members.[20] It is the author's opinion that this unfortunate quarrel caused a split in the church which eventually led to its disbandment.

Nathaniel Haynes' exhaustive history of the Disciples of Christ in Illinois, published in 1915, does not list Lytleville as an active congregation in the McLean County congregational report. The church more than likely was inactive as of 1900. It is probable that many of the members transferred to the Christian Church in Heyworth or to the Blooming Grove Christian Church 5 miles south of Bloomington. Terri Ryburn-

---

[14] "A Pleasant Rural Convention of the Christian Churches," *The Pantagraph*, May 30, 1881.

[15] *The Pantagraph*, January 26, 1881.

[16] Haynes, 283.

[17] *Portrait and Biographical Album of McLean County, IL* (Chicago, IL: Chapman Brothers, 1887), 1074.

[18] "Half Johnson and the Other Half Kitchell," *The Pantagraph*, February 23, 1888.

[19] [*Atlas of*] *McLean County, Randolph Township* (Northwest Publishing, 1895).

[20] "A Warm Church Fight: Lytleville Shaken from Center to Circumference over a Door Latch," *The Pantagraph*, February 27, 1897.

LaMonte, in her report on the history of Lytleville, mentions that the church building had a cemetery next to it (unconfirmed by the author or other sources) and the building collapsed sometime in the 1920s.[21]

The Arny Faction in Bloomington, Illinois[22]

Since my retirement in November 2000, I have been on a quest to learn more about my Stone-Campbell religious heritage. The "quest" is really a journey that has included reading numerous books, journals, newspaper articles, scholarly papers, and pamphlets. Marcia and I have attended several church-related conferences and visited some historical sites in the USA. I've held numerous phone conversations and exchanged many emails with people who have been very helpful in assisting me with my quest. Men and women from all three major streams of my religious heritage have helped and continue to help. Occasionally, I've been able to "help back" or "fill in a blank" for someone else. What a treat that's been for me. Although I haven't kept track, I expect that I've logged literally thousands of hours on the Internet, doing what I term "research," and I have thousands of items that I've been able to read and/or download. The fact that Marcia and I have the good fortune to be members of a 175 year old congregation in Bloomington, First Christian Church (Disciples of Christ), constantly reminds me that a "great cloud of saints" have gone before me, and that I continue to be blessed by their faith and witness. Some of you know that for several years, I've been trying to learn what it was that caused the Bloomington church to split for a brief time (1852 - 1859). Was it over personalities? Politics? Doctrine? I wish I knew, just for the sake of understanding my religious heritage, if for no other reason. One person who was a member of the Bloomington church at the time of the trouble was William Frederick Milton Arny (1813-1881), who in February 1850, was released from an 18-year employment by Alexander Campbell of Bethany, Virginia (now West Virginia), after being involved in a flap between Campbell and Alexander Hall over a Disciples' census taken by Hall in 1848. Arny and his family moved to Bloomington in the Spring of 1850. He is listed as family number 558 on page 21 of the June 1, 1850 US Census (William T. Major and his family are listed as family number 555 on the same page!). By December 1850, Arny managed to be elected as one of the Trustees of

---

[21] Terri Ryburn-LaMonte, *Lytleville: The Town, the Myth, the Legend* (Normal, IL: Illinois State University, 1984), 14-16.

[22] Essay by cohort Ken Christensen from Bloomington, Illinois.

the Bloomington church. Imagine that! Trouble soon followed, with Arny in the middle of things, and by September 17, 1852 the church split.[23] The two congregations reunited sometime in late 1859,[24] during the ministry of John Wesley Lanphear. (Lanphear was called from Ohio to be the pastor of the church on Jefferson Street in 1857, sometime after the new brick building was dedicated in January of that year. He resigned on February 11, 1860.) There are many details that I have not mentioned that relate to Arny and his relationship to the Bloomington church. While living in Bloomington (actually North Bloomington, now Normal) he was involved in numerous worthy endeavors outside the church, such as: helping to create the Illinois Farm Bureau, the Illinois State Fair, Illinois State Normal University, the development of the town of Normal, bringing railroads to the community, the formation of the Illinois Republican Party, and was a prime mover with the Kansas National Committee. But, by 1857, Arny and his family had moved to Kansas. He later would be appointed by President Lincoln as an agent to the Indians, replacing Kit Carson, in the New Mexico Territory. He also would serve on multiple occasions as Interim Governor of the New Mexico Territory. He is buried in Santa Fe.[25]

A theory as to the root cause of the split that I've raised is that it could have been over the "anti-slavery" issue and Arny's abolitionist views. In 1842, while at Bethany, Arny participated in helping fleeing slaves make their way along the underground railroad and coordinated with Joseph Bryant and Matthew McKeever (brothers-in-law of Alexander Campbell), and his son Thomas Campbell McKeever, in that effort. He also participated in an 1854 attempt to organize the Republican party in Illinois, which was described by one historian "as a sort of disguised abolitionism." For years, I've suspected that Arny attended the one (and only, as far as I can determine) Disciples Anti-Slavery Convention, which was held in Cleveland on January 11-12, 1854. In 1854, Alexander Campbell stated that no church from Bloomington attended the convention, as it was but a "faction" that attended. He named no names, however.[26] I am

---

[23] *CE*, 3.12 (December 1852) 424, 425.

[24] In the "Church Directory" in the *Bloomington Daily Pantagraph* (November 26, 1859) 1, only one Christian Church is listed.

[25] Details on Arny are from Christensen's research and Lawrence R. Murphy, *Frontier Crusader—William F. M. Arny* (Tucson, Arizona: The University of Arizona Press, 1972).

[26] *MH,* 1854:174. The remark by Campbell reflects the existing animosity he held toward Arny.

happy to report that it was indeed W. F. M. Arny who attended the Cleveland convention.[27] Concerning the split in the Bloomington congregation and his desire to attend the convention, Arny stated:

> The congregation of disciples of which I am present a member, have been separated for more than a year from others in this place, who call themselves a church, but who hold in their communion and fellowship Slaveholders—men who have removed to this state and have slaves "hired out" in Kentucky. This class of slaveholders we have argued are more censurable than any other class—they profess Christianity, and yet hire out to non-professors their fellow beings. Having objected to such received as members of our congregation, the result was that 39 of us were separated, and we organized a separate congregation and as such would like to be represented at the convention.

The Church of Christ in Danville 1912-1989, and in Vermilion County, 1834-1989.[28]

Preface

The 25th year of the East Park Church of Christ was celebrated on September 27, 1987. At that time, a history of the Church of Christ in Vermilion Co. from 1834 to 1987 was prepared. Now, in 1989, we are celebrating the 90th year of the founding, the East Park parent congregation.

The Gilbert and English Church of Christ in 1929.

The Gilbert and English Church was not the first group to meet in Danville. A group first met in 1912, and they merged with The Gilbert and English congregation in 1940. (We can celebrate 80 years in Danville

---

[27] "Disciples' Anti-slavery Convention," *The Anti-Slavery Bugle* (December 10, 1853) 2.

[28] Michael Moss, Professor at Ohio Valley University, and cohort member, who grew up in Danville, Illinois, has provided information on the churches in Vermilion County. Since the beginnings in Vermilion County mentioned come from 1834 to around the end of the nineteenth century we present his information here.

in 1992). The history written in 1987 has been expanded with information made known since 1987. May you enjoy reading this as it has been rewarding for me to assemble it.

Dale E. Hoover
October 7, 1989

THE CHURCH IN VERMILION COUNTY

The first record of the Church of Christ is somewhere near the early 1830's. The group was referred to as the Disciples or Campbellites. *The Millennial Harbinger*, Number 10, volume 7, 1836 has the following item:

Danville, Vermilion County, Ill., July 12, 1836. I moved to this place last August, at which time there was not a congregation of disciples nearer than 18 miles; since that we have constituted four congregations, and one in Danville. I have baptized a goodly number, besides attending to my practice, which has been considerable. Last Lord's Day I went out 22 miles west, and baptized two, and constituted a congregation of fourteen. The gospel is moving onward amidst all the opposition of ignorant sectarians. I find it easy to proselyte when we get people to understand how to read the gospel. But the declaimers of the day keep the people in ignorance, not knowing the right way themselves.

Dr. W. WALTERS.

W. S. Shockley and Hughes Bowles were associated with Dr. Walters in these evangelistic labors in those early days. Named among the early congregations were Walnut Corner, a union church, located northeast of the airport about 1834; Old Union, another union church, located northwest of Danville, one in the Hillery area and one in Georgetown. The churches mentioned above are forerunners of the Christian churches of today. (A union church was one in which several denominations shared in the use of a building.)

The following information was written by Robert L. Benjamin for "Paths from the Past—History of Georgetown":

On July 5, 1841, a small group of Christians, organized by Elder Watson Clark, banded together to worship God after the simple New Testament pattern. At that time, it was known as the Germany or Liberty congregation.

Charter members were John Jordan, Eli Hewitt, Solomon White, John Sherer, David Sherer, William Drollinger, Henry Martin, R. M. Martin, Christian Vandevander, A. M. Martin, Hannah Jones, Elizabeth Sherer, Nancy Vandevander, Nancy Martin, Mary Martin, Mary Ann Hewitt, Ellen Prather, and Mary Jordan. The first addition to the original membership was Eliza Martin Spicer by immersion on August 7, 1841.

For several months the congregation met from house to house, in a barn belonging to Eli Hewitt and in a grove. The first appointment of officers of which there is a record were: John Jordan and Eli Hewitt, elders; Solomon White and C. Vandevander, deacons in 1844. The first ministers were Elders Watson Clark, Michael Combs, Solomon McKinney, Oliver Jones, John Hibs, William P. Shockley, and H. H. Gunn.

The first church build was erected in 1848, about a mile east of the Pleasant Mound Church of Christ, at a cost of $400. On December 31, 1854, R.M. Martin was regularly ordained as an evangelist by fasting, prayer, and laying on of hands by Elders William P. Shockley and Burke. Elder R. M. Martin preached for the congregation for several years, and was instrumental in organizing a number of churches in the county. He is said to have immersed more than 3,000 persons. When the Pleasant Mound building erected in 1882, the old building was used as a barn until 1934, and later torn down and rebuilt into a corn crib.

On October 27, 1882, John C. Jones and his wife, Martha J. Jones, deeded the church lot to the board of trustees as a gift, to be used as church purposes forever. The following conditions were listed on the transfer: (1) No organ or musical instrument shall be used in the said church house or on the grounds thereto belonging. (2) No festival, fair or any other innovation not authorized by the New Testament shall be held in said church or on said grounds. (3) No political meeting of any kind, Epworth League or Christian Endeavor or such like meetings shall be held in said church house or on said, grounds. (4) All revenues, issues or profits arising from insurance in case of loss, or damage to said church house by reason of fire, storm or otherwise shall be used for erection of another such church house on said ground or other site as may be designated or determined hereafter.

Ministers who preached at Pleasant Mound include: Calahan McBroom, Harmon Gregg, Elder J.W. Perkins (1886-1902), W. G. Roberts, J. C. Holloway, Frank Ellmore, Will Ellmore, O. M.

Davis, A. L. Gepford, A. J. McLaughlin, A. L. Russell, Grover Moss, W. W. Adamson, J. H. Allen, D. M. Mathis, Luther Tolliver, W. F. Mathis, C. F. Peck, J. Horney, James Finney, Harvey Martin, Luther Toliver, E. Adamson, Dan Mathis, Max Ray, John Allen, Harry Dubois, Russel Mathis, and Robert L. Benjamin. (Up to 1976 when this was written).

The R. M. (Raleigh or Rolla) Martin referred to above was instrumental in establishing the Church of Christ in Vermilion County. He was born in Monongalia County, Va., in 1816 and died in Danville in 1878. He came to Illinois with his parents in 1820, who settled near Georgetown. At 25 he was ordained to the ministry and continued therein until his death. He also served 2 elected terms as treasurer of Vermilion County.

After preaching for several years at Liberty, he helped organize the following:

• 1860 Marysville (Potomac)

• 1865 Prairie Chapel (5 mi. W. of Rossville).

• 1866 Westville

• 1870 No. 10 (6 mi. SE of Armstrong).

• 1873 Hoopeston

• 1877 Fairmount, Conkytown, and Gorman School House

The introduction of the organ/piano began in the 1860's and caused a problem for the Church. The village of Bismarck was founded in 1872, and a Christian Society was organized on January 11, 1879, by T. L. Stipp. It contained a Bible School. J. J. Cosat and J. C. Myers were also associated in the formation. About 1880 a building was erected at the northwest corner of what is now Bowman Avenue Road Bismarck Road. J. J. Cozat was the first minister. The first officers were Riley Chandler, William Wilson, and Samuel Munnell, elders; with David and Andrew Claypool and William Holland, deacons.

The question of instrumental music in worship, and the question of Sunday school and missions again created problems, and in 1897 the members came to worship one Sunday morning and found an organ had been moved into the building. Those who objected to the organ were locked out. One of my [Dale Hoover's] great-uncles, Bert Hoover, is said to be one of those responsible for putting the organ in the building.

Those who objected to the use of the instrument in church service met for a short period of time in the Bismarck Hotel while constructing a building on the north side of Bismarck. They started meeting there May, 1898. The subject of instrumental music in public worship was debated in 1898 with William Ellmore against and John J. Cosat for.

Early Elders and Deacons were D. L. Ogdon, A. W. Claypool, Luke Horner, J. M. Cunningham, James McCormick, W. F. Claypool, and B. B. Broin. Membership included Mary Claypool, Sarah McCormick, N. R. Ogdon, Thomas Ogdon, Lizzie Ogdon Roderick, Jennie Green, Stella French Brown, Effie G. Horner, Harriet Horner, Nellie Horner, Andrew Perry, John Horner, Ella Ingram Claypool, Edna Finney, Edith Claypool Burroughs, Elsie Claypool, Oma McCormick, F. M. Ogdon and Anna Ogdon. The Rodericks are relatives of Wanda Pickett. The McCormicks are Ben and Andy White's great-grandparents. The Horners are Kenneth and Carl Moss's grandparents and relatives, and A. W. and W. F. Claypool are my great-grandfather and grandfather.

The question of the instrument in worship caused problems in other county churches at the same time. John J. Cosat, Bismarck Christian Church, debated with J. W. Perkins the subject of instrumental music in worship in Georgetown in 1901. In the same year, S. S. Jones of Danville organized a Christian Church in Georgetown. I suspect that this was a split at Pleasant Mound. It is one of few instances where those not using the instrument retained control of the property.

The Old Columbia Church was built northwest of Danville by a split from Old Union. It is commented in the 1915 History of the Disciples in Illinois, "The church was divided through the preaching of ultra-conservatives. These damages have been measurably repaired by the ministry of J. J. Cosat, who is serving the congregation for the 25th year as its pastor." The above information would indicate the split took place in 1889. Histories written by Old Union members ignore this point. I do not have the details of the split. Old Columbia was disbanded in the early 1960s with members going to Bismarck and East Park. Those who did not want the instrument in worship were referred to as "anti's" by the group who did.

Old Columbia was the place my parents (Marion and Bonnie Claypool Hoover) worshipped along with Florence Moss Huffman's parents (Rolla and Merle Hoover Moss). During worship the men all sat on the left side of the building and the women and children on the right. Members I recall were Harold and Marjorie Moss Ping, Fran and Ruth Moss, Paul and Mary Moss, Mattie Moss, Elmer and Mary Moss, Eire and Bradie Moss, Ernie and Bessie Moss, Don and Myrtle Moss, Glen and Ethel Sumner, Frank and Effie Moss Swisher, Grover and Shiloh Moss, and Moses Swisher. I know this list is not complete.

Worship in these congregations consisted of a reading from the scriptures followed by a mutual edification time in which the men and boys would comment on the scripture read. The Lord's Supper (using only 2 cups) was observed following which all members would get up and file past a table in front, depositing their contribution in a collection basket (the right hand is not to know what the left hand is doing) and upon returning to the pews, all who could would kneel for prayer. Prayer was given by the two men waiting on the table. Singing of hymns also took place. If there was a visiting preacher, a sermon was given (this generally lasted an hour). Each congregation held an annual two week protracted meeting during the summer with members from each of the other congregations supporting the meeting. Other items of interest were the women wore a covering on their heads, there were no divided classes, prayer meeting was the mid-week service (many times held in members' homes instead of the building), Bible readings were meetings—usually through the winter—where the Bible was read aloud completely from Genesis to Revelation.

Restorationist Churches in Chicago[29]

Year	Month	Day	Event	Reference
1837	April	27	David Cory, writing from Athens, Cook [sic] county, Illinois, comments on the moral condition of the Chicago area and the state in general. One section states, "Since I have been in the country I have only met two persons who have espoused the cause of the reformation, thirty miles from here. This is different from what I had anticipated. Even many who had never heard that such a reformation was in progress! In the south I am told the brethren are more numerous." "What distraction might not be, saved to this interesting country by having the truth planted now, while in its infancy. Oh! that some of the brethren would take this subject into consideration, and "come over into Macedonia and help us." Cannot, will not some brother who has an eye to the recompense at the resurrection of the just, turn his course in the above direction? A. C.	*MH* 1837 287, 288
			[This Athens is known as Lemont today. "Lemont is at the southwest corner of Cook County southeast of the junctions of I 55 and I 355, and just south of the ship canal to the Illinois River. Lemont was originally known as *Keepataw* (after a Potawatomi chief) and a post office was established in 1840 as *Keepatau*. After that, it was named *Athens* and then *Palmyra*. The name *Lemont* (literally, 'the mountain' in French) was chosen in 1850 at the suggestion of Lemuel Brown, the postmaster and justice of the peace, or perhaps by his brother Nathaniel Brown." Courtesy of Tom Olbricht via email 2.22.2016.	

---

[29] Information compiled by James L. McMillan

1850	Early		"Early in 1850 the first church of the Restoration movement was formed in Chicago. The charter members were Dr. L. S. Major, Platt Saunders and wife, M. H. Baldwin and wife, J. Reese and Miss Laura Balch, who afterward became Mrs. Dickey. Lathrop Cooley, of Ohio, was the preacher. Mr. Baldwin was chosen elder, and Mr. Saunders, deacon. From that day to this the divinely appointed worship has been maintained by the Disciples there on every Lord's Day."	Haynes 151
1851	Sept.		At the 1851 State Meeting of the Illinois brethren, held at Walnut Grove, Woodford County (this village was later was renamed to Eureka, I believe), "The board of managers appointed bros. W. M. Brown and William Davenport to carry the ancient Gospel to Quincy, Peoria, and Chicago, requiring them to labor six months in the current year at these points. These appointments were accepted." (T. J. Matlock, "State Meeting in Illinois," *Western Evangelist* (later the *Christian Evangelist*), Volume 2, Number 10, (October, 1851) page 316.) Matlock's letter was dated "Monmouth, Ills., Sep. 12, 1851."	T. J. Matlock, "State Meeting in Illinois," *Western Evangelist* (later the *Christian Evangelist*), Volume 2.10, (October, 1851) 316.
1853	Nov.		"A correspondent of the *Central Christian Advocate* furnishes a sad picture of the state of morals in Chicago, Ill. According to his statement, the Lord's day-by a large portion of the inhabitants—is known only as a day of fun and frolic—spent in the indulgence of sinful practices, such as drinking, dancing, gambling, horse-racing and other vices (plainly hinted at by the writer) of a still worse character."	*CE*, 4 (November, 1853) 430.
1853	Nov.		Campbell travels to Illinois, going from Toledo through Chicago enroute to Joliet.	*MH* 1853: 6 – 9.
1853	Dec.	3	Campbell spends a night at the Sherman House in Chicago, enroute to Toledo, on his way home to Bethany.	*MH* 1854: 50; article on the tour spans pages 40 - 52

| 1853 | | | "Illinois is richer in *fact* than in *promise*. At her State Meeting, a year since, she promised us, by her representatives, in annual convention assembled, only $10,000, towards endowing a Chair in Bethany College. Her promise had this extent, no more. But she has given her bonds for $16,000 for a Chair ever to be called the Illinois Chair in Bethany College, and $9,000 to be a perpetual fund for the boarding of her poor sons, who promise to be useful men in the gospel ministry. The proceeds of this sum, in its annual interest, to be appropriated to such as her annual conventions may select, as young men of Christian character, talent and promise.
Besides this, as already hinted, she has, during one year, subscribed, I presume to say, as much more for other colleges and seminaries of learning. Besides this, she is building, and has been annually building, new meeting-houses, paying her own evangelists for their services, and abounding in works of private charity and benevolence. Although possessing not half the church members in Indiana, thousands less than Ohio, and not many more than Virginia, she has transcended them all in liberality to an institution not in her own territory, and has set them an example which, I trust, will at least be equaled, if not excelled, by each of them.

Missouri will not suffer her younger sister, (Illinois,) to achieve greater honor for Christian philanthropy and magnanimity than herself. So I am led to believe, from good authority."

[Note that 1852 would have been the year of the State Meeting Campbell refers to. It was in 1852 that the Illinois State Convention established an "Education Committee" to make recommendations on establishing educational efforts in Illinois. See *Christian Sentinel* Volume 1 for details.] | *MH* 1854: 51 |

1854	March	8	J. H. Mellinger reports the death of his wife Sarah Ann Mellinger. The letter is post-marked "Chicago, Ill., March 8, 1854."	*MH* 1854: 360
1854	June or earlier		"Illinois: Bro. J. Creath, of Missouri, on a late visit to this State, held a meeting in Bloomington, in conjunction with Bro. Henderson, which resulted in 16 additions. Of Chicago, the point from which Bro. Creath writes, he says: "This city has over 60,000 inhabitants. We have but few brethren here, and no house of public wor-ship." To these facts he wishes to call the attention of the brotherhood at this time. He hopes that the brethren of the State will soon make it their special object to solicit aid from the churches, that a house of worship may be speedily built, and an able preacher sustained to minister therein. This sugges-tion will doubtless be a matter of grave con-sideration at their next State Meeting." Christian Evangelist article by Creath is "Visit to Illinois," relating his time in Springfield and Bloomington. Brief mention of visit to Chicago.	*MH* 1854:356; *CE* 1854 300 - 302
1855	May	9, 10	Alexander Campbell, in a letter to Mr. Jno. Taylor, says he plans to attend the Bible Union meeting in Chicago. No date. The letter is in the June number. Several Illinois SCMers are there including A. J. Kane, P. H. Murphy, and W. T. Major. Campbell gave an address on "the work in which the Union is engaged" in the evening session on Thurs-day, May 10th. (352) Per a letter from Frank Remington on page 465, Mrs. Campbell went with him.	*MH* 1854 343; 352; 465. See also, CE 6 (July 1855) 181; 329.
1856			Samuel Church, on a recent visit to Chica-go, meets a Presbyterian from Fondulac, Wisconsin. Church relates how the small congregation pooled their money to pay their pastor and build a building. He, I think, has it in mind that the SCM in Chicago could do something similar. No date on the letter but it is in the November number.	*MH* 1856 631, 632

1857	April	27	Daniel R. Hundley, writing from Chicago, submits an article, "What is He Worth?" on covetousness.	*MH* 1857: 352, 353
1858	May	28	"After Elder Baldwin closed his services, Charles B. Egan, a brother of the noted Dr. William B. Egan, succeeded to the pulpit. On account of certain difficulties between him and some members of the Society, it was broken up and the Rev. Mr. Egan retired. Only a few of the members remained true to the organization, among whom were H. H. Honore and wife, B. L. Honore and wife, and Dr. L. S. Major. This was in 1857. While affairs were in this chaotic condition, the Rev. M. N. Lord was induced by H. H. Honore to take charge of the congregation; commencing his labors in December, 1857, and remaining until June, 1861. During this period, Allen Robbins, of Ohio, visited Chicago, and was largely instrumental in raising a subscription sufficient to erect the church edifice on Monroe Street already mentioned. It stood about one hundred feet east of Rucker Street, was a frame one-story building, thirty-six by fifty-eight feet in size, with a small tower but no bell. It was commenced May 28, 1858, and was dedicated July 4, 1858. The dedicatory sermon was delivered by Rev. D. P. Henderson. The money employed in the construction of this edifice was contributed mainly by Dr. L. S. Major and H. H. Honore."	"History of the Chicago Christian Church" in *History of Chicago from the Earliest Period to the Present Time, in Three Volumes. Volume 1, Ending with the Year 1857.*
1858	July	4	"It was commenced May 28, 1858, and was dedicated July 4, 1858. The dedicatory sermon was delivered by Rev. D. P. Henderson."	Ibid.
1865			John S. Sweeney is minister at the Monroe street building.	Ibid.
1866			John S. Sweeney moves to Cincinnati. He is succeeded by B. H. Smith. Monroe street building sold and the congregation moved to the North Side, buying the old St. James' church building.	Ibid.
1867			D. P. Henderson succeeds Smith.	Ibid.

1868			"In 1868, the members became dissatisfied with the North Side, most of them living on the South Side. In order to satisfy the desire to move to another location, Dr. L. S. Major and H. H. Honore bought for the use of the Society the church edifice of St. Luke's Episcopal Mission, at the corner of Wabash Avenue and Sixteenth Street. This building had been erected by the Universalists, and sold by them to the Olivet Presbyterian Church. By them it was sold to Mr. Cole, who with the assistance of some others, started this mission. This church building was dedicated by the Christian Church the first Sunday of its occupancy by them, Rev. D. P. Henderson preaching in the morning and in the evening. In the afternoon, at the request of some of the members, the Rev. John S. Sweeney preached, which was so much against the wishes of Elder Henderson, that he resigned. His resignation was accepted, and John S. Sweeney called in his stead."	Ibid.
1869	January		"In January, 1869 a congregation moved into a new building at Chicago, Illinois and placed an organ in it over the protest of the minister, D.P. Henderson." http://truthmagazine.com/archives/volume23/ TM023333.html Bob Tuten, "Historical Study Of Controversy Over Instrumental Music In Worship (2) = The Dawning of Instruments In Worship." Accessed 2.21.2016.	

Existing Illinois Churches of Christ Founded Before 1900

Our research shows that there are sixteen Churches of Christ still existing in 2017 that were founded in the nineteenth century before the 1906 division.[30]

Founded	Town	County	Members	Location	Affiliation
1836	Mattoon, Southside	Coles	50	SW of Charlestown	NI
1851	Modesto	Macoupin	5	SW Springfield	
1853	Thompsonville	Franklin	18	W of Evansville, IN	NI
1855	Nebo, Farmer's Ridge	Calhoun	10	E. Bowling Green, MO	
1860	Hamburg	Calhoun	95	MO River N. of Alton	
1862	Eureka	Woodford	80	E. of Peoria	
1863	Crossville	White	18	NW of Evansville, IN	
1863	Cooksville	Maclean	32	E. of Bloomington	
1867	Browning	Schuyler	18	NW of Springfield, IL River	
1880	Hazel Dell	Cumberland	45	E. of Effingham	NI
1882	Hammond	Piatt	20	E. of Decatur	

---

[30] From *Churches of Christ in the United States*, Carl Royster, compiler. 2012 edition. Illinois 271 congregations of Churches of Christ, 25,659 Adherents. Chart compiled by Thomas H. Olbricht. Comparison of this information with the data in Appendix 4, shows that prior to and shortly after 1900, the number and strength of Illinois Churches of Christ, regardless of their affiliation as non-institutional, non-class, or influenced by Daniel Sommer, is underestimated and needs additional study.

1884	Olney, Eureka	Richland	55	W. of Vincennes, IN	
1886	Greenup	Cumberland	20	E. of Effingham	No Classes
1890	Arcola	Douglas	70	S. of Champaign	
1895	Bismarck	Vermilion	60	N. of Danville	
1897	Paris, Oliver	Edgar		NW of Terre Haute	

Grid of the congregations for which Hayes supplies data in his *History of the Disciples in Illinois*. Total number of congregations above 750.[31]

County	Church	Est.	Size
Adams	Antioch	1843	36
	Camp Point	1865	458
	Clayton		187
	Coatsburg		35
	Columbus	1844	151
	Fowler	1861	36
	Kellerville		54
	Liberty	1852	177
	Lima	1830	110
	Loraine	1842	310
	Marcellene		50
	Mill Creek, Mendon		20
	Mound Prairie, Beverly		90
	Mount Hebron, Mendon		30
	Payson	1868	125
	Pleasant View, Camp Point	1835	125
	Quincy, First	1840	530
	Quincy, East End		71
	Richfield, Plainview		20
	Ursa	1833	152
	Wolf Ridge, Camp Point	1892	40
Alexander	Cairo first	1866	157
	Cairo Second	1908	51
Bond	Greenville	1878	300
	Mulberry Grove	1864	200
	Smithboro		30
	Tamalco		99
	Woburn	1859	50
Boone	No congregations		

[31] We can only approximate the total number of existing congregations in 1914. Haynes is inconsistent on the existence of some congregations, stating in some cases the founding date of a congregation but not detailing the congregation's status in 1914. In the chart, a blank cell means Haynes does not provide a year and/ or a number.

Brown	Cooperstown	1881	103
	Hazel Dell, Mt. Sterling	1870	70
	Mt. Sterling	1838	300
	New Salem, Mt. Sterling	1875	50
	Ripley	1842	72
	Timewell	1868	194
	Versailles	1869	
Bureau	Boyd's Grove, Milo	1850	weak
	New Bedford	1866	130
	Princeton	1840	282
	Walnut	1882	242
	Yorktown	1891	20
Calhoun	Bay (Mozier)	1897	60
	Farmer's Ridge, Nebo	1856	123
	Indian Creek (Hamburg)		60
Carroll	Lanark	1843	122
	Savanna	1904	25
	Thomson	1852	105
Cass	Ashland	1892	126
	Beardstown reestablished	1910	137
	Chandlerville	1865	199
	Philadelphia	1837	20
	Virginia	1839	160
Champaign	Champaign	1883	975
	Fisher	1885	236
	Gifford	1880	60
	Homer	1856	107
	Longview		
	Ludlow	1869	183
	Ogden	1871	60
	Rantoul	1892	278
	Sidney	1856	68
	St. Joseph	1845	237

Christian	Assumption	1874	120
	Berea (Mt. Auburn)	1868	100
	Edinburg	1856	299
	Morganville (Blue Mound)	1891	100
	Mt. Auburn	1840	200
	Pana	1905	60
	Pleasant Hill (Pawnee)		138
	Taylorville	1853	410
Clark	Blue Grass	1836	
	Darwin	1840	
Clay	Bethel (Louisville)	1882	224
	Bethlehem (Flora)		24
	Bible Grove		139
	Clay City	1871	88
	Flora	1855	328
	Ingraham	1839	
	Liberty Chapel (Flora)	1911	22
	Louisville		82
	McKinney	1871	96
	New Bethlehem		
	North Harter (Flora)	1905	140
	Oak Mound (Xenia)		98
	Old Union (Xenia)		60
	Red Brush (Louisville)		31
	Sailor Springs		80
	Union Chapel (Louisville)		71
	Xenia	1865	45
Clinton	Keyesport		100
Coles	Brick (Westfield)		90
	Bushtown	1873	200
	Charleston	1840	1,150
	Etna		65
	Humbolt	1858	161
	Mattoon	1859	903
	Oakland		70
	Prairie Union (Kansas)	1868	26
	Rural Retreat (Hindboro)	1857	86
	Walnut Grove (Humbolt)	1887	12

Cook	Chicago		120
	Armitage Avenue	1871	150
	Amour Avenue CC	1888	298
	Ashland, CC	1899	
	Austin	1893	
	Chicago Heights	300	
	Douglas Park CoC	1895	150
	Englewood CoC	1885	600
	Evanston, CC	1896	135
	Harvey, CC	1892	209
	Hyde Park, DoC	1894	200
	Irving Park	1898	240
	Jackson Boulevard	1873	800
	Kendall Street	1865	
	Memorial CoC	1908	600
	Metropolitan CoC	1897	500
	Monroe Street	1891	140
	Russian Mission	1909	40
	Sheffield Avenue	1890	200
	South Chicago, CC	1906	50
	West End		76
	West Pullman		64
Crawford	East Union	1848	150
	Hardinville	1850	103
	Hutsonville	1841	121
	Landes		48
	Oblong		144
	Palestine	1863	250
	Portersville	1875	65
	Robinson	1867	300
	West Harmony (Bell Air)		103
	Wirt Chapel	1862	

Cumberland	Antioch (Greenup)	1891	90
	Brush Creek	1890	25
	Corinth	1876	45
	Greenup	1887	43
	Hazel Dell		80
	Janesville		70
	Jewett	1843	40
	Johnstown (Toledo)		58
	Neoga	1896	35
	Plum Grove (Hidalgo)	1900	80
	Plum Grove (Greenup)	1900	
	Toledo	1875	200
	Webster (Janesville)	1864	
DeKalb	No congregations		
De Witt	Clinton	1852	560
	Fairview (Heyworth)	1887	
	Farmer City	1864	147
	Hallsville (for. Old Union)	1832	211
	Kenney	1883	140
	Lane	1850	55
	Long Point (Wapella)	1851	51
	Rock Creek (Waynesville)	1837	80
	Texas (Clinton)	1850	77
	Wapella	1868	123
	Waynesville	1894	225
Douglas	Arcola	1858	270
	Carmargo		106
	Hindsboro	1863	150
	Murdock	1902	50
	Newman	1869	450
	Tuscola	1863	285
	Villa Grove	1906	110
DuPage	No congregations		

Edgar	Asher (Paris)	1907	139
	Bell Ridge (Paris)		
	Brocton	1873	50
	Chrisman	1890	12
	Conlogue	1872	
	Dudley	1868	
	Hume	1875	167
	Kansas	1856	350
	Little Grove (Vermilion)	1826	40
	Metcalf		125
	Nevins	1858	19
	Oliver	1895	100
	Paris	1855	1714
	Pleasant Hill (Kansas)	1870	207
	Redmon	1907	80
	State Line (Paris)	1862	30
	Success (Vermilion)	1895	75
Edwards	Albion	1841	331
	Bone Gap	1886	154
	Brown	1894	144
	Ellery	1890	150
	Shiloh (West Salem)	1862	125
	West Salem	1858	175
	West Village (Albion)	1858	293
	Little Prairie (Ellery)	1823	100
	Marion	1843	150
	New Hope (Brown)		44
Effingham	Beecher City	1902	161
	Dieterich		65
	Edgewood	1890	110
	Effingham	1890	
	Elliottstown (Dieterich)		54
	Mason	1890	125
	Watson		30

Fayette	Arne Prairie (Brownstown)	1907	17
	Bethany (Brownstown)		61
	Bingham	1911	15
	Brownstown	1871	206
	Four-Mile Prairie(Brown-stown)	1843	20
	Liberty (Brownstown)		75
	Macedonia (Loogootee)	1868	75
	Pittsburg (Vandalia)		34
	Ramsey	1851	123
	St. Elmo		167
	Union (Ramsey)		35
	Antioch		
Ford	Gibson	1872	430
	Mt. Olivet (Paxton)	1857	84
	Paxton		150
Franklin	Benton	1889	200
	Christopher		385
	Long Prairie (Benton)		50
	Miner (Mulkeytown)		108
	Mulkeytown	1830	380
	Six-Mile (Elkville)	1848	88
	Sesser	1905	48
	West Frankfurt	1902	132
	White (Plainfield)	1866	40
Fulton	Astoria	1863	175
	Bryant	1852	48
	Canton	1890	500
	Cuba	1832	226
	Ellisville	1887	25
	Ipava	1842	225
	Kerton Valley (Havana)	1889	30
	Lewistown	1874	175
	London Mills	1887	111
	Summum	1859	200
	Table Grove	1851	112
	Vermont	1847	376
	Antioch Mission		
Gallatin	No congregations		

Greene	Athensville		75
	Carrollton	1832	90
	Kane		100
	Roodhouse	1890	138
	Union (Greenfield)	1854	40
	White Hall	1883	230
Grundy	No congregations		
Hamilton	Broughton	1872	43
	Dahlgren	1906	42
	Dale		35
	Liberty (Thompsonville)	1857	55
	McLeansboro	1876	194
	Mt. Pleasant (McLeansboro)		
	New White Oak (Springerton)	1851	69
		1885	75
Hancock	Adrian		98
	Augusta	1850	251
	Bowen	1890	250
	Breckenridge (Sutter)		56
	Burnside	1875	68
	Carthage	1864	360
	Dallas City		334
	Denver	1875	181
	East Durham (Colusa)		40
	Golden Point (Hamilton)		75
	Hamilton	1893	225
	La Crosse		90
	La Harpe	1877	552
	Mt, Pleasant (Plymouth)	1833	70
	Oak Grove (Carthage)		70
	Plymouth	1855	73
	Stillwell		110
	West Point	1864	160
	Wythe (Sutter)	1865	30
Hardin	Cave in Rock		66
	Rosiclare		146
	Stone Church (Elizabethtown)		
			132

Henderson	Lomax		150
	Raritan		20
	Stronghurst		71
Henry	Kewanee	1901	366
Iroquois	Cissna Park	1906	57
	Darrow	1911	62
	Donovan	1856	140
	Fairview (Wellington)	1892	42
	Iroquois		10
	Martinton	1893	92
	Milford	1877	160
	Onarga	1877	75
	Pittwood	1894	80
	Prairie Green (Wellington)	1872	60
	Sheldon	1890	150
	Watseka	1881	350
	Woodland	1887	34
Jackson	Carbondale	1862	450
	Elkville	1887	145
	Murphysboro	1899	225
	Oak Grove (Carbondale)		25
	Pleasant Hill (Ava)	1878	100
	Six Mile (Elkville)	1848	88
Jasper	Bogota	1851	150
	Christian Chapel (Winter-rowd)	1888	42
	Lotona	1855	150
	Lis	1905	30
	Newton	1881	140
	Wheeler	1883	\65
Jefferson	Boyd		70
	Ebenezer (Mt. Vernon)	1899	22
	Elk Prairie (Ina)	1852	150
	Fouts (Cravat)		
	Hickory Hill (Mt. Vernon)	1880	5
	Ina	1911	25
	Little Grove (Walnut Hill)	1841	100
	Mt. Catherine (Woodlawn)		95
	Mt. Vernon	1853	300
	Union (Woodlawn)	1842	50

Jersey	No congregations		
Jo Daviess	No congregations		
Johnson	Belnap	1896	44
	Berea (Vienna)		
	Bethlehem (Vienna)	1847	30
	Grantsburg	1902	24
	New Burnside	1875	50
	Vienna	1866	56
Kane	Batavia	1852	72
Kankakee	No congregations		
Kendall	No congregations		
Knox	1st Henderson	1838	
	Abingdon	1850	450
	East Galesburg	1902	75
	Galesburg	1871	878
	Hermon		116
	Knoxville	1869	255
	Meridian (Abingdon)	1839	80
	St. Augustine		110
La Salle	Lostant	1865	30
	Dana	1865	57
	Ottawa	1913	20
	Rutland	1868	180
	Streator	1870	385
	Tonica	1912	19
Lake	Antioch	1841	
	Gurnee	1860	75
	Waukegan, First	1888	90
	Waukegan, West Side	1905	89

Lawrence	Allison	1815	170
	Bethany (Lawrenceville)	1879	35
	Bridgeport	1866	252
	Chauncey	1890	35
	Lawrenceville	1833	450
	Mt. Erie (Sumner)		25
	Mt. Zion (Sumner)	1815	40
	Pleasant Hill (Bridgeport)	1843	110
	Pleasant Ridge	1834	60
	(Lawrenceville)	1877	40
	Rising Sun (Russellville)	1840	50
	St. Francisville	1894	121
	Sumner	1850	124
Lee	Dixon	1894	260
Livingston	Ancona	1859	191
	Antioch (Long Point)	1912	24
	Fairbury	1868	163
	Flanagan	1862	195
	Forrest	1868	18
	Indian Grove (Fairbury)	1861	35
	Long Point	1889	151
	Pontiac	1859	377
	Saunemin	1874	139
Logan	Bridge church Pulaski	1848	
	Armington	1828	222
	Atlanta	1855	300
	Bethel (Emden)	1853	75
	Broadwell	1863	99
	Copeland (Mt. Pulaski)	1866	100
	Cornland	1874	120
	Emden	1888	94
	Eminence (Atlanta)	1838	180
	Hartsburg	1870	29
	Lake Fork	1905	100
	Latham	1891	250
	Lincoln	1856	695
	Mt. Pulaski	1868	361

McDonough	North of Blandinsville	1832	140
	Blandinsville	1849	384
	Bushnell		20
	Brandenburg Central		50
	Colchester	1867	190
	Colmar	1906	140
	Fandon	1898	80
	Macomb	1845	500
	New Philadelphia		86
	New Salem (Adair)	1859	
	Old Bedford (Stronghurst)	1849	
	Sciota		62
McHenry	North Crystal Lake		30
McLean	Anchor	1884	17
	Arrowsmith	1879	142
	Bellflower	1891	139
	Bloomington First	1837	1666
	Bloomington, Second		565
	Bloomington, Third	1902	40
	Bloomington, Centennial	1901	241
	Buck Creek (Lexington)	1910	30
	Carlock	1850	250
	Colfax	1836	308
	Cooksville	1867	144
	Ellsworth	1902	100
	Grindley	1867	50
	Heyworth	1872	261
	Holder	1867	35
	Hudson	1877	89
	Leroy	1888	240
	Lexington	1860	285
	McLean	1903	50
	Normal, First	1873	420
	Normal, Second	1884	28
	Saybrook	1868	292
	Shirley	1869	168
	Stanford	1870	323
	Twin Grove(Bloomington)	1841	40

Macon	Antioch (Decatur)	1850	70
	Argenta	1848	65
	Blue Mound	1861	224
	Center Ridge (Maroa)	1867	60
	Harristown	1861	180
	Oreana	1864	125
	Maroa	1862	210
	Niantic	1868	364
	Long Point (Niantic)	1850	
	Decatur, Central	1834	800
	Decatur, First Christian		879
	Decatur, East Side	1908	75
Macoupin	Atwater		143
	Blooming Grove(Nilwood)	1873	
	Berean (Modesto)	1830	25
	Boston Chapel (Girard)		60
	Carlinville	1896	132
	Gillespie	1859	84
	Girard	1860	177
	Modesto	1890	61
	Oak Grove (Rhorer)		36
	Palmyra	1867	392
	Round Prairie(Bunker Hill)	1845	20
	Scottville		160
	Shaw's Point (Barnett)	1882	64
	Stanton		50
	West Pairie (Dorchester)		12
	Virden	1882	240
Madison	Edwardsville	1889	37
	Granite City		260
	Marine		60
	New Douglas		90
	Ridgely	1850	10
	Worden	1892	112

Marion	Alma	1867	50
	Cartter	1866	35
	Centralia	1856	675
	Donahue Prairie Kell)	1898	100
	Gaston Grove (Cartter)	1884	89
	Kell	1896	15
	Kinmundy	1899	110
	Lovel Grove (Iuka)		60
	Mt. Moriah (Mt. Vernon)	1829	135
	Odin	1878	188
	Patona	1875	125
	Salem	1866	265
	Sandoval	1889	320
	Smith Grove (Kinmundy)	1882	25
	Turkey Creek (Odin)	1867	
	Young's Chapel (Salem)	1883	82
Marshall	Crow Creek	1836	
	Belle Plain (La Rosa)	1845	115
	Henry	1889	54
	Toluca	1858	170
Mason	Quiver	1840	
	Bath		
	Havana	1900	
	Mason City	1880	
	Pleasant Plains		
Massac	Bethel (Grand Chain)	1885	60
	Brookport	1885	60
	Joppa	1881	40
	Liberty Ridge (Metropolis)	1867	40
	Little Rock (Unionville)	1875	80
	Metropolis	1864	300
	Mt. Pleasant (Brookport)		24
	Samouth		40
	Unionville	1865	100
Menard	Athens	1838	201
	Greenview	1869	215
	Petersburg	1863	620
	Sweet Water	1825	115
	Tallula	1834	200

Mercer	Keithsburg	1864	142
	New Boston	1902	152
	Ohio Grove (Aledo)		40
Monroe	No congregations		
Montgomery	Barnett	1887	40
	Harvel	1888	89
	Hillsboro	1905	60
	Irving	1853	100
	Litchfield	1856	742
	Pleasant Hill (Barnett)		71
	Raymond	1871	156
	Waggoner	1889	114
	Walshville	1874	50
Morgan	Antioch (Jacksonville)	1833	40
	Berea (Prentice)	1852	75
	Chapin	1875	240
	Concord	1868	96
	Franklin		140
	Jacksonville (Central)	1832	1200
	Jacksonville (Negro)	1904	35
	Literberry	1869	160
	Lynnville (Jacksonville)	1833	140
	Oak Ridge (Prentice)	1876	
	Waverly	1847	131
	Woodson	1869	151
Moultrie	West Crow	1832	
	Allenville	1884	200
	Arthur	1882	132
	Bethany	1881	180
	Cadwell	1902	86
	Dalton City	1865	75
	Gays	1869	150
	Jonathan'sCreek (Sullivan)	1859	70
	Lake City	1886	33
	Lovington	1832	408
	Smyser (Gays)	1837	180
	Sullivan	1840	561
	Union Prairie (Arthur)	1870	47

Ogle	Grand Detour	1897	27
	Mt. Morris	1880	83
	Pine Rock (Polo)	1860	98
	Polo	1904	94
Peoria	Peoria Central	1845	792
	Peoria West Bluff Chapel	1910	
	Peoria Howett Street	1909	192
	Mt. Hawley	1841	
Perry	Duquoin	1857	
	Friendship (Tamaroa)	1867	60
	Tamaroa		50
Piatt	Antioch (Atwood)	1854	50
	Atwood	1879	112
	Bement	1862	120
	Cerro Gordo	1833	74
	De Land	1877	199
	Hammond	1875	
	Monticello	1911	39
Pike	Atlas	1908	140
	Barry	1842	275
	Bee Creek (Pearl)	1911	60
	Chambersburg		326
	Detroit	1882	133
	El Dara	1873	190
	Green Pond (Pearl)		160
	Griggsville	1876	116
	Independence (Pittsfield)	1858	160
	Martinsburg		75
	Milton		250
	Nebo	1885	200
	New Canton		75
	New Hartford	1851	150
	Old Pearl (Straut)		60
	Pearl	1885	277
	Perry	1837	330
	Pittsfield	1836	600
	Pleasant Hill		231
	Rock Hill (Nebo)		
	Rockport	1869	44
	Time (Pittsfield)		15

The History of the Restoration Movement in Illinois

Pope	Dixon Springs Delwood	1912	12
Pulaski	America	1889	55
	Christian Chapel	1890	75
	Grand Chain	1858	73
Putnam	Putnam	1850	100
Randolph	Mt. Summit (Leanderville)	1887	40
Richland	Antioch (Olney)		81
	Berryville (Parkersburg)		80
	Calhoun	1864	66
	Noble	1884	72
	Olney	1866	280
	Parkersburg		124
	Prairie Hill (Claremont)		35
Rock Island	Moline	1906	152
	Rapids City	1847	10
	Rock Island, First	1868	725
	Rock Island, Second		36
Saline	Eldorado	1903	100
	Harrisburg		100
	Stone Fort	1898	25

136

Sangamon	Auburn	1868	70
	Barclay (Wolf Creek?)	1841	
	Berlin	1825	80
	Buffalo	1875	125
	Cantrall	1820	125
	Clear Lake (Springfield)	1865	
	Dawson	1887	30
	Illiopolis	1866	408
	Loami	1892	150
	Mechanicsburg	1845	175
	Pleasant Plains	1869	102
	Riverton	1876	90
	Rochester	1841	90
	Springfield, First	1833	992
	Springfield, Stewart Street	1905	550
	Springfield, West Side	1902	674
	Salisbury	1875	50
	South Fork (Rochester)	1832	75
	Williamsville	1842	200
Schuyler	Bader		90
	Bethany (Rushville)	1871	30
	Browning	1894	12
	Camden	1865	92
	Frederick	1890	12
	Pleasant View		
	Ray	1895	75
	Rushville	1855	225
Scott	Exeter		88
	Glasgow		45
	Manchester	1864	68
	Winchester	1832	300

Shelby	Ash Grove (Windsor)	1832	400
	Brunswick	1860	
	Cowden	1899	120
	Findlay	1906	90
	Henton	1850	127
	Herrick		25
	Mode	1880	51
	Moweaqua	1896	258
	New Liberty (Windsor)	1871	
	Rocky Branch(Tower Hill)	1850	
	Sand Creek (Windsor)	1834	25
	Shelbyville	1831	500
	Stewardson		320
	Tower Hill		50
	Windsor	1857	273
St. Clair	East St. Louis, First	1890	445
	East St. Louis(Lansdowne)	1905	120
Stark	La Fayette	1847	62
	Toulson	1849	82
Stephenson	Freeport	1906	60
	Oneca, called Mt. Pleasant	1847	
Tazewell	Concord (Minier)	1870	90
	Deer Creek	1906	91
	Lilly	1837	79
	Mackinaw	1837	509
	Malone (Green Valley)	1866	20
	Minier	1874	222
	Pekin	1876	250
	Washington	1834	110
Union	Ana		115
	Toledo (Cobden)	1836	50

Vermilion	Danville	1836	
	Alvin	1897	60
	Antioch (Rossville)	1866	195
	Bethany	1875	20
	Bismark	1880	100
	Catlin		212
	Central Park (Danville)	1909	47
	Center Point (Fairmount)	1891	50
	Cheneyville	1891	109
	Danville, First	1871	407
	Danville, Second	1899	100
	Danville, Third	1902	770
	Danville, Fourth	1904	120
	Fithian	1884	11
	Georgetown	1901	198
	Henning	1898	140
	Hoopestown	1873	535
	Indianola		68
	Lowe's Chapel	1876	68
	Number Eight (Amstrong)	1888	23
	No. Ten (Potomac)	1870	270
	Oakwood	1886	129
	Potomac		125
	Prairie Chapel	1865	74
	Ridge Farm	1899	50
	Rossville	1894	264
	Sidell	1895	125
	Union (Danville)	1838	60
	Walnut Corners (Danville)	1843	98
	Westville	1866	40
	Willow Springs(Grape Crk	1870	40
Wabash	Adam's Corner (Allendale)	1851	75
	Allendale	1891	117
	Antioch (Keensburg)	1886	70
	Barney'sPrairie(Allendale)	1819	40
	Bellmont	1896	110
	Keensburg	1819	180
	Lancaster (Mt. Carmel)	1842	95
	Lick Prairie (Mt. Carmel)	1830	125
	Maud (Mt. Carmel)	1896	90
	Mt. Carmel	1862	760

Warren	Alexis	1902	60
	Berwick	1902	58
	Cameron	1831	290
	Coldbrook No. 2 (Cameron	1839	200
	Gerlaw	1859	100
	Monmouth	1839	930
	Roseville		160
	Youngtown		230
Washington	Ashley	1871	90
Wayne	Bailey	1867	65
	Beech Bluff (Fairfield)	1912	26
	Black Oak (Fairfield)	1909	
	Boyleston	1890	
	Buckeye (Jefffersonville)	1840	85
	Cisne	1854	150
	Fairfield	1853	320
	Frame (Mill Shoals)	1842	65
	Jeffersonville	1861	83
	Keenes	1911	
	Middleton (Keenes)		85
	Mount Erie	1911	52
	Oakwood (Goldengate)	1895	130
	Pleasant Grove(Jeffersonv)	1854	200
	Pleasant Hill (Cisne)	1873	65
	Renard	1909	40
	Six Mile		
	Turney's Prairie	1839	
	Wayne City	1887	125
	Zif (Clay City)	1878	42
White	Ashland (Mill Shoals)	1883	57
	Bryant's Valley (Crossville		100
	Carmi	1851	125
	Endfield	1868	77
	Grayville	1840	165
	Mill Shoals	1911	62
	Seven Mile (Carmi)	1839	90
	Springerton		100

Whiteside	Coleta	1847	71
	Erie	1870	100
	Fulton	1896	40
	Rock Falls	1905	200
	Sterling	1875	276
	Tampico	1900	95
Will	Joliet, First	1897	50
Williamson	Carterville	1885	290
	Creal Springs	1895	50
	Fordville (Carterville)	1868	25
	Herrin	1864	145
	Johnson City	1904	90
	Marion	1865	430
	Reeves	1905	125
	Shiloh (Marion)	1866	100
	West Chapel (Carbondale)	1897	35
Winnebago	Rockford	1856	291
Woodford	Cazenovia	1903	
	El Paso	1864	250
	Eureka	1832	805
	Minonk	1865	69
	Mt. Zion (Eureka)	1855	40
	Roanoke	1872	20
	Secor	1862	30
	Washburn	1864	250

7. Church Covenants, Church Officers, The Role of Women

Not only were the Restorationists faced with the primitive conditions of the frontier, they experienced resistance from the religious groups who arrived earlier. While most Protestant groups claimed the authority of the Scriptures and even the supremacy of the New Testament over the Old Testament, they did not agree with some of the Restorationist convictions as to the contours of New Testament Christianity. In this chapter we will consider the expressed views of others on Illinois Restoration efforts and set out characteristics of church life in regard to church covenants, officers, and the role of women.

Attitudes regarding the Restoration Movement

Since members of the Restoration Movement viewed other groups as defective in regard to weekly communion, the importance of baptism, congregational independence, the failure to denounce denominational creeds, and an effort to restore of the doctrine and life of the early church, they were often looked upon with suspicion. In 1868, at Atlanta, near Lincoln, two members experienced overtly this disapproval.

> The Atlanta Christian Church was feeble at that time and held in contempt by the other churches of the place. Two of its members, Andrew Wright and Jefferson Houser, went to the "union" prayer-meeting that was held the first week in January, and were met at the door of the M. E. Church and requested to leave, as no "Campbellites" were wanted in the meeting, they having been unanimously voted out as arch-heretics.[1]

In 1865 in Marion County a congregation was denounced as Campbellite and not Christian.

---

[1] Haynes, 76.

The invitation was soon withdrawn. Min. G. W. Hughey, of the M. E. Church, denounced Mr. Dugger as a "Baptist infidel," and of his brethren in faith he said: "They are not Christians, but Campbellites, and Campbellites they shall be called." However, a church was organized that aimed to be Christian only. A small church building was erected which was the first owned by the Disciples in the county. Another and better house has since been built.[2]

Near Jacksonville a Methodist preacher spoke at length to prevent the "Campbellites" from using a union chapel. "In the union chapel Min. Peter Akers, of the M. E. Church, on one Sunday preached four hours in order "to keep the Campbellites from occupying the house the same day."[3]

A preacher moving from New York experienced the same prejudice when he became a restorationist.

> Mr. Bastian's studies of the New Testament had unsettled his thoughts on the subject of Christian baptism. Finding himself more in harmony with the Baptist than with the Methodist Church, he peaceably changed his ecclesiastical affiliation. Coming West, he soon fell in with the Disciples. He was at once attracted and charmed by the Scripturalness of their preaching and the simplicity of their plea; hence, he was not long in casting in his lot with the people whose teaching and practice were so fully in accord with his own conclusions. Some of his Methodist brethren said that the fact of his "joining the Campbellites" was proof that "he was rattled;" whereas, his thoughts and aims were only moving in wider orbits."[4]

In some areas restorationists were better respected.

The criticisms of E. P. Brand who published a history of the Baptists in Illinois are instructive.[5]

> In 1823 Alexander Campbell and a part of his church were dismissed by the [Redstone Baptist] association and received into an

---

[2] Ibid., 323, 324.

[3] Ibid., 339.

[4] Ibid., 469.

[5] E. P. Brand, *History of the Baptists in Illinois*, (Bloomington: Pantagraph Printing & Sta. Co., 1930) 111-113.

[Mahoning Baptist] Association in Ohio. Here he published a little monthly, the *"Christian Baptist,"* which in 1830 became the *"Millennial Harbinger."* It was antimission; denouncing missionary, temperance and Bible societies and Sunday schools as evil. Mr. Campbell was at that time merely an eccentric hardshell Baptist preacher. In accordance with his Sandemanian views he baptized persons who professed a historical faith in Christ, requiring from them no evidence of regeneration or repentance. He taught that salvation was in baptism:

> God has opened a fountain for sin; he has given it an extension as far and as wide as water flows. Wherever water, faith, and the name of Father, Son and Holy Spirit are, there will be found the efficacy of the blood of Jesus.

He joined hands with the Romanists in making repentance an outward act. "Do penance and be baptized," says one. "Reform and be immersed," echoes the other. It harmonizes with the intellectual theory of saving faith. This teaching is welcome to the unsaved man, who will do anything if he is not required to submit to God. His anti-mission teachings commended Campbell in some quarters. The name "Reformation" misled others, who supposed it to mean a reformation of the spiritual life. For a few years, from 1827 onward, this teaching spread among Baptists like a forest fire, on a line west and south of west from Pennsylvania. In the northern, southern and eastern states it never made much headway. In 1827 the Pennsylvania Baptists Association that fellowshipped Mr. Campbell's church, announced a disfellowship. The example was followed by other surrounding Baptist Associations. From that time the movement was a separate sect. They were known as, Reformers, then as Christians, then as Disciples, etc., all unobjectionable; only they cannot be distinctive names for there are other disciples and other christians.

Many Baptist churches were divided, and some went entirely over. But this generally happened through the manipulation of the pastor. In 1830 the Sycamore Street Baptist church, Cincinnati, under the personal influence of Mr. Campbell accepted his teachings and changed their name to the "First Christian Baptist Church" of Cincinnati. After a time the "Baptist" was dropped and all that was left was the

145

plain christian; and yet one might question whether it was christian or not. In 1832 the pastor of the Shelbyville [Illinois] Baptist church became "Campbellite," and succeeded in having "Baptist" stricken from the name of the church, and "christian" substituted. It was many years before there was another Baptist church in Shelbyville. Decatur, two years afterwards, had a similar experience. The church was organized as the "Christian Baptist church," and when the suitable time had come the "Baptist" was stricken off. The Friendship Baptist church, Perry county, three miles from Tamaroa, as late as 1869 went the same road. Missouri Baptists suffered most, Indiana next, Illinois came third. Butler University, Ind., was the gift of one of the Baptist families that lapsed to Campbell in those days. Silver Creek church, the oldest Baptist church in Indiana, passing this resolution in 1830:

> This church deems it disorder to invite any preacher to preach, or administer in the church among us, who is of the pretended reformation, or who vindicates or circulates Alexander Campbell's pamphlets or his new translation of the New Testament.

The translation, that is, in which reformation is substituted for repentance, and thereby change of behavior is accepted instead of change of mind. Even the antimission churches, pleased as they were at first, discovered their mistake and withdrew their favor. In 1830 the Circular Letter of the old Illinois Association, antimission at that time, was written by Thomas Ray, pastor of the Second Cantine Creek church. His choice of Campbellism as his topic shows that the Campbellites were pressing them hard. He made three points against the system, referring especially to the denial of the Holy Spirit: (1) If the Spirit is in the word, and there only, why was Paul not converted by the word of God rather than by a miraculous appearance of Jesus? (2) What is the use of praying, if God has no means outside of his word of communicating to us the answer? (3) Was the Reformation under Luther and the subsequent revivals, brought about by the word of God or by the Spirit? Much has been done since Campbell's day to restate his teachings and chip off the corners, but not so as to make any essential change.

Church Covenants

Restoration congregations were normally started by an ordained preacher or at least someone with preacher credentials. A covenant was written up and signed by all the charter members both male and female. A congregational covenant was common among the major denominations with Reformed, that is, Congregational, Presbyterian, Baptist, and also Methodist, backgrounds.[6] These covenants or agreements can be found from the earliest times through the nineteenth century. Haynes quotes several of these "agreements." The churches employed this means of establishment throughout the nineteenth century. Members basically affirmed that the church would be subject to the Bible and the Bible alone. By doing so they denounced the detailed creeds of the various denominations.

One of the earliest congregations was in the town of Cantrall in Sangmon County, Illinois, organized in 1820 by Stephen England. Regarding the founding of the church in Cantrall, Haynes wrote,

> Mr. England was a Baptist preacher in Kentucky, but was never known as such in Sangamon County. In June, 1819, he first preached to his neighbors who assembled in his home. The next year (May 15) he formed a church with the following members: Stephen and Anna England, Jachoniah and Nancy Langston, Levi and Fanny Cantrall, Mrs. Adelphia Wood, Mrs. Sarah Cantrall and Mrs. Lucy Scott. This was the first church organized in this county. These nine people then signed the following agreement: We, members of the church of Jesus Christ, being providentially moved from our former place of residence from distant part, and being baptized on the profession of our faith and met at the house of Stephen England, on a branch of Higgins Creek, in order to form a constitution, having first given ourselves to the Lord and then to one another, agree that our constitution shall be on the Holy Scriptures of Old and New Testaments, believing them to be the only rule of faith and practice.
> In 1823 a log meeting-house was built one and a half miles southeast of the site of Cantrall, near what is now known as the

---

[6] William Eleazar Barton, *Congregational Creeds and Covenants* (Chicago: Advance Publishing Company) 1917; Champlin Burrage, *The Church Covenant Idea: Its Origin and its Development* (Philadelphia: American Baptist Publication Society) 1904.

Britten Cemetery. The cracks were chinked, and greased paper was used for the windows. This primitive temple was built by the volunteer labor of the settlement. In 1846 the second house was built in the village, and the third in 1873. Mr. England continued to serve the church till his death, preaching his last sermon sitting. He solemnized the first marriage in the county in his own home. On one occasion a couple came from Fort Clark, now Peoria, to be married by him.[7]

The Cameron Church in Warren County also had such a statement in its founding in 1831.

On the 30th day of April, 1831, this church was constituted upon the belief that the Scriptures of the Old and New Testaments are the only rule of faith and practice and sufficient for the government of the church." The names of the seventeen persons who signed this covenant were these: William M:, Elizabeth, Elijah, Sr., Margaret, Sr., Elijah, Jr., Margaret, Jr., Davidson ; Henry E., Elizabeth and John G. Haley; John E. and Frances Murphy; Richard and Nancy Ragland, and William, Sarah, Josiah and Julia Whitman. Three of these men were preachers William Whitman, John E. Murphy and Elijah Davidson and as many as eight of them were good public speakers.[8]

This agreement signed by the Berea Church organized in 1852 in Morgan County is a bit more detailed.

The church was organized August 15, with twenty-five charter members. A part of the agreement was as follows: We, the body of Christ, agree to organize ourselves after the primitive practice; to watch over one another and to admonish each other, for our good; to take the Scriptures of the Old and New Testaments for our rule of faith and practice. . . . We agree to continue steadfastly in the apostles' doctrine, in fellowship, in breaking of bread and in prayers ... to be known as the church of Christ on Indian Creek, meeting at Morgan Schoolhouse No. 2. Charles Rowe was chosen elder, and Joel Robinson and Wesley Corrington, deacons.[9]

[7] Haynes, 372, 373.
[8] Ibid., 423.
[9] Ibid., 335.

That these covenants continued is indicated at the founding of the Atwood Church in Piatt County in 1879.

> The following is the church covenant: We, whose names are subscribed, agree with each other, that we will take the Scriptures of the Old and New Testaments, known as the Bible, as the only rule of faith and practice, and that we will take the name "Christian" as the only divinely authorized name and will be known as the Church of Christ at Atwood, Douglas and Piatt Counties.[10]

What was affirmed by these creeds or agreements complied with a later professed slogan of the Restoration Movement. "No book but the Bible, no creed but Christ, no name but the Divine name."[11] Such a covenant at that time was not perceived as being a doctrinal creed.

Elders, Deacons, Pastors

For the early preachers Haynes employs the term, Elder, preacher, minister. For later preachers who only served one church year around he sometimes uses the word pastor. In the Illinois Churches of Christ in the 1960s, such a preaching minister was called a minister or evangelist. Another designation was "a located preacher" as opposed to one who preached various places probably holding Gospel meetings throughout the year. The latter might be designated an evangelist.

One of the first Illinois congregations of the Restoration Movement was established in Wabash County in 1819 by at Barney's Prairie. It seems that James Poole functioned as the preacher, but also Seth Gard, who was appointed a single elder.

> Evidently Mr. Gard was one of the leading citizens of that section. He, with Minister James Pool and others, on the 17th of July, 1819, organized the Barney's Prairie Christian Church. Seth Gard was elected elder and Joseph Wood deacon.[12]

The appointment of one elder who was not the preacher was almost standard at this time in Illinois. The congregation at Virginia in Cass County was founded in 1839. According to Haynes' report, "Among the charter members there were probably the following: Mr. and Airs.

---

[10] Ibid., 355.

[11] Brand, *Illinois Baptists*, 112, 113.

[12] Haynes, 22, 23.

Alexander Naylor, Mr. and Mrs. Charles Brady, Mr. and Mrs. John Mosely and Mr. and Mrs. Thomas Mosely. Mr. Naylor was the elder of the church."[13]

The practice of appointing one elder, but also a preacher, is indicated by the Albion Church in Edwards County founded in 1841. By 1914 it had 331 members.

> The first elder was Daniel Orange, and the first deacons were
> Alvin Kenner and George Goodwin. Elijah Goodwin was em-
> ployed one-fourth of the time at $50 the year.[14]

The Woburn congregation founded in 1858, the first Disciples church in Bond County, with 50 members, had one elder and two deacons. "The first officers were Henry Allen, elder; Jonathan Skates and D. V. Tabor, deacons."[15]

The Mulberry Grove congregation in Bond County was founded in 1864. By 1914 the congregation had 200 members. By this time preaching ministers were no longer identified as elders but sometimes as pastors. The congregation had multiple elders and deacons and apparently to meet the state's legal requirements trustees who may or may not have been elders or deacons. They also had a clerk which likely was a State of Illinois legal term. Haynes declared, "Twelve or more pastors have followed him. The congregation has half-time preaching. There are seven elders, six deacons and five trustees. Evert Elam is clerk."[16]

At first the word pastor was not employed but by the twentieth century its use became more frequent and obviously it was used synonymously with minister or preacher. The below is a statement about a congregation in Cairo founded in 1866.

More than forty ministers have served the church. Some of the earlier were Peter Vogel, T. W. Caskey, B. F. Manire, J. C. Mason, David Walk, Alfred Flower and Clark Braden, whose term was particularly helpful. The present building was erected during the pastorate of Frank Thompson. Alden R. Wallace is now the pastor.[17]

---

13 Ibid.. 129.
14 Ibid.. 190.
15 Ibid., 117.
16 Ibid.. 116.
17 Ibid., 110.

Women

Regarding women proclaimers, Haynes wrote,

WOMEN AS PREACHERS AND PASTORAL HELPERS. The entrance of women into the public ministry of the churches of Christ in Illinois was as quiet as the rising sun. They had served with efficiency in so many semi-public relations and places that this final step was easily taken. It seemed to have been Providential. To Mrs. C. C. Babcock, of the Sterling Church, belongs the honor of having been the pioneer in this service. All of her valuable public ministry had the cordial approval of her husband. As far as learned, the other women who have entered the Christian ministry in Illinois are the following: Mary Pickens Buckner, of Augusta; Miss Rachel Crouch, who married Mr. Neil Derrick; Miss Rachel Dangerfield; Miss Daisy Finger; Mrs. Lew D. Hill, wife of Minister Hill; Mrs. Rochester Irwin, wife of Minister Irwin; Mrs. Ida K. Jordon, wife of O. F. Jordon; Miss Bertha Merrill; Mrs. H. E. Monser, wife of Minister Monser; Miss Sadie McCoy, who married Min. J. R. Crank she was employed by the State Mission Board in 1893 and added 127 people to the churches in 188 days of service; Miss Sadie Olive; Miss Myrtle Park, who married Min. W. H. Storm after a successful pastorate of five years with the Carlock Church ; Miss Myrtle Very, Miss Ava S. Walton and Miss Lou Watson. Among the women missionaries who have gone out from the churches in Illinois there are: Miss Frances Irene Banta, and Miss Nellie Daugherty, who married Dr. James Butchart, to China ; Miss Mary Kingsbury, Mrs. Kate Lawrence Brown and Miss Myra Harris McLeoud, to India; Mrs. Marie Jackson McCoy to Japan, and Mrs. Lillian Boyer Hedges to Africa. In the public ministry of the gospel, women have acquitted themselves well in every way.[18]

Considerable information is available in regard to Clara Cesleste Hale-Babcock (1850-1924). She was born in Fitzville, Ohio, and ordained by the congregation in Erie, Illinois, after she visited there to speak on behalf of the Women's Temperance Union. She served in Erie for 15 years, followed by Thompson for nine years, LeClaire for twelve, Dixon for nine, Ellendale, North Dakota, for three and she had just commenced

---

[18] Ibid., 650, 651.

serving the congregation in Savanna when she became ill and died. She had baptized 1502 people. She became well known in the communities where she labored and became actively involved in various organizations. Most of the congregation she served were located along the Rock River east of Rock Island, Illinois.[19]

Haynes gave additional information regarding Rachel Dangerfield as a woman pastor. Notice in the second paragraph Haynes uses pastors for male preachers. This includes the well-known J. H. Garrison, Editor of the *Christian-Evangelist*. Miss Racheal Dangerfield was called pastor in Walshville church. Whether she was the only pastor in the Walshville church at that time isn't clear, but perhaps.

> Walshville Mercer County, just south of Rock Island. Organized 1874, by T. J. Shelton ; present membership, 50…Min. A. D. Northcutt was prominent in the beginning of this effort. The organization was made in the town hall with ten charter members. With little social influence or means, and overshadowed by three strong denominations, this little band trusted God, went to prayer and work and grew up to an influential position. The pastors were L. M. Linn, J. H. Garrison, J. H.Smart, H. P. Tandy and L. F. Wood. For several years the Baptist chapel was used. In 1878 a very neat house of worship was built. A number of ministers preached for the congregation through several years. In 1904 their chapel was destroyed by fire. The Bible school secured the privilege of using the M. E. chapel, but was turned out the next year. The second building was finished early in 1908. J. E. Story, Miss Rachael Dangerfield and Isaac Beckelhymer have served the congregation in recent years. Miss Dangerfield was the pastor when the last house was built.[20]

Women were also active in the women auxiliary organizations as Haynes reported with considerable detail.

> On the first Sunday afternoon following the meeting in Cincinnati, Elder Tyra Montgomery formed a woman's auxiliary in the church at Mattoon, of which Mrs. Caroline Montgomery was the first president. Miss Dickinson was chosen the first president at the formation of the Illinois Society, and for a decade thereafter did the difficult and heroic pioneer work that was needed

---

[19] Ibid. See also *http://www.angelfire.com/folk/foec/babc001.html*
[20] Ibid., 333, 334.

to lay the foundation of a splendid superstructure. Those who followed in the presidency were Mrs. James Kirk, Mrs. Emma Campbell Ewing, Mrs. O. A. Burgess, Mrs. Persis L. Christian, Miss Anna May Hale, Miss Annie E. Davidson, Mrs. Carrie F. Zeller and now Mrs. Lura Thompson Porter. The corresponding secretaries have been Mrs. Ella Myers Huffman, Mrs. Happy, Mrs. M. M. Lindsay, Mrs. J. G. Waggoner, Miss Lura V. Thompson (two terms), Miss Rachael Crouch, Miss Gussie Courson and Miss Anna M. Hale, The treasurers in their order of service were Mrs. John Darst, Mrs. H. W. Everest, Mrs. Cassell, Mrs. M. B. Hawk, Mrs. S. J. Crawford, Miss Clara L. Davidson and now Miss Henrietta Clark. The superintendents of the Young People's Department were Miss Frank Haynes, Miss Annie E. Davidson, Miss Gussie Courson, Miss Minnie Dennis, Miss Lola V. Hale, Miss Irene Ridgely, Miss Clara B. Griffin, Miss Dora Gutherie and now Miss Effie L. Gaddis. Miss Dickinson gave the society, in various official capacities, about thirty years of service; Mrs. S. J. Crawford was treasurer twenty-two years; Miss Annie E. Davidson in a dual capacity fourteen years, and Mrs. Porter fifteen years to September, 1913. Twelve of the women above named have been "field workers;" that is, they have gone through the State as educators and organizers. It may be truthfully said that all of these women in every official position have done their best; hence the work has grown steadily from its beginning. The pioneers in this movement overcame, by their Christ-like devotion, uninformed indifference and out- spoken prejudice and opposition, and they merit the greater honor. At the first meeting in 1874 there was "a collection taken of $5.41 for the State development;" the total offerings for the year closing with June, 1913, were $24,392. Starting with nothing save prayer, purpose and promise, the auxiliaries and circles reported at the same time were 266, with a membership of 6277. In January, 1901, a State paper was started to help in this work. It was called The Illinois Quarterly, but became Mission Leaves in 1906. It was first issued from Athens, with Miss Anna M. Hale as editor; in 1904 from Eureka, with Miss Annie E. Davidson as editor, and in 1909, first from Cuba, then from Petersburg, with Mrs. Carrie F. Zeller as editor to August, 1913. There were eighteen hundred of these Leaves then in circulation. The headquarters of the society have been Eureka for two periods, Jacksonville and Springfield[21]

On one occasion Haynes employs the term "deaconess" but the use of the term does not seem common. This designation is applied to Mary Bennett of the Princeton congregation north of Peoria which was founded in 1840. By 1914 the congregation had 282 members. Chosen when the church was launched were a bishop (elder), deacon and deaconess. It may be that Mr. Bennett the deacon was the husband of Mary, the deaconess. "Mr. Yearnshaw was chosen bishop, Mr. Bennett, deacon, and Mary Bennett, deaconess, on March 8."[22]

Clearly the burden of leadership of the Restoration Movement in Illinois resided with the members or we might say the laity, both male and female. Certain leaders, however, received special designations that set them apart for various forms of service to the specific congregational body of which they were members.

Despite the opposition, especially the anti-Campbellite ire of the Baptists, the Restoration churches in Illinois prospered exponentially after 1820. Those who migrated to Illinois from the east, the border states, and the south became leading citizens and several grew affluent for the time and place. These widely respected Illinois citizens became the leaders in the restoration congregations, both men and women.

[21] Ibid., 103 - 105.
[22] Ibid., 122.

8. Nineteenth Century Illinois Periodicals

If the history of journalism among us should ever be written fully, it would constitute one of the most heroic, and even pathetic, chapters in our history. (J. H. Garrison)[1]

Introduction

The establishment of periodicals can mark the inauguration, growth or the maturation of a movement.[2] At the outset of the Campbell movement, in the Postscript of the *Declaration and Address*, Thomas Campbell proposed a periodical as one of two seminal publications of the Christian Association of Washington:

> The second thing intended is a periodical publication, for the express purpose of detecting and exposing the various anti-christian [sic] enormities, innovations and corruptions, which infect the christian [sic] church...Such a publication from the

---

[1] J. H. Garrison, *Memories and Experiences: a Brief Story of a Long Life, an Autobiography.* (St. Louis: Christian Board of Publication, 1926) 61.

[2] For examples of dissertations with analysis of SCM periodicals, see James Brooks Major, *The Role of Periodicals in the Development of the Disciples of Christ, 1850-1910.* (Nashville: Vanderbilt University, 1985.) William Charles Creasy, *A Study of the Development of the Popular Motives of Health, Wealth, Power, and Success in Practical Theology of the Early Disciples of Christ: As It Appeared in Their Periodicals Through 1850, with Some Consideration of Their Meaning for Today's Preacher.* 1978. For a dated but the most complete to date list of SCM periodicals, see Claude E. Spencer, *Periodicals of the Disciples of Christ and Related Religious Groups,* (Canton, Missouri: Disciples of Christ Historical Society, 1943). For the location of periodicals held by Churches of Christ libraries, Don Meredith, *Union List of Serials in Churches of Christ,* unpublished monograph, 1999. Robert L. Friedly, "Journalism" *ESCM* 434 – 438 surveys the important periodicals for all three streams.

nature and design of it, might with propriety be denominated The Christian Monitor.[3]

The *Christian Monitor* never saw the light of day. His son Alexander's *Christian Baptist*, established in July 1823, was the first paper from the Campbell orbit.

Stone's *Christian Messenger* began in Kentucky in November 1826 and was published at Jacksonville, Illinois, from 1835 until it merged in 1847 with John R. Howard's *Bible Advocate*.

> By our removal here, we have also been able to effect another most important object; a union with the late "Christian Messenger," of Illinois, long edited, principally, by the venerable, beloved, and lamented Bro. Barton W. Stone, who now sleeps in Christ.[4]

With the establishment in September 1853 of the *Christian Sentinel* at Springfield, from then until the close of the century, periodicals thrived in Illinois, even to the point of saturation, causing Missouri editor D. T. Wright in 1867 to doubt whether the Illinois brethren could add any more periodicals, let alone sustain what they already had:

> THE CHURCH REPORTER—Such is the title of a very neatly printed, double-column octavo monthly of 16 pages, published at Quincy, Illinois, by bro. E. P. Belshe. The first No., the only one as yet received, is quite creditable, both in its matter and me- chanical appearance. Bro. Belshe has in this taken the right view of the matter, that which is worth doing at all, is worth well do- ing, hence the Reporter is issued in first-class style. We find no fault, as far as noticed, with the paper, and think that all will like it much. But while it assumes to occupy a place not yet specially filled by any other publication among us—that of a compiled report of the cause from every possible quarter—it will yet op- erate against worthy publications in the State that have long struggled for an existence. For instance, the Gospel Echo, edited

---

[3] Thomas Campbell, *Declaration and Address*, 55, 56. The Christian Monitor was to be a 24 page monthly, and would be published as soon as "500 annual subscribers can be obtained." Our reading of Gorman, *Early Evangelicals*, 162, brought this periodical to our attention.
[4] John R. Howard, "Introduction to Volume V." *Messenger and Advocate* (5.1, January, 1847) 1, 2

by bro. E. L Craig. Bro. Craig has justly earned, by his untiring efforts and faithful labors to publish a religious paper, a large circulation and a liberal support, which we believe he is not receiving, and the Reporter by bro. Belshe, we fear, will still further lessen his already too small support. But possibly the brethren of Illinois may sustain the four papers[5] now published in that State, and asking their patronage; but we very much question it. They can do it if they will, but will they do it? D. T. W.[6]

N. S. Haynes briefly describes some of the periodicals published in Illinois in his Miscellanea chapter. Of that number, we give detailed stories in this chapter for four Illinois SCM periodicals. Alexander Graham's *Berean*, digitized for this project, emerges from the shadow of brief notices to get some overdue attention. Three closely related Illinois periodicals, clearly misunderstood by Haynes, receive detailed attention here because of their connection to the W. S. Russell faction: the *Christian Sentinel* (1853 – 1858), the *Bible Advocate* (1858 – 1862) and the *Christian Freeman* (1860 – 1861).

Before we get to their stories, we suggest some reasons why periodicals are important and ponder why new periodicals are started. Having laid that groundwork, we show how their stories illustrate some of these points.

The Importance of Periodicals

The reader should note that periodicals, both within and without a movement, are a major primary source for historians. Reports from churches document growth and list the preachers and evangelists for gospel meetings. Reports from conventions or "cooperative meetings" detail who attended, the strategies for reaching new areas and fund raising efforts. Articles on doctrines laid the groundwork for the movement as it strove to share its understanding of the scriptures to its readers, be they followers or detractors. Advertisements for books got the word out and helped line the worn pockets of editors who dabbled in bookselling. The sad news of the deaths of the young and old found their way into the pages of the journals, more often than not with genealogical data that today supplies the missing information for a family tree and the answer to the question, was my forebear a believer?

---

[5] The four papers were the *Gospel Echo*, Carrollton; *Herald of Truth*, Carbondale; *Christian Herald*, Eureka, *Church Reporter*, Quincy.
[6] David T. Wright, *CP* 7.33 (September 5, 1867) 528.

Why were so many new periodicals published?

For this discussion, *new* means a periodical without any previous appearances. This eliminates *mergers* from the discussion, when the editors and publishers used a new name that included part of the name of the old periodical. For example, John R. Howard, who was editing the *Bible Advocate* when he took over the *Christian Messenger*, named the journal *The Christian Messenger and Bible Advocate*. This is not a new periodical. In some cases, an editor used a new name, but continued an already established paper. For example, E. L. Craig started the *Gospel Echo* in 1863, which succeeded the *Bible Advocate*, with no break in publication and no change of editor.

According to Robert L. Friedly "As many as 400 journals related to the Stone-Campbell Movement were founded, 100 of them in the four decades prior to the Civil War."[7] Editors of the larger, well established papers were quick to speak out against the proliferation of papers. In his ex-cathedra style Alexander Campbell griped:

> We have already too many periodicals, and glad would I be if I could retire wholly from the laborious toils I have had so long to endure. Some one has said that the multiplicity of our denominational ephemeral reading, and the difficulty of finding a few grains of wheat in a bushel of chaff, has discouraged them from reading either a weekly, a monthly, or a quarterly, in the hope of an adequate reward: therefore, it would be better to have a very few well matured and well assorted articles in one, two, or, at most, three periodicals, than a score of those undertaken at private impulse and for personal advantage.[8]

Later that year, under the guise of saving the Movement substantial amounts of money, Campbell had the audacity to narrow the number needed even further:

> I do not wish to call names, nor to relate the comic-tragedy of our fallen scribes and infant sages. We have never needed, nor shall we ever need in the present generation, but three periodicals—one weekly, one monthly and one quarterly. The weekly sheet, with departments for every State, as to important movements, meeting news, passing events, &c. One monthly, for dis-

---

[7] "Journals," *ESCM* 434.
[8] *MH* 1852: 3, 4.

cussing all great subjects; and one quarterly, for reviews of books and theses connected with church literature, history, biography, &c. &c. These ably conducted, well sustained, and widely circulated, with reputable contributors from all the land, would meet the entire wants of this age, and save the community many thousands of dollars per annum for better purposes than for the readings of diluted ideas in Homeopathic doses, as we now have them dispensed in invisible pills, in the ratio of one to a gallon of water.[9]

In November 1867 D. P. Henderson wrote Benjamin Franklin about the possibility of Franklin taking over the struggling *Christian Standard*. Franklin's reply mirrors much of Campbell's thoughts from fifteen years earlier. Franklin is brash enough to state how other papers have been his rivals and have been in the way of his desire for "one good paper":

Dear Sir: Yours of Nov. 30th has been forwarded to me here and I hasten to reply. I have been perfectly satisfied for many years, that a *few good papers*, would do much more good, than many poor ones. Nothing is now clearer to my mind than this. But I had no hand in creating the *Standard*, or any of the other papers not needed. They have all been rivals of the *Review*, and in the way of my efforts to make *one good paper*. I have no power to stop any of the papers now not needed. The *Standard* has nothing that I want. I have a full corps of assistant editors, much better and more acceptable writers than any belonging to the *Standard* office. If the *Standard* brethren have become satisfied that the *Standard* is a *fifth wheel*, and desire to transfer its list of subscribers to the *Review* and will do so, *free of debt, advancing money to pay* cost of sending the paper to the subscribers, their subscription terms out, we will take them the list and thus unite the two papers. God has given me my birth-right, and I do not intend to sell it for a mess of potage.[10]

Despite the strong wishes of powerful editors like Campbell and Franklin, "fallen scribes and infant sages" continued their existing papers and started new papers. We suggest these reasons:

---

[9] Ibid., 391.

[10] Benjamin Franklin to D. P. Henderson, December 9, 1867. (D. P. Henderson Papers, Disciples of Christ Historical Society, Bethany, West Virginia)

1. In spite of Campbell's 1852 suggestion that one weekly could publish items for each state, the idea went unheeded. Illinois brethren wrote articles for and submitted news to regional monthly papers like the *Christian Record* in Indiana and the *Christian Evangelist* in Iowa and Missouri. The only SCM weekly in 1852 when Campbell made his dictum, the *Christian Age* in Cincinnati, shows no evidence of adopting Campbell's suggestions.

2. As we show in greater detail below concerning the *Christian Sentinel*, individual states felt that a paper dedicated to their interests warranted starting such papers.

3. New periodicals gave new editing and writing opportunities for younger men. Interestingly, Franklin himself made this suggestion when he announced his quarterly in 1862:

> We have now the *broad space* for a hundred pens to battle for the Lord, and, we trust, they will not be idle. We have hosts of young men, well educated, and hosts more educating, who must have such a space upon which to battle for righteousness; and the time has come now for the young men, the old men and all the men, to whet the sword, gird on the armor, and go forth, in the strength of Israel's God, against the combined powers with which we have to contend, and battle with both tongue and pen.[11]

4. Much to the chagrin of insiders and the delight of outsiders, personality conflicts and doctrinal squabbles led to new journals. Writers marginalized by the mainstream, if they still wanted their voices heard, had the option of starting a new paper.

5. Felt needs gave rise to new papers. A conviction that existing journals neglected giving a full report of the additions to the Movement prompted E. P. Belshe to start the Church Reporter.

6. Dissatisfaction with the status quo—a wish for new direction—called for new periodicals. From that sense of urgency sprang, for example, the *Christian Standard*.

---

[11] Benjamin Franklin, "The Quarterly Review," *ACR* 5.18 (May 6, 1862) 2. In this case, Franklin wanted his new paper to be where the writers submitted their essays.

The More Complete Story of Four Illinois Periodicals

In this section we begin by quoting what Haynes stated about each of the four periodicals: the *Berean, Christian Sentinel, Bible Advocate* and *Christian Freeman*.[12] We then contextualize the journals with the results of our research.

> *The Berean.* Alexander Graham came from Tuscaloosa, Ala., where he had published *The Disciple*, to Springfield, Ill., in 1838. There he founded *The Berean*. It was a "monthly magazine, neatly gotten up on good paper and contained much sense and valuable information." Evidently it was short-lived.

For this history we arranged for the digitization of the copy of the *Berean* in the collection of the Disciples of Christ Historical Society. As Haynes suspected, the journal was short-lived, only published for one year, in twelve issues of twenty-four pages. When Graham decided to leave Springfield in late 1838, he wrote to John T. Jones, an associate of Barton W. Stone. Stone then contacted Bro Hill:

> *Jacksonville, January 11th, 1839*
>
> Brother Hill,
>
> Brother Graham has just forwarded a letter to brother J. T. Jones, informing him that he fears he can not continue the Berean longer than the close of the present volume; and asks the question," Can not brother Jones or myself continue it." After consultation with brothers Jones and Henderson, the conclusion is that the work should continue, under the title of the *Christian Messenger and Berean*. I will continue to edit it, assisted by J. T. Jones, D. Henderson and other talented brethren, when fifteen hundred subscribers shall be obtained. The pamphlet will contain 32 octavo pages each number, for $1 25 per annum, or 12 numbers.
>
> Should the subscribers to the Berean wish to patronize this work, let them signify it through their agents to you by letter post paid. We will advise brother Graham of this arrangement.

---

[12] It is clear from his descriptions that Haynes did not have access to any of the four periodicals. It is unclear what source(s) he drew upon.

This you can publish in the last number of the Berean. Grace, mercy and peace be with you. B. W. STONE

Reading between the lines of the letter, the *Berean* was struggling financially. Bro. Hill appears to have agreed to look after the paper's affairs since he is responsible for the last issue of the paper. A biographical sketch by Graham's nephew notes that "perfectly penniless," Graham left Illinois at the end of December, 1838, to return to Alabama. Of his uncle's articles in the Berean, P. B. Lawson, in typical hagiographical style, surmised:

> Some of his best compositions are found in this work, which, for its terseness, conspicuity and laconic elegance, would bear a comparison with the best of the numerous papers at that time being published by the advocates of the reformation, and was perhaps not surpassed by any except the *Millennial Harbinger,* edited by Mr. Campbell, a work that stands unrivalled in editorial theology.[13]

The *Berean* does have a significant number of original articles by Graham. To fill the *Berean,* he also copied articles from the *Christian Palladium* (Christian Connection), *Western Pioneer* (Baptist) and SCM journals, the *Disciple,* the *Millennial Harbinger* and the *Christian Preacher.* The typical doctrinal controversies are there (the August number relates a skirmish with Baptist J. M. Peck); news from churches (Springfield; Winchester; Jacksonville; Salt Creek; Wolf Creek, to name a few); and a few pseudonymous articles to leave readers now and then guessing who wrote that?

Unravelling the Story of Three Related Illinois Periodicals

The following three Illinois periodicals are related to the W. S. Russell defection discussed in Chapter 10. To show the sequence of their publication, we have arranged them in a different order than Haynes.

- *The Christian Sentinel.* A monthly magazine, edited by Dr. W. A. Mallory. He began its publication in Springfield in 1855. John F. Rowe was

---

13 P. B. Lawson, *The Life and Character, to which are Added Some of the Addresses and Sermons of Alexander Graham, Teacher of the Christian Church in Marion. Alabama.* (New York: John F. Trow, Printer, 49 Ann-Street, 1853) 11, 12.

associate editor. In 1857 it was published in Peoria, with I. N. Carman and O. A. Burgess as editors. Shortly thereafter it disappeared.

• *The Bible Advocate*. The place of publication was changed from Jacksonville to Carrollton in 1860. E. L. Craig and J. S. Sweeney were its editors. It is highly improbable that two Christian papers were published in Jacksonville the same year; hence, it may be that the *Advocate* was a new name for the *Freeman*.

• *The Christian Freeman* was published at Jacksonville in 1860. Of it nothing more is known.

The Christian Sentinel

In a letter dated March 20, 1853, using the pseudonym "Luther," a reader of the *Evangelist* of Iowa commented on the number of periodicals published by the Stone-Campbell Movement in the "West":

> I have read with much interest, the March number of the Evangelist, and feel delighted that we have such a paper in the West. Besides the Evangelist, we have no paper in the West advocating our views of Christianity; and the young, great, and growing states of Illinois, Iowa and Missouri certainly can, and will, well support a good periodical.[14]

Later that year, in September, the *Christian Sentinel* debuted at Springfield, Illinois. Perhaps the statement by Luther encouraged some of the Illinois brethren to begin the enterprise? In the first article by W. A. Mallory, one of the founding editors, we note he anticipates there will be objections to a new paper and presents the counter argument that Illinois has the right to and the need for its own paper:

> We are aware that our enterprise will be objected to, on the ground that we already have sufficient number of papers to satisfy the demand for them... It has been a settled conviction with us that each state in the Union, where we have raised the standard of reformation and where we have the means of supporting it, should have in its territory a periodical to serve as a medium of communication, so that our local matters may be properly attended to...[15]

---

[14] Luther [pseudonym], "Periodicals," *CE*, 4.6 (June, 1853) 221 - 224.
[15] W. A. Mallory, "Introduction," *CSent*, 1.1 (September 1853) 3 – 6.

Andrew Jackson Kane, another prominent SCM Illinois pioneer, was not at first favorable to the *Christian Sentinel*. We include the majority of his article because it shows that he had weighed the issues about starting periodicals carefully. Kane is aware of the current discussions about the number of periodicals and hints that he had been in favor of Alexander Campbell's proposal for a "large weekly paper for the benefit of the brotherhood generally."

> Brethren of Illinois: It may seem strange to some of you that I should recommend to your favorable consideration the Christian Sentinel, as I have been of the opinion heretofore that a periodical in our state was not the best plan that could be adopted for the promotion of truth in Illinois. Being rather in favor of a large weekly paper for the benefit of the brotherhood generally, I was opposed to any more state papers in the west.
>
> The Christian Sentinel was conceived and born before I was aware any such project was in contemplation. It originated with brethren Mallory and Underwood, and perhaps the brethren of Sangamon county. At the time of our state meeting held in Jacksonville, September of the present year, the paper was presented to the State Missionary Society for its approval, which was done, so far as making it the 'medium' of all its communications is concerned. Since then, and in fact, at the time, my mind has undergone some change, and I am now fully committed in its favor.
>
> It may be necessary to state some of the reasons which led me to take a stand for a paper devoted more particularly to the interest of the cause in Illinois, they are the following:
>
> First, Indiana, Kentucky, Missouri and Iowa have papers of their own. If the periodicals published for these states respectively, are of any real advantage to the brotherhoods therein and it is conceded that they are doing great good, then is it right for us to engage in the same enterprise; nay more, it is our duty to obtain the same or similar benefits by using the same means.
>
> In the next place, the brethren of this state are considerably dispersed over its extensive territory, which makes it very difficult to get our organizations before them. There are several portions of the state that have never co-operated with us in our missionary labors. They are unacquainted with us and we with them. A state paper generally circulated would enable us to bring before the congregations without any inconvenience, all mea-

sures of common interest within a very short time. None of the papers published around us furnished these facilities. There is no one of them that circulates generally through the state of Illinois, and consequently will not answer as a medium of communication among our brotherhood.

The Christian Sentinel proposes to meet all these demands, and remove the obstacles which have hindered our progress heretofore.

Again, our state is being organized into missionary districts for a more permanent and successful co-operation. The synoptical [sic] reports of the various districts, together with the 'church news,' coming before the brethren through the medium of our paper, will not only impart to them information in regard to the success of the cause of Christ, but will cheer their hearts and lead them to thank God and take courage. Claiming to be neither a prophet, nor the Son of a prophet, yet we venture the prediction that in five years from this, our paper, if prudently conducted, will be the means in a great measure of placing the truth fifty per cent in advance of what it would otherwise be without such aid.

Another reason may be drawn from the fact, that a periodical among us will call forth the writing talent of our state, and thus develop another means of usefulness. There is no doubt that an amount of this is now buried sufficient to make a very respectable monthly if it was brought into exercise. The Sentinel will furnish an opportunity for usefulness in this way.

The above are *some* of the reasons presenting themselves to our mind in favor of a state paper. It has my influence because I think it will be productive of all the advantages which we have enumerated, as well as many more too tedious to mention.

If all these favorable results follow the general circulation of the Sentinel, it is the duty of every member of the church in Illinois to use his influence, not only in giving it circulation but to make it an interesting and useful periodical; one that he will not be ashamed to distribute among his neighbors and friends. We therefore, as co-workers with you in this enterprise, ask your aid in the work.[16]

---

[16] A. J. K. [Andrew Jackson Kane], "An Address," *CSent*, 1.5 (January 1854) 141, 142.

Kane's prediction proved incorrect. In less than five years, the *Christian Sentinel* met its demise; it was not "prudently conducted" as we chronicle in Chapter 10. At this point we detail the relationship between the *Christian Sentinel* and the *Bible Advocate*.

The Bible Advocate

In December 1857, at the end of its fourth year of publication, John Lindsey stepped aside as associate editor of the *Christian Sentinel*. His recap of the early struggles for subscribers and the recent growth in subscribers made him optimistic:

> According to a previous arrangement, our connection with the *Christian Sentinel*, as one of its editors, must now terminate. We can but feel to rejoice that the *Sentinel*, which, when our connection as proprietor and one of its editors commenced, was by no means popular, and its list of subscribers reduced to some two or three hundred, should have become, in the space of a single year, one of the most popular monthlies in our entire ranks. And, although we cannot fully indorse all that its pages contain, it has excited more admiration, more joy, and more jealousy too, than any paper of its circulation now in the religious world. And its list of subscribers is most rapidly increasing, all the time.[17]

The loaded statement "although we cannot fully indorse all that its pages contain" would bring to most readers' minds the way the *Christian Sentinel* had become the mouthpiece for W. S. Russell and his controversial beliefs on the Holy Spirit.

The *Christian Sentinel* continued publication in 1858, making it as far the fourth number, April.[18] Sometime later in the year, certainly as early as

---

[17] John Lindsey, "Valedictory," *CSent* 4.12 (December 1857) 378.

[18] *ACR* 2.20 (May 17, 1859) 78-79 copies an article from the *Bible Advocate* by E. L. Craig in which pages 100, 101 of volume five of the *Christian Sentinel* are quoted. If the number of pages in volume 5 was the same as volume 4, 32 pages, volume 5 had reached at least four numbers.

August, but possibly earlier,[19] E. L. Craig and J. S. Sweeney, in a hostile takeover, bought out the *Christian Sentinel*. Sweeney's recollections of some of the details are flawed but the buyout and its intent are clear:

> Yours of the 16th, requesting me to write a short article giving an account of my connection with the Bible Advocate, etc., is received. I should be pleased to accommodate you, but my recollection of the matters is entirely too indistinct for me to venture anything in the form of an article for publication.
>
> There was a monthly, called the Christian Sentinel I think, published in Illinois, under the control of J. [sic "I"] N. Carman and others. It was about the time of the Russell, Melish, Carman defection, so called. My recollection is that Bro. Craig and I bought out that paper, mainly to get it out of the hands of that interest, moved it to Jacksonville, and called it the Bible Advocate. We were for some time joint editors and proprietors. It was thus edited and published during the stormy times growing out of the above mentioned alleged defection. When that storm had somewhat abated, I retired, I think, in 1859.
>
> The paper was changed from monthly to weekly, and its name from Bible Advocate to Gospel Echo, and its place from Jacksonville to Carrolton about the time I so retired, whether awhile before or after, I can't say now. If I was connected with it at all after it went to Carrollton, it was only nominally so.[20]

Throughout its first four years of existence, 1858 – 1861, the *Bible Advocate* gave considerable attention to the Russell defection. The lead article in earliest issue of the *Bible Advocate* available to us (Volume 2, Number 7, July 1859) has a nine page article by J. S. Sweeney, "President Russell Fully Understood and Fairly Represented," in which Sweeney reviews two of

---

[19] Aaron. Chatterton, "Editors' Table," *CE*, 9.10 (October 1858) 482: "The first two numbers of *"The Bible Advocate,"* edited and published by E. L. CRAIG, Jacksonville, Ill., are received at this office. This Publication takes the place of *"The Christian Sentinel."* The *Advocate* comes freighted with good matter, and we wish it abundant success in "the promotion of an earnest church and a higher christian [sic] life."

[20] J. S. Sweeney, "The Christian Sentinel," *C-E* 1885: 23. Sweeney retired at the end of 1860 rather than 1859, writing articles throughout 1860. The *Gospel Echo* was started in 1863. Craig proposed establishing a *Weekly Bible Advocate* in addition to the monthly *Bible Advocate* if sufficient numbers subscribed to the weekly. "Proposals to Publish the Weekly Bible Advocate," *BA* 4.9 (September 1861) 524.

W. S. Russell's sermons preached in the Christian Church at Jacksonville and subsequently published. Sweeney is relentless in his attack on Russell's doctrines.[21]

The Christian Freeman

Haynes speculated, "It is highly improbable that two Christian papers were published in Jacksonville the same year; hence, it may be that the *Advocate* was a new name for the *Freeman.*" This guess shows that Haynes did not have access to primary sources on the Russell defection. There were, in fact, two papers published in Jacksonville at the same time. Alexander Johnston's letter to Benjamin Franklin announced the new paper:

> Bro. Franklin: With your permission, and provided you receive nothing better on the same topic, ere you receive this, I wish to present to the readers of the *Review* a review of several things now going on in our midst, some of which are being brought to light through the medium of *The Christian Freeman*, W. S. Russell, editor, and T. J. Melish and I. N. Carman, *corresponding editors*. An *interesting trio* truly! Their objects and reasons assigned for their paper we will notice in another place. This seems to be the last desperate effort of these three self-conceited young men, backed up by one whom we call out here "Captain Happy," in view I suppose of laurels won by him in the political field, where he labored about as long as it would "pay" before he turned preacher.[22]

Our research shows a few references to the *Christian Freeman* in SCM periodicals during 1860 and early 1861. No copies are extant. It began as an eight page monthly. In September 1861, E. L. Craig noted the *Christian Freeman* had been suspended or died but he does not give the exact time:

> Mr. Russell's paper has been suspended, for the present at least. That Providence which Mr. Russell thinks brought about the present war, seems to have brought his editorial labors to a sud-

---

21 W. S. Russell, *Two Discourses On the Father, Son, and Holy Spirit Delivered before the Christian Congregation at Jacksonville, Ill., by Its Pastor, W. S. Russell* (Jacksonville: Young America Book and Job Office Print, 1859).

22 Alexander Johnston, "Letter from Brother Johnston," *ACR*, 3.13 (March 27, 1860) 51.

den close. He once said "Prayer in this house [the house in which he was,] would, if made in faith, convert the Chinese empire into a Christian land." Well, whether this be true or not, one thing is certain, prayer could not, or did not, keep his paper from dying. Indeed it never had any life in it, and was only kept along by the depletion to which his partisan friends subjected their pockets.[23]

From the excerpts of the *Christian Freeman* in SCM papers, it is clear that Russell, Carman, Melish, and S. T. Callaway continued their attacks upon the mainstream of the Movement and aired their grievances. As we document in Chapter 10, all four and a few others left the Movement.

Concluding Thoughts

Other 19th century Illinois periodicals await writers who will do the hard work of reading them to tell their stories. At the end of the century, conservative Illinois brethren did not publish a major periodical, relying instead on conservative papers published in other states. They especially reported and contributed to the successor to Franklin's *American Christian Review* the *Octographic Review* (Indiana). Less so, they relied upon the *Firm Foundation* (Texas), *Gospel Advocate* (Tennessee), the *Apostolic Times* (Kentucky).

---

[23] E. L. Craig, "Papers in Illinois," *BA*, 4.9 (September 1861) 528.

9. Restorationist Colleges in Illinois

Restorationists believed in an educated citizenry. Alexander Campbell spent considerable effort encouraging states to establish universal education, as it was then called, and the founding of normal schools to train teachers. He argued that literacy was required in order to discern the ancient order in the Scripture. The charge to read and write was appropriate for all the church members, not just the preachers. They too were responsible for creating their churches after the New Testament patterns.

Alexander Campbell's interest in repositioning American education was subordinate only to his interest in restoring the New Testament church. In fact, for Campbell the two are inextricably related. In his thinking Christianity can flourish only where the people are literate.

Campbell's "Baccalaureate Address to the Graduates of Bethany College" on July 4 1846, was basically a charge to the graduates to support universal education, a matter at that time before many state legislatures. "But especially are you under obligation to advocate just views of education, and to plead for its universal diffusion throughout society."[1] Among his reasons Campbell advanced the argument that religion is dependent upon people who can read.

> Religion is founded upon learning so far as it is founded
> upon truth and the knowledge of truth. The Bible is a writ-
> ten communication from Heaven to man, and must be read
> in order to be understood, believed and obeyed.... While it is
> possible--barely possible--to communicate a saving portion
> of religious knowledge to those who cannot read, certain it
> is that it is impossible to make any one, however gifted, mas-

---

[1] Alexander Campbell, "Baccalaureate Address to the Graduate of Bethany College," *Popular Lectures and Address* (Nashville: Harbinger Book Club, n. d.) 507. Additional material in regard to Alexander Campbell on universal education may be found in Thomas H. Olbricht, "Alexander Campbell as an Educator," *Lectures in Honor of the Alexander Campbell Bicentennial, 1788—1988*, ed. James M. Seale (Nashville: Disciples of Christ Historical Society, 1988) 79-100.

ter of any book, human or divine, which he cannot read. To withhold from the myriads the means of reading and understanding the Book of God--the volume of human destiny-- is the greatest sin of omission of duty to God and man that any community, acknowledging the Divine authority of that volume, can be guilty of.[2]

In Illinois, like other states, "the academy was the dominant educational institution...The academies represented the coming of the great middle class into its own, and this brought universal education one step nearer."[3] As part of its efforts to support universal education, the Stone-Campbell Movement founded colleges. The rise and fall of Berean College, Jacksonville, Illinois, (1854 – 1860) will receive special attention in this chapter because it is a tale of high expectations for success, bolstered by the area churches' fund raising efforts; yet a tragic tale of a highly respected Christian minister and his followers trying, and failing, when they tested the parameters of orthodoxy in an emerging religious movement. To unravel this tale, it is necessary to document the Stone-Campbell Movement's efforts to establish and support its colleges, with a focus on its earliest colleges in Illinois and a careful analysis of Berean College's history, to which we will return later in this chapter.

The Stone-Campbell Movement and Colleges

The establishment of colleges should mark a religious movement as respected, successful and mature. Dwight Stevenson, however, notes that the SCM's first educational institute, Bacon College, "blundered into existence without a charter, without a board of trustees, and even without a name."[4] The fervor for establishing colleges in America between 1830 and 1860 created hundreds of colleges but more than seven hundred had died by 1860.[5] Of the tendency to start colleges in Illinois, one writer wryly remarked:

---

2 "Baccalaureate Address," 512f.

3 James Ellsworth Wooters, *A History of Academies in Illinois* (MA Thesis, University of Illinois, 1913) 4.

4 Dwight E. Stevenson, "The Bacon College Story: 1836-1865," *The College of the Bible Quarterly*, Vol. XXXIX, No. 4, (October 1962): 7 – 14.

5 D. Duane Cummins, *The Disciples Colleges: A History* (St. Louis: CBP Press, 1987) 18

After these early years [up to 1847] colleges have rained down. A settler could hardly encamp on the prairie but a college would spring up by his wagon.[6]

The Stone-Campbell Movement started establishing colleges in the late 1830s and by 1860 had many successful starts; but there were colleges that were proposed but never begun, and the Movement had its share of failures. Of those that survived, some proved to be national, but most were provincial. Illinois efforts were more provincial than national; of the three Illinois colleges established in the 1850s, only Eureka College still exists and it has never achieved the national status of other Stone-Campbell Movement colleges such as Bethany College, Texas Christian University, Milligan College, and Pepperdine University.

Early College Efforts in Illinois

One goal of Barton W. Stone's move to Jacksonville, Illinois, in 1832 was to establish a college.

In 1832, Stone visited Jacksonville, Illinois. His purposes were to evangelize, to seek location for a new home, and to establish a Christian college. Associated with him was T. F. Johnson, whose wife was a relative of Stone. Johnson taught mathematics and engineering in Georgetown College, a Baptist school, but preferred to teach in some Christian institution. Stone was desirous of a school to be controlled bodily by the Christians. A misguided project at New Albany, Indiana, about this time sought to effect this, and named Stone on its directorate without his knowledge. This provoked caustic criticism of John Mason Peck, Baptist leader, who charged Stone with a sectarian motive in his educational ideals. Stone replied: "This I boldly deny as to myself; never have I imbibed the spirit of a barbarian to prostrate any literary institution, or to retard, if I could, the march of science." Johnson was favorable to the initiating of a Christian col-

---

[6] *The Past and Present of Woodford County, Illinois.* (Chicago: Wm. Le Baron, Jr. & Co., 1878) 129

lege at Jacksonville, but was persuaded to remain at Georgetown, where shortly Bacon College was launched.[7]

The leaders of the Stone-Campbell Movement—Thomas and Alexander Campbell, Barton W. Stone, and Walter Scott—were known for their teaching careers. The focus of this part of the chapter, however, is Stone's involvement in establishing colleges. To track Stone's involvement in funding colleges (and indirectly in founding colleges) we go back to 1796, when, as John T. Jones and D. Pat Henderson document in their discourses at Stone's funeral, Stone was commissioned by the Transylvania Presbytery to "visit the South, and endeavor to make collections for the purpose of establishing a college in the, then infant State of Kentucky." According to them, Stone's fund raising efforts were successful and were "the first of those which resulted in the establishment of Transylvania University."[8]

Stone, however, was cautious about placing too much emphasis upon colleges and he bemoaned the tendency for educated ministers to take on airs and look down on less educated ministers. We listen in on a conversation between "Old Preacher" and "Young Preacher," one of the last articles Stone wrote before his death on November 9, 1844:

O.P. ...I have feared that our attention has been too much distracted from the gospel of salvation by a thirst and exertion to imitate and equal the sects in having Colleges and Seminaries amongst us as our own. Is it to make learned preachers? If so; we shall as a people surely degenerate, and lose what little of the Spirit we may have, and sink into carnality...I have seen that a learned ministry has excluded, and is excluding all the unlearned, however Spiritual, from a participation in the preaching of the

---

[7] Charles Crossfield Ware, *Barton Warren Stone: Pathfinder of Christian Union: A Story of his Life and Times* (St. Louis: Bethany Press, 1932) 295, 296. The college at New Albany, Christian College, marred by John Cook Bennet's misuse of funds, never opened according to Cummins 27, 28.

[8] John T. Jones and D. Pat Henderson, "A Discourse on the Death of Eld. Barton W. Stone," *CM*, 14.10 (February, 1845) 302; Stone's fund raising efforts were "the first of those which resulted in the establishment of Transylvania University." Elder John Rogers, *The Biography of Elder Barton Warren Stone, Written by Himself: with Additions and Reflections*, (Cincinnati: J. A. & U. P. James, 1847) 26, 27; 133. From C. C. Ware's biography of Stone, we learn that Stone raised funds for Kentucky Academy, which merged on December 22, 1798, with Transylvania Seminary to become Transylvania University: 72.

gospel. They have assumed the reigns [sic] of government, and every thing must eminate [sic] from them, and terminate in them. They have a superior order of men—they are the clergy, and the people are the laity. The like may take place again, even amongst us. I have seen young College preachers go forth to labor in the vineyard, and attempt to preach the gospel. The people stare at their wonderful display of learning, and eloquence, as high above the gospel as the heaven's [sic] are above the earth. They have not the Spirit— they know every thing, but the power of truth. Poor Evangelists!

Y. P. Are you opposed to Colleges and human learning?

O. P. No, far from it. I wish we had ten for every one we have.[9]

Stone was clearly in favor of establishing more colleges for the SCM, even though his "ten for every one" is hyperbolic. When he wrote the "Interview," the SCM had a large number of what D. Duane Cummins calls "private high schools variously called academies, institutes or seminaries,"[10] but only four colleges: Bacon College, Georgetown, Kentucky (founded 1837); Irving College, Warren County, Tennessee (founded 1840); Bethany College, Bethany, Virginia (later West Virginia) (founded 1841); and Newton College, Woodville, Mississippi (founded 1843).[11] In contrast, Alexander Campbell emphasized having a limited number of colleges:

---

[9] B. W. S. "The 7th Interview between an Old and Young Preacher," *CM* 14.5 (September, 1844) 147, 148.

[10] Illinois brethren were active in founding and supporting academies. For example, Henry Y. Kellar: "For two years he was Principal of the Moultrie Academy at Sullivan, Ill., which was controlled by the Christian Church." *Portrait and Biographical Record of Effingham, Jasper and Richland Counties, Illinois.* (Chicago: Lake City Publishing Co., 1893) 603. Kellar was principal prior to 1850, when he was ordained and became a Christian Church minister. Z. T. Sweeney attended a Christian Church "seminary" at Scottville, Illinois, possibly from 1864 – 1867. Lester G. McAllister, *Z. T. Sweeney: Preacher and Peacemaker* (St. Louis: Christian Board of Publication, 1968) 18. McAllister calls the town Scottsville rather than Scottville. Around 1850 Jonathan Atkinson lived in Winchester, Illinois, where he "took charge of the Christian church and seminary." https://www.findagrave.com/memorial/35543274/jonathan-atkinson. See also "Major Seminary" later in this chapter.

[11] Cummins 35, 36.

I hope most satisfactorily to show, what I believe to be capable of satisfactory demonstration, that *one* good institution, well organized, well furnished with an able cohort of teachers, well patronized by the brethren and the public, is better than ten such as we are likely to have got up and spirited into life by such arguments and efforts, that tend much more to schism, rivalry, and false ambition, than to union, harmony, and successful action. I hope the brethren will hasten leisurely, and hear all the premises and arguments before they act in such a way as to create half-a-dozen of ill-begotten, misshapen, club-footed, imbecile schools, under the name and title of Colleges and Universities.[12]

In June 1855, Campbell continued to stress the need for the SCM to concentrate its efforts on strong, well-supported colleges. It is not coincidental that he reiterated this during the year the Illinois SCM brethren chartered three colleges within a few days of one another in February, 1855:

It is no common, no easy, no every-day occurrence, to institute, to constitute, to continue, and make useful one good college. We have not yet, in any one case, given full demonstration of the conservative and self-perpetuating power of one college in all our limits. These mere academic colleges—or rather high schools—with three, four, or five officers each, are, however, useful as schools, lean and decrepid [sic] substitutes for colleges or universities worthy of the name. I could, I presume to say, write the history of three-fourths of these contemplated colleges, and presidents, and professors, and boards of trustees, before they shall call their first roll or graduate one Master of Arts. But to assume such an invidious task we have neither leisure nor inclination. I only repeat the wholesome oracle made and provided for such cases—"Hasten Leisurely."[13]

Since we quote John Mason Peck (1789 – 1858) several times in this chapter, we provide readers with more about his role in Illinois history. Peck was a pioneer Baptist missionary, statesman, author, periodical editor, educator and founder of one of the earliest colleges in Illinois, Shurtleff College (now the Southern Illinois Dental College, Alton). Sev-

---

[12] Alexander Campbell, "The North-western Christian University," *MH* (June 1850) 335.

[13] Alexander Campbell, "Our Colleges," *MH* (September 1855) 538.

eral of the histories of Illinois counties have a stock section on Education and parrot this quote about Peck:

> Rev. J. M. Peck was the first educated Protestant minister in the
> State. He settled at Rock Spring, in St. Clair County, 1820, and
> left his impress on the State. Before 1837 only party papers were
> published, but Mr. Peck published a Gazetteer of Illinois.[14]

Among his publications are emigrant guides and gazetteers on Illinois and the western states. The earliest was published in 1834 at Jacksonville. Peck was keenly aware of what was happening in Illinois and his works gave statistics on religion in the West; he eagerly followed the founding of institutions.[15] Along with announcing charters for new colleges and tracking the progress of existing Illinois colleges, he made it his business to "expose" the efforts of Campbell, Stone, and Scott in the ill-advised Christian College in New Albany, Indiana, and asserted Stone and others were constantly attacking denominational educational institutions. Stone sharply rebutted Peck's assertions that Stone was opposed to colleges and seminaries, and pulled no punches in pointing out Peck's sectarianism:

> Mr. Peck, in his great zeal to destroy us in the view of society,
> has made a few truthless assertions of which I hope he will be
> ashamed. He represents me with others, both in our speeches
> and written periodicals, continually crying down every institution
> gotten up by sectarians—against, Colleges and Seminaries, he
> says, we have written volume after volume and made speech af-
> ter speech. This I boldly deny as to myself; never have I imbibed
> the spirit of a barbarian to prostrate any literary institution, or to
> retard, if I could, the march of science. We had thought that Mr.

---

[14] See, for example, *The Past and Present of Lake County, Illinois* (Chicago: Wm. Le Baron & Co., 1877) 129; *History of Grundy County, Illinois* (Chicago: O. L. Baskin & Co., 1882) 84; *The Past and Present of Boone County, Illinois* (Chicago: H. F. Kett & Co., 1877) 129.

[15] John Mason Peck, *A Gazetteer of Illinois: In Three Parts, Containing a General View of the State, a General View of Each County, and a Particular Description of Each Town, Settlement, Stream, Prairie, Bottom, Bluff, Etc.--Alphabetically Arranged.* (Jacksonville [Ill.]: R. Goudy, 1834); a "Second Edition: Entirely Revised, Corrected and Enlarged" was published in 1837, with same title but new publisher (Philadelphia: Grigg & Elliot); see also *New Guide for Emigrants to the West, Containing Sketches of Ohio, Indiana, Illinois, Missouri, Michigan, with the Territories of Wisconsin and Arkansas, and the Adjacent Parts,* (Boston: Gould, Kendall & Lincoln, 1836).

Peck was a gentleman of mind too high, and too well improved to descend so low as he has done, to notice, to our injury, the real or supposed boastings of a few ignorant men among us. As to the charge against us of sectarianism, I devoutly pray that whenever Mr. Peck may see it, he would fearlessly expose it, and level all his artilery [sic] against it, until he shall have destroyed the anti-christian [sic] monster in us—in himself—in his churches—in the whole world. From an enemy we may more certainly learn our faults—a friend cannot easily discover them, and if he does, his charity endeavors to cover them from the gaze of others. Surely, Mr. Peck will not charge any thing upon us as crime, of which himself is guilty! As sectarianism is wrong, and so viewed by him as well as by us, let us all labour to strip ourselves from the evil, and by the light of truth in word and deed endeavor to drive this bane of christianity [sic] from the christian [sic] community. This alone will bring the world to faith and salvation.[16]

Apparently growing impatient with the talk about a starting a college, without any action, Stephen Roach of Bloomington, Indiana, in a letter that covered several subjects, wrote to Barton W. Stone, January 23, 1832. Roach stated, "We are in a sad condition for want of efficient teachers in Indiana…" and suggested:

Much time has past [sic] since we talked of a christian [sic] seminary. The Messenger is devoted entirely to religion; and until religion can be taught without education, I shall think that the best way to propagate religion is by founding institutions of learning. If this conclusion be correct, can the Messenger be better filled than by devoting a fourth or half of its columns in favor of a *C. College*?[17]

Stone's more than two page reply to Roach dealt mostly with other issues, essentially sidestepping the college issue. "Your remarks on Education I

---

[16] Barton W. Stone, "The Christian College," *CM* 7.6 (June, 1833) 190, 191. For the New Albany fiasco from Stone's perspective, B. W. Stone, "Answer to the Above Letter [from J. V. Himes]" *CM* 9.2 (February 1835) 44: "With it [Indiana University] I had no connexion. I never heard that such a thing was in agitation, until I saw the account printed in the New Albany Gazette…"

[17] S. Roach, "[Letter]," *CM* 6.2 (February 1832) 60.

expect will be attended to hereafter by brethren, who feel an interest in the subject," was his terse reply.[18]

As mentioned earlier in this chapter, one of Stone's objectives in moving to Jacksonville was to establish a college. Thornton Fitzhugh Johnson (1805 – 1851) accompanied Stone to Jacksonville in 1832 and was convinced of the probability of success for a college. In 1837 Johnson recalled the visit, providing a timeline for the establishment:

> In the spring of 1834, I was invited by our venerable father, Barton W. Stone, to remove with him to Jacksonville, Illinois, for the purpose of establishing there a Literary and Scientific Academy, of the highest grade, to be conducted by us jointly, and extended as circumstances might warrant. Having visited Jacksonville in 1832 with father Stone, I could not for a moment doubt our success. My wife, who is his near relation, and who accompanied us, was not only reconciled to removal, but very anxious that I should embark in the proposed enterprise.[19]

Johnson, however, decided to remain in Kentucky to revive Georgetown College, and the college efforts at Jacksonville did not materialize.

News of a proposed "Campbellite" college in Jacksonville circulated in Baptist circles as well. Jonathan Going, the first corresponding secretary of the American Baptist Home Mission Society, and in touch with Peck in Jacksonville, who was undoubtedly the source of the news about a Campbellite college, tempted J. G. Hall to accept the ministry of the Jacksonville Baptist church:

> By the way, Jacksonville, Ill., the seat of the Presbyterian College—where the Campbellites have projected one, and where all parties seem to look with special interest, needs and wants an educated minister.[20]

In August, 1834, almost as an afterthought, the *Messenger* editors, Stone and John T. Johnson, answering the pseudonymous "James," who com-

---

[18] B. W. Stone, "Reply to Doct. S. Roach's Letter," *CM* 6.2 (February 1832) 63.

[19] T. F. Johnson, "[Letter to] J. T. Johnson & Walter Scott," *The Christian* 1.1 (January 1837) 12, 13.

[20] Edward E. Ferguson, *Religion on the Prairie: the History of the First Baptist Church of Jacksonville, Illinois, Its Pastors and Its People, in Context, 1841 – 1991.* (Jacksonville, Illinois: Morgan County Historical Society and First Baptist Church, 1995) 19.

plained of the poor way congregants supported preachers, made this suggestion:

> Would it not be proper for us to have a general co-operation meeting on this subject [supporting preachers] in Kentucky; and the brethren from the East, from Virginia, and from the West and South be invited to attend. And that we also consider the propriety of having a college for educating our youth.[21]

No doubt prompted by this suggestion, in March 1836, Guerdon Gates and J. T. Jones wrote the *Millennial Harbinger* and noted:

> In our country there are Catholic Colleges, Baptist colleges, Presbyterian colleges, Methodist colleges, etc., and shall there not be a Christian College?[22]

Although he may have been in Illinois at some point, Gates, who left the Regular Baptists to align with the Campbell Reformers, was probably living in Louisville at the time of the article. Given Stone's stated objective that he wanted a "school to be controlled bodily by the Christians" and that Jones and Gates lived in Jacksonville, it is highly likely Stone was in agreement with the letter's request and was privy to its content.

Jonesboro College

A year earlier, however, and most likely unknown to Gates and Jones, a group of men at Jonesboro in Union County, perhaps affiliated with the Connexion Christians in that area of southern Illinois, had formed a board of trustees and proposed founding Jonesboro College as part of an 1835 Omnibus bill with Alton College, Illinois College, and McKendree College, to have their colleges chartered by the Illinois legislature.

> In 1835 a bill was drawn in the legislature and enacted into law creating four corporations to be known as: "The Trustees of the Alton College of Illinois," "The Trustees of Illinois College," "The Trustees of the McKendreean [sic] College," "The Trustees of the Jonesboro College." The bill named the board

---

[21] Editors, "Editors Remarks," *Christian Messenger* 8.8 (August 1834) 235.

[22] Guerdon Gates and John T. Jones, "Literary Institutions—No. 1," *MH* 1836: 197 – 200. The article was post marked Jacksonville, Illinois; Gates lived in Louisville but may have been in Jacksonville when the letter was composed. There was no follow up article with the same title.

of trustees for each college, and locates the schools respectively in Upper Alton, in Morgan county, in Lebanon, and at or near Jonesboro. This charter contained a clause which shut out any chance for theological departments, for it "provided, however, that nothing herein contained shall authorize the establishment of a theological department in either of said colleges." It provided further that "The said colleges and their preparatory departments shall be open to all denominations of Christians." The four colleges were to serve respectively the four leading denominations in Illinois at that time, namely—the Baptist, the Presbyterian, the Methodist, and the Christian…There is no record or knowledge of any steps having been taken to organize this school [Jonesboro College]. A careful inquiry among the old settlers does not reveal any satisfactory information concerning the project.[23]

The trustees of Jonesboro College were B. [Benjamin] W. Brooks, Augustus Rixleben, Winstead Davie, John S. Hacker, Daniel Spencer, Willis Willard, John W. McGuire, Thomas Sams, James P. Edwards, John Baltzell, William C. Whitlock, and Isaac Bizzle. This list of names opens some nagging questions. The men are said to be affiliated with the Christian denomination, one of the four "leading denominations" in Illinois at that time. It is striking that the "Christians" were considered one of the four leading denominations. This is best explained by the confusion that existed at that time because of the amalgamation of Stone's New Lights and the Campbell Reformers. Peck's disdain for Alexander Campbell—he claimed to have "exposed the sophistry of his [Campbell's] arguments"[24]—and Stone's followers—is clear in his 1836 description of the Reformers. He lumps the two groups together and classes them as a sect—a term he uses to describe only three of the nineteen distinct religious groups he describes (Cumberland Presbyterians, the United Brethren in Christ, and the Christians):

---

[23] George Washington Smith, *A History of Southern Illinois, Volume 1* (Chicago and New York: The Lewis Publishing Company, 1912) 384, 385. It is surprising that J. M. Peck does not mention Jonesboro College, especially since his college, Alton College, appears in the same bill.

[24] Rufus Babcock, *Forty Years of Pioneer Life: Memoir of John Mason Peck, D. D., Edited from his Journals and Correspondence*, (Philadelphia: American Baptist Publication Society, 1864) 261.

13. *Christian Sect*, or *Newlights*, have become to a considerable extent amalgamated with the *"Reformers,"* or *"Campbellites."* I have not data on which to construct a tabular view of this sect,—but from general information, estimate the number of their "bishops," and "proclaimers," at 300, and their communicants at 10,000 or 12,000. They have three or four monthly periodicals.

Alexander Campbell, who may be justly considered the leader of this sect, (though they disclaim the term *sect,*) is a learned, talented, and voluminous writer. He conducts their leading periodical, the *Millennial Harbinger*.[25]

The estimate of 10,000 to 12,000 is for the SCM adherents in all states, not Illinois. An 1827 estimate for the one Christian Connexion Conference in Illinois was 600 adherents. Given the meager number of Illinois "Christians" affiliated with the Reformers stream at that time, we conclude these men might have been affiliated with the Illinois Christian Conference, a Christian Connexion conference, that was established in 1817.[26] Perhaps Smith based the observation on statistics in his time and not 1835. Lacking hard data from SCM sources until 1841, and that only a partial census, we have to rely on J. M. Peck's vague description of the SCM's presence in Illinois in 1834:

The *Reformers*, as they term themselves, or "Campbellites," as others call them, have several large, and a number of small societies, a number of preachers, and several hundred members, including the Christian body with which they are in union. They immerse all who profess to believe in Christ for the remission of sins, but differ widely from orthodox baptists [sic] on some points of doctrine.[27]

Denominational affiliations of the Jonesboro College board of trustees have proven elusive. From the board of trustees, Brooks, Willard, Davie, Hacker, Rixleben, and Whitlock were incorporators of the Jonesboro' and Mississippi Rail Road Company, by an act in force on March 3, 1837.

---

25 Peck, *A New Guide* 357. The numbers possibly reflect adherents in the western states but the numbers seem high unless more easterly states like Kentucky are included in his estimates.

26 Richard H. Taylor, *Illinois Christian Conferences*.

27 Peck, *Gazetteer* (Second Edition, 1837) 73, 74.

Willard, Davie and Rixleben had well established businesses in Union County. The college, therefore, may have been an entrepreneurial venture more than a religious venture.[28]

When Gates and Jones wrote there was already a college in Jacksonville: Illinois College, established in 1829, was the first college in Illinois to grant college degrees.[29] Seeing the thriving condition of a school affiliated with a denominational rival no doubt generated some impetus for Stone's followers to act. These colleges existed or had been proposed in Illinois by that time:

Year	Name	Affiliation	City (County)	Notes
1827	Alton Seminary	Baptist	Alton (Madison)	Became Shurtleff College in 1836
1828	Lebanon Seminary	Methodist	Lebanon (St. Clair)	Now McKendree University
1829	Illinois College	Presbyterian	Jacksonville (Morgan)	1st Illinois college to grant college degrees
1835	Hillsboro Academy	Lutheran	Hillsboro (Montgomery)	Now Augustana College
1835	Jonesboro College	Christian	Jonesboro (Union)	Proposed but never opened

Gates and Jones called for a meeting in Louisville, Kentucky, to discuss establishing a college and even suggested that "some facilities might be realized by locating the institution in the vicinity of that place." Campbell

---

[28] *Incorporation Laws of the State of Illinois, Passed at a Session of the General Assembly, Begun and held at Vandalia the 6th day of December, 1836* (Vandalia: William Walters, 1837) 262 – 267. For their business efforts at the time see https://www.nps.gov/trte/learn/historyculture/upload/Wagner-Sharp-TOT-Illinois-Final-sm-3.pdf.
[29] http://jacksonvilleil.org/local-history-people/ accessed 4.6.2016.

responded to the appeal and suggested the Louisville meeting be delayed to allow time for further reflection and study, in effect killing the effort:

> ...I say, when this question is laid before the brethren, perhaps there may not be the same unanimity—the same deep sense of the necessity—the same clear perception of the utility of such an institution; and, therefore, it appears to me expedient that the matter be calmly, and dispassionately, and profoundly considered; and, therefore, I fear (and I give it as my opinion) that the time mentioned in the preceding letter is too immediate for the intelligent action of the great community to which the matter is submitted. Two or three months, however, may be added without any real detriment; and it is much better to have the matter well examined before any expression of our views be required.

The meeting apparently never took place.[30]

Hanover College

As obscure as the Jonesboro College attempt was, James M. Peck mentions a second obscure, but almost contemporaneous, SCM effort to establish a college in Illinois:

> The "Reformers," or Campbellites, as some term them, have a charter and contemplate establishing a college at Hanover, in Tazewell county.[31]

The legislation for the charter provides the names of the board of trustees:

> Be it enacted by the people of the State of Illinois, represented in the General Assembly, That William Major, William Davenport, Dennis Rockwell, Joshua Jones, Jacob Cassell, David B.

---

[30] Guerdon Gates, J. T. Jones, "Literary Institutions—No. 1" *MH* 1836: 197 – 200; Editor [Alexander Campbell] "Remarks [to Gates and Jones]" Ibid., 200 – 202.

[31] J. M. Peck, *A Gazetteer* (Second Edition) 73; A. D. Jones, *Illinois and the West*, (Boston: Weeks, Jordan and Company, 1838) 123 repeats the information from Peck. Hanover became Metamora in 1845. The sources misspell the names of some of the board of trustees; several are well known SC individuals, including Henderson, Major, Davenport, Warriner and Hewitt. *The Past and Present of Woodford County, Illinois.* (Chicago: Wm. Le Baron, Jr. & Co., 1878) 288. Woodford County was created from the east section of Tazewell County in 1841.

Henderson, Josiah L. James, Isaac G. Israel, Joseph J. Taggart, Samuel R. Smith, R. O. Wariner, William Rockwell, John Hill, Huston Hawks, J. Josephus Hewitt, and their successors be, and they are hereby created a body corporate and politic, by the name of the "Trustees of Hanover College," and by that name and style to remain and have perpetual succession. Said college shall be located at or near to the town of Hanover in Tazewell county. The number of trustees shall not exceed fifteen, exclusive of the president, principal, or presiding officer of the institution, who shall, ex-officio, be a member of the board of trustees.[32]

A group of land speculators, the Hanover Company, had purchased 12,000 acres in Woodford County, where they established Hanover in 1836. Hanover became Metamora in 1845. The Hanover Company included Dr. Warner [sic "Warriner"], of Bloomington, Rev. Wm. Davenport (agent), Dennis and William Rockwell, William Major, Jacob Cassell, John T. Jones, D. P. Henderson, J. L. James, Joseph Taggert, [and] _____ Israel. The name Hanover was based on Hanover, New Hampshire:

> Metamora was founded as *Hanover* in 1836. It was named for Hanover, New Hampshire by a consortium of land speculators called the Hanover Company. New post office conventions required towns to have unique names, forcing the town to differentiate itself from others in Illinois named Hanover. Early post office names included *Black Partridge* (1836) and *Partridge Point* (1837). The name of the village was finally changed to *Metamora* in 1845 based on the character in the popular play *Metamora; or, The Last of the Wampanoags*. The village still has a Hanover Street and Partridge Street, reflecting these earlier names.[33]

Neither Hanover College nor Jonesboro College apparently made it beyond the proposal stage. Barton W. Stone died before the SCM established a college in Illinois. The nucleus of the Hanover Company included William Major and William Davenport; both were involved in Walnut Grove Seminary, founded in 1848 and charted in 1849; it was chartered in 1855 as Eureka College, the earliest SCM College in Illinois. Interest-

---

[32] *Incorporation Laws of the State of Illinois, Passed at a Session of the General Assembly, Begun and held at Vandalia the 6th day of December, 1836* (Vandalia: William Walters, 1837) 101 – 105. The legislation was approved 27th February, 1837.

[33] http://gutenberg.us/articles/Metamora,_Illinois accessed 5.19.2016.

ingly, we have found no mention of Hanover College in the published histories of Eureka College. A Church of Christ had existed in Walnut Grove since "the early 30's," overlapping the existence of the Hanover Company's proposal to found Hanover College.[34]

Although the SCM still had no colleges in Illinois by 1850, the Illinois brotherhood had organized for evangelistic purposes as early as 1839 and for informal fellowship purposes as early as 1830 when they had camp meetings. In 1850, when the Illinois brethren established the Illinois Christian Missionary Society (ICMS hereinafter), Illinois leaders recognized the informal organizations from earlier years needed an additional focus: education and establishing schools.

Discussions on organizing educational efforts at the first three Illinois annual meetings after the establishment of the ICMS gave the impetus and the structure for starting SCM colleges in Illinois.

A Board of Education was established in September 1852 to coordinate educational efforts:

A third item of business was the subject of Education. On this subject great interest was manifested. Many eloquent speeches were listened to with profound attention and admiration. The meeting elected a Board of Education, which, by the successors of the present incumbents, is made perpetual. This Board, it is calculated, will collect all the information, of every kind, on this subject within their power, which will be recorded in a book kept for that purpose, and will be prepared to furnish common schools, high schools, &c., with all needed information in relation to the plan of houses, the kind of text books that will be proper for each school to have, the manner of teaching, &c., &c., so as to have a uniform system of Education throughout the state.[35]

And start colleges, they did![36] Members of the Stone-Campbell Movement in Illinois founded three coeducational "colleges" in Illinois in the late 1840s to the mid-1850s: Eureka College at Eureka (founded in 1848

---

[34] Haynes 31; *A History of Eureka College with Biographical Sketches and Reminiscences* (St. Louis: Christian Publishing Company, 1894) 20.

[35] T. J. M., "Illinois State Meeting," *CE* 3.10 (October 1852) 347. Even though colleges are not mentioned, the establishment of three Illinois colleges shortly after this indicates colleges were included in the discussions.

[36] The Illinois General Assembly approved the charters of three SCM colleges between February 6 and 13, 1855.

as Walnut Grove Academy, with the college being chartered in 1855 and still in operation), Abingdon College at Abingdon (founded in 1853 and chartered in 1855; merged with Eureka College in 1884) and Berean College at Jacksonville (founded in 1854 and chartered in 1855, closed in the summer of 1860).

When the *Christian Sentinel*, the first brotherhood journal in Illinois since 1847,[37] began at Springfield in September of 1853, it soon carried brisk, territorial discussions of where the Illinois brethren should establish colleges.[38] These discussions touched upon decisions that were made in the ICMS meetings in Walnut Grove (1851), Abingdon (1852) and Jacksonville (1853). In 1852, D. P. Henderson had proposed, and the meeting passed, a resolution that Walnut Grove Academy "be recognized as the Institution for the brethren of this State."[39] It is clear, however, that the resolution fell victim to the whims of the autonomous spirit of the Illinois brotherhood. Groups from Jacksonville and Abingdon ignored the resolution and worked to start their own colleges.

It is also clear that Illinois at this time was making financial commitments to educational efforts in other states it would be hard pressed to fulfill. Action items at the 1852 Annual Meeting included a resolution to raise $10,000.00 to endow a Chair in Bethany College and a resolution "sympathizing with Christian University."[40]

In 1854, agents for Christian University visited Illinois to raise funds and complained about the dwindling support from Illinois, eliciting a sharp response from Alexander Johnston:

> In confirmation of the above, we say again, that we are not and
> never have been, opposed to the brethren of Missouri, building
> up as many schools as they need, or sustaining their paper...I
> cannot however agree with them that a college in Canton, or any

---

[37] Barton W. Stone published the *Christian Messenger* at Jacksonville; it ended publication in Illinois in 1845, when it merged with John R. Howard's *Bible Advocate* (published in Paris, Tennessee and St. Louis, Missouri); Alfred Padon published the obscure *Christian* in 1847 at Edwardsville; Alexander Graham published the *Berean* at Springfield in 1838. Haynes 663.

[38] Alexander Johnston, "Suggestions on the Location of Our Schools," *CSent*, 1.7 (March 1854) 214, 215; Alexander Johnston, "The Cause in Illinois," *CSent*, 1.8 (April 1854) 236 – 238; A. J. Kane, "Suggestions on the Location of Our Schools," *CSent*, 1.8 (April 1854) 243 – 245; Alexander Johnston, "Remarks," *CSent*, 1.8 (April 1854) 245, 246.

[39] *A History of Eureka College* 32 - 34.

[40] T. J. M. Op cit.

where else in Missouri, would answer the purpose for the brotherhood of this state, as well as a School or Schools, on our own soil. It is not necessary to give our reasons for so thinking, as they must strike every reflecting mind. Governed by these considerations, the brethren of Illinois have commenced building up at home Schools of the highest order, which when completed will afford all the facilities for a liberal education, that can be offered at Canton, or any where else out of the State.[41]

Alexander Campbell was leery of coeducational colleges and in his dictatorial style cautioned against the efforts.[42] He also questioned the viability of many efforts, likening them to lower class institutions. He had also, to some extent, as we noted above, stalled movement-wide efforts to start a college in 1836. Now that Bethany College existed, Campbell became protective of its interests. In October 1855 in "Our Colleges," he bemoans the lack of cooperation in building church meeting houses and colleges, calling out Illinois for having three colleges. Three different times in the article, he mentions how Bethany College, now in its fourteenth year of existence, was not fully endowed and how that had adversely affected its ability to be as effective as possible.[43]

The proliferation of colleges in the Movement caught the attention of Moses Lard, who, in 1865, expressed his concerns about the number of SCM colleges:

Only we are committing this great folly—we are building ten where we should have but one. One great University, with a single well-endowed college in each State where we number fifty thousand brethren or more, will be found, in the end, in our humble opinion, about as near the consummation of human wisdom as we may expect to attain, until we possess an experience to which at present we can lay no claim. Two or three colleges in the same State, under the control of the same body, we regard as strikingly unwise.[44]

---

[41] Alexander Johnston, "Canton University" *CSent* 1.9 (May 1854) 278.

[42] *MH* 1855: 356, 357; 438

[43] Alexander Campbell, "Our Colleges," *MH* 1855: 578 – 581.

[44] *I.Q*, 2.3 (April 1865) 252; Lard does not mention but hints at Illinois with his statement, "Two or three colleges in the same State…" By then, Illinois was down to two colleges. See also Cummins 43

Major Seminary

An additional Illinois educational institution taxed the SCM's resources in the decade of the 1850s, Major Seminary, in Bloomington:

> In 1856 Rev. Robert Conover established a female seminary in Bloomington, which he successfully conducted for many years. Another attempt to maintain a private girls' school was made by Elder William T. Major, who erected a building in the north part of town, which became known as Major's College. It continued until many other institutions arose and it could not keep pace. The property finally fell to the Wesleyan University and was sold for residence purposes.[45]

Perceptively, J. H. Burnham described the fate of Major Seminary:

> Most of the Grove was purchased, in 1835, by Rev. W. T. Major, and it has since been called Major's Grove. Here he built a residence, and at a later date, in 1855 and 1856, he erected the fine educational building, since called Major's College. Its cost was over $16,000, and its value, with the land, was $20,000. This was occupied as a young ladies' seminary for several years, though at first intended to be a female orphan school. At times, it was well filled with students from Bloomington and Central Illinois, having been occupied as late as 1867. Mr. Major was one of the leading members of the Christian denomination. He gave liberally to schools and colleges of that Church, and finally decided to present it this fine building. A full Board of Trustees was appointed, and an effort made to operate the College as a denominational institution, but it was not very successful, owing, mainly, to the fact that the Christian Church was interested in several other Western colleges. This magnificent gift from one of the noblest Christian gentlemen of the age, is almost without a parallel.[46]

---

[45] Jacob L. Hasbrouck, *History of McLean County Illinois, in Two Volumes* (Topeka-Indianapolis: Historical Publishing Company, 1924) Volume 1, 170. Haynes 62, 63.

[46] *The History of McLean County, Illinois* (Chicago: Wm. Le Baron, Jr., & Co., 1879) 442. Burnham wrote this section of the history; he was not the editor of the volume. It is impossible to determine to what extent Major relied upon others to fund Major Seminary. Its closing is further evidence of how the resources of Illinois brotherhood were over extended.

Of the three major 19th century SCM Illinois colleges established in the 1850s, Berean operated the shortest time. Abingdon College operated for a little more than thirty years before merging with Eureka College in 1885, leaving Eureka as the only SCM college in Illinois that still exists. A fourth SCM effort, Southern Illinois College, was established in the late 1860s, but was only briefly under the Movement's control.[47] Illinois would not have an additional SCM college until Lincoln Bible Institute, affiliated with the Christian Churches/Churches of Christ, was founded in 1945.[48] Nationwide, during the 1850s, the Disciples established twenty colleges, of which only five survived to the present age.[49]

The Story of Berean College, Jacksonville, Illinois

Prospectively viewed *Berean College* will yet shine as one of the first constellations in the horizon of the Reformation. (John F. Rowe, December, 1856)[50]

The large and handsome new College buildings have been completed and furnished, and a largely increased number of pupils are expected. Under the management of President Russell the institution will doubtless continue to flourish. It now bids fair to become the leading institution of learning in the city. (Editor, *Jacksonville Sentinel*, September 25, 1857)[51]

We turn our attention now to Berean College, detailing its history, the people involved and the reasons it closed after only five years.

---

[47] Haynes 63, 64 describes the SCM's involvement in what is now Southern Illinois University at Carbondale.

[48] *A History of Eureka College with Biographical Sketches and Reminiscences. Illustrated.* (St. Louis: Christian Publishing Company, 1894.) Leonard W. H. Charnock, *Eureka College, Eureka, Ill., 1855-1955; A Community of Learning in Search of Truth, Human and Divine.* (Eureka, Illinois: Eureka College, 1955.) Harold Adams, *History of Eureka College.* (Eureka, Illinois: Board of Trustees of Eureka College, 1982.) B. J. Radford, *Sketches of the Early History of Eureka College.* ([Place of publication not identified]: [publisher not identified], n.d.). No detailed history of Abingdon College exists. One is desirable, but beyond the scope of this work on Illinois. The same is true for Southern Illinois College.

[49] Cummins 44.

[50] John F. Rowe, "A Visit to 'Athens of the West.'" *CE*, 8.2 (February 1857) 71 – 75.

[51] [Editor], "Berean College," *Jacksonville Sentinel*, September 25, 1857.

Its Founding

N. S. Haynes describes the establishment:

> This institution was organized at Jacksonville, under the general
> incorporation law of the State, April 25, 1854. Sections 2 and 3
> of the charter read as follows:
> The objects contemplated by this act of incorporation are to
> build up and maintain, in the town of Jacksonville, an institution
> of learning of the highest class, for males and females, to teach
> and inculcate the Christian faith and morality of the sacred
> Scriptures, and for the promotion of the arts and sciences.
> The trustees shall have power to erect the necessary buildings,
> to appoint a president, professors and teachers, and other agents
> and officers; to confer degrees in the liberal arts and sciences,
> and to do all other things for the encouragement of religion and
> learning which are lawfully done by the most approved seminar-
> ies and colleges in the United States.
> The first Board of Trustees was composed of Hon. Joseph
> Morton, President; Jesse Galbraith, Secretary; Joseph J. Cassall
> [sic; Cassell], Treasurer; Nathan M. Knapp , Andrew J. Kane,
> William C. [sic; A.] Mallory, Jacob Ward, James Simpson, [Dr.]
> Samuel G[regg]. Weagley , Samuel T. Galloway [sic "Callaway"],
> Nimrod Deweese, Anderson Foreman, Joel Headington,
> Jonathan Atkinson and William W. Happy, Sr. The Faculty was as
> follows: Minister Jonathan Atkinson, President, Professor of
> Latin and Greek, lecturer on sacred history and instructor in
> French; William W. Happy, Jr., teacher of mathematics and the
> natural sciences and instructor in German; Miss Melinda Bond,
> governess and teacher of history, rhetoric and philosophy;
> William D. Hillis, teacher of vocal music; Mrs. L. E. Hillis,
> teacher of instrumental music. The school opened the first
> Monday in October, 1854. The term was forty weeks of two
> equal semesters. During the first year ninety-six pupils were en-
> rolled fifty-nine males and thirty-seven females. In addition to
> academic courses, the study of the Bible was required of all stu-
> dents, and the president delivered every year a course of lectures
> on sacred history.
> The school was located a short distance east of the town on a
> five-acre campus, a quiet and beautiful place. The first term was
> held in a frame building located on one side of the ground.

Meanwhile, an attractive brick building was erected. It was occupied by the school in 1855.[52]

Why Jacksonville?

As mentioned earlier in this chapter, part of Stone's plan when he moved to Jacksonville was to create a college controlled by the Christians. Jacksonville was called the "Athens of the West" and the "Athens of Illinois." The Methodist, James West, made these observations about Jacksonville after attending a conference there in October, 1860:

> *Jacksonville* is one of the oldest towns in the State, and in the midst of some of the most beautiful and highly cultivated parts of the country. Here are some of the finest sheep-walks, stock pastures, corn fields, and peach and apple orchards in the State. Farms are surrounded and fields divided by hedges of the beautiful osage orange shrub, which makes an excellent fence, stronger than the hawthorn. The town of Jacksonville contains a population of about 12,000 persons, and is called the Athens of Illinois. It is a city of churches, colleges, mansions, and State asylums. There are three or four Methodist churches, three Presbyterian, two Baptist, one Episcopalian, and two Portuguese churches, and there are the State asylums of the deaf and dumb, the blind, and the insane; there is the Jacksonville female college, with about 400 pupils, belonging to the Methodists, under the charge of Dr. Adams; there is the Berean college, belonging to the Campbellites; and the Illinois college, belonging to the Presbyterians. Such a centre [sic] of learning and religion has drawn around it a large amount of piety, intelligence and wealth. Wealthy parents go to educate their families there; and all that taste and refined society can do to make a place beautiful and ornamental is done for this town and its vicinity.[53]

---

[52] Haynes 60, 61. The Illinois legislature approved Berean's charter on February 12, 1855.

[53] James Shaw, *Twelve Years in America: Being Observations on the Country, the People, Institutions and Religion; with Notices of Slavery and the Late War; and Facts and Incidents Illustrative of Ministerial Life and Labor in Illinois, with Notes of Travel Through the United States and Canada*. London: Hamilton, Adams, and Co, 1867: 303, 304. Shaw apparently was not aware it had been publicly announced Berean College was not reopening for the 1860 – 1861 academic year.

Jacksonville became the center of Illinois SCM activity when Stone moved there in the early 1830s. Other areas had an earlier Restorationist history, such as eastern Illinois and Kaskaskia, but those areas were not as highly influenced by Stone. Samuel Lowe, a prominent Illinois SCM pioneer stated the significance of Jacksonville for the SCM:

> As an evidence of its truth, cast about you and observe the discord, strife and ruin, that has been produced in many communities by the innovations of men claiming to be ministers of God, preaching for doctrines, the fine-spun theories and opinions of men, instead of the pure unadulterated word of God. May I instance the Jacksonville Church, once the pride—yea, the Jerusalem of Illinois.[54]

In the following chapter, we document the Russell defection and how it affected Berean College. In this chapter we present a more nuanced history of the college and the reasons why it closed so quickly after its establishment.

First, we survey how local newspapers and SCM and local historians present its history.

Jacksonville newspapers have occasionally featured articles on the history of Berean College. These articles have repeated the limited understanding of the factors involved, citing the split in the Jacksonville Christian Church as the main reason for the closing.[55] D. H. Doyle covers the Russell controversy in some detail but his focus likewise is on the dynamics of the split in the Jackson Christian Church; he seems unaware of the national dynamics of the controversy involving W. S. Russell and adds

---

[54] Sam[ue]l Lowe, *BA*, 2.11(November, 1859) 377. Lowe's disappointment is because of the dissension in the Jacksonville Christian Church caused by W. W. Happy, Sr., and W. S. Russell.

[55] *Jacksonville Journal*, October 21, 1981.

nothing new about why Berean College closed.[56] Morgan County histories also treat Berean College, but have the same narrow understanding
of its failure. SCM historians only briefly mention the college.[57] Haynes
gives some details and has John S. Sweeney as a major player in defeating
the Russell defection, a limited analysis. Reasons given in previous efforts,
with our rebuttal or more nuanced explanations are:

• The dissension in the Jacksonville Christian Church led to its
closing.[58]

Admittedly, the dissension in the congregation contributed to
the closing. As we document in the next chapter and as our extensive research shows, it is important to note that the Russell
controversy was not merely a local issue. It drew national attention among the Disciples and other denominations, especially
the Baptists. According to church records, the congregation felt
so marginalized by the SCM, a merger with the Baptists was
considered during the controversy caused by Russell.[59]

---

[56] Don Harrison Doyle, *The Social Order of a Frontier Community: Jacksonville, Illinois,
1825 – 1870.* (Urbana: University of Illinois Press, 1978) 75: "Berean College was
chartered in 1855 and operated only a few years before it dissolved following an
1859 schism in the local congregation." 158 – 160. [Edited] *History of Morgan
County, Illinois: Its Past and Present* (Chicago: Donnelley, Loyd & Co., Publishers, 1878)
398: "About 1853 or '54 the Christian denomination began the erection of a
building known as the Berean College. A charter was received dated Feb. 12, 1855,
soon after which the building was completed, and the following year school was
opened with Jonathan Atkinson as president. The school was opened under very
favorable auspices, and for several years was continued very successfully…The
college continued until about 1858 or '59, when a division in the church occurred,
and soon after the school was discontinued." Charles M. Eames, *Historic Morgan and
Classic Jacksonville* (Jacksonville: Daily Journal Steam Job Printing Office, 1885) 129
repeats the last sentence.

[57] Cummins 49: A theological controversy involving President Walter Scott Russell,
also a Bethany graduate, led to the closing of the school in 1861. The footnote,
number 90 simply refers to Haynes 60 – 62. The school closed after the spring
semester in 1860.

[58] Doyle and others: "The college continued until about 1858 or '59, when a division
in the church occurred, and soon after the school was discontinued." Doyle 160.

[59] See page 37 for the counter suggestion of Charles E. Russell for the Jacksonville
congregation to seek a merger with the Christian Denomination instead of the
Baptists.

- Competition from "more affluent" colleges in Jacksonville led to its closing.[60]

> After only six years of operation, the college closed its doors in the fall of 1860, primarily because of "disagreements" in the Christian church but probably also because of the competition from Jacksonville's more affluent colleges, Illinois College, Illinois Female College (later Mac-Murray College for Women), and Jacksonville Female Academy.

The above paragraph states the historical facts and then supposes another factor was "competition." While it is true that three colleges in Jacksonville were older than Berean College and were therefore better established, no documentation or statistics are presented in support of the conjecture. It does not follow that members of the SCM would have chosen to send their children to denominational colleges in Jacksonville or other cities in Illinois. Berean College was founded so that Christian Church students could attend a local college with teachers that taught Christian Church principles. On the other hand, as we show in Appendix 3, some Berean College students completed their degrees at Illinois College or other SCM colleges after Berean College closed in the summer of 1860.

- Poor planning and too extravagant a building led to its closing.[61]

---

[60] M. James Kedro, "A Look at Berean College, Jacksonville: City's Coeducational College of the 1850s" *Jacksonville Courier* (December 4, 1977) 46. See also, Greg Olson, "The Way We Were: Learning Curves: Berean College's Short History was Troubled by Religious Squabbling" *Jacksonville Courier* (March 4, 2013) 3. Also note, "This Way We Were story was first published Nov. 29, 2004."

[61] *Jacksonville Daily Journal*, (November 28, 1900) 4. "It was about the breaking out of the civil war that the denomination known as the Disciples of Christ, or 'Christians,' began the erection of a college on a plot of ground on East State street. The new Berean college building was so poorly planned and extravagantly built that both project and contractors were ruined, and it was offered for sale." Extravagance aside, Jacksonville estimated the value of the Berean College building and acreage at $25,000.00 in their proposal to locate the land grant university in Jacksonville in 1867.

Poor planning is subjective and retrospective. The cost of the building was not out of line with similar expenditures by the Movement in Illinois. Eureka College raised $60,000.00 in 1857, $20,000.00 of which was spent on a new building.[62] By comparison, Western Reserve Eclectic Institute at Hiram, Ohio, spent $9,300 in 1849 on its building and acreage in a rural location.[63] In 1867, in the offer Jacksonville made to establish Illinois' land grant college, the Illinois College property had an estimated value of $21,000.00.[64]

From the perspective of the SCM, Berean College closed because the Illinois brotherhood in particular, and the broader movement in general, was not willing to support a college that tolerated trustees, preachers and educators who were sympathetic to the ideology and theology of W. S. Russell. The Illinois SCM overextended itself by establishing three colleges at the same time. Major Seminary, started at nearly the same time, further taxed the resources of Illinois brethren. Colleges in Missouri (Christian University), Indiana (North-western Christian University) and Virginia (Bethany College) continued to receive some support from Illinois. SCM leaders were also involved in local common schools since the 1855 act establishing free public schools was not fully in force and local communities were still bearing the brunt of expenses for schools.[65]

A prominent regional newspaper carried the news of the closing:

Jacksonville Schools – The fall term of the Illinois College began on the 17th, with a full attendance.

The Berean College, it appears, will not open this year, on account, it is stated, of the disagreement in the church which patronizes it.

---

[62] *A History of Eureka College* 51, 52. The financial depression of 1857 adversely impacted the fund raising effort, but the building was started in the spring of 1857 and completed in the summer of 1858.

[63] Cummins 46.

[64] *Journal of the House of Representatives of the Twenty-fifth General Assembly of the State of Illinois at their Regular Session, Begun and Held at Springfield, January 7, 1867.* (Springfield: Baker, Bailhache & Co., Printers, 1867) 266-268.

[65] James Ellsworth Wooters, *A History of Academies in Illinois* (MA Thesis, University of Illinois, 1913) 4, 5.

The Female College and the Academy have both commenced their fall terms, and are, no doubt, as well attended as usual, since both these are now fairly established.[66]

College or Common School?

The Illinois institutions in question were not strictly "colleges" when first established, mirroring many schools across the country, which often had "preparatory" departments. The student body often included younger children. Walnut Grove Academy, established in 1848, had a mixture of college and preparatory classes; it was not officially a college until chartered in February 1855. Melinda Hall, a student at Berean College in the spring of 1855, gave this description of the student body at the time:

> I expect that you are very anxious to know what kind of a place Berean College is. I do not know of any better way of describing it than to compare it to a common school but as it is only in its infancy yet we must look over its defects. I think that from the present prospect it will some day become a place that can with propriety be called a college. The president is a man of considerable talents and is capable of giving good instructions. There are about 60 students the majority of which are small children. Sarah and I are in a class to ourselves in Grammer [sic] and Arithmatic [sic], and in our other studies, we are in a class with the large scholars.[67]

Prominent SCM editor, Benjamin Franklin, who played a major role in forcing W. S. Russell from the SCM, and indirectly caused the college to close, gave this analysis in 1860 of Russell and the college:

> We have, probably, misled the public mind to some extent and flattered Mr. Russell's enormous vanity, in calling him "*President Russell.*" It is true that he is in a college building of some note, erected by the generosity and liberality of good men. But there is nothing there but the building that could, by any common use of language, be called a *college*. It is not even a respectable high

---

[66] *Sangamo Journal* (September 29, 1860) 2.
[67] M. James Kedro, "Letters Home: An Illinois Coed in the 1850s," *Journal of the Illinois State Historical Society*, 70.3 (August, 1977) 196-200. The letter to her brother was written on May 8, 1855, near the close of Berean's first academic year. Jonathan Atkinson (1819-1884) was president at this time.

school. It is scarcely anything more than a small *common* school, of twenty to twenty-five boys.[68]

As Cummins notes, Berean College followed the model of daily lectures on Bible themes by Alexander Campbell in his role as President of Bethany College. Atkinson and Russell lectured the students on Bible themes daily.[69]

Its Presidents

Jonathan Atkinson (1819 – 1884)[70]

Jonathan Atkinson, a native of England, was in Illinois as early as 1850 since he attended the organization of the ICMS at the Shelbyville annual meeting and was elected as one of the Managers. He was president from Berean College's founding in 1854 until an unknown time during the 1857 fall term, when W. S. Russell replaced him. After he was ousted from the presidency, he moved to Missouri and then to Iowa, where he practiced law. Surprisingly, he had aligned with the Methodists shortly before his death, but Christian Church minister J. P. Lucas conducted his funeral. Z. T. Sweeney surmised the Board of Trustees replaced Atkinson because of his physical appearance not because of his academic credentials or because he was a poor teacher or president.

Walter Scott Russell (1831 – 1863)

Walter Scott Russell was born in Cincinnati, Ohio, on June 1, 1831. Russell's mother, Louisa (nee Matthews) Russell joined the Cincinnati, Ohio, Christian Church in 1829. She married Charles Elmer Russell, Sr. in December 1829.[71] C. E. Russell was known as a lay minister but made

---

68 Benjamin Franklin, "Remarks" in reply to "Russell & Company," by J. A. Brooks, *ACR* (May 29, 1860) 86. Franklin does not give the source for his numbers; he is not accurate since his numbers do not include female students. Although the number of female students is not known, the 1860 graduating class of four people included three women.

69 Cummins 49.

70 https://www.findagrave.com/memorial/35543274/jonathan-atkinson which has an obituary published in the *Taylor County Republican* (Bedford, Iowa) Thursday, April 17, 1884: 4.

71 Caroline Russell to Claude E. Spencer, December 2, 1960. (Walter Scott Russell Papers, Disciples of Christ Historical Society.)

his living as a stove dealer.[72] Walter graduated from Bethany College in 1856 and ministered at Louisiana, Missouri, for about a year before he moved to Jacksonville in the summer of 1857 to be the minister of the Jacksonville Christian Church, replacing Atkinson. Sometime that fall, Russell replaced Atkinson as president of Berean College.

Although Russell was known, even admired, for his piety,[73] his controversial beliefs about the Holy Spirit and his open criticism of the lack of spirituality within the Movement led to his downfall and the closing of Berean College.[74]

Berean College's Attendance Figures and Graduates

Berean College graduated its first class in its fifth year of existence.

Academic Year	Male	Female	Total Students	Graduates	Notes
1854 – 1855	59	37	96	NA	Haynes 60 - 62
1855 – 1856	Not available	Not available	121 2 Lit. Societies	NA	*MH* 1856: 475
1856 – 1857	58	38	96	NA	Catalogue for 1857/1858

---

[72] *MH* 1841: 528 locates "Elder C. E. Russell" at Bear Creek, Platt County, Missouri. For his role as stove (or tin) dealer, see the 1860 and 1870 Federal Censuses.

[73] J. J. Summerbell, minister of the Christian Denomination congregation in Jacksonville where C. E. Russell was one of the founding members, although he did not know W. S. Russell, stated: "Elder W. S. Russell, late president of the college at Jacksonville, Ill., was of one of the first families embracing this faith in Cincinnati. He afterward graduated at Bethany College under President Campbell. He was a man of great learning, extensive erudition, exemplary life, and surpassing Christian spirit."

[74] See Chapter 10 for the details of Russell and company's defection from the SCM.

1857 – 1858	58	38	96	NA	*Jack-sonville Courier,* December 4, 1977, page 44.
1858 – 1859	Not avail-able	Not avail-able	Not avail-able	11	1st graduat-ing class.
1859 - 1860	20 - 25	Not avail-able	Not avail-able	4	Last year open; Franklin *ACR.*

Students at Berean College

See Appendix 3 for our list of Students who attended Berean College. Our research results in a distorted demographic: the Berean College students we have discovered tend to be from well to do families and were discoverable because their academics and careers were significant enough to be recorded. For example, those graduating with honors were featured in the college news reported to local newspapers and were more easily discovered.

10. The Walter Scott Russell Defection

Those who came to Illinois from the Ohio Valley had roots in the Second Great Awakening, among whom were Barton W. Stone and those associated with him. In Chapter 4, "Bodily Exercises and Healing," we depicted the unusual "operations" of the Holy Spirit in the great Camp Meetings such as Cane Ridge and how they came to be resisted especially by those from a Campbell-Scott background. By the middle of the nineteenth century the consensus position in the larger Stone-Campbell Movement, as well as in Illinois, was that the unusual outbreakings were human manifestations and not works of the Holy Spirit. Furthermore, leaders concluded that the healing gift of the Spirit had ceased. In the late 1850s a controversy broke out in central Illinois because of the insistence of Walter Scott Russell that it was imperative for Christians to recover these gifts. The estrangement that erupted impacted the brotherhood journals (See Chapter 8) and the Illinois Stone-Campbell colleges (See Chapter 9). This chapter focuses upon the important episode of Walter Scott Russell (1831 – 1863) and his critics.

The W. S. Russell Defection[1]

Walter Scott Russell (1831 – 1863) was the leading figure in a defection that sought to "reform the reformation." From 1856 – 1861, Russell and his compeers received a full scale attack from many of the leading per-

---

[1] This defection is also called by many expressions, including the "Russell, Melish, Carman Defection" (John S. Sweeney 1884); Article titles included: "The Defection," "The Defection Again," etc. (Benjamin Franklin, *ACR* 1859: 54; 58 (bis); 74; 78 (bis); 82), "Russell & Company" (*ACR* 3: 86). For secondary source references to Russell or the Russell defection, with full bibliographical details, see the bibliographical essay included in this chapter. These notes frequently reference the sources.

sonalities[2] of the Stone-Campbell Movement; more than ten ministers or educators were implicated. This chapter includes an exposition of an infamous essay by Moses Lard in which he harshly attacked W. S. Russell. We also detail the treatment of the faction by 19th century and later writers and the dynamics in Illinois: the hostile takeover of a journal, a leadership coup, a closed college, and a rival journal started by the defection.[3]

Lard on Russell

Moses E. Lard included Russell and his faction as one of three schismatic efforts to divide the Stone-Campbell Movement in his article "Can We Divide?"[4]

> After Ferguson and recently came poor Walter Scott Russell, and tried to "reform the reformation," *alias* lead out a sect. Like the gilded candle-moth, he flitted gayly for a little season around the dazzling but dangerous lamp of French philosophy, till at last it scorched his wings, and left him fluttering on the ground in littleness and neglect, himself the ruin he had criminally sought to work in the house of God. A few unstable and erratic spirits, as usually happens in such cases, determined in their madness to die with him, *and they did die*. True, in their death-struggle they well-nigh wrecked a church, and for all their pains now have a name that only a convict might covet.[5]

---

[2] Benjamin Franklin, "Reply," to Elders of the Jacksonville, Illinois, Christian Church, "Elder B. Franklin," *ACR*, 1860: 148: "Russell has been repudiated by more than thirty of the most talented, reliable and permanent writers among us."

[3] Portions of this chapter were presented as one of four papers in a session at the Thomas H. Olbricht Christian Scholars' Conference at Abilene Christian University, Abilene, Texas, in June, 2015. Wesley Dingman read a condensed version of his article, "'Can We Divide?' Revisited: The Rhetoric of Moses Lard's Treatise Against Division," (*Restoration Quarterly* 56: 193 – 207). James L. McMillan responded to Dingman's paper.

[4] Moses Lard, "Can We Divide?" *Lard's Quarterly* 3 (1866): 330–36. The article is online http://www.geocities.ws/moseslard/qtrly/divide.htm

[5] Lard 334. Lard's emphasis.

Who was Walter Scott Russell?

Foster and Casey refer to Walter Scott Russell as "obscure."[6] Although Russell receives little attention today, anyone who read the leading SCM journals from 1857 to 1861 knew who Walter Scott Russell was.[7] Russell was born in Cincinnati in 1831 and moved with his family to Missouri when he was seven. He became a Christian at eighteen under the preaching of W. H. Hopson at Louisiana, Missouri. One source says he was a graduate of "an Eastern university" and was Alexander Campbell's nephew.[8] After graduating from Bethany College in 1856, Russell had a controversial one-year ministry at Louisiana, Missouri, where the congregation was so unhappy with him they offered to pay his salary for the rest of the year if he would just leave. He turned down the offer and refused to leave.[9] In July 1857, he moved to Jacksonville, Illinois, to assume the presidency of Berean College and be the minister of the Jacksonville Christian Church. Because of his controversial articles and sermons, and his schismatic actions, opposition to Russell had begun as early as 1856, intensified from 1857 to 1859, and culminated with his expulsion in 1860.[10] After being forced from the SCM, Russell remained in Jacksonville as minister of the Christian Church. Lard's statement, "*and they did die*" (Lard's italics) is a double entendre referring to the faction's ex-

---

[6] Douglas A. Foster and Michael W. Casey (editors) *Stone-Campbell Movement: An International Religious Tradition* (Knoxville: University of Tennessee Press, 2002) 24

[7] A preliminary bibliography of articles by and about WSR from the *Millennial Harbinger* (*MH*), *American Christian Review* (*ACR*), *Christian Sentinel* (*CSent*), *Gospel Advocate* (*GA*), *Christian Evangelist* (*CE*) and *Bible Advocate* (*BA*) from 1854 – 1861 has more than one hundred and thirty items. C. Leonard Allen, following Sikes: "scores of writers" attacked Russell. (*Things Unseen* 86).

[8] Z. T. Sweeney, "The Walter Scott Russell Crisis" *CS* 1923: 539, 540.

[9] Joseph Franklin and J. A. Headington, *The Life and Times of Benjamin Franklin*, 370.

[10] Alexander Campbell, "Philosophy, Dogmatism, Schism," *MH* 1860: 17, 18: "We do not wonder that some of the readers of the speculations of Bro. Russell have come to the conclusion that he maintains that true believers may yet work miracles, and that this power is still needed and may be yet expected. I have not seen this in these identical words, yet I confess that my fears have been, and yet are, that his progress is in that direction. His positive and dogmatic confidence in his own intuitions, and his philosophy of spiritual influence, are evidently in that direction, and that he is not one of us, is too manifest to be doubted by any discriminating and attentive reader of the outpourings of his dogmata. He has turned aside into vain janglings, and cannot legitimately be regarded as one of us. He is evidently now a schismatic, and as such, cannot be esteemed and regarded as a brother in communion with us."

pulsion from the Movement (a relational death) and Russell's and W. W. Happy, Jr.'s physical deaths. In July, 1863, Russell volunteered with the Christian Commission and went to Vicksburg, Mississippi, to minister to sick and wounded soldiers. While there he contracted disease and became fatally ill. He was able to return home to Jacksonville where he died on November 24th.[11] Happy died in 1862 after leaving the faculty of Berean College when it closed in 1860.[12]

Lard's Attack

Lard's attack of Russell is the earliest reflection on the significance of the Russell defection after Russell's death in November of 1863. Since Lard's object in "Can We Divide?" is to cast the three "heretics" as negatively as possible, his words are abusive. His vitriolic attack details three areas: the effort to "reform the reformation," Russell's dabbling in "French philosophy" and the wreck of a church.

---

[11] Russell's obituary first appeared in the *Jacksonville Sentinel*, Friday, November 27, 1863, and was reprinted in the *Jacksonville Daily Journal*, June 4, 1924: 3. Allen, *Things Unseen* 87, apparently following Haynes 62, incorrectly states he died at Vicksburg. D. H. Hamilton, pastor of the Westminster Presbyterian Church of Jacksonville conducted the service.

[12] Benjamin Franklin *ACR* 1860: 148. In 1860, Happy Jr. was considering moving to Iowa for a teaching position. "We understand that the Russell faction in Jacksonville, Ill., have recently ordained W. W. Happy Jr., to the ministry, and that he is about moving to Iowa. He has been in the midst of the Russell defection, aiding and abetting to the extent of his ability. We explain this, that the brethren may not be imposed upon in Iowa, by a man who is not of us in any sense, but an open enemy. He was one of Russell's *professors*, in college, till they all starved out. After the wickedness these men have practiced in Jacksonville and the mischief they have done, they ought not to be received any place till they repent." Happy became sick in Iowa, returned to Illinois and died at Jacksonville on May 26, 1862. http://www.findagrave.com/cgi-bin/fg.cgi?page=gr&GRid=71430876.

Lard's Abusive Language

Several people mention Russell's piety, and his promise, including Robert Richardson[13] and Alexander Campbell.[14] Lard, even though he did speak favorably of Jesse B. Ferguson's abilities in "Can We Divide?" had nothing good to say about Russell. Russell's actions were criminal in intent, seeking to ruin the "house of God." He is classed with "convicts." Russell and his followers were "unstable" and "erratic."

Why does Lard treat Russell with such contempt? Some writers felt the Movement was too tolerant toward Russell.[15] Early on, Alexander Campbell was ambivalent toward Russell. When Russell's articles on the Holy Spirit appeared in the *Christian Sentinel*, Campbell gave the series "a careful reading" and concluded the articles "are in good keeping with pure Calvinism in its hale and unregenerate days."[16] Ironically, at the very time Campbell's article appeared with its stern warning for Russell to "Preach Christ," Campbell was touring Illinois. After visiting Jacksonville, Illinois, and speaking at Berean College during the trip, Campbell glowingly praised Russell's work at the college and with the Jacksonville Christian Church.[17]

Daniel Bates, editor of the *Christian Evangelist* in Iowa, and an eye witness of many of the events in Illinois during the controversy, felt Russell

---

[13] "Robert Richardson to P. S. Fall, September 25, 1857." (Phillip S. Fall Collection, Frankfort, Kentucky). Quoted by West, *Eye of the Storm* 164. "…he is a young man of piety and ability…" Richardson, "Misrepresentations and Speculations," *Evangelist* 1860: 58 "For Bro. Russell, personally, I have a very high regard, and I deeply regret that by *confiding too much in his own judgment in these matters*, he has destroyed his prospects and his usefulness."

[14] Alexander Campbell, "Berean College," *MH* 1857: 465 "We know brother Russell well. His talents and attainments eminently qualify him for such a position [President of Berean College]." Alexander Campbell, "Brother W. S. Russell," *MH*, 594 "Our much beloved Brother Russell."

[15] Z. T. Sweeney surmises it was because Russell was Campbell's nephew.

[16] Alexander Campbell, "The Christian Sentinel," *MH* 1857: 473.

[17] Alexander Campbell, "Notes on a Tour in Illinois," *MH* 1858: 21 "We spoke twice in the Christian Meeting-house to large assemblies of the brethren and citizens. While there, we also addressed the Students in Berean College, under the presidency of Bro. W. S. Russell, who is admirably qualified for the responsible position which he occupies. He also labors in the church with much satisfaction to the brethren and the citizens in attendance on his ministrations. We doubt not that he will be eminently useful in that city of schools and colleges, so intelligent and capable of appreciating his moral worth, his talents and attainments."

received too much attention and had played this to his advantage.[18] Lard, fully aware of the way the SCM press had handled Russell, and writing when the expulsion of the faction was a fait accompli, had no ambivalence toward Russell. In spite of Russell's education and professorship of 'Intellectual Philosophy,' Lard uses the metaphor of a dying candle-moth to mock Russell's education and supposed expertise in philosophy.[19]

"Reform the Reformation"

Lard associates "reform the reformation" with the Russell faction. Exactly when this phrase became associated with the defection is not clear. The concept, if not the actual phrase, may have been first used by a Baptist minister from Bloomington, Illinois, Herman J. Eddy, who attended as a guest, in Bloomington, the 1858 annual meeting of the Illinois Christian Missionary Society (ICMS). Eddy later stated:

> Rev. Mr. Russell, president of a college in Jacksonville, Illinois, and one of their ablest men, is a leader in this reform; and his views are entertained by Rev. Mr. Murphy and Prof. Loos, likewise connected with Western Colleges, with whom also are connected many of the best and most prominent ministers of the Campbellite body.[20]

Eddy's assertions lit off a firestorm within and outside the Movement. When P. H. Murphy disclaimed sympathy with Russell's teachings, he mentioned how far the Baptists had circulated the news of this "reforming of the reformation:"

---

[18] Daniel Bates, "Let Us Profit by the Past," *EI*1861: 89 - 92.

[19] "Berean College, Jacksonville," *Sangamo Journal*, June 12, 1858: 2. Russell's title was "President, and Professor of Sacred Literature and Intellectual Philosophy."

[20] C. L. Loos, "Rev. Mr. Eddy's Statement in 'The Christian Times,'" *MH* 1860: 78 – 80. "Illinois," "Ancient and Modern Pretenders: Russell, Melish & Co.," *ACR* 1860: 88.

...it [Eddy's article] has gone, as on the wings of the whirlwind, through their numerous periodicals, and, to facilitate circulation, even been struck in handbill-form![21]

The expression is repeated by period[22] and later writers such as W. T. Moore and James A. Meng, when referring to the Russell defection.[23]

The defection's agenda to "reform the reformation" is difficult to document since no issues of their periodical, the *Christian Freeman* survived. The following laundry list by Russell, however, likely represents the main points of their concerns about the Movement:

But we are convinced that the Reformation is in error in the following points:

1. It does not take the teachings of the whole Bible as its guide in preaching the gospel to sinners and instructing the church. But it restricts itself to certain passages in order to make out a consistent theory, and the result is the presentation of a one-sided and fractional view of the truth, and, in frequent instances, instead of accepting the plain and obvious sense of the Word, it holds to the glosses and paraphrases of human reason, and re-

---

[21] P. H. Murphy, "An Important Movement," *MH* 1860: 152. Baptist journals that carried information on Eddy's assertions are the *Christian Times*, Chicago, the *New York Chronicle* (both in *MH* 1860: 78, 79), the *Western Recorder*, Louisville, (Franklin, "Rejoicing in Iniquity," *ACR* 1859: 166), the *Western Watchman*, St. Louis, (*Bible Advocate* 1860: 108 – 113; C. L. Loos, "A Correction: 'Reformers Reforming," *ACR* 1860: 22) and the *Religious Herald*, Richmond, Virginia (Franklin, "Handling 'Defection' 'Without Gloves," *ACR* 1859: 78). The *Presbyterian Herald* also remarked on the Russell controversy: Franklin, "Rejoicing in Iniquity," *ACR* 1859: 166.

[22] Franklin, "Rejoicing in Iniquity," *ACR* 1859: 166: "As to Prest. Russell being a suitable man to reform the Reformation, we have not the least concern...but there was never a greater farce than to talk of his reforming the Reformation."

[23] Moore, *Comprehensive History*: 495, 496: "During the same period they were subjected to some very severe internal contentions. In 1860, a small defection in the ranks began to show itself in Jacksonville, Ill. W. S. Russell, a recent graduate of Bethany College, became convinced that he had a call to reform the Reformation." Moore's timing is too late. Rather than beginning, the defection was mostly over by 1860. Meng, *"No Danger Yet"*: 3: "In 1856, W. S. Russell...delivered his graduating speech on 'The Real and the Ideal,' which speech was bristling throughout with modern progressive ideas...with which he had stuffed his head and crowded out the plain teaching of the Bible. That speech elicited much comment, and indicated the course that he pursued in his attempt to reform the Reformation."

lies upon the writings of certain prominent men—appealing to 'our views' (to use the current phraseology) and the 'views of the Reformation,' instead of to the Bible. This we charge as a grave departure from the original fundamental principle of the church—that the Bible is the only rule of faith and practice— and as the source of the subsequent errors. In what particulars we understand this statement to be true will appear from the following specifications:

2. We strongly dissent from the generally accepted doctrine of the Reformation, that in the conversion of sinners the Spirit of God exerts his influence only through the written or preached Word; and also, from the view held, we have reason to believe, by the large majority of the church, that in the sanctification of believers the Spirit acts only through the Word. Our understanding of the Bible teaching is that the Word is the instrument in both conversion and sanctification, but the Spirit is the agent, acting directly upon the heart, in order to the attainments of these gracious results.

3. We have felt in our own experience, and seen in observing the practice of others, that the effect of the Reformation view above stated is to forbid sinners praying for themselves, and others praying in their behalf, in order to their conversion. Indeed, these godless views have often been openly preached. This view also has led members of the church to so undervalue the power of prayer—indeed, inducing skepticism as to God's answering prayer—as to result in a general neglect of hearty, faithful prayer in private, in the family, and in the public assembly. These evils, which we think are obvious to every impartial observer of Reformation churches, we deeply deplore, and feel it our duty to shield ourselves from their disastrous influence upon our spiritual life and upon the genuine conversion of the sinner; and we take steps to so guard our souls only after having used all reasonable efforts to dissuade from these errors those with whom we have been associated.

4. We have been impressed with the fact that the great scriptural truth of justification by faith is mutilated and weakened in the hands of the Reformation, by their giving undue prominence, in their preaching to unbelievers, to the ordinance of baptism, thus fostering reliance upon the merit of human works, and

making salvation to be not of grace but of debt. From this we dissent, for while we believe that the ordinance of baptism should be solemnly and prayerfully administered to every one believing in Christ with all his heart, yet we believe that the vital, unencumbered truth which it concerns the sinner to have singly fixed in his mind is that of justification through faith in Jesus.

5. We disagree with the Reformation when it denies to the convert the possibility of his having personal evidence of his sins being pardoned, and assurance given through the Spirit on condition of faith in Christ and earnest seeking of God in prayer. The practical influence of this error is to make conversion a superficial work, and is most injurious to the young believer and inconsistent with depth of piety in the church.

6. Finally, we are convinced that the whole tendency of these practical errors is against a devout, joyful, and assured religious life, the denial of a religion of the heart's experience, and, in any church which tolerates the teaching, deadening to the very life-principle of its spiritual activity.

It will be perceived from the above statement that those points in which we agree with the Reformation are mostly of a formal character, while those in which we disagree pertain to the living, practical principles of our holy religion; and the history of the Reformation thus far leads us to the conclusion that, while it has succeeded in restoring the simple *form* of primitive church order and practice, it has been drawn off from the *power* of godliness as it existed in the early church. Our humble endeavor, under God, is to bring about the union of both the power and form of godliness, in order to the full restoration of the primitive church to the world.[24]

---

[24] "President Russell's Statement" = No. 70 in "One Hundred Reasons Why Christian Ministers Do Not Preach Immersion in Water in order to the Remission of Sins…" *Christian Pulpit* 1.11 (November 1869) 389 – 393.

One point that many Movement writers conceded was the group's desire to see a higher level of spirituality.[25] Russell was known for his "innerlightism," his criticism of Baconian methodology, and his beliefs that the Holy Spirit played an immediate role in conversion and supernatural gifts of the Holy Spirit were available in modern times.[26]

Dabbling in "French Philosophy"

Lard uses "French philosophy" to refer to Russell's dependence on the French philosopher Victor Cousin. W. K. Pendleton's "Review of W. S. Russell" goes to great lengths to show how Cousin highly influenced Russell.[27] Other SCM writers explicitly trace Russell's philosophy to Cousin, Kant, et al.[28]

---

[25] Campbell, "Opinionisms No. I," *MH* 1859: 433 – 439: "Our young brother is rather sanguine in his temperament and assumes too much for his strength. I can sympathize with him in all his endeavors to elevate the standard of spirituality amongst our contemporaries, and especially amongst those who are preaching the Gospel of the Son of God." Isaac Errett, "The Church in Monmouth," *MH* 1861: 268: "But while deploring the extreme position into which some of these Jacksonville brethren have been led, let the brethren generally be careful lest they be tempted to neglect the just cause of complaint which is urged as an apology for this movement—the lack of spirituality—the failure to cultivate individual piety, family piety, and spiritual devotion in the churches." Russell, seizing upon the statement, claimed Errett was sympathetic to the defection.

[26] See Allen, *Things Unseen*, and the *ESCM* articles referenced in the bibliography.

[27] W. K. Pendleton, "Review of W. S. Russell," *MH* 1860: 202 – 205.

[28] I. N. Carman, "To the Christian Public," subscribed with Franklin's reply, *ACR* 1860: 10: "but those modern 'Disciples,' not of Jesus, but of Cousin, Kant and Hamilton, and especially some of the 'late pastors of the church of 'Disciples,'" Campbell, "Philosophy, Dogmatism, Schism," *MH* 1860: 13 – 20.

The curriculum at Bethany College included the study of these and other philosophers: "In the Department of Intellectual and Political Philosophy, in addition to the regular recitations of the text-books, lectures will be given, so as to place these topics, both in their history and present phases, fully and fairly before the minds of the students. The characteristic features of the different schools of metaphysics will be distinctly drawn and criticized, and a constant effort made to awaken in the consciousness of the student those mental states, the actions and laws of which he may be studying. Thus it is believed, he may be most successfully taught, not only the learning of the books, but the knowledge of himself. In this course of studies and instruction, reference will be frequently had to Kant, Cousin, Locke, Reid, Stewart, Brown, Coleridge, Sir William Hamilton, &c., &c." *Bethany College Catalogue for 1857*: 18, 19. Moore and Meng, op. cit.

Wrecking a Church

Dingman, downplaying Lard's statement that the Russell defection "well nigh wrecked a church," concluded that Russell did not "destroy a prominent SCM church." The congregation at Jacksonville, if not the largest congregation in Illinois at the time, was among the most prominent and had a rich history tracing back to Barton W. Stone.[29] The circumstances at Jacksonville were as volatile as those in Nashville: A dynamic, but schismatic personality split the church and caused a controversy in the congregation and community that last for more than six years.[30] The situation was so hostile that Franklin was not allowed to preach in the building when he went to Jacksonville in August of 1860.[31] While Lard implies that only one congregation was affected, articles written during the controversy provide three locations: Jacksonville, Illinois, (the location at which Lard hinted), Ashland and Cincinnati, Ohio.[32]

---

[29] J. Rogers, "Notes of a Tour to the West—President Russell, Etc.—No. III," *ACR* 1859: 204: "I grieve, however, over the schism in Jacksonville. I grieve to know that a schism exists—I grieve to know that my brethren and dear friends, and the fast friends and admirers of my venerated father Stone, are in it. And I grieve most of all to know that the name of Stone is used to give countenance to certain errors of Russell with which he had no sympathy. Russell's positions make the word of God a dead letter---a perfect nullity. Stone made the word of God the standard of all religious truth."

[30] As the controversy over Russell became more widely known in the Movement, a vote was taken in August 1859 on whether to keep Russell as minister of the congregation. The vote passed, partially because church members who opposed Russell did not cast ballots. Following the split, Russell's followers took control of the building and occupied it until the case over ownership was decided by the Illinois Supreme Court in favor of the minority who opposed Russell. Doyle, 1978: 158 – 160. "The anti-Russellites lost the election two years straight, issuing formal protests to the congregation before each poll was taken. In 1859 they bolted the church and set up their own "true Church of Christ" in rented space in the courthouse. Later they brought suit against the majority and claimed to be the only rightful heirs of the church founded by Barton Stone."

[31] Franklin, "The Cause in Jacksonville, Illinois," *ACR* 1860: 140. The elders of the Jacksonville congregation gave the reason for denying Franklin access to the building in "Eld. B. Franklin," *ACR*, 1860: 148. The article was first published in the *Christian Freeman*. "This reason is the abusive and unchristian language he has used concerning our pastor, W. S. Russell, in his paper, the *Review*, of Cincinnati."

[32] Franklin, "The Defection Again," *ACR* 1859: 74.

"A Few Unstable and Erratic Spirits"

Admittedly, Lard could have given more detail on W. S. Russell and the "few unstable and erratic spirits" who were his sympathizers. Based on the scant information Lard provides, Dingman underestimates the significance of the defection. By stating Russell was the "only lasting casualty," he overlooks the "few unstable and erratic spirits" Lard mentions.

Besides Russell, these men who were implicated in the defection: I. N. Carman, (editor of the *Christian Sentinel* in 1857); T. J. Melish and George Tait (leaders in the Sixth Street congregation in Cincinnati); O. A. Burgess and B. W. Johnson, (professors at Eureka College in Illinois); W. W. Happy Sr., and S. T. Callaway (both were veteran SCM preachers from Jacksonville, were elders of the Jacksonville congregation and were officers of the ICMS); W. W. Happy Jr., and Philip Lucas (professors at Berean College under Russell's presidency; Lucas was also secretary of the ICMS), Jonathan Atkinson (former president of Berean College) and Francis Apperson (Vermont, Illinois).[33]

People who were stated as sympathetic to Russell, by Russell himself or by other writers, but made public disclaimers of their association or sympathy with him are Isaac Errett,[34] Robert Richardson,[35] P. H. Murphy[36] and C. L. Loos.[37] Writing from the shadow of a pseudonym, "Illinois" asked two Bloomington, Illinois, SCM ministers, Brothers Lamphear [sic] and Smith to declare their status with the defection. Franklin's

---

[33] The list is compiled from *Sweeney's Sermons* 1892; Haynes 1915; Z. T. Sweeney, 1923; Franklin, "The Defection Again," *ACR* 1859: 62. Carman, Callaway, Melish and Happy Sr. left for the Baptists. "Burgess, Johnson, Atkinson and many others had their eyes opened, and kept their places with the brotherhood." "Lucas went to the law." (ZTS) Happy Jr. died in 1862. http://www.findagrave.com/cgi-bin/fg.cgi?page=gr&GRid=71430876; Tait and Apperson's status after the expulsion is not known.

[34] Isaac Errett, "The Church in Monmouth, Illinois," *MH* 1861: 262 – 269; "The Christian Freeman," MH 1861: 475 – 476. "But if the design of the *Freeman's* remarks above quoted, is to intimate that we ever had sympathy, or association with Russell & Co., in the peculiar features of their plea, or in anything different from what we now preach and teach, we have only to meet it with an emphatic denial."

[35] Robert Richardson, "Misrepresentations and Speculations," *Evangelist* 1860: 58: "One of our editors persists in falsely accusing me of holding Pres. Russell's views, and this, not only without evidence, but contrary to evidence."

[36] P. H. Murphy, "An Important Movement," *MH* 1860: 151 – 152.

[37] C. L. Loos, "Rev. Mr. Eddy's Statement in 'The Christian Times,'" *MH* 1860: 78 – 80.

comments on the article show his concern that people come clean about their relationship to Russell:

> We hope, for the honor of the cause, that brethren will state whether they are to be thus named, and by implication accused of such complicity as this, especially the brethren named in Bloomington, Ill.[38]

Additional Developments in Illinois

"Can We Divide?" does not mention these additional developments in Illinois that were a direct result of the Russell controversy:

The Demise of the Christian Sentinel

Started in August of 1853, the *Christian Sentinel* was the fourth Illinois-based periodical published by the brotherhood.[39] Similar to earlier periodical efforts in Illinois, it had a tenuous history and appeared to be destined to a short life. Senior editor, O. A. Burgess, however, was optimistic about its future in January of 1857 when I. N. Carman joined the editorial staff.[40] Associate editor and proprietor, John Lindsey, summarized the prospects for the paper:

> We can but feel to rejoice that the *Sentinel*, which, when our connection as proprietor and one of its editors commenced, was by no means popular, and its list of subscribers reduced to some two or three hundred, should have become, in the space of a single year, one of the most popular monthlies in our entire ranks. And, although we cannot fully indorse all that its pages

---

[38] "Illinois," "An Important Movement," *ACR* 1860: 16, followed by remarks by Franklin. The article touched off a series of *ACR* articles on the subject of heresy hunting: E. W. Bakewell, "Heresy Hunting," *ACR* 1860: 50, 51; B. K. Smith, "Heresy Hunting No. II," *ACR* 1860: 192; "Heresy Hunting No. III," *ACR* 1860: 200.

[39] Haynes, 663, 664.

[40] O. A. Burgess, "Introductory Remarks," *CSent*, 4.1 (January 1857) 1, 2. During 1856 some issues were not printed because of a fire at the printer. Burgess decided to begin a new numbering of the issues with volume four, in January of 1857. There were at least four issues of the *CS* in 1858. E. L. Craig refers to pages 100 – 101 of volume five of the *CS* in "The Issue as it Really Is," an article that appeared in the *Bible Advocate* and was reprinted by Franklin in *ACR* 1859: 78, 79.

contain, it has excited more admiration, more joy, and more jeal-
ousy too, than any paper of its circulation now in the religious
world. And its list of subscribers is most rapidly increasing, all
the time.

During 1857, however, the *Christian Sentinel's* loyalty to the movement
came under growing suspicion because of controversial articles by Carman, Russell and Burgess.[41] Burgess and Lindsey left the editorial staff at
the end of 1857, leaving Carman to take the brunt of attack.[42]

In what can be considered a "hostile takeover," in the late spring of
1858, E. L. Craig and John S. Sweeney bought out the *Christian Sentinel,*
"to get it out of the hands of the defection."[43] The pair established the
Bible Advocate at Jacksonville and with the change in ownership, Russell
and Carman lost control of what had been a ready vehicle for their writings.[44]

---

[41] In addition to articles by Carman (on Conscience) and Russell (on the Holy Spirit)
noted by Allen in *Things Unseen* 96, notes 36 – 45, noteworthy is O. A. Burgess,
"American Scholarship," (*CSent* 1857: 65 -74), an exposition of Baconian
methodology. Opposition to the editors' views first appeared in the *Christian Sentinel*
in April 1857 in an unattributed editorial comment: "We are in receipt of certain
letters which make it proper to say that the *Sentinel* is not to be held accountable for
anything but the contents of its pages, and that any impressions concerning the views of
any of its editors, expressed or rumored to have been expressed by them,
individually, at any time and place, are things for which the *Sentinel* is in no sense
responsible." *CSent* 1857: 126. Sikes wrongly attribute the article to I. N. Carman.
Allen followed suit.

[42] *CSent,* 4.12(December 1857): Burgess, "To the Readers of the Christian Sentinel,"
376. John Lindsey, "Valedictory," 378.

[43] John S. Sweeney, "The Christian Sentinel," *C-E,* 1884: 22, 23.

[44] No issues of the *BA* for 1858 survive. Some 1859 issues are extant in private
collections, including McMillan's. Walter Sikes quotes from two different issues
from 1859. All issues for 1860 and 1861 are available on microfilm at Lincoln
Christian University, Lincoln, Illinois, and Christian Theological Seminary,
Indianapolis, Indiana. No issues from 1862 are extant. Aaron Chatterton, editor of
a sister SCM publication in Davenport, Iowa, noted the appearance of the *BA* and
its relationship to the *CS*: "The first two numbers of *"The Bible Advocate,"* edited
and published by E. L. CRAIG, Jacksonville, Ill., are received at this office. This
Publication takes the place of *"The Christian Sentinel.'"* The *Advocate* comes freighted
with good matter, and we wish it abundant success in "the promotion of an earnest
church and a higher christian [sic] life." *CE* 1858: 432.

A Leadership Coup

In 1859 the churches in Illinois took an organized step. Three Russell sympathizers were officers in the ICMS: W. W. Happy, president; S. T. Callaway, treasurer; and Philip Lucas, secretary.[45] In August 1859, Benjamin Franklin described the history of the Russell defection and its ever-widening attempts to "reform the reformation." Franklin called for the Illinois churches to take action:

> But we should think that the case of Prest. Russell was rendered sufficiently clear for the action of the churches in Illinois now. His palpable errors have been shown up sufficiently by almost every publication in the brotherhood.

Closing the article, Franklin feared a rumored alliance involving the defection would be presented at the State Missionary Meeting:

> We fear one trouble. The State Missionary Meeting in Illinois is at hand, and we fear this matter [the rumored alliance JLM] will create trouble there.[46]

Franklin's fears were not realized. Word came from Illinois:

> We have not seen the minutes of the Illinois meeting, but learn that Russellism and Russellites are cleaned out of the Board, and that sound men are elected... The brethren will put their mark on every one of those factious men throughout the land. Not one of them will find support among the brethren in a short time.[47]

---

[45] *Sweeney's Sermons*; Haynes uses the section with some corrections; Z. T. Sweeney 1923 draws heavily on the *Sweeney's Sermons* account but adds details, most notably, and without documentation, that O. A. Burgess and B. W. Johnson were sympathetic to Russell.

[46] Benjamin Franklin, "President Russell's Case," *ACR* 1859: 134. Minutes of the Jacksonville Christian Church in June 1864 mention that W. W. Happy proposed affiliating with the Baptists. Additionally, I. N. Carman, who became a Baptist after he left the SCM, at the same time preached a trial sermon for the congregation, intending to become the minister.

[47] Benjamin Franklin, "Illinois State Missionary Society," *ACR* 1859: 154.

The Closing of Berean College

Another result of the Russell controversy was the closing of Berean College at Jacksonville in 1860. Chartered in1854, the college opened in 1855 with a $30,000.00 building. Since Russell was president of the college, and others in the faction were involved in its leadership, dropping support was another way to squelch the defection.[48]

The Christian Freeman

Realizing options for voicing their opinions had nearly disappeared in SCM journals, Russell, Carman and Melish established the *Christian Freeman* at Jacksonville in January 1860.[49] No issues of the journal are extant, but there are enough excerpts of the *Christian Freeman* in other Movement periodicals to determine the trio used the journal to continue to their efforts to "reform the reformation."[50]

Conclusions

Russell did not start out to "lead out a sect." His study of the scriptures led him to conclusions that ran counter to the Movement's. In early 1860, Robert Richardson gave Russell the only option that would save him to the Movement:

---

[48] Doyle, *Social Order* 156 – 161. The building, built at a cost of $30,000.00, sold for $12,000.00 at a sheriff's sale in 1863. "Berean College became Original Hospital Building," one page flier in Berean College folder at Jacksonville Public Library, accessed 4.13.2011. Walter's father, Charles E. Russell, and a younger brother, Robert D., were living in the building in 1868. (*Polk City Directory, Jacksonville, Illinois* 100.) That same year, the building was donated to an organization that later became Passavant Hospital. For more detail, see Chapter 9: Restorationist Colleges in Illinois.

[49] "A Disciple," "Mr. Eddy Again," *BA* 1860: 225, 226: "Russell's pieces were published in that periodical [Aaron Chatterton's *Christian Evangelist* Eds.] and replied to by the editor until his readers became tired of reasoning in a circle, and until he had forfeited all claims to be heard in any periodical under the control of the brethren connected with the church of Christ."

[50] Chatterton, *EI* 1860: 190; 287. "Omega," "The Place of Faith in the Gospel Scheme," *MH* 1861: 206 – 214. Errett articles above.

The only proper course for him is candidly to acknowledge his error and forever to abandon all speculation and opinionism.[51]

Russell's decision to stand by his convictions forced the Movement to expel him. As Dingman correctly states, "the SCM press mobilized." The efforts of several SCM editors, especially Benjamin Franklin, and the public censure of Alexander Campbell and his proxy, W. K. Pendleton,[52] combined with the concerted efforts of the Illinois churches, amounted to a "crusade"[53] that dealt the death blow to the Russell defection. Lard's hyperbolic "thousand noble sentinels ... sound[ed] the alarm,"[54] exposed the faction and drove them from the Movement.

---

[51] "Misrepresentations and Speculations," *EI* 1860: 61. The entire article deals with the Russell defection.

[52] Campbell refused to deal any further with Russell and gave Pendleton the task of responding to Russell's letters to Campbell. *MH* 1860: WSR, "Letter from W. S. Russell" 135 – 140; 194 – 198. WKP, "Remarks upon W. S. Russell's Article," 140 – 147; "Review of W. S. Russell," 198 – 207.

[53] Allen, *ESCM* 661 sees a "crusade" led by John S. Sweeney based on Z. T. Sweeney, "The Walter Scott Russell Crisis." Z. T.'s article has several errors. Sweeney places the events in Eureka, Illinois, in late 1860, well after the defection had been expelled. The account is embellished and hagiographic, reflecting Z. T.'s admiration for his older brother. A careful reading of the article shows no evidence of a "crusade" led by John S. Sweeney. According to the article, John's reputation as a debater was known but his status toward the Russell defection was not known until he delivered his sermon on John 16 at the annual meeting of the ICMS. This paper provides strong evidence that there was a crusade against the Russell defection; and John Sweeney may have been involved in the crusade, but Z. T. Sweeney's account of the sermon by JSS at the ICMS meeting gives no basis for concluding John led the crusade or that a single sermon by JSS was the pivotal point in defeating the Russell defection.

[54] Lard, "Can We Divide?" 333: "This attempt [by John Thomas], too, was made at a time when we were comparatively weak,—at a time when we had not, as we now have, a thousand noble sentinels on the walls of Zion, imbued with an intense love of the truth and a never-lessening zeal for its purity, sentinels who, with sleepless eye, watch even the most distant approach of error, and [at] once sound loud the note of alarm. Yet, if the attempt then failed, what, we may confidently ask, would be the end of a similar one now?"

Bibliography of Secondary Source Treatments of the Controversy

This is a select, chronological and annotated bibliography of articles or references, by editors, historians or biographers, to W. S. Russell or the Russell defection written after Russell's death in November 1863.

1866

Moses E. Lard, *Can We Divide?*, Lard's Quarterly, Volume 3, Number 3, April 1866, pages 330 – 335. Page 334 discusses Russell.

Online: http://www.geocities.ws/moseslard/qtrly/divide.htm

While there are numerous articles about the defection during its existence, this is the earliest known reflective article on the defection after Russell's death in November 1863. Lard also mentions John Thomas and Jesse B. Ferguson as schismatic personalities.

Lard's article is reprinted verbatim in Gospel Echo, Volume 4, Number 8, August, 1866, pages 318 – 323, with this introduction: "The following article is from Lard's Quarterly, and we think it should be published in all our papers. It has in it the true metal, and we have no doubt of its representing the feeling of our great brotherhood, generally. There are a few brethren, North and South, who manifest a sectional spirit, but their numbers are very limited, and they will yet learn better. Let us all labor to regain and maintain the unity of the Spirit in the bond of peace, and all will work well. Ed." [Ed. = E. L. Craig]

1869

Editorial ("*Bro. H. T. Anderson's Article*,") by Moses E. Lard, in Apostolic Times, Volume 1, Number 14, July 15, 1869, 108, states: "Finally from Bro. Anderson: 'Man has within him, from God, the power to cognize the true, the beautiful, and the good, and with the Messiah before him revealing these, he can know all that is knowable in the present state.' Here we have it all at last—Cousin, instead of God, innerlightism, instead of the Bible. Contingently, man can know in and of himself all that is knowable in the present state. He can know the true; he hence has no use for the Bible to reveal it to him. He can know the good, know the right, know his duty; he hence has no need of the New Testament to teach him these! Poor Walter Scott Russell is not likely, after all, to sleep alone beneath the shadows and glory of innerlightism. How Bro. H. T. Anderson could ever become the author of such a document as we today reprint from his pen, is a profound mystery to us. To say that such productions fill our souls with deepest sorrow, but mildly expresses our emotions. If these sentiments are to prevail, farewell to the primitive gospel, farewell to all that Alexander [sic] Campbell and Walter Scott exhumed or ever achieved. It has seen its day, spent its force, done it [sic] work, and henceforth sleeps the sleep of death." [Anderson's article to which Lard refers is "Salus Populi Sumprema Lex—The Safety of the People is the Supreme Law," *Apostolic Times*, Volume 1, Number 14, July 15, 1869, page 105.]

1874

James A. Meng, "No Danger Yet," (*Apostolic Times*, 6.29 (October 22, 1874) 3. Besides Russell, the article also lists J. B. Ferguson, Calvin Reasoner and W. C. Dawson as examples of SCM members who were not attacked soon enough after they started teaching unsound doctrines. "In 1856, W. S. Russell, a fellow graduate of mine, delivered his graduating speech on 'The Real and the Ideal,' which speech was bristling throughout with modern progressive ideas, obtained from 'Kant's Critique of Pure Reason,' Morsell's [sic] Philosophy, Cousin's History of Philosophy, Psychology, True Beautiful and good [sic], and other works of kindred style and character, with which he had stuffed his head and crowded out the plain teaching of the Bible. That speech elicited much comment, and indicated the course that he pursued in his attempt to reform the Reformation."

1879

Joseph Franklin and J. A. Headington, *The Life and Times of Benjamin Franklin*. (St. Louis: John Burns, 1879.), 315-317; 356 – 377. Discusses the Richardson versus Fanning controversy; references to 'young men' are undoubtedly to Russell and Carman, who portrayed Franklin as an 'unschooled' editor. On 377, the Baptist minister Herman J. Eddy is mentioned in connection with Russell. Additional context is quoted from Eddy's article in the *Christian Times* where Eddy mentions hearing Russell preach at the Bloomington meeting of the ICMS.

1880

John F. Rowe and G. W. Rice, *Biographical Sketch and Writings of Elder Benjamin Franklin*, Written and Compiled by John F. Rowe, Editor and G. W.

Rice, Co-Editor, American Christian Review, Volume 1. (Cincinnati: Published by G. W. Rice. 4th edition, 1881), 41, 42. Mentions Russell, Carman and Melish.

1884

John S. Sweeney, "The Christian Sentinel," *C-E*, 1884: 22, 23. Sweeney states that he and Elijah L. Craig bought out the *Christian Sentinel* to get it out of the control of the "Russell, Melish Carman defection, so called" and established the *Bible Advocate*.

1892

John S. Sweeney, *Sweeney's Sermons by John S. Sweeney, with a Sketch of the Author's Life by an Intimate Friend*. (Nashville: Gospel Advocate, 1892.) On pages 25-32, the anonymous biographer (undoubtedly Z. T. Sweeney) describes John Sweeney's role in defeating the Russell defection. The account is marred by inaccuracies of date and location but provides the names of several members of the defection. The details from this account are borrowed by N. Haynes in his 1915 history of the Disciples in Illinois (see below), with some details corrected. Sweeney also draws from this account in his 1923 Christian Standard article (see below), adding and changing some details.

1901

J. H. Garrison, editor, *The Reformation of the Nineteenth Century*, section by B. B. Tyler, "The Period of Organization," 158: "To this decade also belongs the founding and failure of Berea [sic; Berean] College, at Jacksonville, Ill., through the heretical teaching of Walter S. Russell, its president."

1902

Frederick D. Power, *Life of William Kimbrough Pendleton, LL. D., President of Bethany College*. (St. Louis: Christian publishing company, 1902), 196. "During the current year he gives much attention to Messrs, Russell and Carman, who had been 'bottling moonshine' on the question of the operation of the Holy Spirit, a subject which Mr. Pendleton always handled with great clearness and force."

1909

W. T. Moore, *A Comprehensive History of the Disciples of Christ.* New York: Fleming H. Revell Company, 1909. 495, 496 (in Chapter XIX, The Turbulent Period), describes "W. S. Russell and I. N. Carmen [sic] bottling 'moon-shine.'"

1915

N. S. Haynes, *History of the Disciples of Christ in Illinois, 1820-1914.* (Cincinnati: Standard Publishing, 1915), 61, 62; 619, 620. Haynes relies heavily upon the account in *Sweeney's Sermons* (see above), correcting some details, including the location of the meeting (Bloomington rather than Eureka, per *Sweeney's Sermons*) and the year (1858 rather than 1860). *ACR* 1859 142 confirms the meeting was at Bloomington in September 1859: "Special Notices: The next State Meeting of the Disciples in Illinois will be held with the church in Bloomington, commencing on Thursday before the fourth Lord's day in September. A general attendance is requested."

1923

Z. T. Sweeney, "The W. S. Russell Crisis," *Christian Standard* 1923: 539, 540. This article is one of a six part series on 'Crises in the Restoration Movement.' John Sweeney's role in defeating the Russell defection is the focus and it adds little information, mostly repeating the information in *Sweeney's Sermons.* The article includes O. A. Burgess and B. W. Johnson as sympathetic to Russell. Neither had been associated by name with the defection until this article.

Prior to 1966

Walter Sikes (1896-1966), Disciples historian and social advocate, had a section on the Russell controversy in his unpublished history of the Disciples, *Responsible Denominationalism,* referenced by C. Leonard Allen in footnote 36 on page 96 in *Things Unseen*: "I am indebted to an unpublished paper by Walter Sikes (located in the Disciples of Christ Historical Society) for first introducing me to the Russell controversy."

1978

Don Harrison Doyle, *The Social Order of a Frontier Community: Jacksonville, Illinois, 1825 – 70* (Urbana: University of Illinois Press, 1978) 156 – 160. Doyle provides details on Russell's ministry, the split in 1858, and the re-uniting of the Jacksonville congregation in 1866.

1981

Leroy Garrett, *The Stone-Campbell Movement: An Anecdotal History of Three Churches.* (Joplin: College Press, 1981) 376-379. Second edition 1994 with title *The Stone-Campbell Movement: The Story of the American Restoration Movement)* 256, 257. Garrett, unaware of Carman's efforts as corresponding editor of the *Christian Freeman* in 1860 and 1861, and Carman's trial sermon in Jacksonville in June 1864, wrongly states of Carman: "He quietly dropped out of the picture."

1983

Earl Irvin West, *Elder Ben Franklin: Eye of the Storm.* (Indianapolis: Religious Book Service, 1983.) West, 49, 119, 161-165, advocated Russell and company were foisting "Christian Perfectionism" upon the brotherhood. West includes numerous footnotes to Franklin's articles on the Russell controversy.

1986

Emanuel Daugherty, *Pioneer Preachers – Benjamin Franklin.* "Material originally presented at Memphis School of Preaching Lectures – 1986."

> "Also during this period, the question of "Christian Perfectionism" with its mystical subjectivism lending itself to spiritual arrogance became a heated issue. W.S. Russell, I. N. Carmen, T.J. Melish, and George Tait were the principle men connected to this new heresy. "Their sermons amd [sic] writings were filled with expression of the 'inner light,' or 'spiritual illumination'." (West, Eye, 162). The biographers of Franklin conclude that it was the teaching of Professor Robert Richardson and his views of the indwelling of the Holy Spirit that started these men toward apostasy. Richardson believed that Campbell and others had dwelt long enough on "first principles but it

was now time to go on to perfection." Richardson stated that there was a "higher law" of human nature, a spiritual perception which is to be quickened by the Holy Spirit, and without which quickening none can be spiritually minded or enjoy the things of the Spirit. (Franklin & Headington, 354-56). (This entire chapter in Franklin & Headington's biography ought to be read and studied extensively in the face of present efforts to compromise truth in regard to the leading of the Spirit - EBD). Franlkin [sic] gives some of his reasons for his vigorous opposition to this error in the Review as quoted by West: "We do not dislike this new phrase that has appeared among us because it aims at a deeper piety in our devotion or a greater spirituality, for we do not believe there is anything of this sort in it; but we dislike it because it turns men's attention away from the Bible and from the obedience which the Lord requires. In the place of turning the attention of man to the teachings of the Holy Spirit in the Bible, it turns his attention to the so-called 'divinity within' the 'voice of conscience' or the 'inner light' for divine instruction or divine direction. In the place of directing men's attention to what God requires him to do, it leads him to theorize on the work of the Spirit. These theorizers appear not to perceive that the Spirit is not induced to act upon man by theorizing about his work, or the manner of it."(West, Eye, 164)."

http://ohiovalleyrestorationresearch.com/preacher-profiles/45-pioneer-preachers-benjamin-franklin

1990

Jimmy Jividen, *Alive in the Spirit!*, (Nashville, Tenn.: Gospel Advocate, 1990), 113: "Within the Restoration Movement were both extreme views of the work of the Holy Spirit in conversion. Alexander Campbell, following John Locke's theory of knowledge, defended the exclusive agency of the Word of God in conversion. Jessie B. Ferguson in Nashville and W. S. Russell in Illinois held to the "direct operation of the Holy Spirit" in conversion. Tolbert Fanning became the most outspoken advocate of the view that the Holy Spirit can work in the world only through the Word of God. More recently Guy N. Woods and Foy E. Wallace Jr. argued this view. Robert Richardson, though denying the work of the Holy Spirit in conversion, advocated that the Holy Spirit did personally dwell in the child of God." [Quoted on page 18, footnote 9, in "The Holy

Spirit: Nashville School of Preaching and Biblical Studies, Winter 2005."
http://www.god-answers.org/Online_Tools/books/Holy%20Spirit.pdf]

1993

Dr. Robert E. Hooper, *A Distinct People: A History of the Churches of Christ in the 20th Century*. (Eugene OR: Wipf and Stock Publishers, 1993) 12:

> "Probably Fanning's strongest argument was against a speech delivered at Bethany College and included in the *Millennial Harbinger*. Written and presented by W. S. Russell, a young graduate of Bethany, it was endorsed by Campbell. An appalled Fanning saw elements of natural theology in the presentation. Richardson was one of Russell's teachers. He [sic; it was Campbell rather than Richardson who gave his blessings for the speech, etc.] gave his blessings to the speech and placed it in the *Harbinger*. The source of Russell's ideas was clear—at least to Fanning."

1999

Darren Ross Johnson, *Tolbert Fanning vs. Robert Richardson: Battling for the Birthrights of the 'People of the Book.'* (M.Div. Thesis, Emanuel School of Religion). Johnson (50 and 97) sees Russell and Carman as 'young Romantics' who pled for a return to apostolic spirituality.

2002

Douglas A. Foster and Michael W. Casey, *The Stone-Campbell Movement: an International Religious Tradition*, (Knoxville: University of Tennessee Press, 2002) 24.

> "Significant work needs to be done in this area. Campbell's view stands in stark contrast to the predominant view of Protestant revivalists and has put the movement on the fringe of Protestantism on this issue for much of its history. The Richardson controversy may indicate that differences over pneumatology played a role in the divisions of the movement. Many reformers of the tradition, from the obscure W. S. Russell (1832-1863) in the nineteenth century to Don Finto (1930-), who played a key role in the development of contemporary Christian music in the twentieth, have turned to revivalist, Holiness, and Pentecostal

notions of the Holy Spirit to initiate change in the tradition. Many in the tradition have left the movement and its rationalistic pneumatology for Pentecostal versions."

2004

C. Leonard Allen, *Things Unseen: Churches of Christ in (and After) the Modern Age*. (Siloam Springs, Arkansas: Leafwood Publishers, 2004.) Allen, 38, 71 and 82-87, provides a detailed analysis of Russell's theology and the surrounding controversy. Allen uncritically accepts Z. T. Sweeney's account of John S. Sweeney's role in leading a 'crusade' against Russell's supporters. Allen incorrectly attributes an article, by O. A. Burgess, detailing weaknesses in Baconianism, to I. N. Carman.

C. Leonard Allen, "Walter Scott Russell" *Encyclopedia of the Stone-Campbell Movement*, (Grand Rapids: Eerdmans, 2004) 660, 661. A condensed version of the section from *Things Unseen*. See also: 170 ('Charismatics' by Thomas H. Olbricht,) 386 ('Heresy, Heretics' by Leroy Garrett) and 641 ('Restoration' by Robert O. Fife).

2014

Wesley F. Dingman, "Can we Divide?" Revisited: The Rhetoric of Moses Lard's Treatise against Division. *Restoration Quarterly* Volume 56, Number 4, Fall 2014, 193 – 207. A section of the article deals with the three schismatics Lard gave as examples of people who tried to, but did not cause a division in the SCM: Dr. John Thomas, Jesse B. Ferguson and Walter Scott Russell. Dingman doesn't cover much new ground in the Russell section, relying mostly on existing research. The section on Russell is weak because Dingman does not realize how many people were sympathetic to Russell and left the Movement with Russell.

11. Illinois and Instrumental Music[1]

The Sand Creek controversy about innovations in the SCM, including instrumental music, took place in Illinois in 1889, drawing national attention to Illinois. This chapter presents earlier IM developments in Illinois, since Sand Creek was a much later controversy. The discussions of instrumental music in Illinois were not unique, nor were they earlier than the developments in other states, but, as we show in this chapter, developments in Illinois are representative of how attitudes toward instrumental music changed from adamant opposition in all quarters to growing acceptance in some quarters by the end of the nineteenth century. To contextual events in Illinois, we also refer to national developments in the SCM.

Along with the existence and support of missionary societies, the introduction of instrumental music in the SCM is the other main point of controversy that led to the division of the Movement into two streams. Heated discussion on the society question began well before the establishment of the American Christian Missionary Society in 1849 and continued to the end of the 19th century and beyond. Light discussion on the instrument question began in the late 1840s, heated up in the early 1860s and became constant through the end of the 19th century. The latent division was formalized in 1906 with the separate listing of a cappella Churches of Christ in the religious census.

It will help the reader to know that virtually every Reformed faith group in North America dealt with the issue of remaining a cappella. Baptists, Congregationalists, Presbyterians, to name a few, had the same discussions on instrumental music as the SCM. A cappella Churches of

---

[1] The number of periodical articles, tracts, pamphlets, monographs and debates—both published and reported—on instrumental music is legion. It is beyond the scope of this work to give a bibliography of items that pertain to Illinois, let alone the entire SCM. We cite a significant number of sources in this chapter.

Christ remain the largest faith group that has not adopted instrumental music and are widely known for that belief.[2]

To develop fully the subject of instrumental music requires investigating ancillary subjects such as tuning forks, choirs, instruments in homes, music tastes, hymnbooks, and singing schools. For example, Alexander Campbell held strong opinions about hymnbooks—urging that the SCM use only one hymnbook—his;[3] he also strongly opposed singing schools.[4] Also important is the tendency for the Movement's leaders to urge congregants to avoid extravagance in personal lives and congregations to build plain meeting houses.

Early Attitudes toward Music in Illinois

Haynes' history does not trace the earliest use of IM in Illinois. He uses "instrumental music" nine different times: eight are references to late nineteenth century debates or controversies on instrumental music, including Sand Creek. In his Miscellanea chapter in "The Old Songs" essay, he describes the songs and singing of the "early churches" of Illinois but does not give the exact years he describes. He clearly has in mind the period before the 1860s, when, as we show in this chapter, music tastes began to evolve:

> The singing, being properly regarded as worship, was never turned over to professionals. God's children praised him. There were no choirs, quartets or soloists nor musical instruments, except sometimes a tuning-fork. A musical brother—generally an officer or the preacher—"raised the tune" or "started the hymns." Frequently he marked the time by a patting of his foot on the floor. Generally he "lined out" the words, for hymnbooks were few and sold high. But the Disciples did not take kindly to "lining out." It was lacking in simplicity and equality, upon which they insisted.[5]

---

[2] Thomas H. Olbricht, "Acappella Singing in Early American Churches," *RQ*, 57.2 (Second Quarter, 2015) 65 – 76.

[3] J. E. Choate and William Woodson, *Sounding Brass and Clanging Cymbals: The History and Significance of Instrumental Music in the Restoration Movement (1827 – 1968)* (Henderson, Tennessee: Williams Printing, 1991) 6 "Campbell never gave up the idea that the Restoration churches should have but one hymnal."

[4] Preface to the 1828 edition of Campbell's *Psalms, Hymns, and Spiritual* Songs, cited by Choate, *Sounding Brass*: 3, 4

[5] Haynes, 668.

Some, however, regarded tuning-forks (and part singing) as unacceptable:

> The following incident illustrates the viewpoint and experiences
> of many Disciples in the fifties and sixties. The services in union
> chapel were by rotation, the preachers taking their days. A young
> man from New England came to the village. Having a good
> voice, he was pleased to assist in the singing at church. He used a
> tuning-fork to help pitch the tunes. He sang the tenor. Here
> were two unheard-of things in the community—a tuning-fork
> and a tenor. This at once brought to his feet one of the aged
> rulers of the assembly. He informed the young man that he
> "must drop that pinching-bug and dry up that mulebraying." His
> indignation spread so that not until the young man was arrested,
> tried and fined $5 for disturbing public worship, was the wrath
> of the righteous man appeased.[6]

Most of the earliest mentions of music in Illinois periodicals deal with
the benefits of singing and do not address accompaniment. In 1828,
however, Barton W. Stone, still in Kentucky, but later to reside in Illinois,
spoke disparagingly of instrumental music:

> We have just received an extraordinary account of about 30,000
> Methodists in England, withdrawing from that church and con-
> nexion, because the Conference disapproved of the introduction
> of instrumental music in the churches. The full account shall
> appear in our next. To us, backwoods Americans, this conduct
> of those seceders [sic] appears to be the extreme of folly, and it
> argues that they have a greater taste for music, than they have for
> religion. Editor.[7]

In September 1843, Stone returned to Jacksonville from a several
months' tour of Indiana, Ohio and Kentucky and reflected on what he
saw as disturbing trends in worship, particularly in congregational singing:

> Another thing which seems to have checked the great excite-
> ment, is the want of solemnity in the worship, and in the house

---

[6] Haynes, 186.

[7] Editor [Barton W. Stone], *CM*, 3.2 (December 1828) 48. Stone here made clear his
distaste for instrumental music. He gives more details about the Methodist
secession in later issues of that volume but instrumental music is not mentioned
again. See No. 3, (January 1829) 72 and No. 4, (February 1829) 89, 90.

of God. When the people meet for worship, no one prays or exhorts till the preachers come. True, they sing, but too often with new theatrical, or piano tunes applied to sacred songs without solemnity either in the tune or singer—only a few join, the rest being unacquainted with the tune or song, and before it is learned, another of the same class is introduced. To me it appeared to be a labored exhibition of skill in music (if music it be) rather than solemn worship.[8]

Associate editor of Stone's *Christian Messenger*, D. Pat Henderson, in a several part series, "The Wants of the Churches," echoes the need for Christians to avoid worldly pleasures associated with dance halls and pianos:

There are too many, who are devoted to fashion and folly...Alas! What a sad picture is opened to our minds when we see professed Christians...moving forward in all the vanity and amusements of this corrupted and degenerate age. Indeed, I find by perusing periodicals, that it is deemed necessary in some places for an Editor to raise his voice—to wield his pen in showing Christians that the ball-room—the dancing party are unfit for Christians to attend...If Christians want amusement, surely God has made proper provision for it...Instead of dancing or drumming on Pianos, let the Christian if merry sing Psalms—cultivate those powers that God has given us, so that in the upper world our voices may be tuned to join the choir of angels and archangels in singing the high and glorious strains of redeeming love.[9]

The Introduction of Instrumental Music in the Stone-Campbell Movement

At this point we document the earliest use of IM in the SCM. Many works state the earliest example is Midway, Kentucky, in 1859, 1860. The earliest documented use of which we are aware, involving a violin, rather than an organ, occurred in 1850.

---

[8] B. W. S., "A Ramble," *CM,* 13.6 (September 1843) 132.
[9] D. P. H., "The Wants of the Churches," *CM*, 13.6 (September, 1843) 134.

Also, in 1850, Leonard wrote of a western preacher on a preaching tour eastward who found a congregation that permitted the use of a violin in sacred worship. On opening worship, he told them "to fiddle and sing the hymn on a certain page."[10]

Everett Ferguson notes an instance at the Sixth Street congregation in Cincinnati, in 1855, but the news item does not specify the instrument used:

> The Sixth Street Church is now provided with instrumental music, which together with its *crimson cushions* and *rented pews*, gives it quite an aristocratic caste.[11]

The Leonard and Cincinnati incidents escaped the notice of the brotherhood then and most historians now. The Midway instance, however, created widespread reaction in the Movement; the majority of the articles expressed displeasure with Pinkerton.

In October 1861, a nuanced, nine page essay on church music by Isaac Errett noted that some congregations saw choirs and instrumental music as possible solutions for poor quality congregational singing. Errett surveyed references to music in the Old and New Testaments; he then made these observations:

> To a sense of this great imperfection the churches are waking up. But, *What shall be done?* is the question. Some are seeking for remedy in choir singing. Others are urging the necessity of instrumental music, alike to guide and elevate the taste of our churches.

Later in the essay he sounded this warning:

> The innovation of choirs and instruments will not be checked by captious objections. The only way to stop it, is *to set to work diligently to train the churches in vocal music.* Take away the cause of complaint. We forewarn the brethren, especially in the cities and large towns, that if they wish to block the way against the introduction of choirs and organs, and the formalism resulting therefrom, they must employ suitable teachers of vocal music, and

---

[10] S. W. Leonard, "Church Music, No. 4," *Proclamation and Reformer* 1.5 (January, 1850) 59, cited by Choate, op. cit, 20, and endnote 5.

[11] J. B. [John Boggs]"City Items," *NWCM*, 2.6 (December, 1855) 191. Everett Ferguson, "Instrumental Music," *ESCM*: 414.

spend a portion of every year in training all the voices in the churches in the knowledge of musical science and the practice of suitable tunes...[12]

Even though Errett said, "We do not intend here to enter into this rising controversy," and opined that "the genius of this reformatory movement...is not favorable to choir singing and instrumental music," late the following year after a split in a Detroit congregation, he became the "pastor" of the new congregation composed of the minority. That congregation called itself a "New Interest," adopted instrumental music and declared their support of the missionary society.[13] Errett received sharp criticism for his "Synopsis," the door plate with "Rev.," and his role as the hired pastor of the congregation.[14] The events in Detroit and Errett's involvement therein, prompted L. F. Bittle later to coin the term "Detroit Movement." Bittle saw the "Detroit Movement" as the beginning of a new movement that had abandoned the Campbell movement.[15]

In Illinois in 1861, showing that he was aware of growing tensions about instrumental music in the SCM, E. L. Craig, when suggesting the need to improve the quality of singing in congregations, made clear he was not in favor of instrumental music or choirs:

> We should be delighted to hear of our sweet-singing brother
> Fillmore, when his new work (the Christian Choralist) shall come
> out, being called from congregation to congregation to instruct
> the brethren and sisters, especially the young, in vocal music. We

[12] Isaac Errett, "Church Music," *MH*, October, 1861: 551 – 560; the above quotes are from 558, 559. Choate, *op cit.*, says of the article, "We would dare say that this article proved to be the most influential supporting article written on the subject of hymnody and instrumental music in the whole Restoration Movement up to 1900 or since."

[13] For more on the phrase "New Interest" see G. G. Taylor, *A History of the Plum Street Church of Christ, Detroit, Mich.* (Cincinnati: F. L. Rowe, Pub., 1906) 6; 17 – 19. The New Interest group in Detroit used instrumental music possibly as early as 1862 but certainly in 1863 in the building they occupied on the corner of Jefferson Avenue and Beaubien Street. (Taylor 21, 22.)

[14] Douglas A. Foster, "Isaac Errett," *ESCM*, 302.

[15] L. F. B., "Detroit Movement," *OR*, 43.47 (November 20, 1900) 4. Leonard Fletcher Bittle (1833 – 1905) was an editor, along with Daniel Sommer, of the *Octographic Review*. The phrase appears in the OR as early as 37.6 (February 5, 1894) 4. It also appears in 37.15 (April 10, 1894) 8, where Bittle states Errett "was at the head of the Modern School Discipleism [sic] which [Benjamin] Franklin opposed." Bittle corresponded with Franklin in the *ACR* as early as 1864.

are not advocating *instrumental music* in our churches, nor *choir singing*. To these we are uncompromisingly opposed. We only insist on a development and cultivation of the musical talent among the children of God, for the promotion of his glory, by giving Him the melody of our hearts from a cultivated voice.[16]

It is difficult to give hard data on when, where and which congregations used instrumental music. In 1864 Benjamin Franklin knew of a "dozen" congregations using instrumental music but does not give locations.[17] Our research shows that by 1870 instrumental music was used in Cincinnati, Ohio; Bloomington, Pittsfield and Chicago, Illinois; St. Louis, Missouri; Detroit, Michigan; Indianapolis, Indiana; Midway, Kentucky; and New York, New York.

In February 1880, in response to a request in the *American Christian Review* for a "list of all the churches that use the organ," an unnamed respondent from Pittsfield, Illinois, listed six locations "which surround me" that had "organ strife": Sullivan, Charleston, Summit, Shelbyville, Windsor and Pittsfield. A portion of his letter well summarizes the distressed feelings of numerous others in the Movement:

> I will state to you that they use the organ here in the church and Sunday-school, and they are decidedly on the progressive wing, holding to festivals, fairs, mite societies, preachers' institutes—in fact, every departure that is used by the sects. I have been here eleven years. I put in my letter in reluctantly, it being the first Christian Church I ever saw an organ in. They had new songs and tunes that were only suitable for a theater or concert. Now I have to sit off in one corner and listen to a young, giddy set worship for me, and some of them do not belong to the church. It goes very hard with me, being now over sixty-eight years of age, but I thank God I have my Bible and the Review, which give me great consolation. I attend every Lord's day, to partake of the emblems. I do not go very often at other times. We have no preacher now. They won't have any but a progressionist.[18]

---

[16] E. L. C. [Elijah Lewis Craig], "What We Need, or Fireside Musings—No. 1." *BA*, 4.1, (January 1861) 24.

[17] "Remarks" [to] "St. Louis [pseudonym]," "Instrumental Music in the Churches," *ACR* 7.30 (July 26, 1864) 119.

[18] *ACR* 23.14 (April 6, 1880) 109.

Hymn Books

Another common theme was the announcement and commendation or criticism of hymn books. The Illinois brethren mostly did not toe the party line of Campbell, who, as mentioned above, did not want competition for his hymnbook. That controversy had never died, much to Campbell's chagrin. The announcements served two purposes for editors and publishers: filling space in their issues and the opportunity to sell books to patrons, since some editors and publishers carried inventories of SCM books and hymnals. Examples included John W. Karr (1823 – 1903), founding editor and publisher of the *Christian Herald* at Wapella,[19] and John H. Underwood (1825 – 1883), one of the founding editors of the *Christian Sentinel* in Springfield. Partially funded by the Campbell hymnbook proceeds, Underwood attended Bethany College, graduating in 1856. After his return to Illinois, he established a bookselling business in Carrollton.[20]

D. Pat Henderson felt the design of a hymn book could help with the quality of congregational singing. From Chicago, after seeing proofs of A. S. Hayden's *Christian Hymn and Tune Book. For Use in Churches, and for Social and Family Devotions*, he opined:

> The plan of the work is very much after the style of the 'Plymouth' Book of Church Psalmody. The hymns from our hymn book, are arranged with reference to their metres [sic], and the music is at the head of the page, so that both the music and the words are on the same page. This will be an argument, not easily refuted, in favor of good congregational music.[21]

Appeals for Personal Frugality and Religious Generosity

Another theme is the criticism of Christian families who spend money on pianos and music lessons (and other extravagances), while neglecting to contribute to benevolence (helping the poor) and support evangelists.

---

[19] "Our Table: Fillmore's Christian Psaltery," *CHI*, 5.10 (October, 1868) 320.
[20] In 1856 Underhill, Jeptha Hobbs, Wm. T. Haley and S. S. Earle received equal parts of the Illinois funds from the proceeds of the sale of Campbell's hymn books. *CSent*, 3.6 (March, 1856) 182.
[21] D. P. Henderson, "Reminiscences," *CS* (August 6, 1870) 250.

This was a theme in Stone's writings (1843, 1844) echoed by "Fides" (1857) and E. P. Belshe (1866):

In 1843 and 1844 Barton W. Stone and D. Pat Henderson appealed to the subscribers of the *Christian Messenger* and to the brotherhood at large regarding the need for better stewardship. In 1843 Stone spent several months touring Indiana, Ohio and Kentucky. The tour was enervating for Stone. He returned to his post as editor with renewed vigor but felt he must address trends he observed during the tour, especially among the Kentucky brethren. Two of the subjects he addressed establish the state of affairs that existed then but eventually changed, to make some brethren receptive for the introduction of instrumental music:

> Another thing which checks the work of religion everywhere, but especially in Kentucky, is extravagance in worldly things. Thousands of brethren there are wasting the Lord's goods… Their superb houses, and rich furniture—their pageantry and equipage—their super-abundance of viands and delicacies—all at the expense of the Lord's money—for the want of which millions of men are dying for the lack of knowledge![22]

After addressing how some (1) abused debt and broke contracts, (2) turned from religion to politics, and (3) relied too much on preachers and were "not engaged in the work," Stone, as we mentioned earlier, criticized the style of worship he observed during the tour.

In 1844 D. Pat Henderson continued the appeal for better stewardship:

> We are well satisfied that this age is peculiarly and strongly marked by selfishness. The church is selfish—narrow and contracted in its operations in a comparative point of view. We want an expansive benevolence…I repeat it, we must do more than we have ever done. The times call for it. We must 'deny ourselves' of many luxuries, many comforts, and like Jesus Christ, our great example, cease not in our efforts, till death shall cut the cords of life. This subject shall claim much of our attention during the current year, should life and health permit.[23]

True to Henderson's promise that the subject of expansive benevolence would claim much attention in 1844, in the same issue of the *Christian Messenger*, Stone contributes articles on unfaithfulness and selfishness;

---

[22] B. W. S. "A Ramble." *CM,* 13.6 (September 1843) 130, 131.
[23] D. P. H., "Wants of the Churches—No. 3." *CM,* 14.1 (May 1844) 12-15.

"Clement" expounds the parable of the Rich Man and Lazarus. Instructive are details from Stone's exposition of the Parable of the Talents, wherein he gives an example of a modern servant of the Lord entrusted with $10,000.00, who, having spent $1,000.00 thereof for "Furniture, carpeting, Piano &c." protests giving $10.00 to a needy man, $20.00 for the Bible society, $20.00 for a poor Evangelist and $40.00 for building a "plain chapel."[24]

Moving ahead to 1857 we encounter an article by "Fides," who urges preachers not to be sidetracked by congregants who insist preaching has to touch upon relatively unimportant, debatable questions instead of preaching that allows them to 'leave the first principles of the doctrine of Christ and go on to perfection.' Fides asks more than fifty questions on a wide range of subjects; he feels preachers should not deal with such questions. The questions on music, however, give an insight on what questions Fides thought were current:

> Is it right for christians [sic] to have piano-fortes or any other
> kind of musical instruments in their houses? If christians [sic]
> are permitted to play on instruments, ought they not to be con-
> fined to sacred tunes? Does the Bible allow us to sing any kind
> of songs but sacred, spiritual songs? Should not all members
> who play or sing any other kind of tunes or songs be turned out
> of the church?[25]

Before the instrumental music question was widely discussed in the late 1860s and early 1870s, Illinois editor and evangelist, Elijah Perry Belshe (1825 – 1884), echoing the earlier concerns of Henderson and Stone, bemoans Christians who spend money on pianos and music lessons:

> The accomplished daughter thumps at the piano and sings with
> a sweet and God-given voice, a world's foolish ditty, a war-song,
> a love story, all of which cost money. While this drumming and
> the giddy song are going, the heart of the man of God is listen-
> ing to the song of grief that moans from the mouth of the mul-
> titudes of widows and orphans, and of the poor and unfortu-
> nate, who are destitute of the means of life and education, out
> of the hearing of the voice of the gospel, and without the
> knowledge of God and of the Savior, his heart pays a visit at
> home, and his thought lingers upon the features and counte-

---

[24] B. W. S. "Unfaithfulness." *CM*, 14.1 (May 1844) 20.
[25] Fides, "The Great Work." *CSent*, 4.4, (April, 1857) 101-104.

nance of a lonely companion, who is sad on account of his absence. Little does he enjoy the flip and flaunt of the gay young sister, who thinks to entertain him with a display of her accomplishment as a pianist and the intermingling of her sweet voice, perverted from the worship of God to the silly adoration of vanity.[26]

A lively exchange in 1869 between Elijah L. Craig and Elijah P. Belshe centered on Belshe's criticism of the cost and content of hymnbooks.

Another cause for barrenness in the churches is the destitution of hymn books. Very few of these are found in the congregations throughout the country. The book produced by the Missionary Society is so large and costly, and the familiar and desirable hymns are mixed to such confusion with a multitude of useless pieces that the members of the congregations cannot be induced to purchase it.

We are sorry to see so good a man as Bro. Belshe join in the small clamor of a small class of small men, who seem to think a small hymn book got up by some small man would prove to be such an engine for good as to save the church and the world from sin and ruin; and the smaller the book, the mightier would be its force, seems to be the drift of all these faultfinders, when logically understood.

Now there is no reason in the world, why any one may not have a hymn book if they want one. And here we take occasion to say, that all the clamor about the costliness of the new edition of the Christian hymn book is groundless, false and unjust, as I can buy at the Book Store in this place,[27] a nicely bound copy for sixty cents, and having had some experience in publishing, I here assert that no house in America could afford it to Booksellers, at a figure that would justify selling it at a less price. This objection against the present book is not real, but wholly imaginary on the part of our good Bro. Belshe and all who make the same objection, and their great plea for a cheap book is a false one, as we have a book already as cheap as our own brother Belshe could afford it.

---

[26] E. P. Belshe, "Beware." *GE*, 4.8, (August 1866) 325.

[27] The bookstore Craig had in mind no doubt was John Underwood's in Carrollton, Illinois. Craig lived in the same town at the time and had published the *Bible Advocate* and *Gospel Echo* there since 1860. See Chapter 8 for Craig's tenure as editor of the journals.

Bro. Belshe objects too, to much of the matter in the present hymn book. To this we have nothing to say, only that it is much easier to do this, than to compile a book, or to sustain our objections by solid facts and well-founded reasons. We say nothing of the compliment paid by our brother to the Scriptural intelligence, poetic taste and literary attainments of the committee of publication.[28]

E. L. Craig inferred from Belshe's criticism of the hymn book that the problem was actually with the Missionary Society:

But these brethren object to the hymn book now in use, because put forth by a Society of which the Bible knows nothing, on which account they are opposed to the Society itself. Well, it is true that a Missionary Society as such, is not named in the Bible, and if this is a good reason for opposing the Society, it is just as good a reason for opposing the use of hymn books altogether. Come brethren roll out your heavy artillery and dislodge the enemy of pure speech and practice, who is fortified behind a breastwork of hymn books. 'Verily the legs of the lame are not equal.' This proves too much for anti-society men.

Instrumental Music in Illinois Congregations

To present the earliest references to instrumental music in congregations in Illinois we follow the preaching and writing career of David Pat Henderson (1810 – 1897), one of the leading pioneers of the Stone-Campbell Movement in Kentucky, Missouri and Illinois. His early conservative views regarding instrumental music and its related subjects evolved during his decades of ministry and Movement leadership, mirroring the trends in Illinois and the nation.

It is beyond the scope of our volume to give more than a brief bio-bibliographical sketch of this important Illinois leader, who, in our opinion, ranks among the three most important Illinois SCM patriarchs.[29] Barton W. Stone ranks first; Henderson and John T. Jones round out the triumvirate. We first met DPH in this work in Chapter 9, where he is in the group who developed the Hanover community in Woodford County

---

[28] E. L. C., "Singular Discovery." *GE*, 7.1 (January 1869) 39, 40.

[29] See Haynes 529 for a brief sketch. A more detailed sketch, unfortunately lacking documentation on some events, is http://www.therestorationmovement.com/ _states/illinois/henderson.htm.

and procured a charter for Hanover College, one the earliest proposed, but not established, colleges for the SCM in Illinois. Henderson was an editor of the *Christian Messenger* (Illinois) and the *Christian Evangelist* (Iowa and Missouri). Henderson was deeply involved in founding the *Christian Standard* in 1866, serving as a corresponding editor and fund raiser. His reputation as an evangelist was national.

Henderson wrote on the "Organ question" as early as 1870, prompted by his experience in the Chicago area.[30] In 1878, while visiting Oakland, California, DPH wrote an eight page manuscript *Organs*, from which we quote and draw conclusions. The entire manuscript is found in Appendix 3. Concurrent with the manuscript, DPH wrote a letter to Isaac Errett about his time in California. The letter discussed how DPH superintended the erection of an elaborate church building at Oakland, the extravagant 1878 California state meeting at Woodland in Yolo County, and, because "some" California congregations used organs, DPH condensed his views from the *Organ* manuscript about people who favored or opposed organs, asking Errett for his thoughts on DPH's views on the question.

Congregations where Henderson served where instrumental music was used or caused splits include:

1. Chicago, Illinois, 1868, 1869, where a melodeon was used in spite of his objections.[31]

---

[30] D. P. Henderson, "Reminiscences," *CS*, (August 6, 1870) 250. C. W. Sherwood, "The Cause in Chicago," *CS*, (February 20, 1869) 58.

[31] C. W. Sherwood, "The Cause in Chicago," *CS*, (February 20, 1869) 58. "The organ is but a common melodeon, and even this is tolerated under protest by Bro. D. P. Henderson..."

2. St. Louis, Missouri, 1871, 1872, where Henderson served briefly with a minority who started a new congregation after a disagreement over instrumental music.[32]

3. Oakland, California, 1878, where Henderson sided with the majority who wanted instrumental music.[33]

From the 1878 Errett letter (EL), the *Organs* manuscript (O) and his 1870 *Reminiscences* (R), we note that DPH:

Belief	Reference
Preferred that instrumental music not be used but was willing to sing, regardless.	Personally, my taste has always been for congregational singing without any instrument… Organ or no organ, I sing for myself and try to make melody in my heart to the Lord, and let my brethren enjoy their opinions, without any factious opposition. [EL 4]

---

[32] http://www.therestorationmovement.com/_states/illinois/henderson.htm. Henderson began his ministry on December 17, 1871. "Around the turn of the following decade, D. Pat answered the call to come and help in St. Louis, Missouri. The Central church in St. Louis had met for the first time in December, 1871. This congregation came about as a result of a division that had taken place at the First church when a group of members had unsuccessfully attempted to introduce instrumental music into the worship, As a result twelve members departed and began meeting in a public hall at Fourteenth and Charles streets. D. Pat Henderson served as their first minister, but only for a short time." Autograph letter in the DCHS Henderson Papers: Robert Graham to D. P. Henderson, March 5, 1872, mentions the decision of the committee of Robert Graham, Isaac Errett, Alexander Procter and Joseph K. Rogers overruling the choice of the majority to use instrumental music. That decision apparently did not settle the issue since Henderson went to St. Louis to minister with the minority. For more on the incident, "Report of Committee," *CS*, February 1871: 59. Graham served on the committee with Isaac Errett, Alexander Procter, and Joseph K. Rogers.

[33] E. B. Ware, *History of the Disciples of Christ in California*, (Healdburg, California: F. W. Cooke, Publisher, 1916) 286 - 289.

Worked to build support for a congregation not to use instrumental music	I never questioned the *right* of any church to use the organ if it was desirable, but I always interposed my objections and found a sufficient number to agree [6] with me, so that we had no trouble whatsoever on the subject. [O 5,6]
Preferred robust congregational singing assisted by memorization of the words and tunes	Personally, my taste has always been for congregational singing without any instrument. I prefer indeed, that the members should memorize the hymns, and particularly in invitation songs, around the Lord's Table, and before dismission [sic] that all should sing from the depths of their hearts, without looking at the words and music at the same time. [EL 4]
Believed the design of hymnbooks aided congregational music	...and the music is at the head of the page, so that both the music and the words are on the same page. This will be an argument, not easily refuted, in favor of good congregational music. [R]
Felt the New Testament silence on the subject made any view on the subject an opinion.	Brethren say, that the New Testament is silent on the subject. It says nothing for, nothing against its use, or non use [sic]. It is therefore not a matter of faith at all. It is purely a matter of taste or prejudice—a matter of opinion. [EL 4]

Felt the efforts to prohibit organs gave the issue too much attention, resulting in congregations asking for them	Of this number, one of our preachers from Texas lately has written a tract and circulates it through the state. He will build [4] it up, if I am not mistaken, rather than discourage the use of it. [EL 3, 4] I am confident, that the warfare made against organs, has put many into the churches. So much dogmatism, so much denunciation, have been indulged, that brethren with self respect, have been converted to the use of them—they have asserted their independence, and into the churches they are going constantly through the tyranny, despotism, and bitter denunciation of the organ opposers. [O 4]
Would not make the use of organs a test of fellowship	I do not however, make my <u>taste</u> or <u>opinion</u> a test of fellowship. [EL 4]
Believed in cases where the majority wanted organs, the minority should acquiesce	If I am correct, in all matters of expediency that come before the church, such as the use of organs, tuning forks, building meeting houses, calling preachers, the rule is, that the majority of the members determine all such questions, and the spirit of love will cause the minority to acquiesce and make unanimity. [EL 4]
Admitted that sometimes an organ, piano or violin was useful in practicing to aid memorization of songs that were sung in worship services	"…when we wished to learn new music, we quietly practiced where our leader was the organ. This was in private families however—sometimes we were led by the piano or violin when practicing difficult pieces of music. [O 6]

Mentions in *Organs* three congregations that used organs:

- Bloomington, Illinois[34]
- St. Louis, Missouri[35]
- Indianapolis, Indiana[36]

Conclusions

By 1878, Henderson is near the left on the continuum of opposition to instrumental music. His belief that the minority should acquiesce moves him further to the left than Isaac Errett and others who argued instrumental music could be allowed because of expediency, but insisted, if necessary, the majority should acquiesce "in the spirit of love" to make peace. He was intimately acquainted with the issues since he served congregations that dealt with the question and was aware of developing trends in the SCM, citing examples where instrumental music was used.

Perhaps an anomaly, but worth mentioning because it demonstrates a trend away from personal frugality in Henderson's life and in the Movement, is Henderson's contract with the Chicago congregation in 1867. His negotiated salary total was $3,000.00, a far cry from his appeals for

---

[34] John D. Trefzger, "Pioneer Disciple: William T. Major," *Discipliana* (October, 1967) 48: "On the lighter side we note that the organ in the new church of 1856 caused its share of problems. Mrs. Hunt recalls that one woman tried to push the new organ out of the balcony 'because the Lord should not be worshiped with 'Hollow Sticks'!" Ken Christensen, historian who attends the First Christian Church, Bloomington, states, "I am very much aware of 'the hollow sticks' story, as it is a favorite of John Trefzger, Minister Emeritus of FCC. I have never seen a date associated with the use of an organ in Bloomington, however, I know music lessons were given in the building, shortly after its completion, as the basement was rented out to a school. I have been under the assumption that an organ was in use during the ministry of T. V. Berry, in the early 1860s. I have found no firm date, however." (Email 1.8.2018.) Henderson's statement in *Organs* might point to an earlier time: "Years ago in Bloomington Illinois, where the first organ so far as I know, was ever brought into congregational use by almost the entire membership…"

[35] See page 240 above.

[36] "St. Louis [pseudonym]," "Instrumental Music in the Churches," *ACR* 7.30 (July 26, 1864) 118. "The congregations of our brethren in New York, Indianapolis, St. Louis, and perhaps in one or two other places, employ instrumental music. In some of these congregations it has been used for some time, without apparently attracting much attention, or at least without eliciting much, if any, discussion on the subject."

stewardship in the 1840s.[37] The issue of located "pastors" receiving set salaries developed simultaneously with the instrument and society questions.

During his located ministries Henderson mostly served congregations in large towns or cities, even if the congregations were small. As Errett pointed out in 1861, those locations would be tempted to use instrumental music. Henderson and the Stone-Campbell Movement saw that prediction fulfilled in Illinois and across the nation.

---

[37] D. P. Henderson, [Journal for 1867, 1868] *D. P. Henderson Papers.* DCHS.

12. The Impact of Rising Conservatism on Illinois Restorationist Churches

Theological conservatism or fundamentalism is normally associated with the southern regions of the United States, but perhaps strangely enough, Illinois especially in the Chicago area, was one of the major germinating soils for conservatism both in terms of institutions and leaders. In regard to institutions these included Illinois College, Wheaton College, Moody Bible Institution, and later, Trinity Evangelical Seminary, and their presses, media broadcasting, and the office for publishing the widely heralded twelve volumes on the Fundamentals, 1910-1915. Among the significant leaders who spent at least some years in Illinois were: Peter Cartwright, Dwight L. Moody, William Jennings Bryan, R. A. Torrey, A. C. Dixon, Billy Sunday, Franklin Johnson, George L. Robinson, and John Timothy Stone.[1]

While Northern Illinois also produced leaders of theological liberalism, these modernist institutions were interspersed with conservative churches and with their print and media operations. We will proceed to set out some of the details of these developments and show their impact upon the Restoration Movement in Illinois. The influence of Daniel Sommer merits its own chapter—Chapter 14. Sommer adamantly defended certain foundational motifs of the earlier Restoration Movement and these were theologically different from the post Civil War interdenominational conservative developments in the Chicago area in regard to polity and soteriology.

Leaders of the Illinois Restoration Movement who opposed developing liberalism were Clark Braden, Harvey W. Everest, and J. W. McGarvey. The impact of the new conservatism and its significant role in Illi-

---

[1] These works provide historical insight: George M. Marsden, *Fundamentalism and American Culture* 2nd ed. (New York: Oxford University Press, 2006); Ernest R. Sandeen, *The Roots of Fundamentalism: British and American Millenarianism 1800-1930* (Chicago: University of Chicago Press, 2008); Mark Noll, *American Evangelical Christianity: An Introduction* (Oxford: Malden, MA, Blackwell Publishers, 2001).

nois Restorationism was somewhat delayed until the twentieth century, but the seeds commenced germinating not too long after the Civil War and especially in reaction against the coterie of liberal Restorationists forming around Chicago, and more specifically those associated with the University of Chicago. One concrete eventual outcome was the founding of Lincoln Bible Institute in 1944 and Lincoln Christian Seminary in 1952.[2] The majority of doctoral degrees held by faculty at Lincoln at present were conferred by Trinity Evangelical Seminary in Deerfield, Illinois, founded in Chicago in 1897, a school and seminary that may be designated neo-evangelical. Trinity, however, did not come to the forefront until the latter half of the twentieth century. The current theological outlook at Lincoln Christian is much like that of Wheaton or Trinity.

Theological conservativism

One might argue that conventional theological conservativism was the only Christian outlook in Illinois prior to the Civil War. But in order to do so, conservatism has to be defined in a certain manner. For example to some, the Illinois "new lights" were liberal along with the Restorationists.[3] The conservatives in this case were the old line Calvinists among the Baptists, Congregationalists and Presbyterians. Here we will designate the Illinois "Fundamenatalists" the conservatives for the sake of our discussion which will help establish parameters. The core beliefs of conservatism or Fundamentalism were: (1) Biblical inerrancy, (2) the literalness of Biblical accounts of creation, (3) the virgin birth of Christ, (4) the bodily resurrection and the physical return of Christ and (5) the substitutionary atonement of the crucified Christ.[4] These constructive affirmations exacerbated conservative acrimony toward the rising acceptance of evolution, the higher criticism of the Scriptures, and the social gospel propounded by the liberals.[5] The core beliefs of the fundamentalists were held by the majority of the Illinois Restorationists at the turn of the century even though perspectives on millennialism (4) may have dif-

---

[2] In 2009 Lincoln Christian College and Seminary became Lincoln Christian University.

[3] George A. Rawlyk, *The Canada Fire: Radical Evangelism in British North America, 1771-1812* (Kingston, Buffalo: McGill-Queen's University Press, 1994).

[4] https://www.newsmax.com/FastFeatures/fundamentalist-christians-denominations/2015/04/17/id/639249/

[5] Thomas H. Olbricht, "Rhetoric in the Higher Criticism Controversy," *The Rhetoric of Protest and Reform 1878-1898*, ed. Paul Boase, Ohio University Press, 1980.

fered, the Chicago area conservatives premillennial while the Restorationists tended to be amillennial.[6]

Actually, most of those involved in the first and second great awakenings in the earlier time embraced the later fundamentalist agenda. We have already mentioned Peter Cartwright and his opposition to the miraculous gifts. Professors at Illinois College attended by William Jennings Bryan—an 1881 graduate—basically affirmed the five principles. Illinois College was founded in 1829, and Edward Beecher, brother of Henry Ward Beecher, appointed an early president. Because of certain evangelistically minded Congregationalists, seven students from Yale assisted in founding Illinois College in Jacksonville. Illinois College was also affiliated with the Presbyterian Church. Many in the College supported abolition and in 1903 the College became co-ed. The theological stance was basically conservative well into the twentieth century.[7] In its earlier years the faculty of Eureka College, Restorationist, of Eureka, Illinois, just east of Peoria, embraced the same conservative theological assumptions.[8]

The dispensationalism of such religious leaders as John Nelson Darby (1800-1882)[9] of England and Cyrus I. Scofield (1843-1921)[10] editor of the Scofield Reference Library also constituted a tributary to mainstream conservatism in some quarters, especially in St. Louis and Dallas.

It was professors at Princeton Theological Seminary however who gave fundamentalism its academic credentials, especially with their perspectives on Biblical inerrancy.[11] Charles Hodge (1797-1678), an early professor of the Princeton Theological Seminary asserted that God breathed

---

[6] For the move from conventional to liberal Biblical criticism in the 19th century see: Thomas H. Olbricht, "Biblical Interpretation in North America Through the Nineteenth Century," *History of Biblical Interpretation*, eds. Alan F. Hauser and Duane F. Watson (Grand Rapids: Eerdmans. 2017), Vol. III.

[7] Charles Edward Frank, *Illinois College, 1829-1979* (Carbondale: Southern Illinois Press, 1979).

[8] Alumni Association, *A History of Eureka College with Biographical Sketches and Reminiscences Illustrated* (St. Louis: Christian Publishing Company, 1894).

[9] Donald H. Akenson, *Exporting the Rapture: John Nelson Darby and the Victorian Conquest of North-American Evangelicalism* (New York: Oxford University Press, 2018).

[10] https://en.wikipedia.org/wiki/C._I._Scofield

[11] Hugh T. Kerr, *Sons of the Prophets: Leaders in Protestantism from Princeton Seminary 1909-1992* (Princeton: Princeton University Press, 1963).

his exact thoughts into the text.[12] Other Princeton professors of the same persuasion were: B. B. Warfield (1851-1921), William Henry Green (1825-1900) and John Gresham Machen (1881-1937). According to Hodge and Warfield,

> During the entire history of Christian theology the word Inspiration has been used to express either some or all of the activities of God, cooperating with its human authors in the genesis of Holy Scripture. We prefer to use it in the single sense of God's continued work of superintendence, by which, His providential, gracious, and supernatural contributions having been presupposed, He presided over the sacred writers in their entire work of writing, with the design and effect of rendering that writing an errorless record of the matters He designed them to communicate, and hence constituting the entire volume in all its parts the Word of God to us.[13]

Controversy over evolution became rampant in several Protestant churches shortly after the Civil War and underpinned the second fundamental listed above on creation.

> Protestantism, especially in America, broke out in "acrid polemics" and argument about evolution from 1860 to the 1870s —with the turning point possibly marked by the death of Louis Agassiz in 1873—and by 1880 a form of "Christian evolution" was becoming the consensus. In Britain, while publication of *The Descent of Man* by Darwin in 1871 reinvigorated debate from the previous decade, Sir Henry Chadwick notes a steady acceptance of evolution "among more educated Christians" between 1860 and 1885. As a result, evolutionary theory was "both permissible and respectable" by 1876. Frederick Temple's lectures on *The Relations between Religion and Science* (1884) on how evolution was not "antagonistic" to religion highlighted this trend. Temple's appointment as Archbishop of Canterbury in 1896

---

[12] Thomas H. Olbricht, "Charles Hodge as an American New Testament Interpreter," *Journal of Presbyterian History*, 57 (1979) 117-133.

[13] Charles Hodge and Benjamin Warfield, "Inspiration," *The Presbyterian Review* 6 (April 1881), 225- 60.

demonstrated the broad acceptance of evolution within the church hierarchy.[14]

Since we are specifically interested in theological conservatism in Illinois we will now turn to the publication of the twelve landmark volumes on Fundamentalism which was likely the most significant contribution church leaders in Illinois made to newly emerging fundamentalism. The editors of these volumes were Reuben A. Torrey and A. C. Dixon both of whom had ties with Dwight L. Moody and Moody Bible Institute in Chicago during the time 1910-1915 in which the twelve volumes were published. Because of the close association with Moody we will now turn to Moody himself and the Institute.

Dwight Lyman Moody (1837-1899) was born in Massachusetts to a Unitarian family. Because of stresses in his family's financial situation—his father died young—he went to work in Boston for an uncle who owned a shoe store. His uncle required that he attend a Congregational Church where he was converted at age 18.[15] He immediately started promoting a Sunday school in an old building with great success. In 1856 he moved to Chicago to pursue his fortune but instead founded a church which eventually became the Moody Memorial Church.

> As president of the Chicago YMCA for four years, he champi-
> oned evangelistic causes such as distributing tracts all over the
> city, and he held daily noon prayer meetings. During the Civil
> War, he refused to fight, saying, "In this respect I am a Quaker,"
> but he worked through the YMCA and the United States Christ-
> ian Commission to evangelize the Union troops. He relentlessly
> sought and received financial support for all his projects from
> rich Christian businessmen, such as Cyrus McCormick and John
> Wanamaker. In all this, he tried to mix effective social work with
> evangelism.[16]

Moody's efforts were remarkably successful but he wanted to get into evangelism in a major way. Having heard Ira B. Sankey sing he persuaded

---

[14] https://en.wikipedia.org/wiki/Objections_to_evolution. Jon H. Roberts, *Darwinism and the Divine in America: Protestant Intellectuals and Organic Evolution, 1859-1900* (Madison: University of Wisconsin Press, 1988).

[15] James F. Findlay, *Dwight L. Moody, American Evangelist, 1937-1899* (Chicago: University of Chicago Press, 1969).

[16] http://www.christianitytoday.com/history/people/evangelistsandapologists/dwight-l-moody.html

Sankey to join him in holding evangelistic meetings in large cities. Their successes were modest until they were invited to evangelize in England.

> After preaching for two years in England, Scotland, and Ireland, Moody returned to America as an internationally famous revivalist. Of his fame, Moody admitted, "I know perfectly well that, wherever I go and preach, there are many better preachers ... than I am; all that I can say about it is that the Lord uses me..." Immediately, calls for crusades poured in. During these crusades, Moody pioneered many techniques of evangelism: a house-to-house canvass of residents prior to a crusade; an ecumenical approach enlisting cooperation from all local churches and evangelical lay leaders regardless of denominational affiliations; philanthropic support by the business community; the rental of a large, central building; the showcasing of a gospel soloist; and the use of an inquiry room for those wanting to repent.[17]

Moody was always interested in promoting education that reflected his theological outlooks and therefore founded a boys and a girls school in Northfield, Massachusetts. After much encouragement from others Moody launched what became the Moody Bible Institute.

> Finally, in 1886, Moody started the Bible-Work Institute of the Chicago Evangelization Society (renamed Moody Bible Institute shortly before his death), one of the first in the Bible school movement. From this work, he launched yet another work, the Colportage Association (later Moody Press), an organization using horse-drawn "Gospel wagons" from which students sold low-cost religious books and tracts throughout the nation.[18]

The Institute came into being having emerged from other Moody programs and though suffering financial difficulties in its early years finally grew into a school with more than 5000 students in undergraduate and graduate programs in Chicago and elsewhere. An additional undergraduate program was launched in Spokane, Washington, and a graduate school in Plymouth, Michigan.

> In 1883, Emma Dryer, with Moody's permission, organized and headed what was known as the "May Institute." These were

---

[17] Ibid.
[18] Ibid.

weekly meetings in which church members would meet and pray. Most important however, would be the open discussions among the church members. Many of the church members began to request that Moody open up a new school. This school would serve as a training school for the youth of the Church, a place where future evangelists could learn the skills necessary to carry on in the Revivalist tradition. On January 22, 1886, Moody addressed church members as follows: "I tell you what, and what I have on my heart I believe we have got to have gap-men, men to stand between the laity and the ministers; men who are trained to do city mission work. Take men that have the gifts and train them for the work of reaching the people. This formal meeting, held at Farwell Hall, resulted in the group founding the Chicago Evangelization Society, which was renamed the Moody Bible Institute after Moody died in 1899.[19]

Moody insisted that his theology revolved around the three R's.

- Ruined by the Fall

- Redeemed by the Blood

- Regenerated by the Spirit.[20]

In regard to Biblical criticism Moody denounced higher criticism and the attendant presuppositions,

> Reflecting at least an awareness of developing liberalism in the churches, he warned of any minister who used a "penknife on the Bible, clipping out this and that part because it contains the supernatural or something he cannot understand." Moody had no use for the so-called higher criticism of the Bible. He told a reporter, "You want to know what I think of the effect of higher criticism upon the Bible and upon Christians? Frankly, I don't know anything about the higher critics of late. I haven't seen 'em. I've been six months in the wilderness of Judea calling upon people to repent." Moody had no patience with anything that would undercut the source of Christian belief—the Bible—

---

[19] https://www.google.com/webhp?sourceid=chrome-instant&ion=1&espv=2&ie=UTF-8#q=moody%20bible%20institute

[20] http://www.christianitytoday.com/history/issues/issue-25/three-rs-of-moodys-theology.html

because that source contains the very heart of Christian belief—the gospel.[21]

In 1926 Moody Bible Institute launched a radio program, one of the earliest in the region, and one of the oldest non-commercial radio stations in the United States. The broadcasts could be heard in Northern Illinois, Eastern Iowa, Southern Wisconsin, Western Michigan and northern Indiana. The programming involved readings from the Bible, Bible teaching, preaching, talk shows, and hymns and religious music. The station has had a significant impact in the region. The Moody enterprises now include a major press, as well as correspondence, evening and distant learning schools. It is not known in detail how many church leaders from the Restorationists may have taken correspondence courses from Moody Institute, but the well known C. G. Brewer (1884-1956) of Churches of Christ proudly included such courses in his resume.[22]

R. A. Torrey and A. C. Dixon became involved with the Moody Institute and while in Chicago edited the twelve volumes of *The Fundamentals*, conferring upon Illinois a major role in the anti-modernist crusade. A few other religious leaders in Illinois were involved but we will focus on these two.

R. A. Torrey (1856-1928)

Reuben Archer Torrey was born in Hoboken, New Jersey, and graduated from Yale in 1875 and Yale Divinity School in 1878. He served as a Congregational minister in Garrettsville, Ohio. He then, as did several other Americans, studied in Germany at universities in Leipzig and Erlangen in 1982-83. The scholars at Erlangen, less radical than at Berlin, Tübingen, and Heidelberg, pursued earlier conventional studies giving special attention to history in Scripture under the rubric, "Holy History,"—in German "Heilsgeschichte." Torrey joined Moody in Chicago in 1889 and in 1894 became pastor of the congregation later identified as the Moody Memorial Church. In addition he was Superintendent of the Moody Bible Institute. In 1912 Torrey was persuaded to launch the Bible Institute of Los Angeles, now Biola, where he served as Dean from 1912-1924. He published a number of books, some of which were about Scripture, and were reprinted in several editions. These were widely read by Illinois conservatives and others throughout the world. The import of

---

[21] Ibid. Gene A. Getz, *MBI, The Story of Moody Bible Institute*, Revised and updated by James M. Vincent (Chicago: Moody Press, 1986).

[22] Thomas H. Olbricht, "G. C. Brewer," *ESCM*, 97, 98.

these works can be discerned in a volume combating modernism: R. A. Torrey, *Is the Bible the Inerrant Word of God? And was the Body of Jesus Raised from the Dead?* (1922).

A. C. Dixon (1854-1925)

Amzi Clarence Dixon was born in Shelby, North Carolina, and graduated from Wake Forest in 1875. He also attended Southern Baptist Theological Seminary then located at Greenville, South Carolina. He served churches in North Carolina, Baltimore, Brooklyn, and Boston, moving on to the Moody Church, Chicago, 1906-1911. After Chicago he preached in London taking over the Metropolitan Tabernacle of Charles Spurgeon (1911—1919). In regard to his focus it was said,

> Dixon was a staunch advocate of Fundamentalist Christianity during that movement's developmental period. His preaching was often fiery and direct, confronting various forms of Protestant apostasy, Roman Catholicism, Henry Ward Beecher's liberalism, Robert Ingersoll's agnosticism, Christian Science, Unitarianism, and higher criticism of the Bible.[23]

The Fundamentals: A Testimony to the Truth

The well-publicized twelve volume *Fundamentals*, an effort to combat modernistic tendencies in the mainstream Protestant churches, consisted of 90 essays published by the Bible Institute of Los Angeles from 1910 to 1915.[24] Sixty-four different authors were involved most of whom were Americans, but some from Great Britain. The publication costs were anonymously contributed by two brothers in Los Angeles, California—businessmen Lyman and Milton Stewart. The volumes were sent free to ministers, missionaries, professors, YMCA and YWCA secretaries, Sunday school teachers and superintendants. Over 250,000 sets were sent out.

> The volumes defended orthodox Protestant beliefs and attacked higher criticism, liberal theology, Roman Catholicism (also called Romanism by them), socialism, Modernism, atheism, Christian

---

[23] https://en.wikipedia.org/wiki/A._C._Dixon.

[24] *The Fundamentals: A Testimony to the Truth* (Chicago: Testimony Publishing Co. 1910-15). HathiTrust Digital Library.

Science, Mormonism, Millennial Dawn, Spiritualism, and evolutionism.[25]

These volumes were widely considered to be the defining platform for twentieth century conservatism or fundamentalism. The conservatives in Northern Illinois contributed to their production and dissemination.

Wheaton College

Another Illinois bastion of American theological conservatism was Wheaton College of Wheaton, Illinois. The first president of Wheaton, Jonathan Blanchard (1811-1882), served from 1859 to 1882. He was a graduate of Middlebury College in Vermont and Lane Theological Seminary in Cincinnati where Lyman Beecher administered as president. Prior to his Wheaton presidency Dixon was a Methodist pastor, and for a time president of Knox College in Galesburg, Illinois. Knox College evolved from the Illinois Institute founded by the Wesleyans in 1853. Blanchard was a consummate abolitionist and a crusader for social reforms such as anti-Masonic and anti-alcohol. Warren L. Wheaton gave the new college land and Blanchard insisted on naming the college Wheaton. Blanchard also worked hard to involve Congregationalists on the corporate board of Wheaton giving the school a non-denominational flavor.

Blanchard's son, Charles Albert Blanchard (1848-1925) succeeded him as Wheaton president and served from 1882 to 1925. Charles had ties with the Moody Church inasmuch as he served as senior pastor there for two years. Charles insisted on creating a liberal arts college which addressed the current culture, but that inculcated conservative Christian values in respect to modes of dress and morality, for example, no cosmetics or the drinking of alcohol. In the late 1940s Wheaton became the standard bearer for evangelicalism and essentially adopted the fundamentalist theological agenda.

Wheaton's most famous graduate is Billy Graham, the evangelist par excellence. Both Billy and Ruth Bell Graham graduated from Wheaton in the early 1940s.

Wheaton also has a connection with a Restorationist college since J. Richard Chase, president of Wheaton 1982-1993, received two degrees from Pepperdine University. Chase, however, was always a Presbyterian. Several Restorationists attended Wheaton after World War II for graduate

---

[25] https://en.wikipedia.org/wiki/The_Fundamentals

work in religion including Keith Coleman and Don Horn, graduates of Harding College, later University.

In the early 1920s thought was given to turning out a Wheaton statement of faith. The result was a nine point platform dated to 1926. A summary of these nine points follows:

1. The Old and New Testaments are verbally inspired and inerrant in the original manuscripts.

2. One God: Father, Son and Holy Spirit.

3. Jesus Christ was born of the Holy Spirit to the Virgin Mary. He was the true God and True Man.

4. Humans are created in the image of God. They are born sinful.

5. Jesus Christ died for sins as a substitute.

6. Jesus was resurrected bodily and ascended to the right hand of God.

7. Christ will return to earth personally for a millennial rule on earth.

8. All who receive Christ by faith are born of the Holy Spirit.

9. The resurrection of humankind will result in bliss for the just and punishment for the unjust.[26]

The Wheaton declaration incorporates the same five points of fundamentalism. These affirmations countered many presuppositions of liberal theology found at the University of Chicago.

In the nineteenth century, McCormick Theological Seminary was basically conservative. It had some of the same supporters as did Dwight L. Moody for his activities--Cyrus McCormick (1809-1984) of Chicago and John Wannamaker (1838-1922) of Philadelphia. The seminary was named McCormick after Cyrus' death. The first phase of the Seminary was founded in Hanover, Indiana, on the Ohio River between Louisville, Kentucky, and Evansville, Indiana in 1829. Because of the pending War Between the States the seminary moved to Chicago in 1860. The Seminary prospered in the middle of the twentieth century, but later, because of dwindling student numbers, refocused and in addition trained a different clientele consisting of Hispanics, African Americans and various ethnic groups. The theological stance became moderately liberal.

---

[26] W. Wyheth Willard, *Frie on the Prairie: The Story of Wheaton College* (Wheaton: Van Kampen Press, 1950) 192.

Billy Sunday

On the grass roots level, one of the many successful conservative evangelists in the history of the United States, Billy Sunday (1852-1935), lived in Illinois most of time after he grew to adulthood. Sunday was born near Ames, Iowa. At the death of his father he was sent to orphanages, one the last being the Soldier's Orphanage in Chicago. Sunday possessed superior athleticism and began playing baseball as well as working on farms in Iowa. His greatest asset was his base running ability and he became notorious for stealing bases. He played for the Chicago White Stockings and the Philadelphia Phillies in the latter part of the 1880s. He was converted when listening to a sermon at the Pacific Garden Mission in Chicago in 1891. He became secretary of the Chicago YMCA and decided to dedicate his life to religious activities rather than to baseball. He entered into evangelism and gradually, following much in the footsteps of Dwight L. Moody, developed a major evangelistic team and became highly successful in massive crowd meetings in wooden tabernacles constructed in or near major cities in the United States.[27]

Sunday provides a conventional profile of what conservative preachers of the time believed and preached. He criticized many of the popular amusements such as dancing, playing cards, attending the theatre, reading novels and Sunday newspapers. He opposed evolution and eugenics along with new immigrations from southern and eastern Europe. He was not opposed to sports, especially baseball, as long as the games weren't played on Sunday. He criticized the drinking of alcohol and widely supported prohibition in his lecturing and preaching.

Sunday's theological views were compatible with those of Moody and the twelve volumes on the Fundamentals.

Sunday was a conservative evangelical who accepted fundamentalist doctrines. He affirmed and preached the inerrancy of the Bible, the virgin birth of Christ, the doctrine of substitutionary atonement, the bodily resurrection of Christ, a literal devil and hell, and the imminent return of Jesus Christ. Sunday refused to hold meetings in cities where he was not welcomed by the vast majority of the Protestant churches and their clergy. He went out of his way to avoid criticizing the Roman Catholic Church. Also, cards filled out by "trail hitters" were faithfully returned to the church or denomination that the writers had indicated as their choice, including Catholic and Unitarian. Although

---

[27] https://en.wikipedia.org/wiki/Billy_Sunday. William Gerald McLoughlin, *Billy Sunday was His Real Name* (Chicago: University of Chicago Press 1955).

Sunday was ordained by the Presbyterian Church in 1903, his ministry was nondenominational and he was not a strict Calvinist. He preached that individuals were, at least in part, responsible for their own salvation.

Sunday's homespun preaching had a wide appeal to his audiences, who were "entertained, reproached, exhorted, and astonished." Sunday claimed to be "an old-fashioned preacher of the old-time religion"[28] and his uncomplicated sermons spoke of a personal God, salvation through Jesus Christ, and following the moral lessons of the Bible. Sunday's theology, although sometimes denigrated as simplistic, was situated within the mainstream Protestantism of his time.

Conservative Restoration Leaders

We know of three Restorationist religious leaders in Illinois who maintained a conservative outlook and were critical of rising theological liberalism among Restorationists as well as other religious groups. These were Clark Braden who opposed especially evolution, Harvey W. Everest, who published a major work *The Divine Demonstration* on the authenticity of the Scriptures, and J. W. McGarvey who excoriated radical Biblical criticism. We will present these leaders as representative of numerous other Restorationists in Illinois who opposed the liberal agenda.

Clark Braden (1831-1911)

Clark Braden lived elsewhere in the Midwest, but also in Illinois. He was a noted debater, especially as an opponent to the Mormons, but he also entered into the fray with rising liberalism. We are chiefly interested in his anti-evolution views. He was born in Gustavus, Ohio, northeast of Warren. He was a graduate of Hiram College where James A. Garfield served as a teacher. For a time he considered himself an infidel, but Braden then converted to Christianity and became a major apologist. By 1909 he had preached for over 55 years and served as president of Elgin College, Abingdon College, Southern Illinois College and Southern Illinois Christian College. He was involved in 132 debates on infidelity, materialism, and spiritualism.

> Most of the time during his ministry he was a teacher and he organized the first teachers' institute ever held in Southern Illinois. He was a great controversialist, and not many months

[28] Ibid.

passed when he was not debating either with some infidel or some preacher of another denomination…Braden was a fighter and sometimes an intemperate one. He seemed to glory in controversy, as the people of Liberal [Missouri] learned on his visit here, He debated with C.W. Steward ten times in Liberal, and there are some still living here who remember Braden's visit to the town. This was in February 1885.[29]

One of Braden's often reprinted works involved an extended polemic against evolution. His approach basically was to point out in detail that life in its various forms is so complex it is impossible that higher species of plants and animals were generated by material alone. Braden started his attack on Darwinism not too long after Darwin published his *Origin of the Species* in 1859. Braden's book came out in 1877.

The germ is made up of cells. Was this germ in form and cellular structure evolved out of matter, destitute of either by blind force ; destitute of and destructive of the force manifested in them and of such cellular structure or germ? But when we have the germ, whence came the wonderful co-ordination of matter and its properties and physical forces below vital force, to the growth and development of the germ ? How came the force in the germ to control and co-ordinate matter and force destructive of the germ and its growth and antagonistic to vital force, and subordinate them to this growth and development? Then whence came the types and varieties of vegetable growth; the almost infinite varieties of form, reproduction and products ? Whence came these results of these processes of reproduction and growth? Whence the almost infinite variety of co-ordination, adaptation and adjustments to the surroundings and to each other? It is thought that there are over three hundred thousand varieties differing from each other in almost every one of these particulars, in almost infinite diversity. Whence came they all, and their still more wonderful co-ordination and adaptation and adjustment to surroundings and to each other, and the co-ordination of surrounding nature to them ? Let us take a single illustration. Certain plants, orchids of certain species, are fertilized only by certain insects. Certain insects, moths, perform for these plants this process necessary to reproduction. In the plant there are, Darwin says, traps, gins, pitfalls and spring guns, and snares, to allure the moth and compel it to do this work of carrying the pollen from one sex of the plant to the other. Whence came this co-ordination, contrivance and wonderful design? This is but a single specimen. Thousands, yea millions of such illustrations could be cited. Our problem demands, Whence came all this? Is all this the product of blind, irrational matter, and blind, irrational physical force? Can these results, which require the highest efforts of master minds to apprehend them and construe them — these results so concurrent with and analogous to the highest conceptions of reason, be the result of mere blind irrational matter and force ?[30]

Braden continued to be admired by later Restorationists in Illinois and his books were kept in print. His insights into evolution were of a cutting edge nature for his time and he overwhelmed most laymen with the depths of his understanding and articulate exposition.

Harvey W. Everest (1831-1980)

Harvey W. Everest was born at North Hudson, Essex County, New York. His parents grew up in New England. He graduated at Crown Point and then taught school for a year. In 1849 he entered Hiram College and after enrolling in several courses stayed on as a teacher of Natural sciences. He graduated from Oberlin College having completed the classical curriculum. By 1861 he was an ordained minister in the Disciples of Christ.

His career as a public man may be briefly sketched as follows: President of Hiram College, succeeding President James A. Garfield, 1861-64; President of Eureka College, Illinois, 1864-72; Pastor of the Christian Church, at Springfield, Ill., 1872-74; Professor in Kentucky University, Lexington, Ky., 1874-76; Pastor for one year at Normal, Ill.; President, a second time, at Eureka College, 1877-81; President of Butler University, Irvington, Ind, 1881-86; Chancellor of Garfield University [Wichita, Kansas], 1886 to the present time, May, 1888.

---

[30] http://abarc.org/legacy/Resources/BoyceMouton/Books/Liberal%20Missouri/
Liberal%20Missouri%20Chapter%209.pdf

As a public lecturer and as a Christian minister, the subject of this sketch has been very successful, always making a good impression by his earnest, persuasive manner, and delighting and convincing his hearers by his clear, cogent reasoning. His style is his own, his manner of speaking and his thoughts are more a part of himself, and give the listener more nearly a correct idea of the man than is usually the case with public speakers. Always clear in his thoughts; inclined to be analytical in his treatment of a subject, though comprehensive in his grasp of it; never impetuous or boisterous, though often grand in style, he resembles more the quiet, clear river, than the rushing torrent.

As a scholar, Chancellor Everest is comprehensive and thorough. At Hiram College he filled for eight years the Chair of Chemistry and natural science; in Kentucky University, that of Sacred History; in Eureka College, Butler and Garfield Universities, that of Philosophy and Political Economy. Still he has been mainly given to the investigation and defense of the Sacred Scriptures.

As an instructor, he has always been popular; his affable manner, punctuality, laboriousness and enthusiasm, are among the chief elements of his success. His long experience as a presiding officer in college life sufficiently indicates his more than average ability in this respect.

Chancellor Everest possesses a good physique and has enjoyed almost uninterrupted good health. This has enabled him to perform double work--the work of a professor and that of a preacher and lecturer--with great efficiency during nearly the whole of his public life. He is well known to the readers of the current literature of the Christian church, is the author of many magazine articles, and of a valuable work on Christian evidence, entitled, "The Divine Demonstration." He is also the recipient of literary honors, having received the degree of A. M. in 1864, and subsequently that of LL. D

Since coming to Wichita Dr. Everest has been occupied with the organization and inauguration of Garfield University.

How well he and his associates have succeeded in this work may be seen in the fact that during the first session, which is now drawing to a close, the enrollment has reached thirty-seven professors and instructors and 730 students.

As one of the foremost scholars of the State, and at the head of one of the most prominent educational institutions of the West, and one of the leading and enterprising citizens of Wichita, the publishers take pleasure in presenting, the portrait of Chancellor Everest.[31]

Regarding his presidency at Eureka,

For more than half a century his influence was a potent factor in the lives of many who ever counted his guiding friendship a privilege. During the first three years of his administration the number of students increased from 125 to 225. The close of the Civil War and the resumption of normal conditions contributed to this result. Then he was assisted by some able coadjutors in the school H. O. Newcomb, a graduate of the University of Michigan, a kindly teacher upon whom "the boys" could always depend in "emergencies," and Dr. J. M. Allen, a lovable and stimulating instructor. In 1863 the deficit in current expenses became serious. A canvass of the community was made and enough money was secured to tide over for a time. At the close of eight years' service Mr. Everest resigned in 1872…H. W. Everest returned to the presidency of the college in 1877. For three years more he led the school with his fine energy and scholarship. During this time a boardinghouse for young men, with a capacity for forty-eight, was built. But this hall and that one erected in 1854, having served well their purposes, have gone the way of all earth. Each in its time was full of the romances of youth its joyous laughter and midnight oil but now there remain of them only a few fading memories.[32]

Everest's chief book to combat unbelief and in a sense liberalism is his *The Divine Demonstration* (Christian Publishing Company, 1884). The book is still in print. It appears that Everest has taken some of his clues as to

[31] Haynes, 43-45.
[32] http://www.ksgenweb.org/sedgwick/PortBio/PBios1/Everest_HW.htm

focus from Walter Scott who likewise identifies Jesus as the Christ, the grand proposition. Scott himself published *The Messiahship: The Great Demonstration*. Everest's approach, however, is considerably different. He brings to bear many more non-Biblical arguments and does not lay out the scheme of redemption in the manner of Scott. Everest is also much more involved in establishing the authenticity of the Biblical text than was Scott. Everest sets forth his basic approach in the introduction. It is clear that in his arguments on the similarities of nature and the Bible that Everest has taken basic affirmations from Joseph Butler's (1692-1752) *The Analogy of Religion, Natural and Revealed* and updated the details. As far as his arguments regarding the Biblical texts go he has incorporated a large stash of evidences much the same as those found in the debate of Alexander Campbell with Robert Owen (1829) in Cincinnati.

> Now, the proposition announced by the Father and the Holy Spirit, which is to be believed and confessed by man, and upon which the Church is founded, is the following: Jesus is the Christ the Son of God. The proof of this grand proposition is given, men could not be held accountable for their unbelief. This proof consists of the testimony of the Apostles, the character of Christ and of his religion, and the evidence from prophecy. The providence of God also determined the order in which these arguments should be applied for the construction of the proposition. It is a divine demonstration, because the proposition, the proof, and the order of proof, were divinely given; it is called a demonstration because in normal or probable reasoning a proposition may be as certainly established as in mathematics. We may know whom we have believed as the discussion goes on among men it is more and more evident that the whole question turns on the authority and nature of Jesus. Was he but a man then all is lost; was he divine? Then all else will follow. Men may quibble about various things in the Old Testament and in the New, but the main question, and the one that carries every thing else, is this: Who was Jesus? The army of the Lord must rally around the cross if it would be United and victorious. In following out this plan of the argument room has been found for every class of evidence bearing on the subject. The Proof of the genuineness and credibility of the New Testament has been condensed and presented in one view. The relations of Christianity and science, and the several questions which arise out of this relation, are fully discussed. The adaptation of Christianity

to man—to his mental, moral, and social natures,-is assigned ample space in the argument. Objections are classified and answered. The reliability, and inspiration of the writers of the Old Testament are established, and the testimony of these reliable and inspired writers is brought to sustain the claims of Christ. The Messianic prophecies occupy, in this discussion, as prominent a place as they in the Holy Scriptures...

The author expresses his indebtedness to the writers on Christian Evidences who have preceded him, but especially to the divine word, whence he has endeavored mainly to derive the material and the method of this demonstration.[33]

Everest manifests a sense of certainty regarding the inspiration and authenticity of the Scriptures. His outlook is a major contrast with the liberal theologians at the University of Chicago.

Everest believed that he had established without fail the veracity and authenticity of the Scriptures. He certainly compounded multiple arguments and evidence that brought him to that conclusion. His conclusion in regard to the inspiration of the Scriptures was both euphoric and elegant.

The proposition that the Holy Scriptures were given by inspiration is confirmed when we find no inharmonious or contradictory facts. (a) There is nothing adverse in the form of the Bible. Given for the guidance of human beings it had to be in human language. Man can not use the dictionary and grammar of angels. That the Bible should have great variety of style, that it should sweep through the whole literary gamut, from historic annals to the sublimest poetry, and that it should be the scholar's task to gather up and classify its great truths, are points of excellence rather than defects. (b) There are no portions unworthy of so high a source. Nature has her monotonous plains and her mountain scenery of surpassing grandeur; her leaden skies and her glorious sunsets; so is it in the Bible. Human nature and history had to be portrayed as they were. Portions of seeming insignificance are of great meaning on account of their relation to higher things. History and revelation were developed side by side, and many a link is thrown across with no other purpose than to bind them together. (c) There are no insuperable incon-

---

[33] Harvey W. Everest, *The Divine Demonstration: A Text-book of Christian Evidence* (St. Louis: Christian Publishing Company, 1884) v, vi.

sistencies and oppositions. Deduct from the sum of alleged con-
tradictions all those arising from errors in copying, interpola-
tions, suppressions, mis-translations, ignorance of history, cus-
tom and science, the infirmities of the mind and the moral cor-
ruption of the heart-all difficulties of our own manufacture-and
what would be left to antagonize inspiration? Now, when there is
scarcely a cloud in the sky, when true scholarship has cleared
away nearly every difficulty, and when there is no need of hasty
conclusions, it is no time for Christian defenders to become
weak-kneed and to begin stammering forth their confessions of
Bible errors in behalf of prophets and Apostles.[34]

J. W. McGarvery (1829-1911)

J. W. McGarvey was born in Hopkinville, Kentucky. His mother was a
former student of Barton W. Stone. From Kentucky his family moved to
Tremont, Illinois, south of Peoria, in 1839 and though McGarvey attended Bethany College 1847-1850 Illinois was his home state until he graduated from Bethany in 1850.[35] McGarvey was baptized by W. K. Pendleton
in 1848. He was encouraged by Alexander Campbell to remain at
Bethany as a teacher of the classical languages, but he preferred to preach
and spent 1850-61 at congregations in Missouri. Because of Missouri
requirements on loyalty to the Union he left Missouri in 1861 at the start
of the Civil War and accepted a position as the minister of the Main
Street Christian Church in Lexington, Kentucky. In 1865 he became a
teacher at the College of the Bible in Lexington where he remained
achieving increasing acclaim until his death in 1911. He served as president from 1895-1911.

At the time of his death he was the best known Bible teacher in the
Restoration Movement in part due to his extensive publications. He was
especially known for his commentary on *Acts of the Apostles* (1863, 1892)
which is still in print. He also published a book on *Evidences of Christianity*
(1886) which has much the same approach as that of Everest, but Mc-
Garvey advanced additional arguments affirming the credibility of the
Biblical text. His reading was obviously far reaching and involved both
conventional and liberal critics. His opposition to liberalism is obvious as
he proceeds to clinch his conclusions.

---

[34] Ibid., 390-91.

[35] W. C. Morro, *"Brother McGarvey": The Life of J. W. McGarvey of the College of the Bible*
(Lexington: College of the Bible, 1940)

As to the credibility of these writers, we may say in general terms, in advance of a more critical inquiry, that their high character, indicated by the unvarying purity of the sentiments found in their writings, lifts them above the suspicion of being untrustworthy, and secures to them a credibility at least equal to that of the best secular historian. This consideration unites with the preceding to place them among the most credible of writers, and to render any event which they record, concerning which there is no special ground of doubt, as probable as any of the factors that make up history. This much is conceded by all, even among unbelievers, whose opinions are respected by intelligent men; and it is conceded on the ground which we have stated.[36]

McGarvey, possibly more than any other Restoration leader of the time kept up with the growing liberalism in Christendom, and was uniquely aware of those from the Movement in the Chicago area.[37] In 1895 McGarvey commenced publishing short essays on Biblical criticism in the *Christian Standard*. These were later collected and published as a book.[38] Several times he responded to essays published by Professor Herbert Willett, for example one on "Creation" in the *Chicago Tribune*.[39] The specific focus was on the Babylonian creation myths, The Enuma Elish and the *Gilgamesh*.

This, now, is the string of nonsense by the curtailing of which "the prophetic teachers of Israel"— that is, J and P — drew up the accounts of creation in the Book of Genesis! Professor Willett may believe it if he can, and if he so desires, but to my mind it would be about as sensible to say that the parable of the prodigal son was derived from Peck's "Bad Boy," or from Mark Twain's "Tom Sawyer."

If I were to pass judgment on this "Creation Epic," as destructive critics fondly call it, I would say that it was written by some unbeliever in the gods of Babylon, some Bob Ingersoll of

---

[36] J. W. McGarvey, *Evidences of Christianity*. Cincinnati: Guide Printing and Publishing Co. (Reprinted 1891; Cincinnati: Standard Publishing Co., 1912; Nashville:Gospel Advocate, 1956, 1964, 1974)

[37] M. Eugene Boring, *Disciples and the Bible: A History of Disciples Biblical Interpretation in North America* (St. Louis: Bethany Press, 1997).

[38] J. W. McGarvey, *Short Essays on Biblical Criticism* (Cincinnati: Standard Publishing Company, 1910). Reprinted from *Christian Standard*, 1895-1904.

[39] June 14, 1902, *Chicago Tribune*. 390 in *Short Essays*.

that day, for the purpose of ridiculing the gods out of existence in the minds of the people. Certainly no sensible man who read it and believed it could ever afterward offer incense or prayer to any one of the brutal gang.

This is not all. I scarcely think that the craziest of the critics would claim that this satire on the Babylonian gods was written before the days of Moses. It is only after robbing Moses of all connection with the Bible account of creation, and relegating it to unknown authors of later centuries, that they can claim priority for the Babylonian account. For, be it remembered, this account was found on clay tablets dug out of the ruins of Asurbanipal's library at Nineveh. But Asurbanipal reigned from 667 to 625 B. C, and within this period his library building was erected and his tablets collected or written. There is no historical evidence that these creation tablets had been in existence for any considerable period prior to this. But Moses lived at least seven hundred years earlier, and if he wrote the Book of Genesis, his account preceded by a long interval this Babylonian satire. And if, as is highly probable, Moses received the account of creation either from oral tradition or in a written form, this carries the origin of it back to a still earlier date. The critical theory on the subject, then, although it has been adopted by men who ought to have more judgment, is but a wild and groundless conjecture resulting from their equally groundless analytical theory of the Pentateuch.

In a similar vein McGarvey published a lengthy book *The Authorship of the Book of Deuteronomy*, (1902).[40] McGarvey had a significant influence which showed up in a younger generation of conservative Restorationist leaders in Illinois.

McGarvey, like many of his contemporaries, including those at Princeton Theological Seminary, held that valid Biblical interpretation is "scientific."

The Scriptures are not to be tested by the science of chemistry, or that of astronomy, or that of geology, or that of mathematics, but they are to be tested by the science of logic. Demonstration is not the right word. Demonstrations are addressed to the eye. But scientific proof—that is, logical proof—is the test by which

---

[40] J. W. McGarvey, *Authorship of the Book of Deuteronomy, with its Bearings on the Higher Criticism of the Pentateuch* (Cincinnati: Standard Publishing Company, 1902).

the Scriptures are to be tried; and no man is required to believe them except on such proof. "Is reason the supreme guide in religion?" No. Reason must determine for us whether the Bible is from God; must detect and correct all mistakes and changes made by copyists, and must ascertain as best it can the meaning of all obscure passages; but here her work terminates. These questions being settled, the Bible itself is our sole guide and authority. (McGarvey, *Short Essays* 1910:226-27).[41]

McGarvey and Willett differed over both how the Bible was to be interpreted and the manner of teaching students the text. According to Boring in the judgment of McGarvey,

Ministers were to give one, clear, authoritative answer to every question. Biblical criticism was the enemy of *this*. This was what higher criticism took away. It was therefore the enemy of all that Disciples stood for, in McGarvey's view. Thus the passion (and vitriol) with which McGarvey defended his view of the Bible and opposed higher criticism. This was the peculiarly Disciples issue at stake in the battle over Biblical criticism for both McGarvey and Willett. Willett saw biblical criticism as the liberating means of *attracting* people to the Bible, of showing them the variety in the Bible, and its record of the growth and development of a religious community toward ever higher truth. *This* is what Willett wanted his students to see in the Bible. Willett was thus not an opponent of evangelism. He saw higher criticism not as the opponent of evangelism but as that which allowed evangelism to remain honest. It was not a dogmatic theory about the Bible as such that was the particular issue that bothered Disciples, but how it impacted their understanding of the way the Bible is to be used in the propagation of the faith. McGarvey's pedagogy was indoctrination. There was thus hardly any reference to secondary works on the Bible. Students who studied under McGarvey for four years of Bible class, two semesters per year, could not recall that McGarvey referred them to any books except the Bible and his own *Lands of the Bible*. The College of the Bible library thus did not need to be large or up to date, and it was not, for it was barely used.[42]

---

[41] Quoted in Boring, 231
[42] Ibid., 237.

Clearly Restorationists in Illinois were impacted by the coming of liberalism to the state. Some welcomed the new non-conventional insights. Others resisted Biblical criticism, evolution, and the social gospel adamantly. Those without theological training were largely oblivious to the new perspectives but that would change before the twentieth century gained a firm toe-hold.

Conclusions

The theological conservatives in Illinois were sometimes pugnacious in their reactions against the modernists. Liberals were often near at hand. But the conservatives were also constructive in declaring the major convictions of Christianity which they alleged were age-long fundamental tenants. The Illinois Restorationists increased their opposition to modernism as the nineteenth century wound down and in the early part of the twentieth century. The Restorationists were not a major force in the larger religious world, nevertheless they made an impact, especially on their own congregations, so that in the twentieth century new schools and forces were at work to change the face of the Restoration Movement in Illinois.

13. The Impact of Religious Liberalism on the Restorationist Churches in Illinois

Religious liberalism has many forms. The earliest religious liberals in America were likely Deists. Deism had its roots in the British Isles, but was taken up by the German and French Enlightenments. In Britain prominent Deists were Herbert of Cherbury (1583-1648) and Matthew Tindal (1657-1733). In Germany the philosopher Gottfried Leibnitz (1646-1716) and Gotthold Lessing (1729-1781), and in France the renown Voltaire (1694-1778) held Deistic views. More to the point for our purposes were the American Deists: Benjamin Franklin (1706-1790), George Washington (1732-1799), Thomas Jefferson (1743-1826), Ethan Allen (1738-1789) and Thomas Paine (1837-1809).[1]

According to Lord Herbert, Deists believed in one supreme God, who desired worship in virtue and piety, repentance of sins, and who assigned rewards and punishments in this life and in the one to come. They rejected Trinitarianism, revealed Scriptures, and miracles among other more orthodox perspectives.[2] The Restoration forefathers opposed Deism, for example, in 1929 Alexander Campbell debated Robert Owen the Welsh Deist who established a colony in southern Indiana.

Deists weren't strong in Illinois, but in the nineteenth century the state was the home of two famous agnostics, Robert Ingersoll (1833-1899) and Clarence Darrow (1857-1938).

Robert Ingersoll (1833-1899)

Robert Ingersoll, an eloquent attorney and lecturer, was born in New York State into the family of a Congregational minister.[3] The father, a

---

[1] Kerry S. Walters, *The American Deists: Voices of Reason and Dissent in the Early Republic* (Lawrence, KS: University Press of Kansas, 1992); *Revolutionary Deists: Early America's Rational Infidels* (Amherst, NY: Prometheus Books, 2011).

[2] https://en.wikipedia.org/wiki/
Edward_Herbert,_1st_Baron_Herbert_of_Cherbury

[3] Frank Smith, *Robert G. Ingersoll: A Life* (Buffalo: Prometheus Books, 1990).

right wing extremist, was forced to move about and later lived in Wisconsin then Southern Illinois in the region around Marion and east in the early 1850s. Robert lived for a time in Shawneetown, but then settled in Peoria in 1857. He was a Colonel in the Civil War and after the war Illinois attorney general. He was best known far and wide for his eloquent lectures especially focused on the foibles of religion and Scripture. Though sometimes identified as a Deist he was more properly an agnostic. His influence was generally independent of Biblical scholarship but some of his criticisms later, though not directly from Ingersoll, were taken up by the liberal critics, for example, his charges in his lectures on "Some Mistakes of Moses."[4]

Clarence Darrow (1857-1938).

Another Illinois agnostic was Clarence Darrow (1857-1938) famous for his debates with Williams Jennings Bryan (1860-1925) in 1925 in the Dayton, Tennessee, Scopes Trial.[5] Both Darrow and Bryan had ties with Illinois.

Though in early life Bryan lived in Illinois he was later more identified with Nebraska from which he ran for the presidency on the Democratic ticket three times. Bryan was born in Salem, Illinois, and educated in an academy attached to Illinois College at Jacksonville.[6] He graduated from Illinois College in 1881, studied at Union Law School in Chicago and practiced in Jacksonville, 1883-1887. In 1887 he with his wife, also a lawyer, moved to Lincoln, Nebraska, for the greater challenges it offered. Bryan was a member of the Cumberland Presbyterian Church and later, the larger Presbyterian body. He was a very active Christian, spoke widely for Christian causes across the nation, and became closely identified with pacifism and anti-evolution views. He was widely herald by conservatives as an exemplary Christian leader.

Clarence Darrow was born in Kinman, in Northeastern Ohio, and studied at Allegheny College, Meadville, Pennsylvania, but did not complete a degree.[7] He also studied at the University of Michigan Law

[4] Robert Ingersoll, *Some Mistakes of Moses* (Washington, D. C.: C. P. Farrell, 1879).

[5] Edward J. Larson, *When Science & Christianity Meet: The Scopes Trial in History and in Legend* (Chicago: University of Chicago Press, 2003).

[6] Paolo Enrico Coletta, *William Jennings Bryan* (Lincoln: University of Nebraska Press, 1964-69).

[7] John A. Farrell, *Clarence Darrow: Attorney for the Damned* (New York: Doubleday, 2011).

School, but rather than taking a degree spent his time in a law office preparing for the bar exam which he passed in 1878. His father was an iconoclast and Free Thinker. His mother pushed women's rights and suffrage. He launched his law career in Ashtabula, northeastern Ohio, but moved to Chicago in 1880. In Chicago he became a noted pro-labor attorney, defending Eugene V. Debs and later those who violated Civil Laws, his most important case being the defense of Leopold and Loeb who murdered fourteen year old Bobby Frank.[8] Darrow opposed the death penalty.

Darrow became known as an opponent of orthodox Christianity because of the widespread dissemination of his views expressed in the Scopes Trial which included among other items, support for evolution and opposition to Biblical teachings. While he was not a scholarly liberal religious thinker whose affirmations infiltrated the left-leaning seminaries, the populist fundamentalist preachers quickly identified him as an infidel and he became the recipient of blatant invective in many a fundamentalistic sermon.

In fact the proponents of evolution and higher Biblical criticism soon became the two identifying markers of liberal Christianity late in the nineteenth century. Proponents of higher criticism found many reasons to question orthodox claims regarding the Mosaic authorship and the Scriptures as authentic history and theology. These perspectives toward the 1890s became widely known and opened up rifts in the major denominations.[9] Some of these liberal views were taught at the University of Chicago and other Illinois seminaries and came to impact the Restoration Movement especially in the Chicago area.

Unitarian/Universalist

Another source of liberalism which arrived in Illinois early was Unitarianism and Universalism. In the late eighteenth century certain ministers in the Boston area started questioning the deterministic Calvin doctrines of predestination and eternal security. They also came to believe that though Jesus was divine he was not God, a view that might be labeled

---

[8] https://en.wikipedia.org/wiki/Clarence_Darrow

[9] Thomas H. Olbricht, "Rhetoric in the Higher Criticism Controversy," *The Rhetoric of Protest and Reform 1878-1898,* ed. Paul Boase, (Athens: Ohio University Press, 1980). Thomas H. Olbricht, "Preaching on Biblical Criticism in the United States and Great Britain in the Nineteenth Century," *A New History of the Sermon: Nineteenth Century,* Ed. Robert Ellison (Leiden: Brill, 2010), 115-136.

Arian. These proponents of broader church views were labeled Arminian as opposed to Calvinistic Congregationalists. Stresses and strains continued until in 1825 the Arminian heirs of Puritanism created the American Unitarian Association. Some of the foremost leaders were William Ellery Channing and Ralph Waldo Emerson. The Arminians essentially won Harvard College to their cause, leading to the founding of Andover Theological Seminary in Andover, MA, in 1808. Even earlier certain preachers, mostly in the back country of upper New England turned to universalism which declared that all humans would ultimately be accepted by God.[10]

The second generation of the Jones/Smith movement entered into significant rapprochement with the Unitarians; and Elias Smith with the Universalists especially beginning in 1817.[11] Both the Universalists and Unitarians opposed many of the fundamentals of Calvinism, were antitrinitarian and emphasized the goodness of man and the immanence of God. The Unitarians markedly became more open to Biblical criticism.[12]

Universalists

The Universalist Church in America was founded in 1833, however, various persons of Universalist outlooks could be found in Boston and Philadelphia several years prior to that time. Central to the Universalist vision is the declaration that eventually all humanity will be saved. Their numbers were largely in the Northeast, but in small towns and rural areas in contrast with the Unitarians. It was not uncommon to find Universalists in the frontier regions westward. Noted early Universalists were John Murray (1741-1815) of Boston, Elhanan Winchester (1751-1797) who evangelized widely in the northeast and in England, and Hosea Ballou (1771-1852) of upper New England and Boston. Elias Smith no doubt came in contact with Ballou at some point in his career. In 1961 the Universalist Church of America merged with the Unitarians to form the Unitarian Universalist Association.[13]

---

[10] Jerry Wayne Brown, *The Rise of Biblical Criticism in America, 1800-1870: The New England Scholars* (Middletown, CT: Wesleyan University Press, 1969).

[11] Thomas H. Olbricht, "Universalists," *ESCM* 760.

[12] Thomas H. Olbricht, "Unitarians," *ESCM* 749-780; also, Thomas H. Olbricht, "Christian Connexion and Unitarian Relations 1800-1844) *RQ*, 9 (1966) 160-186.

[13] Elmo Arnold Robinson, American Universalism; its Origins, Organization, and Heritage (New York: Exposition Press, 1970).

The Universalists and the New England Christians often appealed to same socio-economic level, that is, small town and middle class. Certain women preachers, for example, Abigail Roberts (1791-1841), sometimes preached in congregations of both groups. In 1817 Elias Smith who had toyed with universalism, or restorationism as it was sometimes called (that is, the restoration of all things, Acts 3:21), departed for the Universalists and preached among them. More than once before his death in 1846 he returned to the Christians, but then went back to the Universalists.

Unitarians

The American Unitarian Association was formed in Boston 1825 after years of controversies regarding Calvinism within the Congregational (original Puritan) Churches. A century earlier Arminian views emerged and religious leaders in eastern Massachusetts grew more open to the Arminian, Deistic, and rationalistic views coming from England and Germany. Noted early Unitarians were Noah Worchester (1758-1837), Henry Ware (1764-1845), William Ellery Channing (1780-1842) and Ralph Waldo Emerson (1803-1882). The Unitarians promoted human ability in self improvement, the newly developing German Biblical criticism, and a Christology in which Christ was God's special son, and divine, yet not equal with the Father.[14]

Second generation preachers from the New England Christians were strongly influenced by the same theological changes, especially David Millard (1794-1873) and Joseph Badger (1792-1852). As both Abner Jones and Elias Smith worked their way out of the Calvinistic Baptists they became Arminian, and soon anti-trinitarian, especially Smith. Boston Unitarian leaders referred to these Christians as evangelical Unitarians because of their awakening methods which the forerunners of the Unitarians eschewed. Badger spent a few weeks in Boston among the Unitarians, and Unitarians were sometimes present at the Christian conferences. Unitarians invited the Christians to participate in educational enterprises,

---

[14] *A Stream of Light: a Short History of American Unitarianism*, ed. Conrad Wright (Boston: Skinner House Books, 1989). On the early Unitarians and Biblical Criticism see: Thomas H. Olbricht, "Biblical Interpretation in North America," in *A History of Biblical Interpretation: The Enlightenment through the Nineteenth Century*, Volume 3, eds. Alan J. Hauser and Duane F. Watson (Grand Rapids: Eerdmans Publishing Company, 2017) 344-358.

especially Meadville Theological Seminary, founded in 1844 and Antioch College in Yellow Springs, Ohio launched in 1850.

When Alexander Campbell and Tolbert Fanning traveled to New England in 1836, first crossing upper state New York, they often preached in Unitarian Churches as the only buildings available to them. While in Boston Campbell preached in William Ellery Channing's "cathedral." Tolbert Fanning spoke before a group of Unitarian men who later published his address.[15] Campbell, however, believed the Unitarian anti-trinitarian stance was too doctrinaire, and did not feel comfortable with Unitarian "ostentation" and their propensity to central organization.

Both Unitarians and Universalists were found in Illinois by at least 1830.

Olbricht wrote, regarding the Unitarians traveling west.[16]

> In 1825 the American Unitarian Association was formed, over some objection, for the primary purpose of publishing tracts and circulars. The following year students from Harvard Divinity School commenced traveling west in the summers, making contacts for liberal Christianity on the frontier. In 1827 Moses G. Thomas traveled by horseback as far west as St. Louis, making many contacts with people of the Christian Connexion.[17]

Thomas no doubt stopped along the way at certain towns in Illinois.

Meadville Theological Seminary founded by the Unitarians in 1844 moved to Chicago in 1926 and affiliated with the University of Chicago. In the founding years in the early nineteenth century it was hoped that the seminary would be jointly hosted with Christian Connexion leaders.[18] In 1930 after merger of Meadeville with the Universalist Lombard College founded in Galesburg in 1853 the resultant combine affiliated with the University of Chicago. Earlier Lombard had a seminary—The Ryder School of Divinity 1880-1913.[19]

At various times Restoration Movement churches were accused of being Unitarian. As we have shown, the two groups at times held similar outlooks, but over the years the Unitarians became more humanistic and

---

[15] Tolbert Fanning, *A discourse delivered in Boston, July 17, 1836* (Boston: B.H. Greene, 1836).

[16] Olbricht, "Christian Connexion Unitarian Relations, 34 in digitized version.

[17] American Unitarian Association, *Second Annual Report*, 1827, 49.

[18] Thomas H. Olbricht, "Christian Connexion and Unitarian Relations" (Full citation above.)

[19] https://en.wikipedia.org/wiki/Meadville_Lombard_Theological_School.

less amenable to the Restorationists in Illinois. Certain critics wished to
accuse the "Campbellites" of Unitarian predilections.

> Speaking of his observations at Niantic, Illinois, Mr. Shaw says
> on page 294: In and around this town there was a large number
> of Campbellites, a sect to whom I have referred in Chapter X.
> on "American Churches." They viewed with jealousy the en-
> croachments of the Methodists. As they were generally fond of
> controversy, and their preachers flippant proclaimers of the
> "Gospel in the Water," their sermons are a strange medley of all
> sorts of stuff about salvation by immersion. Their style that of
> an auctioneer, reserving their wit and railing for other churches,
> and their praises for their own. Bible, missionary societies, Sun-
> day schools, and colleges, received their loudest denunciations.
> Things the most sacred they ridiculed and institutions the most
> solemn they reviled. The Sabbath they disregarded; the forgive-
> ness of sins, a change of heart, they laughed at, unless what was
> connected with immersion. The divinity of Christ they did not
> generally believe in; the personality and operation of the Holy
> Spirit they scoffed at. They were literally immersed infidels, hav-
> ing little of the form or power of godliness. Where evangelical
> churches were cold and lukewarm, these prospered; but when
> alive and earnest, the Campbellites sank to their coverts by the
> waters.[20]

Another form of liberalism had to do with charismatic actions of the
Holy Spirit in conversion, extraordinary spirit manifestations, healings
and even Spiritualism. In regard to these actions and exercises see Chapter 10, The Walter Scott Russell Defection in Illinois.

Main Stream Liberalism

Trajectories of main stream liberalism began to impact Protestant
Churches in America after the Civil War, but it wasn't until the later part
of the nineteenth century that church members became aware of the
new views regarding the authorship and inspiration of Biblical documents and the creation of earthly fauna and flora. The social gospel, fo-
cusing upon humans building the kingdom of God on earth by addressing social inequities, also came into mix. The first persons to embrace

---

[20] Haynes, 71

these changes were Presbyterians, Northern Baptists, Congregationalists and somewhat later Methodists and Lutherans.[21]

Training in Biblical criticism in North America toward the close of the nineteenth century was in service of the church and its ministers. Even major Biblical Scholars such as Charles A. Briggs (1841-1913) a Presbyterian of Union Theological Seminary, New York, positioned Biblical scholarship as a science which enabled the church to appreciate its heritage and provide a clearer view of its mission.[22] William Rainey Harper a University of Chicago Baptist (1856-1906) hoped to bring technical Biblical studies to the masses through correspondence courses in Hebrew, Chautauqua lectures, and later study guides written by University of Chicago scholars and published by the University of Chicago Press.[23] The presuppositions of these scholars basically retained reformation consensus positions in regard to the authority of the Scriptures, Trinitarianism, Chalcedonian Christology, reformation soteriology, and ecclesiology. Charles Briggs was dismayed in the 1910s when younger colleagues openly denigrated the virgin birth of Jesus.

North American scholars in the 1880s in some quarters began to diverge from the consensus. A significant influence was the great influx of Americans studying in German Universities. In the 1890s above four hundred Americans studied in German theological faculties most years. Not all received German degrees, but several did. Some were professors who spent a year or more in Germany under the supposition that in order to keep abreast of cutting edge Biblical scholarship, a stint in Germany was imperative. Benjamin W. Bacon a Congregationalist of Yale (1860-1932) attended lectures in several German universities in the 1890s. James Frederick McCurdy (1847-1935) of the University of Toronto studied at Göttingen and Leipzig in the early 1880's. Also studying in Germany were Jewish professors Louis Ginzberg (1873-1953) at Strassburg and Heidelberg, and Julian Morgenstern (1881-1976) at Berlin and Heidelberg. Roman Catholic scholars studied in Paris, for example Joseph Bruneau (1866-1933) of St. John's Seminary, Brighton, MA, and Henry

[21] Gary J. Dorrien, *The Making of American Liberal Theology: Idealism, Realism, and Modernity 1900-1950* (Louisville: Westminster John Knox Press, 2003).

[22] Thomas H. Olbricht, "Charles A. Briggs," *Historical Handbook of Major Biblical Interpreters*, ed. Donald K. McKim (Carol Stream: InterVarsity Press, 1998).

[23] Thomas H. Olbricht, "William Rainey Harper," *Dictionary of Biblical Interpretation*, ed. John H. Hayes (Nashville:Abingdon Press, 1999). James P. Wind, *The Bible and the University: the Messianic Vision of William Rainey Harper* (Atlanta: Scholars Press, 1987).

Poels (1868-1948) at Louvain. Poels taught for a time at the Catholic University of America. Even persons of conservative commitments went to Germany, for example, J. Gresham Machen (1881-1937) who studied at Marburg and Göttingen in 1905-06.[24]

At first, the new higher critical positions which attained consensus status in Germany, met with considerable resistance in North America. Church bodies evicted resolute scholars, for example, the Presbyterians, Charles A. Briggs, and the Southern Baptists, Crawford Toy (1836-1919). Toy later accepted an appointment at Harvard. By 1910, several Biblical critics in the older seminaries had embraced critical German positions. Princeton was one of the few exceptions and remained so until 1929 when it was reorganized to bring about a more inclusive theological spectrum. These consensus critical perspectives regarding reconstructed history, the documentary hypothesis of the Pentateuch, the rejection of traditional authors of several Old Testament books, as well as some New Testament books, for example, the pastorals, were not widely disseminated in the churches. At this time, as yet, most of the seminaries were denominational and remained in the service of the churches.[25] The result was a developing rift in mainstream Christian and Jewish seminaries which flowed over into the churches and synagogues. Those on the left openly embraced modernism, while those on the right congealed as fundamentalistic movements, the Protestant movement producing a famous set of twelve volumes on the fundamentals from 1910 to 1915.

As the Presbyterians, Congregationalists and Baptists immigrated across the country they tended to become more liberal and were distinguished by new light and old light.

> The terms were first used during the First Great Awakening, which spread through the British North American colonies in the middle of the 18th century. In *A Faithful Narrative of the Surprising Work of God* (1737), Jonathan Edwards, a leader in the Awakening, describes his congregants vivid experiences with grace as causing a "new light" in their perspective on sin and atonement. Old Lights and New Lights generally referred to Congregationalists and Baptists in New England who took different positions on the Awakening than the traditional branches

---

[24] Thomas H. Olbricht, "Biblical Interpretation in North America in the Twentieth Century," *Historical Handbook,* 89; "Histories of American Bible Scholarship," *Currents in Biblical Scholarship* (1999) 237-256.

[25] Olbricht, "Biblical Interpretation," 90-91.

of their denominations. New Lights embraced the revivals that spread through the colonies, while Old Lights were suspicious of the revivals (and their seeming threat to authority). Historian Richard Bushman credits the division between Old Lights and New Lights for the creation of political factionalism in Connecticut in the mid-eighteenth century. Often many "new light" Congregationalists who had been converted under the preaching of George Whitefield left that connection to become "new light" Baptists when they found no evidence of infant baptism in the apostolic church. When told of this development, Whitefield famously quipped that he was glad to hear about the fervent faith of his followers but regretted that "so many of his chickens had become ducks." The Presbyterian Church in Pennsylvania would experience a division during the Great Awakening, with those elements of the denomination embracing the revivals called "New Side" and those opposed to the revivals called "Old Side."

In the Church of Scotland in the 1790s the "Old Lights" followed the principles of the Covenanters, while the "New Lights" were more focused on personal salvation and considered the strictures of the Covenants as less binding.

The terms were also used during the Second Great Awakening in America, in the early 19th century. New Lights were distinctive from the Old Lights in that they were more evangelical and, as historian Patricia Bonomi describes, carried "ferocity peculiar to zealots...with extravagant doctrinal and moral enormities."[26]

Seminaries and schools sided with one or the other in many cases. Notable new light schools were Oberlin College in Ohio which very early was coed and Lane Theological Seminary in Cincinnati. Various factions in these schools of both faculty and students embraced abolition and resulted in some of the faculty and students relocating at Oberlin. Lane seminary was connected with Lyman Beecher and his family originally from Connecticut.

---

[26] https://en.wikipedia.org/wiki/Old_and_New_Light.

McCormick Theological Seminary

Another Presbyterian school was McCormick Theological Seminary founded in Hanover, Indiana, on the Ohio River between Cincinnati and Evansville, Indiana, in 1829. The Seminary moved to Chicago in 1860, was chiefly supported by benefactor Cyrus McCormick and his wife. After his death it was renamed McCormick Theological Seminary. The seminary was mostly mainstream evangelical, but some of the professors started moving toward the left by the end of the century though not radically so. The Seminary continues to exist in Chicago in conjunction with the Lutheran Theological Seminary near the loop and specializes in programs for different ethnic groups.[27]

The Divinity School of the University of Chicago

A new North American school of Biblical criticism influenced by German predecessors developed at the University of Chicago late in the nineteenth century. The new perspective was empirically and sociologically undergirded. The Chicago approach centered in upon a so-called scientific methodology, that is, that the Scriptures are to be scrutinized from a philological, exegetical, historical, and developing sociological perspective. The Chicago School emulated a North American empirical and pragmatic cast. But also, in contrast with the consensus sola scriptura, that the weight of experience is equal with, and later, and more important than the witness of the Scriptures. Four persons were chief progenitors of the Chicago school apart from William Rainey Harper, who in 1892 became president of the university: Ernest Dewitt Burton (1856-1925), Shailer Mathews (1863-1941), Edward J. Goodspeed (1871-1962) and Shirley Jackson Case (1872-1947). All four spent time in Germany: Burton at Leipzig in 1887, Mathews at Berlin in 1890, Case at Marburg 1910, and Goodspeed at Berlin 1898-1900, though he traveled also to Great Britain, the near east, and Egypt.[28]

The views of Shailer Mathews were typical of the school. Mathews published several books on the New Testament with Burton, and even

---

[27] http://mccormick.edu/content/our-history; ; Leroy J. Jones, *A History of the McCormick Theological Seminary of the Presbyterian Church* (Chicago: The Seminary, 1893).

[28] Thomas H. Olbricht, "New Testament Studies at the University of Chicago: The First Decade 1892-1902 (*RQ*, 22:1, 2 (1979) 87. Peden Creighton, *The Chicago School: Voices in Liberal Religious Thought* (Bristol, IN: Wyndham Hall Press, 1987).

more books by himself. In *The Social Teaching of Jesus* Mathews set out Jesus' perspectives on man, society, the family, the state, wealth, social life, forces of human progress, and the process of social regeneration. Such depiction is now designated Biblical anthropology. He pointed out that while the Gospels contain various corruptions and editorial additions, these may be easily ascertained through criticism, leaving a sizable body of authentic Jesus material. He argued that "divine sonship and consequent human brotherliness" comprised the core of Jesus' social doctrine. In The *Faith of Modernism*, Mathews criticized early Protestantism because it "detached the Bible from history and declared it to be the sole and divinely given basis of revealed truth." He declared that a modernist is one who "implicitly trusts the historical method." He further argued that the Bible as understood by grammatico-historical criticism "is a trustworthy record of human experience of God." He rejected the inerrancy of the scriptures, and accepted standard critical positions, but affirmed inspiration of the Bible in regard to those persons (rather than words) who had experienced the Spirit of God.[29]

It was at Chicago that the largest numbers of Restoration Movement scholars were influenced to take up liberal positions. The University of Chicago opened its doors October 1, 1892, making a widely heralded debut as an innovative and research-oriented university. The Baptist Union Theological Seminary, its predecessor, was founded in Chicago in 1867. In 1877 the seminary moved to Morgan Park. On January 1, 1879, William Rainey Harper at the Baptist Union, and later founding president of the new university in 1892, was called to the chair of Hebrew, where he remained until called to a similar professorship at Yale in 1886. The University of Chicago was established as a Baptist university and the university planners, not desiring duplication, arranged for the Morgan Park School to move on the university campus and become the Divinity School.[30]

William Rainey Harper (1856-1906)

William Rainey Harper (1856-1906) was born in New Concord, Ohio, east of Columbus. He attended Muskingum College and graduated at the

---

[29] Thomas H. Olbricht, "Shailer Mathews," *Dictionary of Biblical Interpretation.*

[30] Edgar J. Goodspeed, *As I Remember* (New York: Harper & Brothers, 1953), 47-50; Charley Harvey Arnold, *Near the Edge of the Battle: A Short History of the Divinity School and the Chicago School of Theology 1866-1966* (Divinity School Association, 1966).

age fourteen. He did graduate work at Yale obtaining the Ph.D. in Semitic Studies in 1876. He first taught at Denison University, then back to Yale in 1886, where he was Professor of Biblical Literature. He was active in the Chautauqua program in Western New York State and by time he became President at Chicago he had above 3000 students studying Hebrew in correspondence courses. He launched at the University the first courses in Egyptology and sociology in American universities.

As head Professor of New Testament Literature and Exegesis, Harper sought and finally secured Ernest D. Burton, Professor of New Testament Interpretation at Newton Theological Seminary, a Baptist seminary located in Newton Center, Massachusetts, just west of Boston. The 1895-96 Circular of Information of the Divinity School listed Burton as Head and Shailer Mathews as Associate Professor of New Testament History and Interpretation. In the 1900-1901 Circular, Edgar Johnson Goodspeed is listed as Associate Professor in Biblical and Patristic Greek.

Several scholars have commented on the emerging "Chicago School" and its characteristics.[31] Those who taught New Testament accepted the developing viewpoints regarding Biblical criticism and in fact contributed their New Testament expertise to the directions in which it went. Perhaps the most succinct expression of the platform and direction of the Chicago School is a statement by Gerald Birney Smith in *A Guide to the Study of the Christian Religion*. This volume, a collection of essays, comprised something of a Chicago School encyclopedia. In the preface, Smith wrote:

> The only common presuppositions of the various portions are the acceptance of the historical method and the belief that the interpretation of Christianity must be in accord with the rightful tests of scientific truthfulness and actual vitality in the modern world.[32]

The mood of America in the late nineteenth century can be summed up by the word "science." All enterprises were called upon to be scientific, even those normally associated with personalistic and humanistic pursuits. It was the untiring effort of William Rainey Harper to bring persons of scientific outlook to Chicago irrespective of discipline. He assembled an impressive array of professors in the natural sciences including William Gardner Hale in astronomy and A. A. Michelson in physics.

---

[31] C. H. Arnold, *Near the Edge of Battle* (Chicago: Divinity School Association, New Testament Studies) 89.

[32] *A Guide to the Study of the Christian Religion*, Gerald Birney Smith, ed. (Chicago: University of Chicago Press, 1916) vii.

He brought in Harry Pratt Judson to head the Department of Political Science and Albion W. Small to head Sociology, almost the first such departments in America. These appointments surprised the numerous critics of Harper's new university. "They thought I was going to organize a theological seminary," he observed.[33] As Harper staffed the Biblical departments, he searched for men with a historical and scientific turn of mind. And these departments were some of the larger in the University. In his autobiography, Shailer Mathews observed, "There were as many in the field of the Biblical and Semitic studies as in all the other departments combined. Biblical study was representative of the new scientific interest in religion. . . . It was inevitable that we should share in the enthusiasm for scientific research which has always marked the University of Chicago. But scientific research is tentative, and theology has always been the organization of an authoritative group belief." In Harper's vision Biblical studies were to take their place alongside the other disciplines and as scientifically respectable. He believed this goal could be attained through the critical, historical approaches to the Scriptures generated and championed in Germany. He was aware of dangers inherent in these studies, but he was convinced that in this manner the church could face the intellectual currents of the times. He was sure that through scientific study the Scriptures would be vindicated rather than deprecated.

Funk has incisively summed up Harper's program and outlook:

> Harper assumed that the battle with science and with religious orthodoxy would be fought on biblical ground. It was an assumption widely shared in his day. He also assumed that a victory for Scripture and the historical method required the creation of a new high scholarship in America. This scholarship had to

---

[33] Bernard E. Meland "The Chicago School of Theology," in *Twentieth Century Encyclopedia of Religious Knowledge*, Lefferts A. Loetscher, ed. (Grand Rapids: Wm. B. Eerdmans, 1955); Bernard E. Meland, "The Empirical Tradition in Theology at Chicago," *The Future of Empirical Theology* (Chicago: The University of Chicago Press, 1969); John E. Smith, "The Forging of an American Theological Tradition: the 'Chicago School,'" mimeographed paper, delivered at the Vanderbilt Conference on the Chicago School, February 27, 1969); and Larry E. Axel, "Modernism and the 'Chicago School,' of Theology," mimeographed paper presented at the 1974 Annual Meeting of the American Academy of Religion. Robert W. Funk, "The Watershed of the American Biblical Tradition: The Chicago School, First Phase, 1892-1920," *Journal of Biblical Literature* 95 (1976), 4-22. C.H. Arnold, *Near the Edge of the Battle*, 27. Gerald Birney Smith, ed., *A Guide to the Study of the Christian Religion* (Chicago: University of Chicago Press, 1916), vii.

specialize in those areas most closely associated with a sacro-
sanct text, viz., biblical languages, textual criticism, grammar,
lexicography, verse-by-verse interpretation, and translation. Such
scholarship would be motivated by an evangelical respect for the
text—or at least by the memory of it—and by a desire to control the battleground. Textual criticism became the surest means,
for example, of combating the verbal inerrancy of Scripture.
The victory would come in the form of a new respect for Scripture, in the spirit but not the letter of orthodoxy, and in accordance with the canons of historical science.[34]

We shall better understand the beginnings of the department of New
Testament at Chicago by scrutinizing the two pivotal figures, that is,
Ernest DeWitt Burton and Shailer Mathews.

Ernest DeWitt Burton (1856-1925)

Ernest DeWitt Burton (1856-1925) was born in Granville, Ohio, and
graduated from Denison University in 1876, where he excelled in Greek.
That same year William Rainey Harper came to Denison as a tutor and
stayed until moving to Morgan Park Seminary in 1879. After teaching for
three years in Michigan and Ohio, Burton entered the Rochester Theological Seminary as assistant to William Arnold Stevens in Greek. He
served as instructor in New Testament Greek 1882-83 during Professor
Stevens' leave of absence. In 1883 Burton was elected associate professor
of New Testament Greek at Newton Theological Institution, Newton,
Massachusetts. In 1887 he was given a year's leave to study abroad. He
hoped to spend most of the time studying at Leipzig, but ill health prevented more than short spans of attending lectures. In Leipzig Burton
made the acquaintance of Caspar Rene Gregory. In 1891 Burton was invited by President Harper to become chairman of the New Testament
Department at Chicago. After much conversation and inner struggle Burton accepted.[35] In Burton he secured a man of great energy, dedicated to
scholarship and publication. Burton proved more than equal to his position, despite the lack of graduate training beyond seminary. In the spring
of 1884 Burton was once again in Europe, this time at the University of
Berlin. From then until 1920 Burton was busy teaching, writing, and lec-

---

[34] Funk, "The Watershed," 16.

[35] John W. Boyer, *"A Hell of a job getting it Squared around": Three Presidents in Times of
Fundamental Change: Earnest D. Burton, Lawrence A. Kimpton, and Edward H. Levi*
(Chicago: The University of Chicago, 2013).

turing in various parts of the country, especially in the summer. He also was heavily involved in the Chicago journals, being associate editor of *Biblical World* and managing editor of *The American*.

Burton served the University of Chicago in many ways. He was head of the Department of New Testament and Early Christian Literature until he was chosen president in 1923. By 1902 Burton had published a number of books, mostly as aids to Biblical studies for persons from high school up and in class situations all the way from high school through seminary. These were books on New Testament Greek grammar, the Gospels, the life of Christ, and Paul and the apostolic age. Mostly printed by the University of Chicago Press, they were for popular consumption. Several of these works were coauthored either with William A. Stevens or Shailer Mathews. Most went through multi-editions and printings, indicating a considerable demand for such material and the fulfilling of the aim of Harper, Burton, and others at Chicago to educate not only Chicago students but all interested church and lay persons.

Each of these works represents the commitment of Burton to the view that "true Christian religion" is grounded in a proper understanding of the grammar, literary features, and historical settings of the New Testament. In his works Burton shows a progressive break with traditional American views of the nineteenth century. But such views as he held by 1902 would generally be looked upon as moderately conservative in our time. In 1906 Burton responded to a critic:

> All my predilections have been for the traditional views. My sympathies have been always most strongly with those who held the conservative positions, and who are pained and grieved by any departure from them. I have moved in my own thinking, but never save under the stress of evidence which seemed to me im-

possible to resist.[36] If I have erred in this matter I think it has
been from over-caution and over-reluctance to accept the evidence which required modification of view…To all criticisms of
myself I have only the answer that I stand where I do in my
convictions because I am forced to stand there as an honest student of the evidence and that the views which I hold do not di-
minish but increase my enthusiasm for Christianity and my hope
for its rapid progress in the world.[37]

Burton's position on four matters show him essentially traditional. (1) In
A Harmony of the Gospels, Burton utilizes the Johannine accounts of Jesus'
early visits to Jerusalem in constructing his basic outline. (2) In reflecting
on the parallel sayings of Jesus for which different occasions are presented, Burton wrote: "We simply maintain that in the present state of New
Testament criticism it is impossible to determine to which historical situation each of the parallel sayings belongs, and which of them were actually repeated on more than one occasion. He never suggests that the occasions are simply provided by church tradition or the evangelists. (3) He
affirmed an empty tomb, the bodily resurrection of Christ, and his "abid-
ing with, and working in, his kingdom on earth." (4) In conversations
with Harper late in 1905, Burton professed the mounting evidence to his
way of thinking for personal immortality. "…I am almost compelled to
think of the life to come as personal."[38] In his first decade at Chicago,
Burton always found experience coming out at the same place as the
Scripture rather than going beyond or contradicting it.

---

[36] "The following books were published by Burton before 1902, in alphabetical
order: with Mathews, *Constructive Studies in the Life of Christ* (Chicago: University of
Chicago, 1900). *The Ethical Teachings of Jesus in Relation to the Ethics of the Pharisees and
of the Old Testament* (Chicago: University of Chicago, 1897). *A Handbook of the Life
of the Apostle Paul* (Chicago: University of Chicago, 1897). With Wm. A. Stevens, *A
Harmony of the Gospels for Historical Study* (Chicago: University of Chicago, 1894).
With Mathews, *The Life of Christ* (Chicago: University of Chicago, 1900). *Notes on
New Testament Grammar* (Chicago: University of Chicago, rev. 1904). With Stevens,
An Outline Handbook of the Life of Christ from the Four Gospels, (Boston: The Bible
Study Publishing Co., 1892). *The Purpose and Plan of the Four Gospels* (Chicago:
University of Chicago, 1898). The Records and Letters of the Apostolic Age (New
York: C. Scribner's Sons, 1895). *Syntax of Moods and Tenses in the New Testament Greek*
(Boston: N. J. Bartlett and Co., 1892).

[37] Olbricht, "University of Chicago," 93.

[38] Ibid., 94.

Shailer Mathews

Mathews (1863-1941) was born in Portland, Maine. After graduating from Colby College in 1884, he entered Newton Theological Institution. Burton had arrived at Newton the previous year. Mathews was not particularly committed to the ministry but felt the attraction of a theological education. He was impressed by the persons, but not so much by the teaching methods. He felt the attention to detail and accuracy required by the Biblical languages was valuable. He particularly singled out the study of Biblical theology inasmuch as he was impressed with the manner in which it undermined "the basis of evangelical orthodoxy." After a summer serving a Baptist church in Maine he decided to become a teacher.[39] Upon graduation from Newton he was appointed Assistant Professor of Rhetoric at Colby College. A year later when Albion W. Small, professor of history and political economy, became president, Mathews was switched to that department. In that capacity he also taught courses in sociology. In 1890, with the help of Small, Matthews went to Germany for a year. He and his new bride moved to Berlin in order to study history and political economy at the university there.[40]

Upon his return to Colby he spent the next three years teaching the subjects in which he had prepared. In Germany he had little contact with those in theology. For example, he did not attend a single lecture of Harnack. His work in history progressed and he also prepared to teach sociology since Small, who went to Chicago to become head of the department of Sociology, had in mind that Mathews transfer to Chicago to teach sociology. But in 1894 Burton invited him to Chicago as Associate Professor of New Testament History. Mathews had substituted for Burton two winters at Newton, but did not feel inclined to teach in a seminary, prepared in New Testament, or favorably disposed toward Chicago. He had turned down an invitation to teach at Newton. Mathews' own statement indicates his outlook as he took up the position at Chicago.

> ...I knew I was not adapted to conventional New Testament instructing. I had never worked in the field proposed and knew nothing about it. In that I had plenty of company for the historical method had not yet been applied in any serious way to the study of the New Testament. I doubt if Dr. Burton himself

---

[39] William D. Lindsey, *Shailer Mathews's Lives of Jesus: The Search for a Theological Foundation for the Social Gospel* (Albany, State University of New York Press, 1997).
[40] Olbricht, ibid., 96.

foresaw the revolutionary effect of such a method . . . But Professor Burton overcame our hesitation. I caught his enthusiasm for a university in the making. My inherited interest in religion took form in an ambition to have a part in extending its frontiers. A new age was in the making and religion was needed in social change. I had at least some mastery of historical method which could be applied to the New Testament field."[41]

By 1905 Mathews had shifted to the Department of Systematic Theology and from 1908-1933 served as Dean of the Divinity School. Much like Harper and Burton, Mathews was a person of considerable drive and energy. He published several books in a number of different areas. He also published a work of the Burton handbook sort. But he had also begun to write books of a more specialized nature, which would be chiefly of interest to professors, seminary students, and academically inclined clergymen. Mathews was to publish many other works, but these mentioned were completed or in progress before 1902. A brief look at the last two works will indicate the ideas and methodologies Matthews brought to bear in New Testament studies. In his *The Social Teaching of Jesus*, Mathews, under his own admission, undertook a response to the "Zeitgeist." In justification, he argued that since the Reformation "individualistic philosophy . . . has largely dominated the theological and exegetical study of the New Testament." The result has been that "our religious teachers have to a considerable degree overlooked the essential sociability of human nature, and unconsciously have developed exegetical presumptions that have biased interpretation."[42] Mathews sought to present a more balanced view of Christianity but not so as simply to shed new light on Christianity. For him more was at stake than a change of direction in New Testament studies. He undertook this sociological study for his contemporaries so they could discover "the social philosophy and teachings of the historical person Jesus the Christ." Non-Biblical scholars were asking the questions. Mathews was providing the answers from a careful exegetical study of the New Testament texts. "There is but one way to the apprehension of the teachings of Jesus, whether religious or social, and that is the patient study of the gospels with the aid of all modern critical and exegetical methods. The only thoroughly safe method is the inductive gathering of teachings from the gospel sources,

---

[41] *Ibid.*, 96.

[42] Shailer Mathews, *The French Revolution: A Sketch* (Cleveland: The Chautauqua Press, 1900) 50, 51

and their subsequent classification into a system.[43] Mathews was not traditional in his approach to the Gospels, but then neither did he raise doubts as to whether, for example, the sayings of Jesus are authentic. He declared that the Gospels consisted of the teachings of Jesus and the editorial material added by the writers. He identified the second as "introductions, transpositions, explanations, reflections, prophetic antitypes, and verbal changes." These he considered self-evident to the careful reader. The editorial comments, according to Mathews, have varying merit, but are of considerable value. But the narrative sections, also editorial, are of utmost value. "In most cases such narrative is demonstrably from eyewitnesses and in its essential elements is beyond suspicion." The significance of the teachings of Jesus is not in scientific sociological description of his contemporaries, but rather the ideal society which he heralded. If it should appear that Jesus occasionally characterized life as he found it, it will also be clear that such characterization was but a part of this effort at portraying an ideal society and the enforcing of effort for its attainment. Human experience, therefore, in a sense supersedes the Scriptures in its analysis, but not in the goals toward which man should be tending.[44]

Mathews takes up this matter again in *Messianic Hope*[45]. At this later date he seems more open to "tampered" sayings but basically comes out for authenticity, even in regard to Jesus' sayings in the Gospel of John. In the latter area, the views of Jesus, as reported in the Scriptures, remained authoritative at least for the Mathews of 1897. Mathews characterized his *The Messianic Hope in the New Testament* as a pioneering scientific study. "The book was the outgrowth of a growing perception of the real meaning of the history of New Testament times as the history of ideas and social attitudes." He saw the book "as a step forward in the application of historical method to and understanding of Christian attitudes and doctrines." In this work Mathews examined the Jewish extra-Biblical sources with considerable rigor as well as those of the New Testament. But the book now seems from another generation in that Mathews is not content just to set forth the messianic hope of New Testament times, but wishes to declare what significance this hope might have for modern man. The messianic views of New Testament writers thus have authority,

---

[43] Shailer Mathews, *The Social Teaching of Jesus: An Essay in Christian Sociology* (New York: The Macmillan Company, 1897) 4f.

[44] Ibid., 3-13.

[45] Shailer Mathews, *The Messianic Hope in the New Testament* (Chicago: The University of Chicago, 1905), 57-61.

but that authority is different from what the orthodox envision, as shall be seen. The manner in which the New Testament scholar assists in determining what a concept means in modern times is to locate its true essence apart from the historical setting in which it is found. Theological reconstruction that shall in any true measure be based upon the New Testament is dependent, not only upon strictly philological exegesis, but also upon that larger historical exegetical process that endeavors to separate the content of a correctly apprehended teaching from the historical form in which it is cast. It is only when this form is resolved that the content stands clear, and it is in the content of biblical teaching alone that men of today can feel more than an antiquarian interest. The separating of the form from the content is admittedly an undertaking of the interpreter, but not a purely arbitrary undertaking. It requires that one be a rigorous historical scholar and exegete and that he proceed according to clearly delineated steps. The first step is "an exact estimate of the place any concept holds in a given system of thought." After that has been determined, the second step is to decide whether the concept is formal, that is, historically acculturated, or whether it is essential. This step, too, must be undertaken by one historically informed since he ascertains whether the concept is an outgrowth of faith or is in fact grounded in experience. The concept in the final analysis must "square with historical and scientific facts." Mathews comes out, not turning his back on Scripture, but locating in modern experience support and meaning for its "essential content." The third step, according to Mathews is a "presentation of these facts, through the use of such interpretative and pedagogical concepts as will do for today what the various concepts of the New Testament did for their day. Mathews thus concludes that messianism has meaning today in respect to certain essential teachings of Jesus. And with these teachings even the orthodox of Mathews' time could concur. In a word, to remove or to allow for messianism is not to destroy the essentials of the gospel—the personality, the teaching, and the resurrection of Jesus; a rational faith in God as Father; a certainty of divine forgiveness; and experience of the eternal life; and assurance of a complete life beyond and because of death. It is rather to make them more intelligible, more convincing, more certain, and more dynamic. They become this because messianism encourages an expectancy about the future in which all the strata of life both in individual and social units will be revolutionized.

Matthews with Burton, though from a different working perspective, believed that the correct sort of modern New Testament studies could add to the deepening of faith and the advancement of Christianity in an age which increasingly tended to look upon Christianity as outmoded. The first decade of the New Testament Department at the University of Chicago is characterized by a commitment to a scientific approach, which meant that the Scriptures were to be scrutinized from a philological, exegetical, and historical perspective. Such studies presuppose the best training available, and Chicago, like most other American schools of the time, depended in part upon German training, obvious in the case of both Burton and Mathews. These men were prolific writers, but in the early period their works ranged from popular study guides to seminary handbooks, rather than scholarly monographs. The weight of experience began to have considerable influence with Burton and Mathews as they set out to determine the manner in which the Scripture has relevance for modern man. But they saw this experience as confirming the "essential" message of the New Testament. These beginnings at Chicago, however we may evaluate them, set the pattern for early twentieth century New Testament studies, especially in the Midwest.

Restoration Movement Liberalism in Chicago

Theological liberalism among the Restorationists in Illinois in the last decade of the nineteenth century centered in Chicago and more specifically at and around the University of Chicago. Three men were principally involved: Herbert Lockwood Willett (1864-1944), Winfred Ernest Garrison (1874-1969) and Edward Scribner Ames (1870-1958).[46] These leaders created the Disciples Divinity House (1894), the Campbell Institute (1896) and its publications, and the outlook of the University Christian Church (1894). These men and institutions reflected and were involved in the changing perspectives at the University of Chicago.[47]

---

[46] For the perspectives of earlier restorationists on Biblical interpretation see: Thomas H. Olbricht, "Alexander Campbell in the Context of American Biblical Studies, 1810-1874)," *RQ*, 33:1 (1991) 13-28; and Thomas H. Olbricht, "Walter Scott as Biblical Interpreter," in *Walter Scott: A Nineteenth-Century Evangelical*, ed. Mark G. Toulouse (St. Louis: Chalice Press, 1999); M. Eugene Boring, *Disciples and the Bible: A History of Disciples Biblical Interpretation* in North America (St. Louis: Bethany Press, 1997).

[47] Considerable information about the Stone-Campbell professors, ministers and churches around Chicago in this period is supplied by Perry J. Rice in an unpublished manuscript held at the Christian Theological Seminary Library in Indianapolis. "The Disciples of Christ in Chicago and Northern Illinois 1839-1939."

Herbert Lockwood Willett (1864-1944)

The most obvious early outcroppings of liberalism in the restoration movement in and around Chicago revolved about Herbert Lockwood Willett. Willett attended Yale Divinity School in 1891 and there had William Rainey Harper as a professor who persuaded Willett to transfer to the new university of which he was becoming president. Willett pursued the Ph.D. at Chicago in Semitic languages and literature receiving the degree in 1896. He then stayed at Chicago as a professor in these subjects. Willett was born in Ionia, Michigan, in 1864. He received the A.B. and M.A. degrees from the Bethany College, founded by Alexander Campbell in West Virginia.[48] With the encouragement of Harper he helped founded the Disciples Divinity House in 1894. He served as the first dean which post he held until his retirement from the University in 1921. He was also active in the formation of the University Christian Church and served as its first pastor.

Willett was foremost a Biblical and more specifically an Old Testament scholar. He sought to infuse the growing higher criticism of the main stream Protestant Churches into the bloodstream of the Restorationist Churches. His views were much like those of the other professors at the University of Chicago. Eugene Boring described him as the "first liberal Disciples Bible scholar." Not only did he study at Yale and Chicago he attended the Lectures of Adolf Harnack a famous church historian and Hermann Gunkel a major Old Testament scholar at the University of Berlin. He sought to wean the Disciples away from the recovery of a normative past, in the pursuit of a progressive future. He received heavy criticism from writers in the *Christian Standard*, especially from J. W. Mc-Garvey who wrote a regular column on Biblical criticism and latched onto Willett as a useful foil. Willett responded in kind on such subjects as the Mosaic authorship of the Pentateuch and the order and authorship of the Gospels. He wrote regular essays for the left leaning *Christian Century* and the *Christian-Evangelist*. Willett also favored open membership which entailed including unimmersed persons on the membership rolls.

As was true of most American Biblical critics of the time Willet embraced the "new" views on the Old Testament, but remained essentially conventional in regard to the New Testament until later. Boring wrote,

---

[48] Larry D. Bouchard, "Willett, Herbert Lockwood (1864-1944) *ESCM*, 774. Also M. Eugene Boring, *Disciples and the Bible: A History of Disciples Biblical Interpretation in North America* (St. Louis: Bethany Press, 1997).

Willett accepted some of the results of the German and British higher criticism of the Old Testament, at least tentatively, and thus revised his date for the Book of Daniel, his view of Mosaic authorship of the Pentateuch, and his view of the unity of Isaiah (three cardinal litmus tests of one's stance on Old Testament criticism). All of this McGarvey considered heresy. But on the New Testament, Willett's conclusions on such matters were not so different from McGarvey's, during the period McGarvey was debating with him in the pages of the *Christian Standard*.

In 1899 Willett was completely traditional in his view of the authorship of the Gospels: the apostle Matthew wrote Matthew, Mark the companion of Peter and Paul wrote Mark, Luke the companion of Paul wrote Luke and Acts, and the apostle John wrote John. Within this traditional view, Willett was beginning to make room for critical methods and conclusions, but the traditional conclusions were still firmly in place. Paul wrote all the letters attributed to him in the tradition (except Hebrews), writing the Pastorals during a postulated "second Roman imprisonment" according to the traditional, but not the critical, pattern of Paul's life. James the Lord's brother wrote the Epistle of James. Only about 2 Peter does he express doubts, and then does not pronounce against it, but says it adds interest to read the Epistle as from Peter, even if only in a secondary sense, and that the inspiration of the book is in any case unquestionable. These are almost exactly the critical conclusions postulated in B. W. Johnson's *People's New Testament with Notes.* Willett even leans toward apostolic authorship of Revelation. (Willett and Campbell 1899, 1901, ad loc.)[49]

To understand the manner in which the Chicago liberalism developed over the years it is important to see that Willet changed his 1899 views on the New Testament in later life.

All the information on Willett's 1899 views is taken from *The Teaching of the Books* published that year. Eighteen years later, he had changed his mind on the authorship of the Pastorals and had accepted the critical consensus that 2 Corinthians was composite. (See *Our Bible* 1917, ad loc.) Twelve years later still, he was expressing doubts about the authorship of the Fourth Gospel.

---

[49] Boring, 232.

(*The Bible through the Centuries* 1929) All this was after the critical
period in which he was debating with McGarvey. During that
period, Willett and McGarvey held essentially the same views on
the origin of the New Testament books. Willett and McGarvey
had their differences, but it is not the case that Willett was the
progressive critic who accepted the radical views of higher criticism's judgment on matters of authorship and date of New Testament books, whereas McGarvey was the reactionary who rejected them. They both rejected them, and in doing so were in
step with the American biblical scholarship of their day.[50]

Willett, much like other liberals and perhaps especially those at the University of Chicago continued to believe in the evangelistic mission of the
church. They saw Biblical criticism as supporting that mission rather than
destroying it.

Willett saw biblical criticism as the liberating means of *attracting*
people to the Bible, of showing them the variety in the Bible,
and its record of the growth and development of a religious
community toward ever higher truth. *This* is what Willett wanted
his students to see in the Bible. Willett was thus not an opponent
of evangelism. He saw higher criticism not as the opponent of
evangelism but as that which allowed evangelism to remain honest. It was not a dogmatic theory about the Bible as such that
was the particular issue that bothered Disciples, but how it impacted their understanding of the way the Bible is to be used in
the propagation of the faith.[51]

Winfred Ernest Garrison (1884-1969)

Winfred Ernest Garrison had impeccable Restorationist credentials
through his famous parents James Harvey (1842-1931) and Judith Elizabeth Garrison as well as strong ties to Illinois. J. H. Garrison was born in
Missouri south of Springfield, but after the Civil War entered Abingdon
College in Illinois which was soon absorbed by Eureka College near Peoria. J. H. early on was involved with Restorationist periodicals and ended
up editor of the *Christian-Evangelist*. Garrison was perceived as someone
who welcomed newer approaches to the Christian faith and not so much

---

[50] Ibid., 233.
[51] Ibid., 237.

wed to primitivism.[52] Garrison lived in Illinois until he moved to St. Louis in 1882. His son Winfred Ernest was reared in St. Louis, but pursued a B.A. at Eureka College (1892) as well as one at Yale (1894). In 1897 he received a Ph.D. in church history from the University of Chicago writing his dissertation on the Theology of Alexander Campbell, published in 1900 as *Alexander Campbell's Theology*. He then taught at Butler University in Indianapolis where he also served as President 1904-1906. Because of an effort to combat tuberculosis he moved to New Mexico where he taught at New Mexico State University 1908-1913 and served as President. He moved to Claremont, California, and became founder and headmaster of a boys school. In 1921 he returned to Chicago as Dean of the Disciples Divinity House and as associate professor of church history at the University of Chicago.[53] He served as dean of the Disciples Divinity House from 1921-1927 during which he raised money for a building modeled after a residential college at Oxford University. Garrison took up a new career at age seventy-seven as professor of philosophy and religion at the University of Houston in 1951.

Garrison did not impact the Restoration Movement in Illinois in his early years as he did later, which is past the time frame for this history. Garrison turned out major volumes, some focused on Restoration history, after he retired from administrative responsibilities in 1927. These volumes include: *Christian Unity and the Disciples of Christ,* (1955), *Religion Follows the Frontier: A History of the Disciples of Christ (*1931), and with A. T. DeGroot, *The Disciples of Christ: A History* (1948, rev. 1958).

To obtain some sense of Garrison's approach to history we turn to his early volume *Alexander Campbell's Theology.*[54] In this publication Garrison focused on development or in some sense progress as the new method for history. These were front leading or liberal views of history writing for which the University of Chicago was noted.

> He who undertakes to estimate the intellectual achievements of the nineteenth century and to generalize upon the history of thought in this period, cannot fail to admit that the most fruitful and far-reaching general conception which this age has brought into prominence is the idea of development. Based upon a metaphysics which finds the essence of reality to consist, not in

---

[52] William E. Tucker, "James Harvey Garrison," *ESCM*, 350.

[53] W. Clark Gilpin, "Winfred Ernest Garrison" (1874-1969) *ESCM*, 351-353.

[54] Winfred Ernest Garrison, *Alexander Campbell's Theology* (St. Louis: Christian Publishing Company, 1900) 9-13.

the changeless identity of an unknowable "substance" in which
all attributes inhere, but in the process by which functions are
fulfilled, forms developed and new adaptations made to changing conditions, it quickly passed beyond the limits of speculative
philosophy and found application in the fields of science, history, theology...

According to the historical method, it is maintained that any
object of knowledge, whether it be an organic formation, an
idea or an institution, is not known as the scientific observer
seeks to know it until one knows the sources from which it
sprang, the processes by which it came into being, and the
changes which it has undergone in adaptation to varying conditions. The effect of the application of this conception in the various fields of thought has been little short of revolutionary. The
general principle of evolution (of which the Darwinian theory
of the origin of species is a mere detail) is the most notable
product of the idea of development, or the historical method, as
applied to the understanding of the natural world. The scientific
study of an organ of an animal or a plant, viewed from this
standpoint, includes not only anatomy, which studies the organ
statically as a mere complex of tissues, but morphology, which
investigates the origin and development of the organ in the
species, and physiology, which inquires how it performs its functions at the present time. It is not possible to attain a complete
scientific knowledge of any organic formation, either plant or
animal, without these three elements.

Applied to the study of the phenomena which constitute the
recognized domain of history, the idea of development has produced what is sometimes called the "new historical method." It
is the method which treats history as an organism whose parts
grew together and cannot be understood separately; as a succession of events causally related, the ultimate essence of which lies
in their causal connection. History is no longer a heap of facts, a
collection of anecdotes which may be told in any order without
substantial loss. It is not viewed as a mere review of facts, succeeding each other in a definite order but with only a chronological sequence, as the old annalists represented it. It is a chain of
facts logically linked together, and the essential reality of it all
lies in the fact that it represents a continuous process of development. Applied to the study of political, social and religious
institutions and ideas, there has been produced what may be

broadly termed the historical method. An idea or an institution is a growth. As a plant grows out of a seed, so an idea develops from earlier ideas. Varying conditions of soil, moisture, heat and light influence the growth of the plant; varying local and temporary needs, individual abilities and personal adaptations determine the form of the idea....

If this method as here described be applied to the study of a system of theology, it will mean that for the time the critical process is laid aside and no attempt is made to determine whether or not the development which actually took place ever ought to have taken place, or to judge whether it meets the requirement and embodies the best thought of a time other than that which gave rise to it. The study will inquire into the philosophical presuppositions of the system, its affinity with other systems preceding and contemporary, and the special conditions which influenced its leaders apart from the general current of thought which influenced all alike; but, in so far as this method is employed in its purity, it will not attempt to perform the function of an apologetic or a polemic. It will orient the system in the general history of Christian doctrine. It will be a study of sources and historical setting and development, but it will not profess to be either critical or constructive, although it is the necessary preparation for a consideration of that sort.

Later Garrison set out to show how the Disciples were impacted by the westward migration in the United States. He took up the Frederick Turner thesis that growth in the American denominations followed the frontier and the leaders in outlook were molded by the democratic mindset of frontiersmen. Indeed his history of the Disciples written with DeGroot contained more church growth data than any such history before or since.

The Campbell Institute

It will be appropriate here to mention the founding of the Campbell Institute. We will also take up the influence and importance of the Disciples Divinity House of the University of Chicago in which Garrison was also involved, but before that introduce Edward Scribner Ames (1870-1958). The seminary of choice of Disciples' students other than Disciples' seminaries in the decade before the establishment of the Di-

vinity School at the University of Chicago was Yale Divinity School.[55] By
1920, 105 Disciples ministers had received a seminary degree from Yale
and 48 from the University of Chicago Divinity School. In order to encourage Disciples students to retain their commitment to their Restorationist heritage a group of Yale students proposed launching an academic
society to be named The Campbell Institute. After considerable discussion the organization was founded at a Disciples' National Convention in
Springfield, Illinois, in 1896. Among the fourteen charter members were
Garrison, Herbert W. Willett, and Ames. All of three at one time had
been students at Yale. The members were expected to hold either the
B.D. or the Ph.D. Twenty years later the membership was reported as
200. The leaders also founded a journal *The Scroll* in 1906, but it soon ex-
pired due to continued carping over its theological liberalism. The Institute held an annual meeting normally in Chicago. The Institute ceased to
exist in 1975 because of decreased interest.

To celebrate the twentieth year The Institute published *Progress: An-
niversary Volume of the Campbell Institute on the Completion of Twenty Years*.[56]
The essays exuded the conviction of the times that progress was apparent in many areas of life. Included was a declaration regarding the purpose of the Institute. (1) To encourage a deep scholarly spirit involving
free discussion. (2) To develop a quiet self culture exhibiting higher spiritually in the churches. (3) Positive productive work and scholarship in
Disciples' circles. The outcome was a liberalizing of Disciples' priorities
which in turn generated criticism among those of a more conservative
bent.

Edward Scribner Ames (1870-1958)

Edward Ames was another important Disciple who taught at the Univer-
sity of Chicago and reflected the predilections of the Chicago School.[57]
He was born in Eau Claire, Wisconsin, in 1870 where his father was a
Disciples' minister. He received a B.A. and M.A. from Drake, a Disciples'
University in Des Moines, Iowa. From Drake he entered Yale Divinity

---

[55] Edwin L. Becker, *Yale Divinity School and the Disciples of Christ 1872-1989* (Nashville:
The Disciples of Christ Historical Society, 1990).

[56] (Chicago: *Christian Century*, 1917).

[57] Edward Scribner Ames, *Beyond Theology: the Autobiography of Edward Scriber Ames*
(Chicago: University of Chicago Press, 1959); Creighton Peden, *Christian Pragmatism:
An Intellectual Biography of Edward Scribner Ames, 1870-1958* (Newcastle upon Tyne:
Cambridge Scholars Publishing, 2011).

School receiving the B.D. in 1892. From New Haven he entered a Ph. D. program at the University of Chicago receiving the degree in 1895. He studied with such well known philosophers who identified themselves as pragmatists, John Dewey (1859-1952) and James Tufts (1862-1942). Ames launched his teaching career at Butler University, Indianapolis in 1897. In 1900 he was offered a teaching position at the University of Chicago in the philosophy department where he taught until 1936. His main focus was on psychology and religion and published more than a half dozen major works.[58]

In outlook Ames' work had similarities with William James' *Will to Believe, and other Essays in Popular Philosophy* and the better known *Varieties of Religious Experience*. His basic positions were highly influenced by the Pragmatism of John Dewey. He pursued the empiricism of John Locke, the Pragmatism of John Dewey and William James, and approached the Scriptures employing the presuppositions of the higher critics. Because of his liberal views he was widely criticized by conservative ministers and professors including those in the Restorationist congregations.

> Ames's distinctively liberal and humanistic approach to both theology and ministerial leadership brought him into repeated conflicts with more conservative elements of the denomination. Among the specific doctrinal questions for which Ames is remembered is the humanity of Jesus, the denial of an afterlife, the diminished role of baptism, and open membership.[59]

Ames did not publish much on Biblical criticism, but he did develop a "liberal" perspective on Jesus detailing somewhat similar views to those of the Frenchman, Ernst Renan. About him Boring wrote,

---

[58] *The Psychology of Religious Experience.* (Boston: Houghton Mifflin Co., 1910) Reprinted (New York: Red Label Reprint, 1931); *The Divinity of Christ.* (Chicago: New Christian Century Co., 1911); *The Higher Individualism.* (Boston: Houghton Mifflin, 1915); *The Psychology of Religion: A Professional Reading Course.* (Chicago: University of Chicago Press, 1917); *The New Orthodoxy.* (Chicago: University of Chicago Press, 1918); 2nd edition (Chicago: University of Chicago Press, 1925); *Religion.* (New York: Henry Holt and Co., 1929); Reprinted (New York: Red Label Reprint, 1931); *Beyond Theology: The Autobiography of Edward Scribner Ames.* Edited by Van Meter Ames. (Chicago: University of Chicago Press, 1959); *Prayers and Meditations of Edward Scribner Ames.* Edited by Van Meter Ames. (Chicago: Disciples Divinity House of the University of Chicago, 1970).

[59] https://nl.wikipedia.org/wiki/Edward_Ames

Ames saw this religion of spirit and social Christianity as a recovery of the original religion of Jesus. Thus Ames, like several
advocates of the "Jesus research" two generations later, had his
own version of the "restoration movement." Instead of restoring the "ancient order" of the church that had been perverted
by "denominationalism," he wanted to restore the "simple religion" of Jesus that had been perverted by the church as such.
The pattern is constant; only the content is different. Late in life,
a trip to Israel gave Ames opportunity to reformulate his understanding of Jesus somewhat along the romantic lines of Ernst
Renan, picturing Jesus as the simple, wholesome Galilean lover
of nature who "lived an out of door life, close to nature, and
there he found the scenes and the traditions which he made into
parables everyone could understand."(Ames1918: 157) The
Pharisees became the evil formulators of dogma and Jesus the
advocate of simple human reason who "had precisely the attitude of a modern man." Mixed in with this was the typical liberal understanding of Jesus as one who "based his hopes upon the
great possibilities of man, including that of building a kingdom
of heaven on earth." (Ames1918: 188).[60]

Ames was also influential in certain Disciples quarters because he served
as minister of the Hyde Park Christian Church located near the University of Chicago campus from 1900-1940. He emphasized the goals of the
"Social Gospel" and the congregation gave attention to the needs of the
community surrounding the University. In later years the demographics
changed and Ames gave successful attention to integrating the church.
Ames lived to be 88, dying in 1958.

The Disciple Divinity House

The Disciple Divinity House was chartered in 1894 and Herbert Willett
was appointed the first Dean. He was followed by W. E. Garrison
1921-1927 and Edward Ames 1927-1945. It was not until Garrison became dean in 1921 that funds were raised to build a complex after the
fashion of an Oxford University college. The House was officially connected with the University of Chicago Divinity School and its printed
purpose was (1) Instruction beyond the undergraduate degree, (2) Scientific and historical studies in religion in the context of a major research

---

[60] Boring, 219.

university, (3) application of theological reasoning to the problems of contemporary society, and (4) creating a Disciples' self understanding community in the midst of an ecumenically high level academic institution.[61]

Conclusion

The Restoration Movement in Illinois may not have been a key player as it was around Indianapolis, Indiana, and Lexington, Kentucky, nevertheless the moves toward theological liberalism were as pronounced in Illinois especially around Chicago as in any other region in the Restoration Movement.

---

[61] Scott D. Seay, "Disciples Divinity House," *ESCM*, 273 – 274; William Barnett Blakemore, *Quest for Intelligence in Ministry: The Story of the First Seventy Five Years of the Disciples Divinity House of the University of Chicago* (Chicago: Disciples Divinity House, 1970).

14. Daniel Sommer and Illinois Conservatives

In Chapter 12 we set out a broader perspective on Protestant religious conservatism in Illinois and how it impacted the peoples of the Stone-Campbell Movement. We now turn to the churches themselves that professed conservatism. The "progressive/conservative" confrontation resulted in a division between Disciples of Christ or Christian Churches and Churches of Christ. The conservative congregations' self-appellation was "Churches of Christ." The comparatively small number of the conservatives is clear from the 1906 Federal Religious Census. That census reported 769 Disciples of Christ or progressive congregations in Illinois and only 58[1] churches of Christ, or conservatives.[2] The former reported 101,516 members and the latter 3,582.

In the nineteenth century some of the conservative congregations came to identify with Daniel Sommer (1850-1940), a major religious journal editor from Indiana.[3] It is not easy to distinguish completely the congregations influenced by Daniel Sommer and those that weren't. We will return to this question when we take up the available data. Since in this volume we are limiting the observations to the nineteenth century and the first decade and a half of the twentieth century, the conservative congregations, both non-Sommerite and Sommerite will be the focus.

The readers of this volume live in the twenty-first century. Over the long haul of the twentieth century major shifts occurred in congregations

---

[1] By examining Haynes and conservative periodicals such as the *Octographic Review* and the *Christian Leader*, we have located more than one hundred conservative congregations in Illinois. See Appendix 4 for the data.

[2] Department of Commerce and Labor, U. S. Bureau of the Census, E. Dana Durward, Director. Special Reports: Religious Bodies 1906 (Washington, D. C.: Government Printing Office, 1910) 182.

[3] Works on Sommer include James Stephen Wolfgang, *A Life of Humble Fear: the Biography of Daniel Sommer, 1850-1940*, (M.A. Thesis, Butler University, 1975). James Stephen Wolfgang, "Sommer, Daniel (1850 – 1940" *ESCM* 692 – 694.William E. Wallace, *Daniel Sommer, 1850 -1940: A Biography*. (No place of publication: no publisher, 1969). Matthew C. Morrison, *Like a Lion: Daniel Sommer's Seventy Years of Preaching*, (Murfreesboro, TN: Dehoff Publications, 1975).

identified as Churches of Christ. We cannot therefore simply project back what we know about Churches of Christ in Illinois today and understand the conservative congregations of the nineteenth century. For that reason brief observations on developments in Churches of Christ in Illinois in the twentieth century plus two decades in the twenty-first are offered.

In the first half of the twentieth century the views of Daniel Sommer persisted in certain Illinois Churches of Christ, promoted later by W. Carl Ketcherside (1908-1989) of the neighboring state of Missouri, on whom Daniel Sommer conferred his mantle. But despite the significance of Sommer in the upper Midwest, his influence failed to reach far into the border-states or the southwest where the majority of members of the Churches of Christ lived: Kentucky, Tennessee, Alabama, Arkansas, Oklahoma and Texas. In fact by the nineteen twenties, few Churches of Christ members in these states opposed located preachers and "Christian" colleges as did Sommer, and frequently established new congregations open to both in the Illinois towns where Sommer congregations were located. By the nineteen twenties these new non-Sommerite Churches of Christ were planted in Illinois by migrants from the border-states and the southwest, especially in the larger towns and cities. They settled in Peoria, Springfield, Decatur, Bloomington, Rockford, and Rock Island where employment was available, unlike in the small rural towns from which they migrated. By the 1930s the members of the non-Sommerite Churches of Christ in Illinois outnumbered those influenced by Sommer. The 2018 edition of the Royster *Churches of Christ in the United States* only lists five remaining Sommerite congregations, mostly in the region around St. Louis. With one exception these were founded since 1950.

The mainstream Churches of Christ have dominated the Illinois landscape significantly as compared with the Sommerite congregations. In the 1960s the mainstream congregations began to experience divisions over institutionalism that for the most part occurred in the more southerly and southwest American states. The non-institutional influence in Illinois from the late 1950s and for the following decade was around Chicago, nurtured by Leslie Dietzelkamp (1911-1995) and his sons. The congregations that became non-institutional in southeast and southern Illinois were prevailed upon by church leaders from Indiana and Kentucky. A major journal of these people, *Truth Magazine,* was once published in Indiana. The non-institutional leaders continued some of the complaints of Daniel Sommer but focused on newer developments such as the Herald of Truth national broadcasting on radio and television from Abilene,

Texas, orphanages under board of directors, kitchens and recreation centers in church buildings, large mission efforts under the control of one congregation, and all forms of parachurch organizations. Because of the issues at stake they were designated Non-Institutional Churches of Christ. In 2018, forty-nine of two hundred sixty-six Illinois congregations are identified as non-institutional churches, a percentage higher, about twenty percent, than the United States as a whole where the numbers are fifteen percent. The chief centers of the NI Illinois congregations are around Chicago, Peoria and between Terre Haute, Indiana and Effingham, Illinois, according to truthdirectory.org. The congregations tend to be small with only five over a hundred members and most of the congregations clustering around fifty members or less.

It will be helpful to commence with a list of viewpoints that predominated in Sommer influenced congregations compiled by the publishers of the *Apostolic Review*, in June 1932, advanced principally by Daniel Sommer, along with some of our own remarks.[4]

1. The Lord's Supper observed each Sunday. 2. Church membership through obeying the preaching of the gospel and immersion. No testimony of conversion experience required. 3. The teaching and preaching decided by each church. Sommer added mutual edification rather than one preacher. 4. No pastors except for the elders, each congregation with elders and deacons. 5. Edifying singing, no instruments. 6. Contributions are for spreading the Gospel and taking care of the poor. 7. Fair discipline of members. 8. All teaching activities of the church under the elders. No outside, for example, Sunday School organizations. 9. Preachers have good character. 10. Sommer declared that church treasury can only support activities of the church and not such outside entities such as colleges, orphan homes and benevolent organizations. 11. Attendance at Bible classes according to personal preference. 12. Individuals may support foreign missions but the church may not contribute to mission societies. The church is the only avenue through which to do religious work. One might add that preachers are to be called elders, preachers, or ministers, but not reverend and preference is given to church of Christ for the congregation name. However one may access the Biblical authority of each of the views, those who held them persisted in maintaining these pre-1850 practices and were appropriately designated the conservatives. Those who embraced such items as mission societies, instrumental music, the pastor system, and "church" colleges were the progressives or liberals. Weekly celebration of the Lord's Supper, the means of conversion,

---

[4] *Apostolic* Review, 86.25, 26 (June 21, 1932) 1. Cited in Wolfgang, *A Life* 160 – 164.

decisions about preachers and teachers made by the local congregations, church discipline and preacher attributes were held in common by both conservatives and liberals in the Stone-Campbell movement.

Alexander Campbell founded Bethany College West Virginia, in 1840. This established a pattern Sommer opposed as a work of the church. Colleges were founded in Illinois by Disciples in middle of the century at Jacksonville, Eureka and Abingdon. The existence of these colleges became widely accepted among Illinois Disciples by 1889, the date of the Sand Creek declaration. The views represented by Sommer by no means reflected even a small percentage of the views of the Illinois Disciples. Less than 80 congregations out of nearly 800 were sympathetic to the platform supported at Sand Creek. Neither did any sizable group within the Illinois Disciples oppose state evangelistic societies. Cooperative evangelistic efforts were started as early as 1840. Opposition to the American Christian Missionary Society founded in 1850 with Alexander Campbell as the president was minor in Illinois.

Daniel Sommer (1850-1940) never lived in Illinois but through his publications left an indelible imprint on some of the conservative Christians in Illinois. He helped orchestrate a split in the Illinois Stone-Campbell movement in the nineteenth century through events that transpired at Sand Creek, Shelby County, Illinois, southwest of Mattoon. For that reason we will first present a brief life of Sommer, then comment on events at Sand Creek.

Daniel Sommer

Daniel Sommer was born in Saint Mary's County Maryland, on the southern tip projecting out into Chesapeake Bay. His parents were both German and Lutheran and immigrated to America in 1835. His father, John Sommer was a Hessian and his mother, Magdalena Wyman, a Bavarian. His father was a blacksmith, but died young and Daniel had few memories of him. The family, before John's death, moved to Queen Ann, Maryland, about thirty miles east of Annapolis around 1855. The widow, with a large family, worked as an independent tailor to support them. The family lived in a log cabin and Daniel added to the coffers through trapping; putting wild rabbit, along with cornbread on the table as the principal food. Daniel was hired out at age nine to work on a road building construction crew. He walked to and from the construction sites often some distance away. Plenty of opportunities for work opened up during the Civil War years 1861-65.

Sommer entered school at age seven and was identified as a slow learner, but he persisted and became a better than average student. His schooling continued for the next five years until 1862 when he dropped out. Daniel pursued no additional class room education until he enrolled at Bethany College, West Virginia, the college founded by Alexander Campbell in 1840. It was because of growing religious interests that Sommer pursued a college education. Before the spring of 1863 Sommer gave little attention to religion. That spring Miss Louisa Harwood, an adopted daughter of the store-keeper, opened a Sunday School in a private house. Because the young teacher presented her lessons in an appealing manner, Sommer became interested. She encouraged her students to repent and pray and consider the direction of their life. In 1864 Sommer attended a Methodist revival. Members of the Methodist church encouraged him to come to the mourner's bench and seek religion, but he persuaded them that he was already a Christian. He joined the Methodist Church and regularly attended Bible classes. In 1866 he heard of a Disciples of Christ group and attended a Gospel Meeting held by D. S. Burnet, a well-known Disciples' evangelist. This led to more contacts. In 1866 Sommer moved to Hartford County, Maryland, north of Baltimore on the Pennsylvania border. He went to work for John Dallas Everitt a Disciples' minister and from him learned the Biblical teaching on adult believer's immersion. Finally in August of 1869 Daniel Sommers was baptized by T. A. Crenshaw of Middletown, Pennsylvania, just south of Harrisburg. Daniel struggled for a time over a profession and decided he wanted to preach. When he informed some elderly members of his desire, they told him he needed additional education and recommended Bethany College in West Virginia. Though Alexander Campbell was deceased, the school thrived under W. K. Pendleton, his son-in-law, C. L. Loos, the new president, and Robert Richardson, Campbell's biographer. Sommer entered Bethany with inadequate preparation, but he was determined and did reputable work even though he departed before graduating.[5]

At this point Sommer began to develop an antipathy for the Christians at Bethany and their church activities. He concluded that some of the leaders believed that instructions in the Scriptures applied to both believers and sinners while others believed that they were addressed to sinners and that the Christians "should love God and do as they pleased." He objected to efforts to raise funds for new curtains, carpets and paint for the church building through an organization, "Ladies' Mite Society."

[5] James Stephen Wolfgang, "Daniel Sommer" *ESCM* 692.

Sommer spoke against the fund raising society, but was not applauded for his objection and over the months his denouncing of such actions cost him numerous friends. In 1871 Sommer met Benjamin Franklin, editor of the *American Christian Review* with the result that mutual admiration developed. Franklin, a descendant of the famous Benjamin Franklin's brother, lived in Ohio and Indiana. In 1864 Franklin moved to Anderson, Indiana, and there edited *The American Christian Review* until his death in 1878. *The Review* was widely read, perhaps more than any other journal of the Stone-Campbell Movement, and after the death of Alexander Campbell in 1866, Franklin was likely the most influential spokesperson in the Movement. Franklin, who earlier was supportive of missionary societies, later became critical of them and other para-church organizations.[6]

After two years at Bethany, Sommer got married, preached briefly in Baltimore then settled in Kelton, Pennsylvania northwest of Newark, Delaware, for six years. He wrote his first essay for Franklin in 1871. He evangelized widely and became better known. In the summer of 1886 Edwin Alden the owner of Franklin's *American Christian Review* offered the journal for sale; Sommer purchased it, changing the name to *Octographic Review*. Sommer published the renamed paper in Cincinnati and Richwood, but moved to Indianapolis in 1894 five years after the "Declaration" at Sand Creek, Illinois. He identified with the North Congregation in Indianapolis and preached off and on for the congregation until his death in 1940. In the last decade of his life Sommer made a concentrated effort to establish relationships with many church leaders from whom he had become estranged.[7] These efforts are significant but are well into the twentieth century and beyond the scope of this volume.

Sand Creek

We turn now to the Sand Creek "Address and Declaration." Leroy Garrett has especially pinpointed these documents and their affirmation at Sand Creek as the first indication in the Stone-Campbell movement that a major division was underway. By 1906 the divergences resulted to a separation of Disciples of Christ from Churches of Christ in the 1906 Federal religious census.[8] The Sand Creek developments are indeed significant for the areas where Sommer had influence in Ohio, Indiana, Illinois and

[6] James Stephen Wolfgang, "Benjamin Franklin," Ibid., 342-3.
[7] James Stephen Wolfgang, "Sommer," Ibid., 693.
[8] Leroy Garrett, *The Stone-Campbell Movement: An Anecdotal History of Three Churches* (Joplin, Mo.: College Press Publishing Co., 1981, rev. 1994).

Missouri. In regard to Churches of Christ, however, the predominant membership was located in Tennessee, Texas, Alabama, Oklahoma, and Kentucky. In 1906 131,940 out of 159,658 were located in the Border States and the south [9] The major influences in these regions were David Lipscomb, editor of the *Gospel Advocate,* and various Texas leaders, including Austin McGary and J. D. Tant connected with the *Firm Foundation.* It is pretty clear that whatever Lipscomb heard about the affirmation at Sand Creek, he did not read the documents until 1892, three years later. When he read them he opposed the call for division at Sand Creek and declared it sectarian.[10] But Lipscomb was not oblivious to the rising differences in the movement and finally, when approached by the Census Bureau, agreed to help solicit data for Churches of Christ for the 1906 census. Regardless of how to assess the significance of Sand Creek for the larger Stone-Campbell Movement, the "Address and Declaration" did impact the churches in Illinois from 1889 through the rest of the nineteenth century even though only about ten percent of the churches were in the conservative coalition.

The Sand Creek congregation was founded in 1834.[11] Over the next several decades they had a role in establishing at least six additional congregations in surrounding towns. In 1874 Sand Creek built a new brick building. When they started using the building they initiated an annual summer gathering which eventually became so large that it rivaled camp meetings. Church members from elsewhere traveled some distances to be involved. The 1889 meeting was the 17th annual gathering. Daniel Sommer had addressed the annual meeting three years prior in 1886.[12] Before the 1889 meeting, wheels were set in motion, encouraged by Daniel Sommer, to make a statement regarding the need to separate those who stood for the ancient paths from the innovators.[13] A declaration was jointly written and signed on August 17, 1889 by representatives from five different congregations in the area and two additional persons who signed as individuals. The next day, Sunday, August 18, the "Declaration was read to those assembled." Following the reading, Daniel Sommer spoke for an hour and forty minutes, that is "The Address." His speech was written up later and published in the *Octographic Review.* Several sources confirmed that above 5000 persons were present. Five thousand

---

[9] James Stephen Wolfgang, "A Life of Humble Fear..." p. 15

[10] David Lipscomb, *Gospel Advocate*, November 7, 1892.

[11] A. K. Guthrie on the history in "Documents—Sand Creek"

[12] Ibid. Sommer so stated in his "Address."

[13] Carson Reed, "Sand Creek 'Address and Declaration'" *ESCM* 669.

seems unrealistic since in the 1906 Federal Religious Census only 3582 members of the Churches of Christ were reported for the state of Illinois. The 1906 census count, however, was likely low, and no doubt people were present from Indiana and Missouri as well as perhaps Michigan and Wisconsin.

Three items should be noted in regard to the "Declaration." First, the designation "Address and Declaration" was intentionally designed to bring to mind Thomas Campbell's famous "Declaration and Address" of 1809. Campbell's plea was for the unity of believers. The Sand Creek entreaty was for the breach of one set of believers from another.

Second, instrumental music was not mentioned in the version Sommer printed in the *Octographic Review*. It was, however, included in the version published by F. L. Rowe in *The Christian Leader*. It is not altogether clear why Sommer didn't include condemnation of instrumental music in his version; nevertheless he spent considerable time discussing a cappella versus instrumental music in his hour, forty minute address.

Third, the statement in closing demanded immediate separation of those considered Biblically focused, from the innovative progressives.

"The Declaration"
OFFICERS IN A MASS MEETING ASSEMBLED AT SAND CREEK, SHELBY CO., ILL., AUG. 17th, A. D. 1889

TO ALL THOSE WHO IT MAY CONCERN:

Greeting
Brethren: You doubtless know that we as disciples of Christ (with scarcely an exception) many long years ago took the position that in matters of doctrine and practice, religiously, that "where the Bible speaks we speak, and where the Bible is silent we are silent;" and that further, we held that nothing should be taught, received or practiced for which we could not produce a "thus saith the Lord." And doubtless many of you also know that as long as the above principles were constantly and faithfully observed, that we were a happy and prosperous people. Then we were of one heart and of one soul, we lived in peace and prospered in the things pertaining to the kingdom of God and the name of our Lord Jesus Christ. Then what was written as doctrine and for practice was taught and observed by the disciples. And, it may not be

amiss in this connection to say that many, yes, very many in the sectarian churches saw the beauty, consistency and wonderful strength and harmony in the plea, as set forth by the disciples, for the restoration of primitive or apostolic Christianity in spirit and in practice; and so came and united with us in the same great and godly work. It is, perhaps, needless for us to add in this connection that we, as a people, discarded all man-made laws, disciplines, and confessions of faith, as means of governing the church. We have always acknowledged and do now acknowledge the all-sufficiency of the Holy Scriptures to govern us as individuals and as congregations. As an apostle has said, "All scripture is given by inspiration of God; and is profitable for doctrine, for reproof, for correction, and for instruction in righteousness, that the man of God may be perfect, thoroughly furnished unto all good works."

And now, please allow us to call attention to more painful facts and considerations. There are those among us who do teach and practice things not taught nor found in the New Testament, which have been received by many well meaning disciples, but rejected by those more thoughtful and, in most instances, better informed in the scriptures, and who have repeatedly protested against this false teaching and these corrupt practices among the disciples. Some of the things against which we protest are the unlawful methods resorted to in order to raise or get money for religious purposes, NAMELY, that of the church holding festivals of various kinds in the house of the Lord or elsewhere, demanding sometimes that each participant shall pay a certain sum for an admittance fee; the select choir to the virtual, if not the real, abandonment of congregational singing; likewise the manmade society for missionary work, and the one man, imported preacher-pastor to take the oversight of the church. These with many other objectionable and unauthorized things are now taught and practiced in many of the congregations, and that to the great grief and mortification of some of the members of said congregations.

And, now, brethren, you that teach such things, and such like things, and those who practice the same, must certainly know that they are not only not in harmony with the gospel, but are in opposition thereto. You surely will admit that it is safe, and only safe to teach and practice what the divine record enjoins upon the disciples. To this none can reasonably object, and this is exactly what we want and for which we contend. And, now, we say, that we beg of you to turn away speedily and at once from such things, and remember that though we are the Lord's freemen yet we are bound by the authority of our Lord Jesus Christ. You know that by keeping His commandments and not the commandments of men that we have the assurance of his approval. Therefore, brethren, without addressing you further by using other arguments, and without going further in detailing these unpleasant, and as we see them, vicious things, you must allow us in kindness, and in Christian courtesy, and at the same time with firmness, to declare that we cannot tolerate the things of which we complain; for if we do, then we are (in a measure at least) blamable ourselves. And, let it be distinctly understood, that this "Address and Declaration" is not made in any spirit of envy or hate, or malice or any such thing. But we are only actuated from a sense of duty to ourselves and to all concerned; for we feel that the time has fully come when something of a more definite character ought to be known and recognized between the church and the world. Especially is this apparent when we consider the scriptural teachings in the matters to which we have herein referred—such for instance as the following: "Be not conformed to this world, but be ye transformed, by the renewing of your mind, that ye may prove what is that good and acceptable and perfect will of God."

It is therefore, with the view, if possible, of counteracting the usages and practices that have crept into the church, that this effort on the part of the congregations hereafter named is made. And now, in closing up this address and declaration, we state that we are impelled from a sense of duty to say, that all such as are guilty of teaching, or allowing and practicing the many innovations to which we have referred, that after being admonished and having had sufficient time for reflection, if they do not turn away from such abominations, that we can not and will not regard them as brethren.

[Signed] P. P. Warren, A. J. Nance, Daniel Baker, Peter Robertson, J. K. P. Rose, James W. Warren, Officers of Sand Creek Church. Randolph Miller, Charles Erwin, W. K. Baker, Wm. Cozier, Officers of Liberty Church.
[Signed] Wm. R. Storm, Ash Grove Church. J. H. Hagan, Union Church. Isaac Walters, Mode Church.

The brethren whose names stand alone in signing this document, represented the churches from which they came. Beside these, Elder Colson, of Gays, and Elder Hoke, of Stricklyn congregation, signed as individuals only, because the congregations whence they came had not been called together and formally sent them.

Green Creek congregation was represented by letter from Bro. Jesse Baker, indorsing the movement.

The "Address" of Sommer was written out after he presented it on Sunday the 18th and published by Sommer in the *Octographic Review*, September 5, 1889. In his long address, Sommer employed the rhetorical strategy of first advancing positions on which he presumed, with justification, the conservatives and progressives agreed. They agreed upon faith that resulted from hearing or reading the testimony of the word of God. Therefore what was not in Scripture was not the will of God. Sommer further asserted that repentance has to do with salvation as well as baptism by immersion. He eschewed human creeds and sprinkling instead of immersion. He argued that "Christian" is the proper designation for the church member and that church of Christ and churches of Christ are the proper name for the church. He charged that a plurality of elders is the Biblical approach, not a one man pastor. He insisted that funds should be given freely and not through launching festivals or any other fund raising approaches. He claimed that instrumental music was added to Jewish worship by king David, and absent in the early churches of Christ. Organs drown out vocal lyrics hence impede worship. Sommer insisted that church buildings, lamps, stoves, etc. were approved in the Scripture when dedicated persons searched. His broader thesis was that inference, opinion, supposition, and presumption cannot be safe means through which to enter heaven.

What happened at Sand Creek apparently had a dramatic impression on most of those present. They went away determined to separate from the innovators. The impact on the larger Churches of Christ brotherhood was slow in coming. Lipscomb reported that he agreed with most of the objections to the progressive's conclusions and actions expressed by Sommer. But he didn't believe that a group of self-appointed critics should write up a declaration in concert to divide the brotherhood of believers.[14] J. D. Tant, referencing the sect baptism controversy, noted that Sand Creek was not the first time a group had declared non-fellowship with others in the Movement.[15] Responses in the progressive journals, the Christian-Evangelist and Christian Standard, surprisingly did not appear immediately, but were severe in their condemnation of the event.[16]

However important August 18, 1889 was to later Churches of Christ, it certainly impacted the future of the Stone-Campbell Movement in Illinois even though if only of a small percentage of believers.

---

[14] David Lipscomb, "He Wants to Divide," *Gospel Advocate* 33.4 (January 28, 1891) 49 and "Be Firm But Patient," *Gospel Advocate* 34.1 (January 7, 1892) 5, cited by Wolfgang, *A Life* 88, 89.

[15] J. D. Tant, "The Thirty-three," Firm Foundation 6.3 (February 6, 1890) 1.

[16] Russell Errett, "A Divisive Work," *Christian Standard* (June 18, 1892) 520, 521; Wolfgang, footnote 45, page 90, gathers eight additional references in the *Standard* to Sand Creek and its results. See also, J. B. Graves, "Sand Creek," *Christian-Evangelist* 1890: 53.

15. African American Christians and Churches in Illinois[1]

No group was more deeply affected by the Civil War and its outcome than formerly enslaved African Americans. For these people, the end of the war meant freedom to develop and exercise leadership in ways never afforded under slavery. In the church it provided the prospect of organizing congregations free of white oversight, starting extra-congregational organizations of their own, and establishing schools. Yet racism challenged these efforts at every point. Whites often tried to control the destiny of blacks, disregarding their desires and newly gained rights.[2]

Our research confirms the marginalization of, even apathy toward, African Americans in Illinois mirrors or exceeds national trends in the SCM.

The exponential growth of African American Disciples from around 7,000 in 1862 to 56,300 at the turn of the century occurred mostly in the former slave states of Kentucky, Tennessee, Georgia, Virginia, and North Carolina.[3] In Illinois, it was a decade after the Civil War ended before the first congregation of African Americans began; rather than "free of white oversight," it was started with the guidance of a white preacher. As

---

[1] For African Americans and the SCM see "Black Disciples" in David Edwin Harrell, Jr. *Quest for a Christian America: The Disciples of Christ and American Society to 1866* (Nashville: Disciples of Christ Historical Society, 1966) 93 - 97; in *GH*, Slavery and Race in "Developments in the United States to 1866" (35 – 39) and "Growth of African American Institutions to 1920," (46 – 60); Hap Lyda, *A History of Black Christian Churches (Disciples of Christ) in the United States through 1899* (Unpublished PhD Dissertation, Vanderbilt University, 1972); Sheila Hope Gillams, *Principle and Practice: The Quandry of African American Restorationists in the History and Theology of the Church of Christ, Disciples of Christ, 1850 – 1950* (Unpublished PhD Dissertation, Union Theological Seminary, 2002).

[2] *GH* 46.

[3] Ibid. 47.

we document in this chapter, only three African American congregations were started in Illinois before 1900.

There is no evidence of any organized work for African Americans in Illinois until a canvas by the white-led Board of Negro Evangelization and Education near the end of the century.[4] Nineteenth century educational institutions established for African Americans were located in the South.

A Voice through Periodicals

A lack of their own resources after the Civil War no doubt caused African American Disciples to be unable to publish periodicals devoted to their news and thoughts. The *Christian Standard* began a column, "Our Colored Brethren," in 1879, edited by Preston Taylor. The column, sometimes subtitled "An Official Organ for the Disciples of Christ (Colored)," continued until 1886; it carried valuable information on founding of African American congregations; activities in colored congregations; marriages, brief death notices and obituaries. Articles in 1882 and 1884 mention Illinois.[5]

The earliest known African American SCM periodical was the *Christian Star* of Dallas, Texas, started around 1882, with H. S. Howell as editor. M. F. Robinson and Annie Marshall started a paper with the same name at Louisville, Kentucky circa 1888. Since no issues of these papers seem to be extant, it is impossible to determine any correlation between the two papers.[6]

African Americans published the *Christian Soldier* at Lexington, Kentucky in 1888.[7] Regrettably, no issues of this paper seem to have survived.

---

[4] C. C. Smith, "Closing Days of the B. N. E. E. Canvas in Illinois," *CS* (January 4 1896) 20. As a subject for a later volume on Illinois is Gillams' note: "Other independent, unaffiliated African American Disciple fellowships are found in Texas, Illinois, and Indiana." *Principles...* 12.

[5] November 18, 1882 365: W. Hancock plans to organize a colored congregation at Jacksonville.

January 19, 1884 22: Frank and Amelia Thomas, with assistance of white minister G. M. Goode, are establishing a congregation in Normal, Illinois.

June 21, 1884 195: Death notice for Clara McFadden at Normal, Illinois.

September 20, 1884 301: R. M. Chamberlain moved to Normal, Illinois, and "has taken charge of the work there."

[6] Spencer, *Periodicals* 45.

[7] Ibid.

The first major paper for African Americans was the *Christian Plea: Official Organ of the Negro Disciples of Christ* (also called *Gospel Plea*) published in Mississippi and Tennessee from 1889 – 1924.[8]

Illinois did not have a paper published by African Americans in the 19th century.

African American Membership in Stone-Campbell Congregations

The American Restorationist churches were by majority white, but blacks also attended the white congregations or formed congregations of their own.[9] Most of the black Restorationists before the Civil War were slaves, most of whom were born in the United States in Virginia, the Carolinas, Georgia, Alabama, Mississippi, Tennessee and Kentucky.[10] Slaves attended white congregations, but in some cases they were delegated to a back balcony and were forced to climb to their "loft" on an exterior ladder. Various leaders of the Restoration Movement at one time owned slaves including Alexander Campbell, Barton W. Stone and David Lipscomb.[11]

Restorationist churches had Black members almost from the beginning. The Brush Run Church in Pennsylvania and the Cane Ridge Congregation in Kentucky reported African-Americans.[12] In the 1820s African American members were reported in Pleasant Grove, Kentucky, Walnut Spring, Virginia and Old Union, Kentucky. The earliest Black congregations were in Kentucky, first at Midway in 1834 and then several other locations until Hancock Hill was founded in Louisville in the 1850s. Black churches were reported in North Carolina in 1854, Tennessee in 1859, and in Georgia before the Civil War. By 1861 the number of

---

[8] Ibid. 41.

[9] Portions of this chapter are by Jan Staggs. Of his research, he states, "This study began when I prepared a "History of the Stone-Campbell Church in Springfield, Illinois" for Professor Aaron Berkowitz at Lincoln Land Community College. I then worked on a History of the Church of Christ in Champaign-Urbana, Illinois, where I was raised. This led me to study the history of the Stone-Campbell movement in Illinois. Based on that work, I decided to study the Black Stone-Campbell ministers in Illinois. I was not aware of any other person who had conducted research on Black Stone-Campbell ministers and congregations in Illinois."

[10] Hap F. C. Lyda, "African-Americans in the Movement," *ESCM* ,11-13.

[11] Paul M. Blowers and Robert O. Fife, "Slavery in the Movement," ibid., 685-688.

[12] Lyda, Ibid., 11.

African-Americans in integrated congregations totaled 5,500 and those in Black congregations about 1500.[13]

Early Black Religious History in Illinois

Illinois has a long history of faith communities in which Blacks participated.[14] The presence of a sizable number of Blacks commences in 1721 at Prairie Du Rocher, south of St. Louis. The first area settlement was Fort Chartes, on the Mississippi River, in about 1721. St. Josephs Catholic church was established at Fort Chartes about the same time. In 1722, Phillip Francois Renault, acting on behalf of King Louis XV, arrived in the region to search out gold and silver. On his way to Illinois, Renault stopped at Santa Domingo Island to purchase 500 slaves to assist in locating and the mining of these precious metals. Renault and his expedition spent 20 years looking for gold and silver without success. He did, however, discover lead which is still mined in eastern Missouri and southern Illinois. In 1742, Renault departed Illinois territory and returned to France, leaving behind the slaves and their descendants.

The San Domingo slaves, whose forbears were born in Africa, were largely Roman Catholic because of their Santa Domingo French cultural upbringing. It is claimed that for the next 150 years the black population of Randolph County, Illinois, and Saint Genevieve County, Missouri, were descendants of these slaves.[15]

By 1765 the population in this region declined and the settlements deteriorated. Captain Sterling wrote to General Gage on December 15, 1765 regarding the French withdrawal from the area and commented on the African-American slaves.

> I have not been able to get an Exact Account of the number of the Inhabitants, as there is always a number of them at N Orleans, trading with the Indians, or Hunting which they go to as regularly as the Savages, the Village of Caskaskias has about Fifty Familys, and at Caho, about Forty, those of Prairie du Rocher, Fort Chartes, and St. Phillip are almost totally Aban-

---

[13] Ibid.

[14] To gain an appreciation of the black experience with Christianity in the United States read Albert J. Raboteau, *Slave Religion: The "Invisible Institution" in the Antebellum South,* (New York: Oxford University Press, 2004).

[15] Craig Manson, *The Catholic Gene: Exploring Our Catholic Family History,* February 5, 2016.

doned; This settlement has been declining Since the com-
mencement of the War, and when it was Ceded to us, many
Familys went away for fear of the English, and want of Troops
to protect them from the Indians, they have formed a Settlement
Since the Peace, opposite to Caho called St. Louis, where there is
now About Fifty Familys, and they have another opposite to
Caskaskias, which has been Settled Thirty Years ago, Called St.
Genevieve...

I have Enquired into the affairs of the Jesuits, and find that
they were Dispossest, and their Estates and Goods Sold by
an Order, from the Council at N Orleans, for the behoof of
the King; Their Houses, Lands, and goods here, were Sold
for a Hundred & some odd Thousand Livres, besides about
Fifty Negro's that were send down to Orleans, and there
Sold: They Carried away the Papers of Sale so that I could
not get an exact amount...[16]

An egregious example of the early mistreatment of slaves in Illinois is
the salt mines in Gallatin County:

In 1803 a slave owning company Kentucky company salt operator earned the first lease from the government to produce
120,000 thousand bushels of salt with wells near Eagle Creek.
He didn't last long. Over the next few years a series of businesses would take control of the wells, increasing the needs of
slaves. The Illinois Treaty adopted the indenture laws of Indiana,
which had been updated over the course of six years, when it
was adopted in 1809. The slave owners, in fact, demanded more,
no one, more so, than the salt well owners near Eagle Creek. If
anything, history has immortalized the act of slavery in name
alone. The Great Salt Spring near Eagle Creek dates historical
maps as N----r Well or N----r furnace. It still remains the Negro
Spring today.

---

[16] Punctuation, spelling and capitalization follow the text in "Stirling to Gage,
December 15, 1765" in Clarence Walworth Alvord and Clarence Edwin Carter,
*Collections of the Illinois State Historical Library, Volume XI, = British Series, Volume II:
The New Regime, 1765 – 1767.* (Springfield: Illinois State Historical Library, 1916)
125, 126.

By 1810, an estimated 1,000 black slaves toiled in the forested area as woodcutters and salt kettle attendants. Some had been temporarily brought over from Kentucky and Tennessee. To the dismay of emancipationists around the country, Illinois ratified its state 1818 constitution with two jarring clauses. No slavery or involuntary servitude would be allowed, though unlike Indiana constitution, previously enslaved and indentured servants remained the same in their same status. More important, the constitution had one exception: legal slaves would be allowed within the tract reserved for the salt works near "Shawneetown" until 1825 - the heart of the salt and coal fields near Eagle Creek. These same salt works employed the same slaves to dig out coal for the furnaces. The slavery provisions were removed in a fight over the 1824 constitutional convention.

The unsung credit, according to southern Illinois historian Ron Nelson, went to the backwoods Baptists and their "Friends of Humanity" anti-slavery movement, which confronted the slave-owning salt and coal traders in the forests of Eagle Creek.[17]

The Methodists reported having Blacks in their congregations from in the 1810s. In the 1820s they reported for 1823, 3,155 whites, 53 colored and 10 Indians. In 1827 there was an increase to 5,335 whites and 55 colored.[18]

Several Black Baptist congregations were founded beginning in 1819. The Salem Baptist church, in Alton, Illinois, first organized in 1819, still stands as the only predominately African American congregation in Madison County, and is situated along the Mississippi River across from Missouri. African American stonemason Madison Banks and white contractor Samuel Marshall, both from Alton, built the church sometime in the early1820s. They were assisted by two members of the congregation, John Walker and William Emery. It is believed that Salem Baptist Church's first congregants were organized in 1819 on a local farm, by a Baptist missionary named James Ely Welch.

A Zion Missionary Baptist Church was founded in 1838 as the colored Baptist church at 1601 East Laurel, Springfield, Illinois. The Rev. John

---

[17] Jeff Biggers, *Illinois Teachable Moment: The True Cost of Coal, Slavery, and Historical Markers.* https://www.huffpost.com/entry/illinois-teachable-moment_b_4172108. January 23, 2014.

[18] James Leaton, *History of Methodism in Illinois from 1793 to 1832.* (Cincinnati: Walden and Stone, 1883) 192; 264

Livingston, a travelling Baptist evangelist (and the first ordained black minister in Illinois), and 18 black residents of Springfield organized the church at a meeting in the home of Anderson Cooper on April 21, 1838. Livingston briefly served as pastor. He was succeeded in 1838 by the Rev. Luther Arnold.[19]

The Stone Campbell Movement did not have any known Black congregations until 1875 at Little Rock (Unionville) in Massac County. As an example of the delay in establishing a Black congregation, consider Springfield, the state capital. The white First Christian Church was established in 1833. Barton Stone came over from Jacksonville to help Joseph Hewitt plant this congregation. First Christian did not have any known effort to establish a black Disciples Christian Church. They did help establish West Side Christian in 1901 and Stuart Street in 1905. It was not until 1973 when West Side Christian helped establish the Monroe Street Christian Church, 140 years later.[20]

Disciples as Slaveholders

A startling statistic is that an 1851 census of slaveholders revealed that Disciples held 101,000 slaves, making the SCM, per capita, the largest slave-owning religious body in the United States.[21]

Clear evidence of Restorationists in Illinois struggling over the relationships of the slaves and the free is W. F. M. Arny, an ardent abolitionist from Bloomington, Illinois. Before moving to Illinois, Arny was active in the Underground Railroad.[22] Arny described an 1852 split in the Disciples church there because some members were slaveholders:

> The congregation of disciples of which I am present a member, have been separated for more than a year from others in this place, who call themselves a church, but who hold in their com-

---

[19] "Zion Missionary Baptist Church," published October 3, 2013. http:// sangamoncountyhistory.org/wp/?p=949

[20] Jan Staggs, *History of the Stone-Campbell Movement in Springfield, Illinois.* (Unpublished manuscript.)

[21] *GH* 39. *Annual Report of the American and Foreign Anti-Slavery Society* (New York: William Harned, Office Agent, 1851) 56. David Edwin Harrell, Jr. points out the difficulty of arriving at an accurate count of slaves owned by ante-bellum Disciples: *Quest for a Christian America: The Disciples of Christ and American Society to 1866* (Nashville: Disciples of Christ Historical Society, 1966) 93.

[22] Earle R. Forrest, *History of Washington County, Pennsylvania* (Chicago: S. J. Clarke Pub. Co., 1926) Volume 1, 426, 427.

munion and fellowship *Slaveholders*—men who have removed to this state and have slaves "hired out" in Kentucky. This class of slaveholders we have argued are more censurable than any other class—they profess Christianity, and yet hire out to non-professors their fellow beings. Having objected to such received as members of our congregation, the result was that 39 of us were separated, and we organized a separate congregation and as such would like to be represented at the convention.

Arny's letter was an appeal for his congregation to be represented at a "Disciples' Anti-Slavery Convention" to be held in Cleveland, Ohio, January 11 and 12, 1854. Brethren from the United States and Canada were invited. Among the concerns and agenda for the convention regarding slavery:

- [Slavery's] existence is greatly detrimental to the progress of Christianity in this country

- To consider and decide upon the most efficient plan we can with propriety adopt to aid in removing these evils, and to free ourselves from all responsibility for them while they exist.

- This call is a sort of Declaration of Independence on the part of those who have signed it, of Alexander Campbell. His name and influence have long bound many members of that church reluctantly to the support of slavery, and this indication of purpose to be free is encouraging.[23]

Additional Views on Slavery in Illinois

Here we present quotes from Haynes representative of the dichotomy of beliefs of the Illinois brethren toward slavery in the nineteenth century.

What was the attitude of the Disciples in Illinois toward slavery? By 1861 the Illinois Disciples had grown to possibly about 20,000. In all the discussions on slavery that culminated in the Dred Scott decision—the deepest and most damning nadir of our national annals—Disciples were active participants. In the eighteen thirties, forties and fifties many disciples came into Illi-

[23] "Disciples' Anti-slavery Convention," *The Anti-Slavery Bugle* (December 10, 1853). Ken Christensen, E-Mail, April 26, 2016 to Jan Staggs, brought this to our attention.

nois from Kentucky, Tennessee and Virginia. Some, who settled in border counties were pro-slavery, but most of those relocating to Illinois came because of their aversion to the "peculiar institution." For example, Ben Major, who came from Kentucky and settled in Walnut Grove in the early thirties, freed his slaves and sent his agent with them to New York City in 1834 to pay passage to Liberia. Of those disciples who came into Illinois during these three decades from the states east of us, nearly all were anti-slavery except those from southern Indiana. In the early forties two colonies of Ohio people migrated to Illinois. Of these, Dr. J. P. Walters, now, a resident of Fairfield, wrote:

> The two colonies of Christians who came from Ohio and settled in Wayne County in earlier years were decidedly anti-slavery in their political convictions, there being abolitionists in each of the companies. These new comers were important factors in molding the political sentiment in this County in the years 1840-1861. The attitudes of the Disciples of Christ during these those years throughout this portion of the state was decidedly anti-slavery, but in border counties pro-slavery sentiment prevailed. In evidence of which is the fact that Wayne County, east of Mt. Vernon, raised more than its quota of soldiers in every call for volunteers, and that the prevailing religious convictions in quite a number of the military organizations in this part of the state was that of the Disciples of Christ...

The writer is indebted to Professor B. J. Radford, the Sage of Eureka, for the following:

> Of the Disciples of Christ who came into Illinois up to 1861 the great majority were immigrants from Kentucky, Tennessee, and Virginia. They were pretty evenly divided between Henry Clay Whigs and Jackson Democrats—the Whigs predominating in the center of the state and the Democrats in the southern portions. The Clay Whigs leaned strongly toward abolitionism and many were supporters of the Liberian Colonization So-

ciety. The democrats were mostly pro-slavery, or indifferent to the slavery.[24]

Illinois Blacks in the Civil War

One of the most interesting of the Illinois regiments serving with the eastern commands was the 29th Regiment U. S. Colored Infantry. The State of Illinois had commenced the creating of this unit in the late months of 1863, when Governor Yates made a decision regarding Negro soldiers and issued an executive order defining the terms under which a colored regiment was to be raised. The 29th was raised slowly, however, for a multitude of reasons, among which was low pay and mistreatment of Negro soldiers captured by the confederates.

The regiment A Company was brought together in the Quincy area, and was filled in the early months of 1864. The remaining companies, up to and including the K company, were recruited slowly but gradually from all sections of the state, including those of "little Egypt." The official date of the mustering-in of the regiment, that is to say, the moment at which the organization was officially accepted for service, was April 24, 1864.[25]

Black Members, Ministers and Congregations in Illinois - Disciples of Christ

The earliest mention of colored members by Haynes is the congregation at Cameron in Warren County near Galesburg, organized in 1831. By 1914 it was a fairly large congregation with a total of 290 members. In regard to colored members, Haynes wrote:

> In May, 1834, the congregation received by immersion "Bro." Richard, a colored man; in 1838, Sister Polly, a colored woman, and in 1843 by commendation Sister Susan Richardson, a colored woman.[26]

---

[24] N. S. Haynes, "The Disciples of Christ in Illinois and Their Attitude toward Slavery," *Transactions of the Illinois State Historical Society for the Year 1913.* (Springfield, Ill.: Illinois State Journal, 1914) 57, 58.

[25] Victor Hickman, *Illinois in the Civil War*, (Urbana: The University of Illinois Press, 1966) 334-335.

[26] Haynes, 424.

Haynes mentions six African American congregations: Little Rock in Massac County (1875);[27] Normal Second (1884);[28] Armour Avenue, Chicago (1888);[29] Bloomington Third (1901);[30] Jacksonville (1904);[31] and Rockford (post-1904).[32] We present more information on the congregations that were established before 1900 later in this chapter after we document African American preachers who labored in Illinois, regardless of whether they served in mixed race or predominantly African American congregations.

African American Illinois Preachers

It is important to note that Haynes does not include any biographical sketches of African American preachers although he does include the history of a few African American congregations in Illinois. In this section we highlight African American preachers known to us who labored in Illinois prior to 1900 but are not mentioned by Haynes in the histories of black congregations.

Andrew Jackson Blackburn (1824 – 1892)

In June 1870 the "Disciples of Christ in Northern Illinois" convened at Rockford. Of the two representatives from Rock Island, one was a colored preacher, A. J. Blackburne.[33] It is unclear if the Rock Island congregation was mixed race or an early, otherwise unattested African American congregation. The other attendee from Rock Island was Edwin Rogers but his ethnicity is not noted. If the congregation was mixed race, it is striking but possible that Blackburn was their preacher.

Blackburn appears in the admittedly incomplete 1880 *Preachers of the Churches of Christ in the United States* in a separate "List of Colored Preach-

---

[27] Ibid., 322

[28] Ibid. 295, 296.

[29] Ibid., 154

[30] Ibid., 287.

[31] Ibid., 338.

[32] Ibid., 98. This African American congregation in Rockford is not mentioned elsewhere by Haynes. It received $50.00 in Living Link support sometime after 1904 when the program was initiated.

[33] "Missionary Meeting in Northern Ill.," *GE* 8.8 (August 1870) 348; 350. The more common spelling of his surname is Blackburn. The 1870 and 1880 Federal Censuses locate him in Rock Island. In the 1870 listing he is a "Reformed Minister"; in 1880 he is a "Minister of the Gospel."

ers," where thirty preachers are listed; A. J. Blackburn, of Illinois and W. H. Brown and David Blackburn of Ohio, are the only colored preachers working outside of the border and southern states.[34]

W. M. Hancock (? - ?)

In November of 1882, Preston Taylor's column, "Our Colored Brethren," carried a notice of the efforts of W. Hancock in Jacksonville, Illinois:

> *Oct. 13, 1882*—I preached eight sermons here, and had 30 addi-
> tions to the church. I thank the Lord, as I am the first colored
> Christian minister that ever preached here. All the additions are
> from the Baptist and the Methodist churches. We baptized on
> the 9th inst. in the white Christian church, and we will organize
> to-night. The prospects are good. I baptized one local preacher,
> from the Methodist church. I will leave for Hannibal to-night,
> where I will dedicate our new church. W. Hancock.[35]

An African American preacher, W. M. Hancock, was active in Hannibal in 1881. He is likely the same person:

> *Hannibal*, March 21.—I commenced a series of meetings in *New
> London*, on the first Sunday in March, for Bro. Scholl, and closed
> yesterday, delivering fourteen discourses in that time, and had 35
> additions—2 from the Catholics, 1 from the Presbyterians, and 3
> from the Methodists; and while there was called on by white
> brethren, and prepared one sermon for them. I am now in Han-
> nibal, and preach here to-night. Had a very exciting time at New

---

[34] F. M. Green, *Preachers of the Churches of Christ in the United States.* (No place of publication: no publisher, [1880]) no pagination. We have not been able to determine if A. J. and David Blackburn were related.

[35] *CS* (November 18, 1882) 365. We have not found any evidence the 1882 African American congregation in Jacksonville was actually constituted. Haynes 338 gives 1904 for the founding of an African American congregation at Jacksonville. There was a "mission Bible school" as early as 1894. This is clearly a different effort than Hancock's in 1882.

London. We had an attendance that had not visited the church in seven years. W. M. Hancock.[36]

Little Rock - Unionville (Massac County)

The earliest well documented African American congregation of the SCM in Illinois was Unionville in Massac County across the Ohio River from Paducah, Kentucky. This congregation was started in 1875 with the help of a white minister, W. W. Dugger. Its building was located in the east end of the county; the congregation met regularly every Lord's Day for worship, with half-time preaching.[37] Dugger, who ministered at Mayfield, Kentucky, before and during the Civil War, moved to Massac County after the war.

This church is also reported in the *History of Massac County* by Elder A. R. Cook who describes all of the Christian congregations in the county.

> This is the only congregation of colored people we have in the county. It was organized in 1875 by Elder W. W. Dugger, and has a membership of twenty-nine. They have no house in which to worship, and no Sunday school, but under the faithful leadership of C. S. Welch meet every Lord's day for the breaking of bread (Acts 2:42) and prayer.[38]

---

[36] *CS* (April 2, 1881) 109. T. P. Haley, *Historical and Biographical Sketches of the Early Churches and Pioneer Preachers of the Christian Church in Missouri* (St. Louis: Christian Publishing Co, 1888) does not mention Hancock and has vague information on only one African American congregation in Missouri: "There were eighteen colored people who came into the church ["Church of Christ at Lamine" Eds.] at the same time ["August 1865" Eds.], but their names we did not succeed in getting. These soon organized a church of their own. (257).

[37] Haynes, 322.

[38] O. J. Page, *History of Massac County, Illinois* (No place of publication given: no publisher given, 1900) 104. By way of contrast, Cook notes that there were fifteen Baptists churches in the county of which five were colored.

A more recent history of the church was prepared by Dorothy Morris Lovelace.[39]

> The Little Rock Christian Church was organized 1874, by Wm. W. Dugger on the old Crag Farm in a little log school house, Elder Wm W. Dugger serving as their first minister. There were six charter members, though small in number, the group was loyal to the faith and under the leadership of Elder Dugger they worked and worshipped together in that school house until the new school building was built. The granters of the land were Mr. and Mrs. George Deen, who were at that time living in Paducah, Ky. But [sic] was [sic] citizens of Pope County, IL. They continued their worship service in the new school house until they bought an acre of land and built the building in which we now worship. The deed for this land was received October 27, 1896 and recorded in Metropolis, Il. By the year 1900 they had a membership of 29 members. Elder Charlie S. Welch was their first superintendent of the Sunday school. The foundation of this building was laid in 1906 by Charlie S. Welch, a faithful leader of the church. Bro. Welch did not live to see the work finished. He departed this life July 24, 1906. Other carpenters were hired to finish the building. Thomas R. Dugger, son of Wm M. Dugger was one of the carpenters.
>
> The work was completed December 20, 1906. The building was insured and needed seats and equipment bought. The church building was dedicated the 3rd Sunday in June 1907. Elder R. E .Pearson was pastor at that time.
>
> None of the charter members are living. We can not dedicate, we can not consecrate, we can not hallow this work for the brave mothers and fathers have consecrated far above our knowledge to add or detract. In looking into the past we can say of those faithful Christians as the great Apostle Paul said to the Gentiles,

---

[39] This history was prepared for the *African Settlement of Massac County: Documenting Historical Structures Project* scrapbook (2006). I spoke to Dorothy by telephone in early 2017 in Metropolis where she is living in a nursing home. Unfortunately, Dorothy did not have a good memory at this time of the events in the past at Little Rock. Dorothy wrote a column *News from Shady Grove* for the Metropolis Planet that sometimes mentioned items about the Little Rock Christian church and its members.

in his closing remarks. They fought the good fight, they kept the faith, they believed in one Lord, one faith and one baptism. They believed that the cordial principals of the doctrine of Christ as taught by the Apostles, were faith, repentance, confession and baptism.

Under the leadership of our present minister, Eld. Cloe Tharpe Jr., we are teaching this same gospel. It is altogether fitting and proper that this date be celebrated. For the past must always be remembered with loving sentimentality, as the church presses forward to the mark of great accomplishments in the name of Jesus Christ our Lord.[40]

Dugger was 69 when he started the white Unionville congregation in 1875. He had been in Massac County since 1865 according to a Census for that date. He and his wife Mary Ann were originally from Tennessee before moving to Kentucky. They were married on July 11, 1841 in Maury County, Tennessee. W. W. Dugger died Sept 23, 1885 at Unionville. He was coming from a baptism when his horse and buggy ran away, hit a stump, and threw him out. He broke his hip and later died of pneumonia.

C. (Charles) S. Welch, the initial leader of the Little Rock Church in Unionville, and his wife Lidia Ann, were from Morganfield, Union County, Kentucky. He was born in 1841 and Lidia in 1847. They had moved to Massac County by 1867 because their first daughter Mary was born there in 1867. They had nine children.

Siloam Baptist Church, located 13 miles west, was built approximately in 1875 and served the African-American population of Unionville and New Liberty. The cemetery may also be the final resting place of mem-

---

[40] The 2006 Document included a copy of the October 4, 1959 "Our 85th Year Little Rock Christian Church." This document included many of the members of the congregation in 1959. It also included the names of 20 "Ministers Who Have served Our Church." Of interest is the name J. E. Anderson. He will be mentioned as helping with a dedication in Bloomington, preaching in Rockford, and finally serving in Champaign from about 1926 until his death in 1960. The 2006 document has twelve photographs of the Little Rock building in 2006.

bers of the Little Rock Christian Church, also African American and built in 1875.[41]

Normal Second (McLean County)

As a promising, albeit slow development, in 1883 the General Convention of the Disciples appointed African American Preston Taylor as a National Evangelist to travel on behalf of African American disciples to evangelize and establish churches. This appointment indicated that white Disciples of Christ began to sense the need to help establish separate black congregations rather than having mixed race congregations.[42]

Taylor went to Normal, Illinois, in January, 1884, where he found some disciples, and constituted a congregation of twenty five charter members. G. M. Goode, pastor of the First Christian Church (white), helped Taylor purchase the old Presbyterian building at Cherry and Linden.[43] This was eight years after W. W. Dugger, a white minister, helped establish the Little Rock congregation in Unionville.

Armour Avenue Christian Church, Chicago (Cook County)

In 1888, on Dearborn Street, William G. F. Reed organized a group of eight people as the first African American SCM congregation in Chicago. With the help of the Chicago Missionary Society, the congregation sold the Dearborn property in 1893 and attempted to arrange other meeting places. Lack of a permanent meeting place hampered their vitality for

[41] https://www.findagrave.com/cemetery/2549633/siloam-baptist-church-cemetery. Harrison and Laura are buried there and two other Welch family members. C.S. Welch died sometime in the late 1890s. Lidia died sometime after the 1920 Census of Massac County. Robert Rice, a member of Little Rock, died in 1977.
[42] *GH* 46.
[43] Rick D. Williams, "African American Churches In Bloomington-Normal: The Development of Baptists, Methodists, and Disciples in the 19th and Early 20th Centuries," (Unpublished Master's Thesis, Illinois State University, 1991) 42. Madlyn Graves "Black-White Relations In The Disciple of Christ Church: A Look At National and Local Segregation," (Unpublished Honors Thesis, Illinois State University, 1981) 23-25. Details on the number of members differ: "When Taylor came to Normal in 1884 he helped organize the Second Christian Church with 16 charter members..." Williams adds, "One local account indicates that the group had been meeting as early as 1882..." (43).

several years until 1906 when the Armour Avenue property was purchased.[44]

The early instability of this congregation was partly caused by the disinterest for African American congregations in Illinois in general and neglect for Chicago in particular. Even white congregations in Chicago struggled before the end of the century.

To increase church planting efforts in their city, the Chicago brethren established the Christian Mission Board (also called the Chicago Missionary Society) in the autumn of 1887. Providentially, shortly later Reed's work in Chicago came to the attention of the Board, who appointed a committee review the opportunity. Rice describes the events:

> On the night of the 18th of November, brethren W. W. Eaton, J. G. Hester, and a brother Hoppy, a colored preacher formerly of Cincinnati, Ohio, met the group above mentioned, and in that meeting two elders, brethren Barnett and Washington, and three deacons, whose names are not given, and a clerk were elected and formally ordained. Writing of this event, Mr. Blackwell said: "The service was indeed an impressive one. The event was one of great importance. These fifty men and women are fine looking and of the very first of character and ability in this city. Among them are lawyers, editors, teachers, preachers, merchants, clerks, and industrial workers. More are uniting at every service.[45]

In 1889 there was a concerted effort to raise funds for the "Chicago Colored Mission," netting $149.44 in contributions, mostly from Illinois individuals and congregations.[46] To raise funds for the Chicago Colored Mission and encourage Reed, S. R. Cassius traveled extensively beginning on October 22, 1889. In mid-February, 1890, he reported:

> I have visited about fifty churches, and sought private aid from about 1,000 individuals. During that time I have raised in cash $120, and in pledges about $235. To raise the money I have been compelled to travel from the Mississippi River to Terre Haute, Ind., and all through Northern and Southern Illinois.

---

[44] Haynes, 154-55. Perry J. Rice, *Disciples of Christ in Chicago*, (Unpublished Manuscript, 1944) 266.

[45] Rice, op. cit, 41, 42. "Fifty" conflicts with Haynes' "eight."

[46] H. H. Hubbard, "Chicago Colored Mission," *CS* (October 12, 1889) 672.

The report's details indicate Cassius bemoaned that he had barely received enough donations to cover his expenses for railroad fares, food and shelter. Wealthy congregations gave pennies rather than dollars. His disappointment—rather, disgust—rang loud and clear:

> ...I have lectured on "The Race Problem" until I have become color blind; I have preached on "Charity" until I am disgusted; I have preached on "The Great Commission" until I am tired; in fact, I have done everything but hold up the congregation with a pair of Colt's revolvers, and we are not yet able to build a house unto them.[47]

Concluding Thoughts

The Black Stone-Campbell churches in Illinois lagged behind the Black Methodist and Black Baptist congregations. The Methodists reported congregations in 1807 in southern Illinois. The Baptists reported the Alton congregation in 1819; Springfield reported a congregation in 1838. No black SCM congregation was established in the nineteenth century in Springfield. Bloomington had the Mount Pisgah Black congregation in 1867, seventeen years before the Normal Second congregation was established in 1884. In Chicago the Olivet Baptist Black congregation was established thirty-three years before Armour Avenue was established.

The earliest documented SCM congregation with Black members in a predominantly white congregation was 1831, the Cameron congregation in Warren County.

The first standalone Black SCM congregation was in 1875 at Little Rock in Unionville in Massac County. W. W. Dugger, a white minister who also served a white congregation in the same town, was the founding minister.

The second established was Third Christian in Normal in 1884. Preston Taylor from Nashville established this congregation. The white congregations in Bloomington-Normal had not helped to establish a Black congregation. The white First Christian Church of Normal did help the Black congregation purchase the old Presbyterian building for a meeting house.

Third was Armour Avenue in Chicago, established in 1888. This congregation struggled to exist.

---

[47] S. R. Cassius, "The Chicago Colored Mission," *CS* (February 22, 1890) 126.

The burning question is why there were only three Black Stone-Campbell congregations in Illinois by 1900. Haynes enumerates over 700 white congregations. As previously mentioned there were several Black Methodist and Baptist congregations in Illinois. This clearly shows that blacks were receptive to the Gospel in its broadest sense. The white congregations did not reach out to the Black community and establish Black congregations.

Mirroring national trends, the establishment of Black Restorationist churches in Illinois accelerated in the twentieth century. We hope to tell that story in a later volume.

Conclusions to the Stone-Campbell Movement in Illinois in the Nineteenth Century

The detailed history of the Stone-Campbell Movement in Illinois in the nineteenth century has taken us on a detailed time journey into an important quest for the roots, sprouts, and limbs of Restorationism in Illinois. The faith and religious predilections of these early Illinois pioneers was a vital dimension in the unfolding of life itself in this dynamic Midwestern state. We have examined carefully the numerous commitments and changes of these peoples over the years. We believe we have given the readers of this volume an adequate overview of the important developments. It is our hope that anyone who seeks information about their own heritage will find in this book various specific details to enhance their insights.

On several subjects we have offered exhaustive comments, for example, on the earliest congregations, congregational organization, colleges, religious journals, major controversies both liberal and conservative, women, African America congregations and preachers, and a number of important church leaders. In other areas much more could have been added, but that would have made the volume unmanageable. It is our expectation that over the coming years, historians of the movement will pursue these undeveloped topics in essays, theses, dissertations and books. We anticipate that this volume will encourage publications to that end and provide a sufficient backdrop for such future efforts.

Many important details are presented in the appendices. We herein offer indices of people, and places. By the people index, bibliography and leaders can be located. The place index includes all the place names in the chapters but not in the appendices. The place names in the appendices are easy to locate since they are alphabetized for the most part.

We now turn to the future. We have gathered much data for a history of the Stone-Campbell Movement in Illinois in the twentieth century. It is our intent to commence working on the twentieth century so as to continue the history. We hope that volume 2 on the succeeding century will be forthcoming in the next two years.

Appendix 1: Statistics for Restorationist Growth, with an Emphasis on Illinois

This timeline lists statistical reports for Restorationists. Various Stone-Campbell Movement publications tracked statistics. When possible, we give Illinois numbers. Statistics for sister movements and other denominations are sometimes included for comparison.

Readers should keep in mind that early statistics are estimates, reflecting loose or no organization. Over time, when the various movements became more organized, the numbers become more accurate.

Year	Event	Reference
1790	Baptists began the publication of the *Baptist Annual Register* in England: "Baptist Journalism may be traced to 1790 when the *Baptist Annual Register* was established in England by Dr. John Ripon, successor to Doctor Gill in the church in Southwark, London. This publication included communications from Americans also and was a means of communication sufficient for their simple purposes at that early stage of the American churches."	Joseph S. Swaim, "The Development of Baptist Journalism," in J. Pressley Barrett, *Modern Light Bearers: Addresses Celebrating the Centennial of Religious Journalism,* (Dayton, Ohio: Christian Publishing Association, 1908) 83.
1793	"But the next year it was recognized that the title of the body did not consort with Mr. O'Kelly's claim of having all things in the church governed by the New Testament, and so the title, Republican Methodist, was dropped in favor of the Bible name, Christian. At that time, in 1793, there were in Virginia and North Carolina about a thousand members in the churches of the new body, and about twenty churches and ministers."	Martyn Summerbell, *An Address on the Origin and Principles of the Christians.* (No place: the New Jersey Christian Conference, 1911) 6.

1808	"In 1808, when proposals for union of the Christians in Virginia, Kentucky and New England were made, there were said to be twenty thousand members in the South and West." The actual statement is "We have members in every state south of the Potomac, also a few churches in Pennsylvania; from the best information I can obtain, I suppose there are about 20,000 people in the Southern and Western states who call themselves by the *christian* [sic] name."	Morrill: 115, citing *HGL* 1:43. W. G. [William Guirey], "Copy of a letter to the editor dated Caroline County, Virginia, Dec. 18th 1808." *HGL* 1.11 (January 19, 1809) 43.
1812	"We are always comforted in hearing from our brethren in North and South Carolina, Georgia, Kentucky, Ohio, Tennessee, Indiana territory, and other places in that quarter. There are some subscribers in Illinois territory; from that part we should be glad of a concise statement of affairs as to the state of religion."	Elias Smith, "To the Patrons of the Herald," *HGL* 5.26 (August 20, 1813) 517, 518.
1813	"Illinois Territory, Nov. 21, 1813. Dear Sir, There appears to be a great inquiry after truth among the people in this part of the country. Truly the harvest is great, and the labourers [sic] are few…I have a circuit of about two hundred and fifty miles, which I have constantly attended to for some time when health & strength would admit…I am your unworthy friend, Joseph Taylor." Humphreys and Kernodle do not have a sketch of Joseph Taylor. Taylor is an agent for the *Herald of Gospel Liberty* per 7.2 (September 6, 1814) 628: "Joseph Taylor, Kaskaskai, Illenois [sic] Territory." There are a few "western" agents in the list: James Lemon, Clark County, Indiana Territory; Griffin Green, Marietta, Ohio.	Joseph Taylor, "Extract of a Letter from Joseph Taylor, to the Editor, dated Illinois Territory, Nov. 21, 1813," *HGL*, 6.15 (March 4, 1814) 574.

1814	"I have lately heard from *Kentucky, Ohio, Tennessee, Indiana Territory—Illinois,* and the *Missouri Territories,* and from all these places the general account is, that knowledge is increasing, while a goodly number are running to and fro for that purpose."	E. Smith, "To the Patrons of the Herald," *HGL* 7.1 (August 19, 1814) 622.
1825	Connection had 13,000 members and 225 ministers in the west: "The available statistics show the strength of western churches in 1825, which numbered nearly 13,000 members and were ministered to by 225 preachers. They were distributed over three conferences in Kentucky (3,350), and one each in Tennessee (1,800) and Alabama (600). The largest membership, however, could be found in the six conferences of Ohio (4,390), and smaller numbers in Indiana (1,200), Illinois (600), and Missouri (1,000). Altogether the statistics also list 64 church buildings as being owned by these churches." (90 – 93). [Note that buildings were included in the stats. Kentucky started doing this in the *Christian Messenger*, listing wood or brick in addition.]	"Proceedings of a Conference in Kentucky, and Address to Elder Badger, &c.," *G L* 2 (1826) 82 - 93.
1827	The whole number of preachers in the above named Conferences is 225. The number of brethren is as follows, as near as can be ascertained:—In three Conferences in Kentucky is about 3350; Tennessee Conference, 1,800; Alabama do. 600; Six [conferences JLM] do. in Ohio, 4,390; Indiana do. 1,200; Illinois do. 600; Missouri, do. 1000; Total, 12,940. In Kentucky, our brethren have built 36 Meeting houses, two of them stone, ten of brick, and 24 of wood. In Ohio they have built 28—three stone, 4 brick, the rest wood." [This seems to be the same report as the Gospel Luminary.]	Ed. [Elias Smith], "Worthy of Notice," *Morning Star and City Watchman,* 1.2 (July 2, 1827) 28, 29.

| 1829 | There is another sect, called "Christians"—by their enemies, "*New Lights*," which have, in little more than the quarter of a century, risen from nothing to 1500 congregations, with a membership of 150,000, and an influence equal to the one-twentieth of the whole population. These are "*poor and ignorant too*." But let Dr. Ely know that these poor and ignorant folks have wrought all the wonders that have been of magnificent influence in the annals of the world. The spoke of the wheel which is now in the mud, will be nighest heaven by and by; and that which is "clean and *dry*," will soon descend. The rich become poor, and the poor become rich; and their children in the third generation generally change seats." (Editor [BWS] "Remarks on the Preceding," = "Presbyterian Statistics," [from the *Christian Baptist*, for April 1829]. | *CM* 3.8 (June 1829) 189, 190 |
| 1829 | "At the present time, the number in Christian fellowship amounts to upwards of seventy thousand, scattered over our widely extended territory." | Unattributed Editorial, "Introductory Remarks," *Christian Repository*, 1.1 (January, 1829) 1. |

1834	"Our Probable Number	John Clark, *Christian Register for the Year of our Lord 1836* (Union Mills, N. Y.: Printed by the Author, 1836)
	Various calculations have been made as to the number of the Christian Society in America. But for want of universal correspondence all representations are at present imperfect. We can find none more condensed and authentic, that that made by Elder Millard in June 1834, found I his letter No. XVIII. Ch. Palladium, 3d. vol. page 112.	
	From my late extensive travels west of the Alleghanies [sic], I have received information which enables me to say there will be no hazard in the following computation of the numbers of the Christian Connection. In Kentucky we have about 11,000 members, and about 80 preachers. In Ohio, we have about 11,000 members, and about 140 preachers. In other sections west of the Alleghanies [sic], I travelled only in Western Virginia and Indiana, but I received information which I think can be depended upon, as to the number of the Christians. West of the Alleghanies we have from 400 to 500 preachers, and from 40,000 to 45,000 communicants. East of the Alleghanies [sic] we have as many preachers and brethren as on the west side. We may then safely calculate the whole number of the Christian Connection in America to be from 80,000 to 100,000, and the whole number of our preachers to be from 800 to 1000. It may also be calculated that the number of those who attend on our ministry statedly, is not less than 350,000 souls. Surely, as a people we have a responsible work on our hands."	

1834	One principal object in view at the time the meeting was appointed, was to collect as many teachers of christianity together as possible, that when assembled, they might form an acquaintance, communicate all the information of which they were possessed, in relation to the different congregations of our Lord Jesus Christ-ascertain the feelings of the brethren on the subject of sending out Evangelists to spread abroad to dying mortals the good news of salvation through Jesus Christ, and to adopt such measures, in other respects, particularly as it regards co-operation, as would insure a spirit of union and perseverance [sic], in the great work.	*Evangelist* 1834: 279, 280.
	The Elders and Brethren who attended, were B. W. Stone, Palmer, (of Ky.) Rigdon, Elders Hewett, Osborne, Baker, Hodgen, Sweet, Jones, Peler, Bledsoe, and others.	
	Brother John Rigdon, a master spirit, was unanimously solicited to act as an Evangelist, for the next six months, with the pledge of $150 dollars being furnished for the support of his family during that time.	
	The brethren from different parts of the state, particularly the north, stated, that the congregations were in number, from 10 to 120, and that there were but few public teachers—that the 'harvest is truly great but laborers few.'	
	A committee was appointed to write an address to the different congregations in the state. In a few days it will appear, and we will forward one to you.	
	We shall now close by commending you to God and the word of his grace, praying that he may ever support, and prosper you while industriously propagating the words of immortal truth to a dying world.	

1836	13. *Christian Sect*, or *Newlights*, have become to a considerable extent amalgamated with the "*Reformers*," or "*Campbellites*." I have not data on which to construct a tabular view of this sect,—but from general information, estimate the number of their "bishops," and "proclaimers," at 300, and their communicants at 10,000 or 12,000. They have three or four monthly periodicals.	Peck, *New Guide* 1836: 357
1837	T. F. Railsback letter to the Millennial Harbinger: "Dear brother, I rejoice to inform you that in the last four years the prospects in favor of the ancient gospel and order of things has much changed in the counties of Tazwell [sic; Tazewell] and M'Clean [sic; McLean]. We have some six or eight intelligent teachers and upwards of five hundred disciples, and many of the brethren are men of intelligence." https://www.findagrave.com/memorial/51169319/thomas-fisher-railsback. [Accessed 1.31.2017.]	*MH* 1837: 329, 330.
1837	"We have no regular statistics —no annual reports, that, with numerical accuracy, enable us to state the increase during the last year throughout the whole United States." Alexander Campbell	"Letters to England--No. 1" *MH* 1837: 271

1839	"There are probably half a dozen Unitarian congregations in the state [Illinois], and three or four ministers." "The *Reformers*, as they term themselves, or "Campbellites," as others call them, have several large, and a number of small societies, a number of preachers, and several hundred members, including the Christian body with which they are in union. They immerse all who profess to believe in Christ, for the remission of sins, but differ widely from orthodox baptists [sic] on some points of doctrine." [This paragraph is copied verbatim from his earlier works. In his earliest work he misspelled Campbellites as Cambellites.]	Peck, *Traveler's Directory for Illinois*, 1839: 136.
1840	STATISTICS OF THE UNITED STATES. The following statistics are gathered from the American Almanac for 1840. *Literary and Religious Institutions.* There are 95 Colleges in the United States. 27 Medical Schools. 37 Theological Schools. 8 Law Schools. *Religious Denominations in the Union.* Baptists, (of different denominations,) 4,300,000 Methodists, 3,000,000 Presbyterians, 2,175,000 Congregationalists, 1,000,000 Episcopalians, 800,000 Christ-ians, 800,000 Universalists, 600,000 Roman Catholics, 800,000 Lutherans, 540,000 Dutch Reformed, 450,000 Besides a great many other denominations, not so numerous as the foregoing. Newspapers, Magazines, &c. : 1,555 Daily Papers, 126 Locomotive and Railroad Engines in the United States, 350 Massachusetts has 37, and Maine 2. There are over 800 Steam-Boats in the Union; 8 of which are in Maine, and 140 in New York.	*MH* 1840: 239.
1841	D. Pat Henderson calls for Illinois congregations to provide data: "Another matter to which I would call their attention is, the necessity of each church preparing a statistical report of the date of her organization—the number of members at the original organization—the present number—the bishops and evangelists." (D. Pat Henderson, "To the Editor of the C. Messenger," *Christian Messenger*, Volume 11, Number 10, June 1841: 358.	*CM* 11.10 (June 1841) 358

1841	John M. Peck, "Brief View of the Baptist Interest in Each of the United States… Part IV: The Western and Southern States and Territories." Page 57: "There is also a class of Baptists, known in the Western States as "Reformers," or "Campbellites," from their affinity to the peculiar views of Alexander Campbell. In Illinois, they have 103 churches, probably 75 preachers and expounders of the word, and 4,929 members."	The *American Quarterly Register*, Volume XIV, August 1841, pages 42 – 58.
1841	Illinois Annual Meeting at Jacksonville. Statistics were reported at this meeting.	
1841	Statistics of the Churches of Christ, in Illinois, reported to their annual meeting in Jacksonville, September, 1841. Summary: 79 congregations 81 named leaders; 7 have the title 'evangelist;' 74 are called 'elders.' The total membership for the report is 3,601. Average size of the congregations is 45.6. The largest congregations are: - Jacksonville 165 - Winchester 157 - Sugar Creek 130 - Ursa 110 - Fork Prairie 102	*CM*, 12.2 (December 1841) 62, 63.
1847	"I still ask a continuance of this aid, and hope you will greatly increase the patronage. In Missouri, Illinois and Iowa, we certainly number 20,000. Can we not raise 5000 subscribers for this paper?"	D. P. Henderson, "To the Readers of the Christian Messenger," *Messenger and Advocate*, 5.1 (January, 1847) 9, 10

1848	"In 1848, Alexander Hall, of Ohio, published the first statistical report of the Christian Churches in Europe and America...A total of 1,983 churches were listed in his *Register*." [Note that W. F. M. Army had collected some statistics already and was miffed that Hall apparently did not include some of his information in the *Register*. Part of the controversy about Hall's statistics was accuracy.] Hall lists 157 churches in Illinois	Henry K. Shaw, *Buckeye Disciples*: 155 – 160.
1850	ICMS officially established. Haynes reports lower numbers than Hall: 104 congregations with aggregate membership of 6,359.	Haynes 91, 92
1855	John Lewis Peyton, *A Statistical View of the State of Illinois, to which is Appended an Article upon the City of Chicago*. (Chicago: Spaulding and Tobey, Printers, June 1855.) Page 33 states the number of churches for the Christian denomination is 67. [Since Hall listed 157 Stone-Campbell congregations in 1848, perhaps the number is for Christian Connection congregations.]	John Lewis Peyton, *A Statistical View of the State of Illinois, to which is Appended an Article upon the City of Chicago*. (Chicago: Spaulding and Tobey, Printers, June 1855.) 33. This item is in the Peck Collection at Mercantile Library in St. Louis.

1857	DISCIPLES' ALMANAC AND STATISTICAL REGISTER. Such is the title of a document proposed to be published by Jas. Challen & Sons, Philadelphia, Pa., It will contain a condensed history of the rise and progress of the Current Reformation, or in their own language, "The Denomination." Name, size, and post office addresses of Churches, Evangelists, Elders, Sunday schools, Colleges, Seminaries, Endowments, Benevolent Institutions, Prospects, &c. &c. If properly gotten up, it will be a work of great labor and should call forth the co-operation of all who can forward to them reliable information. We have just two suggestions to make on the subject, First, that they so change the title as to qualify the word "Disciple," or substitute in its stead the word "Christian." For all that one can tell, it may mean either the followers of Jo. Smith or Tom. Paine. Second, that the congregations in the South report the number of *slaves* and *slaveholders* in their communion, and especially the number and names of their Elders and Evangelists who hold slaves.	John Boggs, "Editors Table," *North-western Christian Magazine*, 3.7 (January 1857) 224.
1860	"Many of the writings of Mr. Campbell and his fellow-laborers, have been republished in England, where the Disciples are becoming numerous. Their churches are found also in Wales and in Ireland. In the United States, they are most numerous in Kentucky, Ohio, Indiana, Illinois, Missouri, and Virginia. There are a few churches in the British Provinces. The whole number of communicants in the United States, so far as has been ascertained, is believed to fall but little short of 350,000." (45) "They have some 2,000 Churches, 2,000 Ordained Ministers, and about 350,000 Members, principally in the Middle, South-western, and Western States." (46)	"Disciples of Christ, or Christians," *The American Christian Record*, (New York: W. R. C. Clark & Meeker, 1860) 42 - 46

1860	"As a denomination, they are strong, numbering about 2,200 ministers, 2,200 churches, and 180,000 communicants." (54)	"Christian Connexion," *The American Christian Record*, New York: W. R. C. Clark & Meeker, 1860: 52 – 54.
1860	"Riding the antebellum tide of rural democracy and westward expansion, Disciples enjoyed substantial growth in numbers and structure during the years between 1840 and 1866. Disciples historians call it the "Age of Cooperative Evangelism." Despite being an ill-regarded sect by European denominations, Disciples developed an effective entourage of district "cooperations" for the purpose of evangelizing the rural frontier population into membership, and the Movement increased from 45,000 in 1840 to more than 200,000 in 1860."	Cummins 54
1860	"40,000" for Illinois.	Green, *History of Missions*, pages 345 – 348.
1865	"By 1865 the Disciples of Christ had over 200,000 members."	Harrell, *Quest*, 11, citing Garrison and DeGroot, 328, 329.
1867	Dowling lists Illinois preachers on pages 39, 40. Page 42 states 150 preachers and 33,000 members, making Illinois fourth in membership, behind Kentucky (75,000); Indiana (70,000); and Ohio (52,000).	L. H. Dowling, *The Christian Almanac for the Year of Our Lord and Saviour 1867* (Indianapolis: Journal Print, 1867)
1868	F. M. Green published a list of SCM ministers in the United States, listing over 250 individuals from Illinois.	F. M. Green, *Preachers of the Churches of Christ in the United States*. (Photocopy with no publication information except date of "December 1, 1880).

1874	Christian Denomination statistics:	Morrill 239
	"The number of churches was estimated at nearly fifteen hundred. Estimates of men then conversant with denominational affairs allowed an average of one hundred members to a church—probably an impossible figure, as scores of churches were small and soon fell to pieces. A total membership of sixty-seven thousand was the estimate given in 1874. [A. H. Morrill, *HGL* June 6 1874.]	
1876	"The Christian Almanac" for 1876 reported eighty-one conference organizations. [fn 1 = "See Ap., p. 386."] The next year names of twelve hundred and sixty ministers were printed in the Almanac, not including three hundred and eight licentiates [fn 2 = "See Ap., p. 386."], or about fifty-three ministers and fourteen licentiates in the Southern Christian Convention. This gives a surprising total of over sixteen hundred preachers and ordained ministers."	Morrill 239

1880	"The national census of 1880 reports the number of the Disciples in the United States as 4681 churches; 3,658 preachers; and 567,448 members. It is quite likely if the exact statistics could be obtained it would be found that the Disciples of Christ in the United States and territories do not number less than six hundred thousand. Perhaps it would not be fruitful of pleasant memories to inquire how many of this number are real and active members and how many "have a name to live and are dead." Whatever may be the merit or demerit of the foregoing table of statistics, the General Christian Missionary Convention is entitled to the credit of having made the first measurably successful attempt to get at the exact numbers." Illinois is 2nd in this list, with 80,275. Indiana = 90,685; Kentucky 70,525; Missouri 65,950; Ohio 48,500.	F. M. Green, *History of Christian Missions*, 192
1881	N. S. Haynes compiles a directory of Illinois congregations and ministers: "This is the first time that anything of the kind has been attempted in Illinois. This list is partial and imperfect, but it is the best possible that could be made. Everyone who receives this report is earnestly requested to correct its errors, help to complete it and notify N. S. Haynes, Decatur, Ills."	The *Christian* (Thursday, October 20, 1881) 2 - 5
1911	"For this denomination, the Christians, it may be briefly said that it has been in existence a little over a century; that it numbers now something more than a hundred thousand communicants, some making it a hundred and forty thousand; that it has some twelve hundred ministers and fifteen hundred churches; that it owns and administers some ten colleges in as many states of the Union."	Martyn Summerbell, *An Address on the Origin and Principles of the Christians.* No place: the New Jersey Christian Conference, 1911: 3

1920	"The Illinois Christian Missionary Society.—The Disciples of Christ have 700 churches and 130,000 members in Illinois. They have in the neighborhood of 600 preachers in the State." [H. H. Peters is mentioned and he likely provided the content of the section. It is slanted toward the Disciples/Campbell background, claiming 1819 as the year when the first church was established.]	*History of McLean County,* Vol. 1 212, 213

Appendix 2: Information on Berean College

Attendance and Graduation Figures

Academic Year	Male	Female	Total Students	Graduates	Notes
1854 – 1855	59	37	96	NA	Haynes 60 – 62; Olson
1855 – 1856	Not avail able	Not avail- able	121	NA	*MH* 1856 475
1856 – 1857	Not avail able	Not avail- able	Not avail- able	NA	
1857 – 1858	58	38	96	NA	Jacksonville Courier, December 4, 1977, page 44. Catalogue for 1857/1858
1858 – 1859	Not avail able	Not avail- able	Not avail- able	11	1st graduating class.
1859 - 1860	20 - 25	Not avail- able	Not avail- able	4	Last year open.

Berean College Students

Abbreviations used in the below chart:

- P. 7.11.1858 = *The Pantagraph*, Bloomington, Illinois, (July 11, 1858) 2.
- ISJ 6.25.1859 = *Sangamo Journal/Illinois State Journal*, (June 25, 1859) 3.
- ISJ 6.23.1860 = *Sangamo Journal/Illinois State Journal*, (June 23, 1860) 2.
- HEI&HMC = Newton Bateman, et al., *Historical Encyclopedia of Illinois and History of Morgan County* (Chicago: Munsell Publishing Company, 1906).

- HM&MC = *The History of Menard and Mason Counties, Illinois* (Chicago: O. L. Baskin & Co., Historical Publishers, 1879).

See our A Find A Grave Virtual Cemetery for Berean College students to track the progress of our research: https://www.findagrave.com/virtual-cemetery/686349

Surname	Given Name	DOB	DOD	Attended	Profession	Notes
Barnes	H. C.			1858		P 7.11.1858
Brown	John W.			1858 1859		P 7.11.1858 ISJ 6.25.1859
Bruce	J. A.			1858		P 7.11.1858
Callaway	Sallie C.	2.1842	1910	1858 1859		Class of 1859; Valedictorian P 7.11.1858 ISJ 6.25.1859
Cassell	Harrison Osborne	10.6.1839	1893	1858	Attorney; States Attorney	P 7.11.1858 Left BC after 1858 academic year; Graduated Illinois College 1861
Cassell	Sue R.			1859		ISJ 6.25.1859
Cherry	John Heber	7.15.1838	?	1856-57	Attorney	Married Katie V. Jackson of Springfield; Attended IC after BC; moved to Little Rock, AR, where she died
Constant	William Francis	2.25.1838	5.14.1916	?		FAG
Daniels	Verrin	11.25.1838	1.18.1919	1859-60		FAG; Attended

Engle	M. M.			?		HM&MC 730. Attended; transferred from Eureka
Ewing	Lidie			1859		ISJ 6.25.1859
Ewing [Brock-man]	Mary Ellen	3.16.1 836	9.20. 1923	?		FAG
Freeman	Louisa			1858		P 7.11.1858
Goodin	Martha Eleanor	3.4.18 39	4.17. 1941	1858	School teacher	P 7.11.1858; Second Honor; Married name is Coley. Older sister of W. A. Goodin.
Goodin	William Alexan-der	3.24.1 841	11.2 0.19 32	1858	Teacher; Farmer; Pike County As-sessor	High schooler at BC
Grafton [Patter-son]	Katharine "Kate"	1.1.18 39	7.16. 1902	1858 1859 1860	Studied to be a missionary; teacher; wife of U. S. Sen-ator Thomas M. Patterson	P 7.11.1858 ISJ 6.25.1859 ISJ 6.23.1860; Class of 1860; Latin Salutato-ry Great niece of Alexander Campbell.
Grafton	Mary E.					Great niece of Alexander Campbell?
Grant	W. B.			1858		P 7.11.1858
Green	Horatio R.	4.2.18 34	4.23. 1896		Farmer; not a member of any church per the Mor-gan and Scott county biographies	Attended

Hall	Melinda			1855		Married Ezra M. Aylesworth
Happy	Emma (Emmy) S. or K.			1859		ISJ 6.25.1859 ISJ 6.23.1860 Class of 1860
Hasel-wood	Willis K.	9.8.18 38	6.8?. 1903		Teacher; Farmer; J of Peace; Democratic nominee for Fifteenth Congressional District in 1900	No FAG located as of 9.5.16.
Hender-son	Amos	11.20.1 841	10.2 7.19 27	-1860	Merchant; Insurance; Justice of Peace	1889 History Graduated
Holand	A. H.					ISJ 6.25.1859
Johnson	Mary Ann	1836	1929	?	School Teacher	Married Cornelius Decker
Kelly	John			1859		ISJ 6.25.1859
Kerr	J. M.			1859		ISJ 6.25.1859 ISJ 6.23.1860 Class of 1860
Larimore	Samuel Hugh	3.14.1 834		?	.	HEI&HMC 878; His father was a Methodist Class of ?
Latham	Kate			1860		ISJ 6.23.1860 Philokalian Society

Laughlin	George Hamilton	12.28. 1838	11.1 6.18 95	1857	President and Professor of Oskaloosa and Hiram Colleges	Left BC during WSR presidency, transferring to Abingdon College; FAG; Portage County, Ohio, history
Lindsey	Mary Eleanor	12.3.1 832	6.26. 1898	1858		Married name Phillips P 7.11.1858
Morton	Francis M.	10.8.1 841			Farmer	HEI&HMC 898 Attended two years
Parker	John F. M.	1838	1906	?	Christian Minister	Haynes 585; Attended
Patton	James William	2.15.1 840	4.27. 1921	?		FAG
Ross	Francis A.	4.1.18 40	9.28. 1898	1860		Thratalethian Society ISJ 6.23.1860; FAG
Routt (Rout and Route)	Kate			1858 1859 1860		Class of 1860; Valedictorian P 7.11.1858 ISJ 6.25.1859
Shuff	John Richard	9.18.1 837	2.18. 1904	1858	Christian Minister	Same birthday as Sims; First Honor P 7.11.1858; FAG
Sims	Aquilla H.	9.18.1 839	6.26. 1866	1859/60	Christian Minister	Attended Illinois College in 1860 after attending BC
Smither	Henry			?	Christian Minister	Attended

Sweeney	Mary					Mary Sweeney attended per Z. T.'s WSR Crisis in CS.
Virgin	Maria					Attended 4 years; Class of ?
Walker	Lucy F.			1859		ISJ 6.25.1859
Whitlock	Herbert G.	11.24.1831		1859	Judge	ISJ 6.25.1859; attended
Withers	Henry Clay	8.29.1831 or 1.10.1839	12.4.1904	?	Attorney	FAG Attended 1856 – 1858

Appendix 3: "Organs" by David Patterson Henderson[1]

Organs

[1] Organs, defined by Webster, mean, instruments or mediums by which an important object is accomplished; especially a material part or feature of a living existence or being, capable of a special function that is essential to the life or well being of the whole, as the lungs, the heart, etc.; also an artificial or conventional structure, which performs a duty or function that is determined by the nature of the welfare of such an existence; as, the organs of government, law, etc.

[2] A medium of communication between one person or body, and another; as the secretary of state is the organ of communication between the government and a foreign power.

[3] A wind instrument containing numerous pipes of various dimensions and kinds, which are filled with wind from a bellows, and played upon by means of keys similar to those of a piano forte.

Such the definition of organs by Webster. About the latter kind of organs, we wish to offer some remarks:

[1] There are hand organs, which by means of a crank are made to play a variety of tunes. Generally, these are owned and used by persons, who are blind, one armed, or affected by some physical ailment. They may be found on the corners of public streets, and make music for a support. Or, wandering stations, accompanied generally by trained monkeys, play and entertain children and idlers.

---

[1] Manuscript from the papers of David Pat Henderson at Disciples of Christ Historical Society. Contextualization and transcript are by James L. McMillan. A letter to Isaac Errett, dated October 23, 1878, at Oakland, California, is signed by DPH. A note on the verso of the last page of the four page letter states: "Letter to Standard. Not sent from Oakland, Cal." The letter and manuscript are written on the same color of paper; the hand writing in both documents is the same. Sentiments on organs and instrumental music on page 3 in the letter reflect the same thoughts as the manuscript. Henderson, therefore, is the author of the manuscript. It is likely Henderson prepared this manuscript as an essay to submit to the *Christian Standard* but, like the letter to Errett, was not sent. See Chapter 11, Instrumental Music in Illinois, for more on Henderson's views on instrumental music.

[2] There are cabinet organs, found in many houses, used to accompany the human voice and entertain the music loving members of the families and friends.

[3] The large thunder toned church organ, used in giving tone and time, while the congregation is singing praises to God.

Now, we are prepared to speak understandingly of [page 2] this instrument, which has caused so many scribes to spread gallons of ink on multitudes of sheets of paper, which the types and presses have thrown off for the entertainment, edification and instruction of the religious people. Now mark, these instruments are of no value whatever in the production of sound unless *wind* is applied. They are wind instruments to be run by steam, water, electricity or foot hand and foot power. A church organ is generally large, placed in a conspicuous part of the edifice and finished very tastefully and elegantly. A cabinet organ, differs in size and form from the church organ. The church organ has a series of pipes, these being filled with wind and producing loud sounds when desired. The hands and feet are used by the organist when playing. The cabinet organ is a small piece of furniture, generally made of black walnut, with reeds, bellows & treadles, which the performer uses in families or Sunday schools, sometimes to give tone and time, aiding the voices of the people singing the praises of God. Organs are mentioned by the Psalmist David, who was a grand poet and musician. Organs are perfectly harmless, make no sound, produce no discord, unless the attempt is made by unskilled persons to play upon them. Then the sounds are unmusical and grating upon the refined ear and heart. On the other hand, when handled by a skilful [sic] operator, it sends out deep solemn and musical notes, which vibrate upon the nervous system and exhilerate [sic], elevate and charm the soul.

[page 3]

No one should attempt to play in public, unless well instructed and fully understanding the nature and character of the instrument. But unfortunately there are many persons who keep their minds so fixed upon this instrument, and are such so much interested in speaking and writing about them, that every time they attempt to play, nothing but harsh discord greets the ear. Indeed they become disgusted with the sounds they make themselves and keep up a perpetual warfare against the organ. As wind is the *motor* power in developing the instrument, so the *windy* performances of these persons who are so afflicted when they touch a key, demand our attention and calls for our sympathy. Organ on the brain. These anti organ people keep the poor instrument tortured constantly, make it a sine que non that you shall discountenance it altogether, else they condemn, disfellowship—divide and ruin. The use of the organ is made by these persons the *test* of fellowship, with these persons who seem to carry organs on the brain, and go almost into spasms when they think how wicked, how demon like, an organ is. Do the scriptures teach any thing upon the use, or non use of organs in congregational service? If so, why cannot those who so bitterly oppose organs, show where Jesus, or the apostles speak authoritively [sic] on the subject? I have remained silent so far as pen or tongue is concerned on this subject. I have closely watched the progress in our papers which the brethren have made, and my calm deliberate judgment is, that the bitter and unceasing condemnation of their use in the churches [page 4] has caused far more division and unpleasant feelings, than any thing else during the years the subject has been before the public. I am confident, that the warfare made against organs, has put many into the churches.[2] So much dogmatism, so much denunciation, have been indulged, that brethren with self respect, have been converted to the use of them—they have asserted their independence, and into the churches they are going constantly through the tyranny, despotism, and bitter denunciation of the organ opposers. Strange indeed, if the comparative few, who denounce organs with such vehemence and zeal, should in so many years have so completely failed in making converts to their theory. In St. Louis the organ was a part of the church building, part of the real estate purchased by the Christian Church from one of the denominations. The question came up whether the congregation should use it or not. No objection being made during the time Bro B. H. Smith was the pastor, it was employed in giving tone and time, strengthening the weaker parts and establishing harmony in

---

[2] A later example is Sand Creek, Illinois: "This church had never used an organ and had no thought of introducing one until the preaching of Mr. Sommer created a desire and a demand for its introduction." Haynes, 390.

singing.[3] In process of time two Kentucky brethren removed to St. Louis and objected to the use of the instrument in the congregation, a few others joined in the objection and it was ceased to be used for a while. This is the true history of that church. After a lapse of several months, the organ was again introduced, and some 8 brethren refused to attend the regular meetings and went to other churches, staid at home or loitered in the city on Lords day. They were expostulated with and the proposition was made, that if they would [page 5] attend to the Lords supper, the organ should not used. This they declined and while hundreds of the brethren and members favored its use, not tens of their number opposed it with bitterness of feeling and denounced its use. Whatever alienations, whatever bitterness and divisions were made were caused by a few prejudiced and determined persons. Years ago in Bloomington Illinois, where the first organ so far as I know, was ever brought into congregational use by almost the entire membership, a few opposed, and indeed one member took the responsibility of pitching [it] out of the gallery and breaking the Instruments. Indianapolis church, was the first one I ever heard in any of our churches, and I never heard of any trouble being caused by its use. So far as I am concerned, unless it can be shown by a 'Thus saith the

---

[3] The exact dates of B. H. Smith's ministry in St. Louis are unclear. One source places him with the 5th Street congregation in St. Louis from 1859 until "around 1862 or '63" when the congregation exchanged the 5th Street property for a building at 17th and Olive. He "resigned shortly after the church moved to 17th and Olive." T. P. Haley, *Historical and Biographical Sketches of the Early Churches and Pioneer Preachers of the Christian Church in Missouri.* (St. Louis: Christian Publishing Co., 1888) 480. Unless Smith was commuting between Bloomington, Illinois, and St. Louis to speak each weekend, Haley has the date of Smith's arrival wrong. Smith was still head of Major's Female College in Bloomington, Illinois, in November 1859. Ken Christensen's research places Smith with the First Christian Church in St. Louis from 1862 – 1865. (Email 12.29.2018). Dr. Hiram Christopher's 1867 pamphlet, *An Address on the Use of Instrumental Music in the Worship of the Church of Christ* (Saint Louis: P. M. Pinckard, 1867) gives a brief background of the purchase of the building with the organ. He notes there was a growing interest to use the organ after a law suit determined the organ legally belonged to the Christian Church. Christopher does not state the congregation used the organ, only that there were those "so strongly in favor of using the organ" that he wrote and read the address to the congregation. This manuscript documents that the organ was in fact used, then not used in the services for a period of time; then used again, only not to be used again when the Kentucky brethren moved to St. Louis. Moses Lard reprinted the address with slight changes in emphasis (removing italics) and capitalization in *Lard's Quarterly*, 4.4 (October, 1867) 349 – 368. Lard does not include the page from Christopher's pamphlet with the historical background.

Lord" that it is sinful to use the organ in aiding the human voice in prais-
ing the Lord, and making melody in the heart, I can have no *conscience* on
the subject—without testimony there can be no faith, without faith, the
faith of the heart, it is impossible to have a conscience either in favor or
against its use or non use. With me it is a matter purely of taste or prejudice, and I am free to say, that my prejudices were always against introducing the instrument into the congregation. I never questioned the *right*
of any church to use the organ if it was desirable, but I always interposed
my objections and found a sufficient number to agree [page 6] with me,
so that we had no trouble whatsoever on the subject. Still, when we
wished to learn new music, we quietly practiced where our leader was the
organ. This was in private families however—sometimes we were led by
the piano or violin when practicing difficult pieces of music. I have often
wondered why pianos, violins, and organs could be used in private families who were church members, without objections or denunciations
from those who make so much opposition to their use in churches. By
the way, I believe I have seen a splendid piano, and a splendid organ
owned by one of the most honest, resolute and uncompromising opposers of the organ in churches. His daughters taught to play at home on
these instruments, without sinning. But if a chord of either was stricken
touched in the church this same honest, zealous good brother, would almost take a spasm. Yes a spasm that would send him out of the house of
worship because in the church the organ would be transformed into a
'*demon*'. In his own house however, played upon by the tiny fingers of
well cultivated and educated daughters it was an angel of sweet sound. To
me, this is passing strange!! Certainly if wrong at church, wrong at home.
The 'Demon' cannot be exorcised by removing senseless matter from
one place to another. The prejudices of a limited few, against the tastes
of the larger number, and their determined opposition, causes the trouble and not the organ. [page 7] Now, who are responsible for making all
the trouble about the instruments? I do not hear any one, make trouble
but these brethren who so bitterly oppose its use in aiding the human
voice to sing praises to God. And these same brethren keep musical instruments in their own houses, lay out money to purchase them, and
spend thousands in having their daughters taught to understand and use
them. 'The legs of the lame are unequal.' I wish to repeat and emphasize
the proposition, that it is simply a matter of *taste* or *prejudice*, on either
side, the New Testament being silent on the subject of either the *use*, or
nonuse of organs in the church, during the worship. No one has *yet shown a
Thus saith the Lord on either side of this question. It is purely a matter of opinion*,
and as such, it should be treated. I have before me, from one of the

strongest opposers, the following frank admission, 'All agree that one must earnestly contend for *the faith,* for all items of faith. But the organ is not of faith. It is clearly and confessedly a matter of opinion; and therefore cannot be contended for or urged, to the disturbance of peace and harmony, without great sins.' Now gentle reader, note, that it is admitted to be an *opinion* and not of faith, and why? Answer, because faith is dependent entirely upon testimony. No testimony, no faith. On what is opinion dependent? On inferences, on circumstances, on human reasoning, without positive testimony. Nothing is said in the New Testament about organs, their use or nonuse. It is *inferred* from this, that they were not used. [8] Grant it and what follows? Why, we must not use the organ, because the early Christians did not use it. The early Christians met in private houses to worship. Not a word is said about building meeting houses by the early Christians in which to worship, therefore we must build meeting houses. But we all are of opinion that we should provide suitable places for the accommodation of Christians, and therefore, there is no division of *opinion* on this subject. It is not a matter of *faith* at all, whether we should erect suitable places for worship, or whether we should invent a tuning fork to give us one the sound of one musical note, or an organ, to give us the key and sounds of all the musical notes. A tuning fork is a musical instrument and who objects to its use? Not one known to me. Why then should we fancy the fork right, and the organ wrong? Simply and only simply, because it is a matter of *taste* or prejudice, or both and this being the case, why on earth keep up such a fruitless warfare, striving to divide, accusing each other of being factionists, and creating so much bickering, heart burnings & alienations? Oh! My heart why? The *opinion* of the friend of organs, stands precisely *equal* with the opposers of organs. The friends of the organ, have the same right to their opinions as those of the opposite side, and neither should denounce the other. How, then can the matter be settled in the churches? By a majority, the minority yielding and making unanimity. I know of no other way.

Appendix 4: Illinois Conservative Preachers and Congregations Mentioned in Haynes and Conservative Papers

> While there were only three baptized during the meeting, the Seed was sown and I believe it will bring forth fruit in the future. I expect to do more preaching there soon, as I realize the need as never before of getting the glorious gospel before the people where we have no congregations. We will find some good honest people wherever we go. F. A. Ditrick, Iuka, Illinois, August 10, 1909.[1]

The 1906 Federal Census of Religious Bodies has 58 Church of Christ "organizations" in Illinois, with 58 "reporting" and a total membership of 3,552; 1,383 are men; 2,169 women.

Our research shows the 1906 Federal Census numbers for Illinois Churches of Christ do not accurately reflect the number of conservative congregations. By electronically searching Haynes and two conservative regional papers, the Octographic Review and Christian Leader, we have found more than one hundred conservative congregations existed by the time Haynes compiled his history in 1914.[2]

As our research in this appendix shows, conservative preachers—those who opposed innovations such as instrumental music in worship services and organizations such as missionary societies—aggressively founded new congregations in communities where there were no SCM congregations. They also worked in existing congregations to keep out instrumental music and missionary societies. In places where they were not able to keep out the innovations, but still had a sustainable nucleus, they started a Church of Christ in the same community.

We present the initial research in tabular format below. We hope our readers can provide more details on other places where conservative congregations existed in Illinois prior to 1914, when Haynes wrote his

---

[1] Department of Commerce and Labor, U. S. Bureau of the Census, E. Dana Durward, Director. Special Reports: Religious Bodies 1906 (Washington, D. C.: Government Printing Office, 1910) 182.

[2] See the *Introduction* for more information on the digitization of significant numbers of SCM periodicals.

history. To track the names and biographical information on conservative Illinois preachers, see our virtual cemetery here: https://www.finda-grave.com/virtual-cemetery/709268

We will continue to add names to that Virtual Cemetery as we find them.

City	County	Name	Notes
Allenville	Shelby		OR 42.4 Jan 24 1899: 6. In "Cullings and Comments" M. J. Walters states, "Through the instrumentality of Bro. Gepford of Findlay, Ill., we expect to visit the faithful congregations at Niantic, Bethany, Allensville and Findlay and converse with them upon things pertaining to the kingdom…"
Annapolis	Crawford		https://www.findagrave.com/memorial/27965146/david-edward-towles "By 1880, David was living in Coles Co, Illinois as a single man in the home of his brother, Henry Clifford Towles. David's history is unknown during the 1880's but in the 1890's we see him becoming an active soldier for the cause of Christ. He did preaching for the Brick Chapel in Hutton, Coles, Illinois...the Liberty Chapel in Hidalgo, Jasper, Illinois...the Church of Christ in Annapolis, Illinois...the Church of Christ in Bell Air, Crawford, Illinois...the Church of Christ in Gila, Jasper, Illinois...the Church of Christ in Iola, Clay, Illinois."

			OR 37.46 Nov 13 1894 p 6 has the report of the founding of the Annapolis congregation by H. C. and D. E. Towles. "Closed last night a four week's meeting at Annapolis, Ill. The disciples had no congregation there. We succeeded in getting eight brethren together and set in order a congregation. Added seven to their number, making in all fifteen members. Their number is few, but they are strong in the faith, and set for the defense of the gospel. There is a union house at Annapolis, and surrounded with sectarianism on every side. But many of them, like Agrippa, were almost persuaded to be Christiana. We found people there who had never heard one of our preachers before. Also a great number were willing to admit that we had been misrepresented." https://www.findagrave.com/memorial/80262316/henry-clifford-towles Haynes does not mention either Towles.
Ash Grove	Shelby	(Lower) Ash Grove	Haynes 387: "It [Ash Grove (Windsor)] was the mother of Windsor, Gays and Lower Ash Grove, a conservative society." OR 51.29 July 21 1908 p 5: A. J. Nance, in "A Brief Sketch of the Life of J. H. Price" states, "Under the training of such teachers as the Ash Grove church then had, he became well grounded in the faith, and thoroughly committed to the simplicity that is in Christ." https://www.findagrave.com/memorial/53844042/john-henry-price.

Bell Air	Craw-ford		"David's history is unknown during the 1880's but in the 1890's we see him becoming an active soldier for the cause of Christ. He did preaching for the Brick Chapel in Hutton, Coles, Illinois...the Liberty Chapel in Hidalgo, Jasper, Illinois...the Church of Christ in Annapolis, Illinois...the Church of Christ in Bell Air, Crawford, Illinois...the Church of Christ in Gila, Jasper, Illinois...the Church of Christ in Iola, Clay, Illinois." Haynes has two references: 85 "1889...At Bellair [sic], Clark Braden and E. S. Kelley discussed Mormonism. 170 "West Harmony (Bell Air). Present membership, 103; value of property, $800; Bible-school enrollment, 65. Inactive. Chapel built in 1871. [This might be the congregation Towles served. More research is needed.]
Berea (?)	Christ-ian	Berea	OR 42.4 Jan 24 1899: 5. In "A Few Thoughts" by Samuel Piety, from Duvall. Mentions Nance had worked with the congregation. Meeting there postponed because of sickness.

| Bethany | Shelby | Bethany Chapel | OR 42.4 Jan 24 1899: 6. In "Cullings and Comments" M. J. Walters states, "Through the instrumentality of Bro. Gepford of Findlay, Ill., we expect to visit the faithful congregations at Niantic, Bethany, Allensville and Findlay and converse with them upon things pertaining to the kingdom…"

Haynes 385: "Minister Warren served Bethany once per month for more than twenty years. The chapel was built in 1871. The congregation gave A. J. Nance to the ministry. It died by conservatism." [Need to confirm that the Bethany congregation had closed by 1914. Seems unlikely.]

OR 51.25 June 23 1908 p 8: [Confirmation that Haynes overstates the status of the Bethany congregation.] "Hammond, Ill., June 10. – On the occasion of our last visit to Cooksville we had two confessions and baptisms. The church there is doing well, although opposition to the truth is very great. We also had one confession at Bethany Chapel on the fifth Lord's day in May. Bethany is one of the two meting houses belonging to the Sand Creek congregation. We were much pleased to have Brother Brady, a faithful preacher of the Word who lives in the vicinity, with us in the meeting. On the third Lord's day in this month we will be with the Long Point Church, near Niantic. A. J. Nance." |
| Bethany | Vermil-ion | Bethany or Lone Oak | Haynes 405, 406: "Organized 1875, by J. C. Myers… The location is five miles northwest of Danville. It is also known as Lone Oak. For years the congregation held large influence for good in a wide community. Preachers who made their opinions of equal authority with the Scripture came and sowed the seeds of dissension. Wrangling supplanted worship, and vilification of men the praise of God. The congregation was divided and feebleness followed." |

Bethel	Massac	Hille-man Post Office; Also spelled Hiller-man; Also Grand Chain.	Haynes 321: "Bethel (Grand Chain). Organized 1885, by George Barrows ; present member-ship, 60; value of property, $1,500; Bible school began 1885; present enrollment, 78. This church is near Hillerman." [Haynes is not aware of the conservative efforts there or this is a different congregation. The latter is unlikely.] OR 54.16 April 18 1911 p 8: "…This congregation was re-established by the writer and his brother last winter. They are carrying out the true apostolic teachings. This congregation was once very strong, but the innovations and additions of men caused the division. For many years this once strong congregation was asleep, but now I believe that they are going to move on nicely if no "wolves" get into the flock. These innovations are our worst enemies. The different sects are not troublesome. The modern missionary societies are what have caused the divisions. The Church is the one great missionary society, hence let men forsake other additions of no importance and work through the Church…*Wiley F. Mathis, Vienna, Ill.*"
			https://www.findagrave.com/memorial/11095613/wiley-f_-mathis. Retrieved 1.31.2019. (1889 – 1973) He was about twenty-two when he wrote to the OR. Haynes lists some people with Mathis surname in Livingston County.
Bismark / Bismarck	Vermil-ion	?	Haynes 406: "Organized 1880…The church was rent with division on the question of instrumental music, Sunday school and missions. Finally, those opposing these things withdrew." [It is not clear yet if the conservatives formed a congregation or attended elsewhere. Nearby congregations are ?] https://www.findagrave.com/memorial/47523259/walter-franklin-cline. Cline is from Bismarck. Mac Lynn's 2003 directory has a starting date of 1895 for the Church of Christ at Bismarck.

Blooming-ton	McLean		OR 54.46 Nov 14 1911 p 3: H. D. Leach writes from Charleston about the tent meeting in Bloomington to establish a congregation. Includes his visit to the ICMS office. https://www.findagrave.com/memorial/51708434/harvey-dean-leach. Retrieved 1.23.2019.
Bourbon	Douglas		Haynes has no entry for a congregation at Bourbon. OR 43.30 July 24 1900 p 8: "Bourbon, Ill, July 12. – We began our meeting June 2, closed 15th with about as good an interest as I ever saw, but other promises call me away. I baptized 22, reclaimed 4, 26 in all. This is a good congregation. 'Loyal to their king,' and reward a man for his work in the Lord. May they ever 'hold fast to the form of sound (incorruptable) [sic] words.' From there I went to Newark; held 12 days; reorganized with 42. This used to be the 'Christian church—having their faires festivals etc., but there is no such work there now. I set my stake deep and built from "the foundation" up. I baptized 8 of these; the 32 were members heretofore. I went from, there to Richland…J. R. Roberts.
Bowling Green	Fayette	Antioch	Haynes 199: "An old congregation called Antioch, in Bowling Green Township, lived in the seventies. Conservatives paralyzed its activities and, later, their own. Some of the members went to Herrick."
Boyleston	Wayne		Haynes 428: "This is a child of the Fairfield Church, six miles west. In this small village five denominations sought to control. The house was completed in 1892 and the little church promised good until an ultra-conservative preacher came in and divided them."
Brookport	Massac	Mt. Pleasant	Haynes 323: "Present membership, 24; value of property, $800. Conservative."

Browning	Schuyler		OR 50.49 Dec 3 1907 p 8: "Browning, Nov. 20 – Our meeting still in progress. One confession, one reclaimed. E. G. Denney." Haynes 382: "Organized 1894, by L. F. Davis; present membership, 12; value of property, $1,000; Bible school began 1894; present enrollment, 48. "Meetings were held in a hall for a year and a half, when the chapel was built." [No hint of a conservative element.] https://www.findagrave.com/memorial/43810580/joseph-marsh-walton. In Ligon's portraiture. See OR 47.12 Mar 22 1904 pp 4, 5 where JMW reports from Browning about a house church in Chicago.
*Bruce	Moultrie	Tent Meeting	https://en.wikipedia.org/wiki/Bruce,_Illinois OR 51.25 June 23 1908 p 8: "Charleston, Ill., June 15 – Brothers Cuppy and Towles are in a tent meeting at Mattoon and are doing some good. One addition so far. Brother Cuppy and I are intending to hold a tent meeting at Bruce in July. A very favorable prospect is before us to do some good there. The people are eager to hear the plain preaching of the gospel. Nothing else will supply the real needs of sinful man. There is no Church of Christ there. Brothers Cuppy and D. A. Sommer expect to be at Villa Grove, with the tent, the first part of July, and the latter part of August in Sullivan. An inviting field is open for seed sowing, but the reapers are few. We pray much good may be done from this contemplated work. W. E. Dudley."

Bryant's Valley / Crossville	White		Haynes 434: "Bryant's Valley (Crossville). Present membership, 100; value of property, $1,000; Bible-school enrollment, 100. OR 49.50 Dec 11 1906 p 8: "Shoals, Ind., Dec 5.-The writer closed a short meeting with the Mt. Zion congregation, Lawrence Co., Ill., last Monday night, Dec. 3. Our meeting was well attended. Two confessed their faith in Christ and were baptized Tuesday morning. I will visit them again over the 4th Lord's day in this month. Will go to Bryant's Valley, near Crossville, Ill., next Saturday - report later. Flat River, Mo. O. M. Davis." OR 49.51 Dec 18 1906 p 8: "Crossville, Ill., Dec. 11 - Meeting here three days old. Dark nights and unfavorable weather hinder much. Interest fairly good. Don't know how long I will stay here. May close next Lord's day night. Very much opposition at this point. May the Lord bless the labors of the faithful, is my humble prayer. O. M. Davis. Flat River, Mo., Box 226."
Byerton (near)	Calhoun		OR 42.8 Feb 21 1899: 5 CFW "Just closed a splendid meeting near Byerton, Ill., with 4 additions and much good done. The meeting was brought to an abrupt close by the sudden change of weather, or we are sure many more would have obeyed."
Calhoun County Congregations	Calhoun		OR 53.1 Jan 4 1910: 2: E. G. Denney, "Denney in Illinois." EGD is in Calhoun County and reports, "Mozier, Ill., Dec. 11, 1909. Brethren: We have been in this county (Calhoun) since Nov. 12. There are five churches of Christ here and one 'digressive.'

Carbon-dale (near)	Jackson	Russell "church house"	Not in Haynes. OR 40.51 Dec 21 1897 p 8: "Carbondale, Ill., Dec. 13.--J. R. Bush and myself are engaged in a meeting at the Russell church house twelve miles North East of this place. The meeting is now 2 weeks old and nine have taken member-ship up to this date. The house has been well filled all the time and great interest is manifest in the work that is being done. This Church is apostolic and we think has elders that will con-tinue it so. We have succeeded in securing enough subscribers for the O. R. that will entitle them to club rates, and we think the 'Old Reli-able" will prove a great benefit to this congre-gation. With such a man as Bro. J. R. Bush (who has a record for accuracy and reverence for God's word) to assist, we have a guarantee that the work that is being done will be of an apostolic order. We will report further result of the meeting at the close. A. J. Peck."
Carterville / Cartersvill e	Franklin	Six Mile	OR 42.50 Dec 12 1899: 8 A. J. Peck had 3 weeks' meeting there. OR 40.9 Mar 2 1897 p 1: "Letters from Cartersville, Ill., inform us that the church at that place has a difficulty on band, which has been thrust into its midst by a preacher from Longview, Texas, named R. S. Robertson. Any of our readers, who know the doctrinal and pri-vate character and reputation of that Longview preacher will benefit the cause of truth by writ-ing out the same in clear form and sending it to A. J. Peck, Cartersville, Ill. The story concern-ing the Cartersville trouble is the old story of innovationism introduced by a preacher who ignores all who oppose him. Let the loyal brethren read Gal. 2: 4, 5, and stand together. We have written the brethren at Cartersville a private letter on the subject."

Casey	Clark	Walnut Chapel	A conservative who preached in Clark County is Christopher C. Boyer, Haynes 481. Haynes has the dates wrong. FAG is: https://www.findagrave.com/memorial/35881970/christopher-columbus-boyer OR 37.46 Nov 13 1894 p 6: H. C. and D. E. Towles "On account of sickness my meeting was delayed at W. Charleston. Will commence at Walnut Chapel next, thence to Charleston, if God wills." Haynes 79: "1870... Mr. Braden this year met Samuel Binns at Casey, in discussing the questions of baptism." http://www.findthechurch.com/congregation.php?ftcID=caseyWalnutChapel is possibly the same congregation.
Cham-paign	Cham-paign	White Street	ACR 9.1 January 2 1866 p 2: J. K. Speer writes concerning the Champaign congregation, "Champaign City, Illinois. The brethren in this new and growing city have just finished a neat little house in which they have met to observe the things commanded. They did not have a 'fair,' a 'supper,' a 'lottery,' to get up the money to defray the building expenses. Neither did they shame every outsider in the city by asking 'alms' of him. They did the work, assisted by a few noble brethren of other congregations....The brethren assemble each first day to observe the ancient order of things in the Lord's house. They are content to have the gospel preached and the commands obeyed. No organ, no hired seats, no new things here. They (though but few) did better singing than I have heard in an 'organ' congregation of five hundred members...

The Church of Christ has three or four young men who can and will preach. They have the old Jerusalem Theological College at Champaign; the same president and professors, and a *live* assistant. The Lord bless these good brethren and sisters.

They did not hire me, but sent me on my way having relieved my necessities according to their ability. If the little societies called 'our societies' will stay out of Champaign, Christianity will be a grand success there...J. K. Speer."

CLead 17.45 Nov 10 1903 p 12: "Vinton, O., November 5 – I will begin a meeting in Champaign, Ill., third Lord's day in November, if the Lord wills. My address until further notice will be Champaign, Ill., 209 W. Park Street. The object of the meeting is to build up apostolic Christianity there. W. H. Devore."

https://www.findagrave.com/memorial/58770162/william-henry-devore

OR 50.14 Apr 2 1907 p 8: "Covington, Ind., March 27 – I was with the brethren at Champaign, Ill., over Lord's day. Two young ladies obeyed the gospel. These brethren seem to be earnest and full of hope. Frank Ellmore."

OR 50.17 Apr 23 1907 p 8: "Covington, Ind., April 15 – I was with the church at Champaign, Ill., over Lord's day. One young lady was baptized and another returned, humbly confessing that she had strayed from the path of duty. These brethren rejoice in the Lord. Frank Ellmore."

| | | | OR 50.25 June 18 1907 p 8: "Covington, Ind., June 12 – Good meetings at Champaign, Ill. Four persons, bearing letters of commendation, united with the congregation. The church meets on East White St. Frank Ellmore."

OR 50.27 July 2 1907 p 5: In "A Good Meeting," Jas. L. White, Georgetown, Ill., R. 3, reports, among other things, "We had a good crowd and the best of behavior all day and all expressed themselves as glad they were there and well paid for their coming. We had visiting brethren from the Churches at Champaign, Indianola, Danville and Columbia, in Illinois, and from Covington, Ind.

In the afternoon the pastor, three elders and several members of the Christian church, in Georgetown, were present. We had two splendid discourses: one at 11 a. m. and one at 3p. m., on the following subjects, being by request of Bro. J. C. Jones, the oldest member of our congregation, (past eighty-six): the morning subject was "Rightly Dividing the Word of Truth" - afternoon, "Christian Union." Those who missed these sermons missed one of the golden opportunities of this life. Bro. Frank Ellmore did justice to them in a masterly, scholarly, Bible and gentlemanly manner; in a fearless, yet kind and persuasive way, calculated to do much good in the Master's cause." |
|---|---|---|---|

				OR 52.35 Aug 31 1909 p 3: "Pearl, Ill., Aug; 18. My meeting at St. Joseph closed last. Lord's day, and from there I went to Champaign, preaching once for the little congregation there. The sexton of the Christian Church house showed me through and I saw many strange things: a kitchen, dining room, class rooms, a room for the Brotherhood (deep down in the basement), and all kinds of musical instruments. From there I came on Pearl and found all things ready for a meeting. I will remain over two Lord's days and then go on to Higbee, Mo…Hoping for a good meeting here at Pearl. Pray for us. J. L. DAVIS." [Haynes helped raise funds for a Champaign congregation during his tenure as State Secretary. See pages 95 and 130; Haynes is listed as the founder.]

			OR 51.14 Apr 7 1908 p 4: In "Echoes from the Field," A. J. Nance reports, "The church of Christ in the city of Champaign has a good house of worship, centrally located, with gaslight, and furnace heat. The building and lot represents several thousand dollars, and is a gift out-right, to the church, by Bro. and Sister Edwards, whose lovely home is situated on a corner lot, almost touching the house of worship. The church house is situated two blocks north from University Place, on East White St., at No. 608. On our regular visit in February we had some of our young friends out to hear us, who are in the State University. The presence also of Bro. and Sister Ponder, from our home church, who are residing in the city during the school year, that they may give their children the benefit of a course in the State University, made our visit seem very home-like. The brethren, of the twin cities, gladly welcome all visitors to their meetings for worship." OR 52.35 Aug 31 1909 p 7: "St. Joseph, Ill., Aug. 7. - The meeting continues with interest and the little congregation is pleased with hearing the truth. Yesterday we had visiting brethren from Champaign. We think to close next Lord's day night. Then I go to Champaign; then to Pearl. Hope to do much good while in this State. J. L. Davis."

Charleston	Coles		OR 51.21 May 26 1908 p 8: "Findlay, Ill., May 19. - I just closed a meeting in Charleston, with nineteen additions, nine by baptism and the rest otherwise. Brother W. E. Dudley began the meeting and preached a week, and I continued it, preaching nearly two weeks. The brethren there are hopeful for the future. Brother Dudley is a good instructor in music as well as preacher, and the churches should use him in that work as well as preaching. Brother Cuppy has bought a tent and intends to pitch it in Mattoon soon to advance the cause there. This is the year when men will be specially interested in politics, but let us who are Christians be interested as never before in the religion of Jesus Christ. D. A. Sommer." https://www.findagrave.com/memorial/ 177944672/william-eli-dudley. Retrieved 1.19.2019. From the obituary at FAG: "Mr. Dudley spent most of his life in Charleston and was well known in religious circles. He established the first congregation of the Church of Christ in Charleston." [Haynes 147 does not mention a conservative congregation in Charleston. The congregation he describes and its 1840 founding mean a conservative congregation did exist as early as 1908, but probably much earlier.]
Chicago	Cook	?	Congregation Al Diestelkamp states was conservative and was started in the 1840s.

Chicago	Cook	Kendall Street	Haynes 162: "Kendall Street Church (Kendall Street, near Polk Street). Organized in 1865. James Bremner, Joseph Badenoch and other worthy Scotchmen formed this congregation. They came from the old First Church while it met on the West Side. They have been ministered to only by their elders, but have given to the kingdom many worthy servants." [NB James Brenner (page 151) is mentioned as involved in the 1850 congregation, of which Haynes says, "Early in 1850 the first church of the Restoration movement was formed in Chicago."]
			OR 47.19 May 10 1904 p 6: In the obituary for Jessie Newberry: "Bro. Horn received the telegram in his Oklahoma home that she was very ill and started to her on the first train he could get, but his heart was saddened when he found her cold and lifeless in the embrace of death. The brethren of Kendall Street extended their sympathy in a brotherly way, one of them speaking words of comfort."
			OR 49.51 Dec 18 1906 p 5: "November 18th I met and worshiped with the church of Christ meeting at Kendall St., near Polk St., Chicago. This is the only church in this great city that is worshiping God after the New Testament plan. I began to preach to attentive audiences at night and continued over three Lord's days and closed Dec. 3...T. L. Gray."
			OR 49.51 Dec 18 1906 p 8: "Chicago, Ill., Dec. 6.- Bro. T. L. Gray has just closed a two weeks' meeting with the disciples who meet on Kendall Street, in this city. His labors here were rewarded with four baptisms, and one addition, and the church led and strengthened as it has not been for years. Our regret was that we could not keep him longer but hope to have him back with us in the near future. May the Lord bless, guide and keep this fearless teacher of the one faith, is our prayer. L. C. Overmeyer."

Chicago	Cook	Leggitt House Church	OR 47.29 July 19 1904 p 3: "Chicago, Ill., July 7, 1904. DEAR BRO. SOMMER:-Bro. Chas. S. Black, of Mentone, Ind., was with us a short time; preached eleven discourses and baptized four. We feel encouraged, and rejoice that some have obeyed the Lord in baptism. We are now thirteen in all, but some of that number cannot meet with us every Lord's day, but there are ten of us the most of the time. We have also decid-ed to have prayer-meeting every Thursday night.
			We still extend the invitation to any and all faithful brethren who can to come our way and lend us a helping hand in our effort to build up the cause in this part of the city. We are your brother and sister in the One faith, LINCOLN LEGGITT, 10223 Union Ave, CORA B. LEGGITT."
			See OR 47.12 Mar 22 1904 pp 4, 5 where JMW reports from Browning about a house church in Chicago. This is the Leggitt family.
			OR 47.21 May 24 1904 p 2: Three weeks' meeting at the Leggitt home. No results. "Since the meeting closed there has been no one at worship on Lord's day except our own family. But the Lord willing, we shall continue the worship as usual in our own house until we can do better."

Cisne	Crawford	House Church	OR 37.46 Nov 13 1894 p 6: Andrew Perry reports, "CISNE, Ill., Nov. 2. I have been at home a few days having been hard at work the greater part of the year in our Master's work, I have delivered two hundred and eleven sermons this year in Illinois, Indiana, Iowa, Missouri and Kansas. Recently I have been in Crawford county, Ill., in a meeting. Political excitement, etc., made against our meeting, and none were added. I learned of and met with a household congregation while I was in Crawford county. On account of the manifest corruptions and departures of the congregation, a few of earnest disciples withdrew themselves, and in the house of a true and worthy member they have been keeping up the worship for quite a while in the past. This is right and all that can be done in some places in this age of apostacy [sic 'apostasy'] and rebellion. The apostles recognized the work of household congregations in several instances and so can we. Congregations wishing my help in meetings this winter may write and we will arrange for the same. Address me at Cisne, Ill., till Nov. 20th, and then to Watseka, Ill. ANDREW PERRY."
Columbia	Monroe		OR 44.2 Jan 8 1901 p 8: "Coxville, Ind., Jan 1. – I was with the church of Christ at Columbia, Ills., over last Lord's day. They have the same sad story to tell as all true, devoted disciples of Christ who have been driven from their church home by innovators. After losing their house of worship they went to work and built a new house and are now worshiping in peace...Josiah Laney." https://www.findagrave.com/memorial/22475854/josiah-laney.

| Conlogue | Edgar | | Haynes 184, 185: "Conlogue. Organized 1872, by Z. T. Sweeney; value of property, $400; never had a Bible school. [185] The house was built in 1873. Preaching now only periodically." [Conservatives have taken up the slack. No indication yet from the OR how often conservatives preached for Conlogue.]

OR 43.34 Aug 28 1900 p 8: Don Carlos Janes states, "Indianapolis, Aug. 16. - I left West, Texas, on last Friday morning and reached Conlogue, Ill., on Friday evening. Preached there that night and at Cooksville over Lord's day…"

https://www.findagrave.com/memorial/43581806/don-carlos-janes. Retrieved 1.21.2019.

OR 47.26 June 28 1904 p 5: "ABYDELL, Ind.- At my last appointment at Conlogue Ill., the 4th Lord's day in last month, 2 were added; 1 noble young woman came from the M. E's, and her husband confessed his Savior and was buried in baptism. Last Lord's day evening, by request, I baptized a neighbor's wife into the one body. J. P. DAVIS." |

Cooksville	McLean		Haynes 290, 291: "Organized 1902 by John R. Golden...present enrollment, 86...In 1894 members from Blue Mound organized a church [291] at Cooksville. A restricting clause was written in the deed to the church lot which led many members to hold themselves aloof..."
			OR 40.31 Aug 3 1897 p 6: "The congregation of the Church of Christ at Cooksville, McLean Co., Ill., invites the brethren to meet with them in a basket meeting or general Assembly, Aug. 26 to 29 inclusive. The object of the meeting is to get acquainted and talk of the things pertaining to the Kingdom of God. Come brethren, let us assemble in the Lord's name and for the good of Zion. Thomas Hensley, Milton Henline [sic], Joseph Arnold, and Marion Pasor, Elders."
			OR 42.20 May 16 1899 p 2: D. Collins from Secor is now editing "Notes from Illinois." He writes "I was with the brethren at Cooksville, Ill., the third Lord's day in April. The brethren are moving along as usual there. It is a pleasure to meet with faithful brethren among whom we have spent so many happy and profitable hours."
			Later he states, "Not. For a moment do I consider that there has been any division in the church. No, there has been no division, but there has been a falling away on the part of those who have left the faith and practice of the apostles. This I think brethren is a point that should be plainly presented to the people. No division has been proclaimed by either those who have remained faithful or the societyites. We have no power nor disposition to make such declaration. They have separated themselves from those who are satisfied with the truth. The faithful stand ready heartily to embrace all who will accept the teaching and practice of Jesus and His

apostles. But it is a sad thing for me to contemplate that they will not return. As one once said, 'Majorities never repent.'"

Denton Collins.

https://www.findagrave.com/memorial/8698073/denton-collins. Retrieved 1.21.2019.

Zollars family genealogy states, "Porter Zollars was baptized by Denton Collins of the Church of Christ, a preacher of Indiana who had baptized his wife several years before, and from the day he united with the church was faithful to his vows." Page 90, Frederick's Hope: A Historical Genealogy of the Zollars Family of Washington County, Pennsylvania and their Descendants.

OR 43.34 Aug 28 1900 p 8: Don Carlos Janes states, "Indianapolis, Aug. 16. - I left West, Texas, on last Friday morning and reached Conlogue, Ill., on Friday evening. Preached there that night and at Cooksville over Lord's day…"

OR 51.25 June 23 1908 p 8: "Hammond, Ill., June 10. – On the occasion of our last visit to Cooksville we had two confessions and baptisms. The church there is doing well, although opposition to the truth is very great."

| County Line School | Pope | County Line School Church of Christ | OR 38.12 March 19 1895 p 3: J. F. Hight, of Samoth (spelled Samouth in Haynes) in "Report of a Debate that Did Not Take Place," says, "I have just returned from Count line school house on the line between Massac and Pope counties, Ill. Held a meeting…" A debate between Hight and D. R. Pryor did not take place because Pryor claimed "the Church of Christ at Samoth, Ill., would not endorse Bro. J. F. Hight." Elder John Kerr of County line Church of Christ had asked Hight to meet Pryor in a debate.

https://www.findagrave.com/memorial/11134189/james-franklin-hight. Retrieved 1.17.2019.

Per Haynes 238 Hight was from the Bethlehem congregation at Vienna. See Samoth, below, where Hight is said to be a member in good standing, of the Samoth Church of Christ.

Haynes 240: "Other Disciples filled various county offices. J. F. Hight has earnestly contended for the faith, and held a public discussion on every occasion for a period of twenty-five years. Now he is serving as county judge. Evidently he is a diplomatist.
But he continues to preach to those who are poor and neglected."
Haynes 85 "1889 – A discussion was held at Creal Springs led by J. F. Hight and Robert Huggins, a Christadelphian."
Haynes 86: Hight debated G. W. Smith in the Azotus Baptist Church, in Pope County in 1896.
"1897. At Joppa, J. F. Hight and R. H. Pique, of the M. E. Church, debated."
"1898. J. F. Hight and C. M. Weaver, Primitive Baptist, met in a debate at New Burnside." |
| | | | Haynes 87: "1911…This led to another discussion at the same place between J. F. Hight and Mr. McLain." |

Creal Springs	William son		OR 50.11 Mar 12 1907 p 5: Addison Pickerill writes from Marion, Indiana "...we have received the following additional communications in which they desire some 'loyal' preacher to locate in their midst, or to go to their assistance: G. S. Dillon, Champaign, Ill...Jas. Springer, Creal Springs, Ill. As the writer can visit but few of the above, we wish someone, who may be more accessible, to go to their relief. In this way their needs may be made known and supplied. No one is desired at any of the above places unless he is strictly 'loyal' to the 'ancient order of things.'"
Danville	Vermil-ion	Lowe's Chapel	Haynes 410: "The church has never been strong, and has been further handicapped by ultra-conservative preachers." OR 43.22 May 29 1900 p 6: "Bro. Eli N. Gants, born in Vermillion Co., Ill., Sept. 27, 1845, died May 6, 1900, at his late residence near where he was born...He was baptized Aug. 17, 1895 by his father-in-law, Bro. Jas. B. Stevens, and at his decease was a member of the church of Christ at Lowe's chapel..." https://www.findagrave.com/memorial/29215738/eli-n_-gants.
Danville	Vermil-ion	Union	Haynes 413: "The church was divided through the preaching of ultra-conservatives. These damages have been measurably repaired by the ministry of J. J. Cosat, who is serving the congregation for the twenty-fifth year as its pastor."
De Soto	Jackson		OR 39.8 Feb 25 1896 p 8: "De Soto, Ill., Feb. 18 – I wish to give to the readers of the O. R. a final report of the meeting which just closed at this place, which was held by the writer and A. J. Peck of Carterville, Ill..." Also see Dix.
Dexter	Effing-ham		OR 55.32 Aug 6 1912 p 8: "De Soto, Ill., July 30. - Closed meeting near Dexter the 28th with a congregation of 10 set in order...W. E. Dudley."

Dix	Jefferson		OR 50.8 Feb 19 1907 p 8: "Champaign, Ills. Feb. 11 – My meeting with the church three miles north-east of Dongola closed yesterday evening. I left home Dec. 26, for Dix; preached eighteen times at the home congregation of Bro. O. A. Timmons. Two took membership. From there I went to De Soto and preached six times. At Dongola I preached forty-five times in twenty-three days; baptized 15, reclaimed 5. Chas. T. Cook." https://www.findagrave.com/memorial/ 36494419/charles-thomas-cook. https://www.findagrave.com/memorial/ 53532538/otto-alfred-timmons.
Dixon Springs	Pope		Haynes 363: "This church is five miles east of Grantsburg, near the road leading from Vienna to Golconda. It is of the ultraconservative class."
Dongola	Union		OR 50.8 Feb 19 1907 p 8: "Champaign, Ills. Feb. 11 – My meeting with the church three miles north-east of Dongola closed yesterday evening. I left home Dec. 26, for Dix; preached eighteen times at the home congregation of Bro. O. A. Timmons. Two took membership. From there I went to De Soto and preached six times. At Dongola I preached forty-five times in twenty-three days; baptized 15, reclaimed 5. Chas. T. Cook." OR 51.21 May 26 1908 p 8: "Dongola, Ill., May 16. - Brother Charles F. [sic T.] Cook came here May 6 and preached over Lord's day to the people in the country. Two were added and large, attentive audiences gathered each night to hear the truth in its simplicity. On Monday and Tuesday nights he preached to the people in town, and then left for his home at Covington, Ind. NAOMI KARRAKER." https://www.findagrave.com/memorial/ 119170905/naomi-josephine-kaufman. Retrieved 1.19.2019. Nee Karraker.

Dudley	Edgar		Haynes 185: "This church is about extinct. Landlordism and ultraconservatism have proved its undoing." OR 33.50 Dec 11 1890 p 3: J. F. Tomson reports, "On last Wednesday night we closed our very interesting meeting with the church of Christ, at Dudley, Edgar Co., Ill., which resulted in seven added to the membership. Two by relation, one from the 'New Lights,' and four by confession and baptism...I will labor for the church at Dudley one fourth of my time next year, and hope to establish a church that will worship in accordance to the teaching of the Bible."
Fairfield	Wayne	Black Oak	Haynes 428: "This is a mission point of the Fairfield Church. It is six miles east and north of there. It was organized with forty-five members and did well for several years. Then a traveling preacher of the ultra-conservatives came in and measurably crippled its usefulness."
Farmer's Ridge			OR 42.8 Feb 21 1899: 3 Claud F Witty in meeting at Farmer's Ridge: "The brethren at this place have just completed a nice, new, house of worship, the deed of which contains the restrictive clause."
Findley / Findlay	Shelby		See also Bethany entry. Haynes 388: "Mr. and Mrs. A. H. Terry moved from Shelbyville to Findley in 1903. The Christian Church there was so conservative that it was doing little. In 1905, through the influence of Mrs. Terry, an auxiliary to the C. W. B. M. of twelve members was formed. A meeting by Mr. Monser in November, 1906, resulted in the organization of a church of eighty-eight members. It is active and aggressive. A brick building was finished and occupied in January, 1909. Miss Olive was set apart to the ministry by this church. There is also a conservative church here."

George-town ("near")	Vermil-ion	Pleasant Mound	OR 42.40 Oct 3 1899 p 5: "The writer recently assisted the Church of Christ near Georgetown, Ill., in a meeting of a few days, resulting in 2 by relation and 6 obeying the gospel. This church has about 200 members, a large per cent of whom are young people, and not anything to draw and hold them together but the magnetism of the gospel of Christ. The above was the 14th meeting of said church in which the writer did the preaching. J. W. Perkins" Perkins regularly reports to the OR additions to this congregation OR 45.45 Nov 11 1902 p 5: "Sumner, Ills., Oct. 28. - I preached over the 4th Lord's day at Pleasant Mound, near Georgetown,' Ills., and 1 young lady confessed her Savior and put on Christ in baptism. Bro. J. W. Perkins preached for these brethren fifteen years and a more welcome visitor could not go there than Bro. Perkins. I will, the Lord willing hold them a meeting in December. W. G. ROBERTS. See under Champaign for the basket meeting hosted by this congregation. OR 50.27 July 2 1907 p 5
Gila	Jasper		"David's history is unknown during the 1880's but in the 1890's we see him becoming an active soldier for the cause of Christ. He did preaching for the Brick Chapel in Hutton, Coles, Illinois...the Liberty Chapel in Hidalgo, Jasper, Illinois...the Church of Christ in Annapolis, Illinois...the Church of Christ in Bell Air, Crawford, Illinois...the Church of Christ in Gila, Jasper, Illinois...the Church of Christ in Iola, Clay, Illinois." Haynes does not mention Gila.

Greenfield	Greene	Union or Old Union	Haynes sometimes spells the county as Green rather than Greene. Haynes 211: "Union (Greenfield). Organized 1854, by John S. Sweeney; present membership, 40; value of property, $1,500, no Bible school. This is in the northeast part of the county." OR 1907 and 1908 details how the digressives took over the building, forcing the conservatives to build their own building. H. W. Cuppy intervened on their behalf without securing the building. "Bro. W. H. Raffety wrote the OR, asking for funds to help with the building. W. H. Prather, kin to one of the congregation's founders, Edward Prather, was handling the funds sent. https://www.findagrave.com/memorial/161632283/w_-h_-raffety. Retrieved 1.19.2019 https://www.findagrave.com/memorial/26602844/william-hiram-prather. (1865 – 1921) https://www.findagrave.com/memorial/99226820/edward-prather. (1854 – 1932) OR 50.48 Nov 26 1907 p 6: H. W. Cuppy, writing from Kemp, Ill. "More Antics of the Christian Church"

			"Dear Brethren: - I thought it might be of interest to the friends of truth, to hear of the good done in Green Co., Ill. It was at a place called "Old Union," about seven miles south-east of Roodhouse, that Bro. W. H Raffety, having endured the conditions of an abandoned field as long as be could, availed himself of the opportunity to make his wishes known through the columns of the Review. After a brief correspondence, I went, and I found that the hand of digression had divided and scattered a once congenial people. For fifty years they had met for worship without the hinderance [sic] of an organ, but a few "heady, high-minded" fellows, 'ever learning and never able to come to the knowledge of the truth" stepped in…" Now here is what I saw in the history of 'Old Union.' Pioneer preachers were good on First Principles, Church Identity, but failed to strengthen the church in its work and worship, (with a well equipped eldership) hence it was not prepared to resist these foreigners… Men going into the church of Christ should know they are not going into a sect and, if coming from a sect, they had just as well understand at first they will be expected to leave their paraphernalia of X-mas entertainment, Sunday-school, Y. P. S. C. E., etc., questionable methods of raising money and instrumental music behind. In holding meetings and reaching the people, the future welfare of the congregation must be considered. Here was the greatest failing of the work done at the above-named place; the proper education of the brethren to avoid any departure from the living God! After fifty years of peaceable possession, those who had done most in building the church-building were driven out. The climax came about eight years ago, and to this day a feeling exists that is not at all pleasant…

			I found a people divided, robbed, naked, half dead; sad indeed was their condition. They were stupid or benumbed by their encounter with the enemy of truth, until they seemed to think they could not do any thing to recover. But they could easily digest good plain food. See .John 4. I stayed with them two weeks. The first of September I returned about two weeks, but was anticipated by a digressive preacher. Came home and went back in two weeks more, and stayed over two Lord's days. During this effort we were compelled to use a dwelling-house and a schoolhouse. The result was about twenty separated themselves from the apostasy, three good men were chosen to act as their overseers, and $575 subscribed to build a house. May the faithful become more aggressive and carry the Word into the regions beyond. We are more than well pleased with the way the brethren take hold. May others be encouraged, and bring forth fruit. H. W. Cuppy."
Green Pond	Pike?	Nebo?	OR 42.8 Feb 21 1899: 3 CFW: "Leaving Nebo, I made my way to the Green Pond congregation, where I remained one week, preaching the Word."
Greenup	Cumberland	Antioch	Haynes 170: "Organized 1891, by H. C. Kuykendall...This church is eight miles northeast of Greenup. Conservatives are in control." OR 49.35 Aug 28 1906 p 8: "Kemp, Ill, Aug. 24.-A few days' labor about 8 miles north of Greenup, resulted in 3 confessions and baptisms. H. W. Cuppy."

Appendix 4: Illinois Conservative Preachers/Congregations Mentioned in Haynes &
Conservative Papers

| Hamburg | Calhoun | Indian Creek | Haynes 124: "A small, ultra-conservative congregation, with little influence for good."

OR 50.49 Dec 3 1907 p 8: "Hamburg, Nov. 20 – We closed a 17 days' meeting last night with the Indian Creek church near the above place. We had 11 baptized and 2 restored, making 13 added. The church had almost completed the cleaning of their record, when the meeting began, which helped much. The interest was fine from the beginning. I was royally entertained and liberally remunerated. I hope to see Bro. T. S. Hutson at The Bay, near this place, to-night on my way home. Bro. John S. Wilson lives at Indian Creek, and preaches for them. His support in this meeting helped us. Nebo. H. D. Leach."
https://www.findagrave.com/memorial/143702172/john-silas-wilson
https://www.findagrave.com/memorial/51708434/harvey-dean-leach
https://www.findagrave.com/memorial/43719082/thaddeus-stevens-hutson. |
| Hammond | Piatt | | Haynes 356: "The ultra-conservatives have long since taken it off the map as an active force for truth and righteousness." |

Hardin	Calhoun		OR 47.4 Jan 26 1904 p 2: J. M. Walton proposes to hold meetings in Hardin to gather a congregation.
			OR 54.34 Aug 22 1911 p 8: "Hamburg, Ill. – Meeting at Hardin begins the 20th with Bro. Baldwin, of St. Louis, preaching. Pray for us. – Anna Schlieper." Baldwin is J. H. Baldwin. No FAG found yet but too many hits so far.
			https://www.findagrave.com/memorial/ 134181123/anna-schlieper. Retrieved 1.19.2019. Nee Martens. (1867 – 1956)
			OR 54.39 Sept 26 1911 p 8: "Hamburg. Ill., Sept. g.-A 12-nights' meeting at Hardin, conducted by Bro. J. H. Baldwin, of St. Louis, was closed Aug. 31. Four persons, members of the church at different places, expressed their desire to unite with 4 others at that place in doing the Lord's will. Some others 'almost persuaded,' and one lady wanted to be baptized, but was prevented by her husband. Brethren, pray for the few there. - Chas. H. Sevier."
			https://www.findagrave.com/memorial/ 15206899/charles-henry-sevier. Retrieved 1.19.2019. (1886 – 1974) Obit reads, "Funeral services were conducted at 2 p.m. today at Indian Creek Church of Christ with the Rev. Wilson Ramsey officiating. Burial was in Indian Creek Cemetery."

			OR 55.30 July 23 1912 p 8: "Fidelity, Ill., July 11. - I was at Green Pond, 5th Lord's day in June, and rejoiced to see 2 come back into the fold, also one from Christian church. Congregation there has had hard battle, but is now gaining ground and doing much good. I hope and pray they will continue. I was with church at Greenfield last Lord's day and had good meeting. A few of as loyal ones there as I ever met; am to be with them in meeting this fall. If the Lord wills, I start a meeting in Hardin next Lord's day, and hope to do much good. Brethren, pray for me. J. C. Roady." OR 55.30 July 23 1912 p 8: Roady reports on the work at Hardin: "Hardin, Ill., July 16. – I am here in meeting which began last Lord's day night. Only 8 members of the Church here, but they have been meeting on 1st day of the week since Bro. Baldwin held them a meeting last year. As they have no house of their own, we are conducting the meeting in the town hall and having very good crowds and very best of order; those coming seem to be interested and I hope and pray much good will be done before we close…If the Lord is willing, I shall go from here to Modesto, where I am to begin meeting Aug. 1…J. C. Roady, Fidelity, Ill."

			OR 55.52 Dec 24 1912 p 8: "Hardin, Ill., Dec. 15. – Meeting here lasted a week. Brethren there in midst of sectism [sic]. Catholics strong there, and represent their church as the only true one. Church of Christ there was started by several congregations. Farmers Ridge, Mozier Bay, Mozier Hollow and Indian Creek all had fellowship in this work. A few weeks ago I spoke of this place as being started by Mozier Hollow, but later learned others had fellowship, so will allow 'honor to whom honor is due.' This is the county seat of Calhoun county. Several have been baptized here and are continuing the work, and people of this community look to the church of Christ to oppose Catholicism. Several books and tracts were sent us to use against them, but the Bible is sufficient. While attendance was not what the brethren desired, we trust some good was done. Thos. Smith, Barnard Mo."
Hidalgo	Jasper	Liberty Chapel	"David's history is unknown during the 1880's but in the 1890's we see him becoming an active soldier for the cause of Christ. He did preaching for the Brick Chapel in Hutton, Coles, Illinois...the Liberty Chapel in Hidalgo, Jasper, Illinois...the Church of Christ in Annapolis, Illinois...the Church of Christ in Bell Air, Crawford, Illinois...the Church of Christ in Gila, Jasper, Illinois...the Church of Christ in Iola, Clay, Illinois." Haynes 234 under Extinct Congregations in Jasper County: "Liberty Church was formed in the forties. It is located a few miles northwest of Hidalgo. The chapel built in 1858 burned down, and the second was built in 1868. The preachers who served there before the Civil War were Daniel Connor, Benj. Duvee, James Duncan and H. J. Sutherland. It did not move to town after the railroad was built, and has gone down."

Hut-sonville	Craw-ford		Haynes 168: "There is also a conservative church here with a Bible school." OR 33.49 Dec 4 1890 p 3: "Next Lord's day I go to Liberty, Sullivan county, Saturday week I go to Hutsonville, Ill., to hold a series of meetings. I hope for better weather than we had at Macy. Marshall Parker." OR 34.6 Feb 5 1891 p 3: Marshall Parker updates his meeting at Hutsonville, writing from Trimble, Ill., where he is holding a meeting: "My meeting at Hutsonville began on Saturday night of the 1st Lord's day in December and continued over three Lord's days. The immediate results were…Not every thing in this congregation is as it should be, but we think the majority want to do right and will do the right as they learn it. The Review has some strong friends there and I think more persons will take it. Two of the four elders take it and one other of them says he is going to send for it soon…"
Hutton	Coles	Brick Chapel	Not in Haynes "By 1880, David was living in Coles Co, Illinois as a single man in the home of his brother, Henry Clifford Towles. David's history is unknown during the 1880's but in the 1890's we see him becoming an active soldier for the cause of Christ. He did preaching for the Brick Chapel in Hutton, Coles, Illinois...the Liberty Chapel in Hidalgo, Jasper, Illinois...the Church of Christ in Annapolis, Illinois...the Church of Christ in Bell Air, Crawford, Illinois...the Church of Christ in Gila, Jasper, Illinois...the Church of Christ in Iola, Clay, Illinois."
Indianola	Vermil-ion		Haynes 410: "Present membership, 68; value of property, $3,500; Bible-school enrollment, 67." No indication the congregation is conservative. See Champaign entry, where Indianola is mentioned and where it might be inferred Indianola was conservative since James White shows an "us versus them" mentality in his report of their basket meeting.

Iola	Clay		Not in Haynes
			"David's history is unknown during the 1880's but in the 1890's we see him becoming an active soldier for the cause of Christ. He did preaching for the Brick Chapel in Hutton, Coles, Illinois...the Liberty Chapel in Hidalgo, Jasper, Illinois...the Church of Christ in Annapolis, Illinois...the Church of Christ in Bell Air, Crawford, Illinois...the Church of Christ in Gila, Jasper, Illinois...the Church of Christ in Iola, Clay, Illinois."
Iuka	Marion		Iuka is not in Haynes. CLead 17.49 Dec 8 1903 p 4: "I [W. H. Devore] preached one sermon at Iuka, Ill., and met again the faithful few there. Bro. Walker [S. A. Walker?], a loyal preacher of the Word, is doing a good work there. I was pleased to meet him. He subscribed for the CL, and I hope to see now and then in the Leader reports of the work he is doing for the Lord. Pick up your pen, Bro. Walker, and give us some of your mature thoughts on the subject of life and salvation." OR 52.35 Aug 31 1909 p 2: In "Illinois Letter," F. A. Ditrick reports,

"Iuka, Ill., Aug. 10, 1909. Bro. Bro. Hade Cuppy on Saturday before the first Lord's day in
July pitched his tent in the north part of Marion
county, Ill., and began preaching the gospel in
that much needed field. The tent was located
between Kinmundy and Omega, and the meeting continued through the month. The writer
joined Bro. Cuppy about the middle of the
meeting and continued until the close. There is
no congregation at that place, but there are a
few members living in that part of the county
that are anxious to see the cause established that
they may have church privileges. The Christian
Church people are all around them and one of
their preachers attended the meeting a part of
the time. W. Simer is his name. I spoke one
night on some of the differences between the
Christian and Church of Christ and Elder Simer
took exceptions to some things I alluded to, so,
after we dismissed that night, he said he would
like to defend the practice of the Christian
Church. He would affirm that the practice of the
Christian Church was permitted by scripture—
that it came under the head of Christian liberty.
So we accepted and on Saturday before the
third Lord's day we discussed differences between the two bodies and the investigation
proved satisfactory with our brethren, *but not
with Elder Simer and his people,* and they
wished to try it over. On the next Saturday we
had another investigation which proved satisfactory to those that are satisfied with what is
written.

			While there were only three baptized during the meeting, the Seed was sown and I believe it will bring forth fruit in the future. I expect to do more preaching there soon, as I realize the need as never before of getting the glorious gospel before the people where we have no congregations. We will find some good honest people wherever we go. Bro. Cuppy is doing a grand work with his tent at a great sacrifice, but he will be rewarded at the end of the race. We hope more of our preaching brethren will do some missionary work as they have opportunity, for it is badly needed. Your brother in Christ, F. A. DITRICK." https://www.findagrave.com/memorial/100363349/frederick-andrew-ditrick https://www.findagrave.com/memorial/26527232/william-jackson-simer
Janesville	Cumberland	Webster	Haynes 173: "This is two and a half miles northeast of Janesville. Min. I. S. McCash constituted a church in 1864 near Hazel Dell, at the Washington Schoolhouse. At that place four of his sons were led to Christ and all of them entered the ministry; namely, Andrew, Levi, Albert and I. N. McCash. Andrew has remained there over forty years. Levi has preached in California and Albert in Washington for nearly as long. I. N. has been more prominent, and, hence, more widely known. This congregation is now divided."

| Jewett | Cum-berland | | Haynes 172: "The first chapel burned in 1900 and the second was built. The church was reorganized in 1911 by Evangelist J. E. Stout with forty members, and is now led by better ideals.

There was a division in this congregation in 1909, and the conservatives formed a church that has now fifteen members and a Bible school, but no chapel."

OR 37.52 Dec 25 1894 p 6: "Charleston, Ill., Dec. 13 – We have just closed a meeting of two weeks at Excelsior, 7 miles south of Jewett, with 12 confessions and baptisms, 2 reclaimed and 1 from the Baptists. We closed with a full house and good interest. To God be all the glory. D. E. Towles, E. A. Armpreister.

OR 52.20 May 18 1909 p 8: "Sullivan, Ind., May 6. – Our meeting at Jewett, Ill., closed on the 3rd and much interest was manifested. The sects put up a hard fight and kept many from hearing the truth. But the brethren were strengthened in the Faith and 37 persons were added—17 baptized; 13 restored and 7 took membership. They have been divided over the organ but now seem to be satisfied with "what is written." J. W. JACKSON."

OR 52.32, August 10 1909 p 3: W. G. Roberts writes "Locked Out," describing events at Jewett around June 30, 1909. Mentions "State Board" man Beabout, who was over congregations in "twenty-two counties." This provides several details of the controversy mentioned by Haynes. Beabout is not in Haynes; it might be a nickname assigned by Roberts. |

			OR 52.41 Oct 12 1909 p 5: News item, "A New House," by "William Ingram, For Building Committee," describes the people on the committees to get a new meeting house built. Typical appeals for help from other locations. See appeal for help in St. Louis meeting house in the same volume: "My Visit," by W. G. Roberts, Number 31, August 3, 1909, page 5. WGR makes a strong appeal for outside support for the St. Louis congregation; he feels more emphasis is needed on city congregations. OR 54.14 April 4 1911 p 8: "Kemp, Ill., March 28 - Closed 2 weeks meeting at Jewett Lord's day night. They are going to build a new house this summer. "Digressives" locked them out, hence they have to go elsewhere in the town and build. The ones that locked me out when I was there before came to hear me preach this time. Held our meeting in the U. B. house, and had large crowds and good attention. One took membership. I "whipped" the "digressives" by treating them kindly and saying nothing at all about them. They expected me to jump on them with both feet, but were disappointed, and the world is now throwing in their teeth the way they treated me. That was strictly a mission meeting—more so than any I ever before held. I go Friday to Cowden for another mission meeting. Bro. Cuppy will be with me. - *W. G, Roberts.*"
			OR 54.16 April 18 1911 p 8: "Kemp, Ill., April 6. - Preached over Lord's day and till Tuesday night at Yale. A new congregation. We are getting several new ones in Illinois. I think there will be about 4 new houses built in this part of the State this summer. Am well pleased with outlook at Yale. Going to build up a good congregation. They, like Jewett, have men and women of influence. Brethren at Yale will build this summer. Restrictive Clause in their deed. Fine people. I promised to visit them again. Begin at Cowden the 15th. – *W. G. Roberts.*"

Kane	Greene		OR 42.6 Feb 7 1899: 5. Thomas Jefferson Roady reports on the work there. https://www.findagrave.com/memorial/62270083/thomas-jefferson-roady Haynes 211: "Present membership, 100 (conservative)."
Kemp	Douglas		OR 50.46 Nov 12 1907 8: "Kemp, Nov. 8 – The meeting at this place was a success from all appearances. Eight were baptized into the one body and eight took membership. The preaching was done by Bro. Jas. M. Briggs. H. W. Cuppy." https://www.findagrave.com/memorial/112406697/hadon-wall-cuppy
Lancaster			OR 42.52 Dec 26 1899: 3. S. O. Pool. Reports obit of Theresa Smith: "In the year of 1889 she obeyed the gospel under the preaching of Bro. G. S. Morel. She said that was the first time she ever understood the gospel. She united with the church of Christ at Lancaster, Ill. She was one of the few which remained faithful when the congregation apostatized."
Macoupin [sic]	Ma-coupin		OR 49.18 May 1 1906 p 4: "On next Lord's day (5th in April) we will be with the little church at Macoupin, Ill. This church was established last October, and we have visited them once, since they were banded together and took up the work of the Master. We found them doing well, and hopeful and joyous in their work. We hope to find them still in the line of duty, and in the enjoyment of their high and holy profession." A. J. Nance reported this.
Martins-burg	Pike		OR 42.6 Feb 7 1899: 5. AJ Nance held a meeting of 3 weeks duration. Haynes 359: "An old church of good but conservative people."

| Mattoon | Coles | | OR 51.21 May 26 1908 p 8: "Mattoon, Ill. – There are a few faithful brethren here who meet every Lord's day at 521 DeWitt avenue for worship in the apostolic way. Brother H. C. Towles preaches for us on the first Lord's day in each month and expects to hold us a tent meeting in June, the Lord willing. G. W. Shull."

See also Charleston.

OR 51.25 June 23 1908 p 8: H. W. Cuppy has bought a tent, suggesting it can be used to start other congregations where there "is a prospect for one."

"Personal Items.

Brother H. W. Cuppy has pitched his tent in Mattoon, Ill., and he and Brother Towles, of Ashmore, are conducting an interesting meeting. Brethren W. E. Dudley, of Charleston, and D. A. Sommer, of Findlay, have been present and helped with their preaching and singing. Some nights the tent will not hold the audiences. The common people are listening attentively to the old, old story. There is a fine prospect for much good to be done there. Brother Cuppy and other brethren propose to keep the tent going all summer. Earnest brethren in central Illinois who have no congregation near, but think there is a prospect for one, might do well to write.to Brother H. W. Cuppy, Kemp, Ill., stating the circumstances and prospect, and he may be able to help you some time."

OR 51.25 June 23 1908 p 8: "Mattoon, Ill., June 17. - The tent meeting here is still being carried on with increasing interest. Ten accessions to date; five last night. The tent is too small to accommodate all. H. C. TOWLES." |
| Metamora (west of) | Woodford | Partridge | Haynes 446: "The Partridge congregation was located west of Metamora, but conservatism finally closed its doors." |

Mode	Shelby		Mode is in Holland Township. One signatory of the Address and Declaration is "Isaac Walters, Mode Church."
Modesto	Ma-coupin	Berean	Haynes 306: "This congregation is located three miles northeast of Modesto. It is "the church of Christ and not the Christian Church." It has Bible classes, but no Bible school. It is opposed to "the pastor," but has preaching one Lord's Day in the month; also is opposed to "so much preach for so much money" and to instrumental music in the public worship. The correspondent is J. C. Roady, Fidelity, Ill." OR 40.35 Aug 31 1897 p 3: Nance is in a meeting here. Says, "Many, and perhaps all, of these old churches might be saved to the master could uniform sacrifice and self-denial be maintained among the members of the same, and cooperation on the basis of equality secured between these churches and faithful preachers and teachers." He mentions John S. Sweeney and Sweeney's father labored there.

			OR 41.4 Jan 25 1898 p 5: A. J. Nance in "Echoes from the Field," writes, "Arriving at St. Louis from the west, we took a train on the Bluff line for Modesto, Ill., and was met at the station by Elder D. L. Goode who conveyed us to his pleasant home. The following evening (being Christmas) in company with Bro. Goode and family, we went to Berean Chapel where we had formerly made an appointment, and were greeted by one of the largest and most attentive audiences we ever had the pleasure of addressing during the holiday season. The order was unexceptionally good and the interest profound, and we have reasons for believing that great good was accomplished by the three discourses delivered during our stay. The Berean church through her officers requested us to visit that place monthly during the present year, and we have consented to assist them in their labor of love at least till such time as they may be able to dispense with our service with less damage to the cause in that community than what they think would result at this time, for lack of such service. This the place at which we assisted the brethren in a grand meeting in August during which time so many precious souls were brought into the kingdom. And these brethren ask our assistance in the matter of training and developing this material." https://www.findagrave.com/memorial/64008154/andrew-jackson-nance. https://www.findagrave.com/memorial/12093455/darwin-l-goode

| Mozier | Calhoun | Mozier Bay or Mozier Creek or simply Mozier? | Haynes 123, 124: "*Bay* (Mozier). Organized 1897, by J. M. Bovee.[124] This congregation was the result of a meeting conducted by Mr. Bovee in the West Panther Creek Schoolhouse. The use of an organ and the beginning of a Sunday school led to a division of the church. Those withdrawing put up a chapel within a stone's-throw of the other house. Then they challenged Mr. Bovee to publicly debate the 'organ question.' He complied."

Haynes 86: "1897... In the West Panther Creek Schoolhouse, in Calhoun County, J. M. Bovee and J. W. Miller discussed instrumental music in public worship."

See CSI page 472 for John McLelland Bovee. Has article on "Church Music" in 1908 4 Apr: 574.

OR 53.1 Jan 4 1910: 2: "The congregation here at Mozier Creek has a good cement house, well finished, and are at peace. We aided them in perfecting their organization by appointing Bishops and Deacons. They are a willing, energetic band, striving together for the advancement of the Redeemer's cause. We can see a bright future for this congregation. In their deed, they are fortified against any foe from without, and they intend to fortify against foes within by exercising church discipline—in withdrawing from any brother that walks disorderly. Neither do they intend to have any man preach for them that holds to the opinions of men. They clearly see the danger along that line. They requested I should write a few lines, hence these. E. G. Denney,

https://www.findagrave.com/memorial/112311260/elias-gaskins-denny |
| Mozier | Calhoun | Mozier Hollow | Congregations at "Mozier and Mozier Hollow" still existed in 1952 per reports in the Old Paths Advocate: https://www.newtestamentchurch.org/OPA/pdf/OPA1952.pdf. Retrieved 1.19.2019. |

Mt. Zion	Lawrenc e		OR 42.9 Feb 28 1899: 6. In obit of Moses Perkins, "He lived a worthy member of the body of Christ at Mt. Zion, Lawrence Co., Ill., and served as a deacon over 20 years."
			OR 51.15 Apr 14 1908: 3: B. F. Stivers reports he visited Mt. Zion, where he was raised and where he "obeyed the gospel." "But there is a band of disciples still meets and worships there, contending for the things that are pure and holy.
			"On Monday I went to Eureka, west of the above place. There I found a band of eight or nine, keeping house for the Lord...I went from there to Shilo [sic 'shiloh'], Richland Co., and preached two sermons. I found this place not doing much, but they said they were going to meet again...I then went to Berryville and was there over Lord's day. Here I found a faithful band, striving together in the work of the Lord.
			"I then came back to Mt. Eora and was stormed out, not getting to meet with them. I would have loved to have had the opportunity of doing so. It was there I did my first preaching and organized them." https://www.findagrave.com/memorial/43817688/benjamin-franklin-stivers

Nebo	Pike?		Haynes 359, 360: "Organized 1885..."
			362: "Rock Hill (Nebo). This is six miles west of Pearl." [No more details.]
			OR 42.6 Feb 7 1899: 5. Alfred Ellmore held a meeting at same time as Nance in Martinsburg.
			OR 49.51 Dec 18 1906 p 8: "Nebo, Ill., Dec. 8. - Closed a. short meeting here last night. The M. E's were also running a meeting, but I don't think it hurt us any. Bros. H. B. Applegate and Samuel Witty are the preaching brethren who attended the meeting, We closed a week sooner than we would have, had it not been for the bad weather. There are about eighty-five names on the church-book here, but only ten and twelve attend the Lord's day meeting. Some of the members live fifteen miles away. These are good brethren, and set for the truth. They have suffered many things from the Christian church. I hope to visit them again. God bless them and all the faithful. W. G. Roberts."
Newark	Kendall		Not in Haynes. Haynes has no congregations in Kendall county.
			OR 43.30 July 24 1900 p 8: "Bourbon, Ill, July 12. – We began our meeting June 2, closed 15th with about as good an interest as I ever saw, but other promises call me away. I baptized 22, reclaimed 4, 26 in all. This is a good congregation. 'Loyal to their king,' and reward a man for his work in the Lord. May they ever 'hold fast to the form of sound (incorruptable) [sic] words.' From there I went to Newark; held 12 days; reorganized with 42. This used to be the 'Christian church—having their fares festivals etc., but there is no such work there now. I set my stake deep and built from "the foundation" up. I baptized 8 of these; the 32 were members heretofore. I went from, there to Richland...J. R. Roberts."

Niantic	Macon	Long Point	OR 42.1 Jan 3 1899: 5. A. L. Gepford worshipped there, but was unexpected. OR 42.8 Feb 21 1899: 5 "We, the Church of Christ at Long Point, Ill., have just closed a four weeks' meeting…The meeting was conducted by Samuel Fisher, our regular minister, who is well able to handle the gospel in its apostolic form. He is about 23 years old and this is his second meeting. Geo. M. Bell." Haynes 303: "Above the entrance door of the chapel is a marble slab, on which are carved the following words : "This building was erected by the Long Point Church of Christ and is dedicated to the worship of almighty God so long as instrumental music is not used therein." "James Dingman and James Sanders were the two strong and unique characters of the community who, in their later years, gave to the congregation its ultra-conservative cast. But the memory of each is rightfully held in high regard."
Ogden	Champaign		CLead 3.5 Jan 29 1889 p 3: In 'Briefs Here and There,' J. C. Myers reports. "Bro. B. N. Anderson, of Gifford, Ill., closed a meeting at Ogden, Champaign County, a few days ago. Two or three were immersed. The church at Ogden has been in the background for some time. Glad to hear of this evidence of new life." J. C. Myers also reports of his labors in Vermilion and Douglas Counties.
Oliver	Edgar		Haynes 188: "A conservative congregation that was re-enforced from the Big Creek Church." OR 47.26 June 28 1904 p 5: "Oliver, Ill., June 24 – Bro. J. P. Davis filled his regular appointment here the 3rd Lord's day in this month, preaching also Monday and Tuesday nights. Four were added to the one body; 2 by confession and baptism, and 2 reclaimed. H. E. Hall."

Palestine	Craw-ford		Haynes 169, 170: "The frame chapel on North Main Street was burned in 1855. The present brick house was built in 1874. In 1893 a number of the members who were opposed to the use of instrumental music in the public worship withdrew and put [170] up a frame chapel two blocks south. This is now unused and stands as a monument to mistaken zeal."
Pearl (South of)	Pike	Old Pearl (Straut) Also Bee Creek?	Haynes 360: "An old church of conservatives five miles south of Pearl." Haynes 357, 358: "Bee Creek (Pearl). Organized 1911, by G. W. Williams; present membership, 60; value of property, $500; Bible-school enrollment, 40. [358] This congregation is five miles south of Pearl. It is feeble." OR 38.41 Oct 8 1895 p 6: "NEBO, Ill., Sept. 22.- Have just closed an interesting and profitable meeting with the Church of Christ at Bee Creek, Ill., of two weeks' duration. The visible results are 11 additions to the One Body; 2 restored, and 9 by obedience, of which 4 were heads of families... The church at Bee Creek is apostolic. Bro. G. W. Williams held them a meeting last winter with some 15 or 20 additions. Bro. Williams, like myself, is young and just entering the field as an evangelist, and is satisfied with what is WRITTEN and is loyal to the divine model, having no use for modern innovators. This is my first effort in a protracted effort and with Bro. Williams' assistance we sowed some good seed in the Master's vineyard. I go from here to East Panther Creek in Calhoun Co., to lay the foundation and build the Church of Christ. I want to be in the field all winter and would like to hear from any one desiring my services. Address me at Nebo, Ill. HARRY WALSTON."

| Perry | Pike | | Haynes 361 details the congregation there. He gives no hint of a split. The congregation built its third building in 1880. Another example of conservatives working separately to establish congregations alongside progressives.

OR 37.17 April 24 1894 p 6: HGG reports from Perry, Ill. "…The Lord is blessing our efforts to build up a strong and loyal congregation here. Bro. Sommer's meetings here did us a great deal of good for which we thank the Lord." HGG gives the wording of the Church of Christ entry in the local church directory but no address is given, just the times for services.

OR 42.3 Jan 17 1899: 3. "The church at Perry, Ill., had recently the labors of Bro. A. L. Gepford, Findlay, Ill., who has made himself useful in the Master's cause. Also that good Bro. J. R. Bush, Parsons, Ill., has visited Perry and edified us with some true gospel sermons. These are two of the noble young brothers in Illinois who are set for the defense of the Master's cause. They desire to devote most of their time to the work of an evangelist. Call them out." [From "Along the Pathway" by D. W. Summers.]

Henry Griffin was a contributor to the OR from Perry.

https://www.findagrave.com/memorial/43711164/henry-g-griffin. Retrieved 1.21.2019. Listed in Ligon's Portraiture. (1865 – 1938). |
| Pleasant Mound | Vermilion | | OR 47.26 June 28 1904 p 3: Lorenzo Bennett reports from Georgetown on June 10, 1904 "…Bro. and Sister Perkins…came to visit the brethren at Pleasant Mound…Bro. Perkins having preached for us nearly fifteen years in days gone by. He began preaching for us at Pleasant Mound in April, 1886, closing his labors here in December, 1900…We rejoiced to see Bro. and Sister Perkins before leaving for their home in Chicago. Their address in the future will be 6341 Wash. Ave., Chicago, Ill." |

Preston	Ran-dolph or Rich-land		OR 38.2 Jan 8 1895 p 6: "Niantic, Ill., Jan. 1. - Elder J. O. Sutherland just closed a six weeks' meeting at Preston, Ill., with seventy-four additions, a full house and good interest. He set in order the church, and it is gone to work to build a house. They met in a hall. M. M. SUTHER-LAND." https://www.findagrave.com/memorial/134618296/jacob-o_-sutherland https://www.findagrave.com/memorial/37991904/martha-malissia-sutherland
			Preston congregation is not in Haynes.
			Biographical sketch of JOS on page 616: "Was born in Marion County, Ind., 1848. He worked at Patoka, Ill., where he began his ministry. He served the church at Sailor Springs and founded the churches at Latham, Riverton, Dawson and Morgansville. He is a plain, sincere man and good preacher, whose thirty years' work in the ministry has been fruitful."
Ramsey	Fayette		OR 49.16 Apr 17 1906 p 8: "Ramsey, Ill., Apr. 11- I am with a. dead congregation: they haven't broken the bread since about October last. We will meet next Lord's day to break bread (D. V.) I will try to start them to working the Lord's way. May the Lord help us all to be faithful. Chas. T. Cook."
			Haynes lists two Ramsey congregations, both in Fayette County: 198 Ramsey and 199 Union (Ramsey)

| Rushville | Schuyler | | OR 38.10 March 5 1895 p 6: "Brief Account of Affairs in Rushville, Illinois"

In second column, "The few brethren had now waited for over sixteen years for a settlement of the trouble and with no immediate prospect in view, Bro. S set a church in order in May, 1893."

OR 38.21 May 21 1895 p 1: DS reports on the end of the meeting at Rushville, stating also, "…the people had no desire for the unmixed gospel, and the preacher was not eloquent. But arrangements were made to buy a lot on which to build a meeting house."

OR 38.39 Sep 24 1895 p 1: DS says, "By the time that the meeting at Lamine, Mo., will draw to a close the new house at Rushville, Ill., will probably be finished, and I hope to be present at the opening thereof." |
| Samoth (Samouth once in Haynes) | Massac | | Haynes 323: "Samouth [sic]. Present membership, 40; Bible-school enrollment, 50. This is a union church."

OR 38.12 March 19 1895 p 3: "Samoth, Ill., Dec. 23, '91. *To all whom it may concern.* Inasmuch as it has been reported that the Church of Christ at Samoth, Ill., would not endorse Bro. J. F. Hight in religious debates, therefore, we, the officers of the Church of Christ at Samoth, Ill., of which Bro. Hight is a member in good standing, do endorse him to defend our teaching and practice with any fair and honorable opponent of any name, creed or doctrine in religion."

OR 39.46 Nov 17 1896 p 2: J. F. Hight reports on his debates with Baptist G. W. Smith at Azotus and Samoth, Illinois.

There are three other debates at Samoth listed in Haynes on 84, 85: Radcliffe-Caldwell (Baptist); Mecoy-Smith (Baptist); Kincaid-Smith (Baptist). |

Secor			OR 42.52 Dec 26 1899: 3. D. Collins reports. Had Mormon debates in KS. WF Cline held meeting there.
			Haynes 451: "The church finally divided on questions of opinion. In 1898 the conservatives received a deed to a lot that specifically pro-scribes the use or placing of any musical in-strument on the premises, the organizing of any societies of any kind, and the permission to preach in the house by any one who favors these prohibited things. That both congregations have maintained only a feeble life under all the circumstances is apparent."
Shel-byville			OR 54.39 Sep 26 1911 p 8: "Shelbyville, Ill., Sept. 17. - Our last 2 meetings have been our best—most encouraging. I have a class of chil-dren (9 to 15 years old) that I rejoice to see at each meeting. There are about 12 and their number has steadily increased. Tent meeting is bearing good fruit. If older ones would attend as well as children do we would have fair crowd. Must have another meeting this fall. Once we get going we ought easily to have good congre-gation in few years. So many "almost persuad-ed." - J. F. Williams."
			OR 55.30 July 23 1912 p 8: "Shelbyville, Ill., July 17. – Our new meeting house will be ready for plasterers ere this reaches O. R. readers (D. V.), but, although many brethren have helped liberally, we lack probably $300 of sufficient amount properly to complete our work…Jerry F. Williams, 2710 Walnut.
			OR 55.43 Oct 22 1912 p 3: W. F. Cline started a meeting; Gepford continued the meeting. No additions. Jesse F. Love also held a meeting. Williams pleas for help on the $500 balance on building.
			Jesse F. Love not in Haynes.
			https://www.findagrave.com/memorial/ 54174522/jesse-f-love. Retrieved 1.20.2019.

Spring Bay	Wood-ford	Par-tridge School House	OR 42.2 Jan 10 1899 p 5: D. Collins held Sommer style Bible Study. JJ Snyder reported. Complains that 'societyites' have church clerk sign letters of commendation (for people trans-ferring membership) rather than the elders.
St. Joseph	Cham-paign		Haynes 133 – 135: "Following the pastorate of Mr. Jones, a schism in the church occurred. This was encouraged and led by a former min-ister, J. W. Perkins. A suit at law followed, which resulted in according the property to those opposed to Mr. Perkins. Two years after this an organ was placed in the church and used...There is also a congregation of conserv-atives here." Heffley's timeline seems to vary.]

CLead 7.41 Oct 10 1893 p 12: George P. Slade reports, "Both of the congregations at St. Joseph, Champaign Co., Ill., are talking of be-ginning a protracted meeting about the fourth Lord's day in this month. Geo. P. Slade."

OR 34.21 May 21 1891 p 6: "Tuscola, Ill., May 9, '91. Two additions since last report. My work is divided this year with three churches—St. Joseph, Prairie Chapel and Brushy Fork. All are doing reasonably well. Your Bro. in Christ, D. W. Honn."

https://www.findagrave.com/memorial/144391219/daniel-william-honn
https://www.findagrave.com/memorial/74755979/peter-k_-honn

[Honn was from a family of Illinois preachers. See CS 1918 13 Apr 885 for a family portrait. The above are the only ones found in FAG as of 1.13.2019. DW Honn in Haynes, page 96; Prairie Union, near Kansas (Coles County) "has given Daniel K. Honn to the ministry." Error for Daniel W.? 148, 149. Additional Honns are on page 149 under Walnut Grove (Humboldt). None is in the CS list.]

			OR 38.53 Dec 31 1895: B. R. Heffley gives the history of the split at "St. Joe" in detail. Of most interest: "To be brief, Bro. Gregg [Harmon Gregg of Tuscola?] was driven out and Jones [from Homer] installed as 'pastor,' the organ introduced in the Sunday-school, thence into the worship of the Church. The fathers and mothers in Israel who had given of their means to build the house…were thrust out, the door locked against them and they driven from home." [More follows.] OR 39.51 Dec 22 1896 p 3: In "Briefs Here and There," J. W. Perkins says, "The Church of Christ, St. Joseph, Ill., is living in peace and gaining ground…The church has a comfortable house, centrally located, and protected from innovations, and the only one in the county which worships the Lord as the Bible directs." [Ironically, later in the article, Perkins praises the work of B. R. Heffley, who preaches for the Champaign congregation. Perhaps the Champaign congregation was not in existence? See following from H. C. Shaw. Perkins' statement, if correct, indicates how widespread instruments were at that time in Champaign County.]

			OR 46.14 Apr 7 1903 p 2: H. C. Shaw holds a meeting at St. Joseph. "But like many other bans of disciples, the spirit of the world found its way into the hearts of some, who like Judas were willing to sell their Lord. At night, the time that honest men should be asleep, they carried the organ into the house that others had built, and with their master, who took Jesus into the mountain, declared they owned the kingdom. To defend their claim they procured the assistance of one known as the Rev. Slade, whom Bro. Perkins met in debate, and gave him for his share of the spoils, what Goliath got from David...Bro. and Sister Edwards who live there [Champaign] were in attendance at almost every service. Sister Edwards leads the singing. On Lord's day Bro. and Sister Heffler [sic Heffley] of Champaign and several others were with us. Bro. Heffler [sic Heffley] is a brother who has preached some and is a kind, generous man."
Tamaroa	Perry		OR 55.16 Apr 16 1912 p 2: From De Soto, Ill., W. E. Dudley, in article dated April 3, reports on visits to several Illinois congregations: Holiday, March 16, 17th. Could not speak at Lower Ash Grove on March 20, 21 because of sleet Bruce March 22 – 25 Charleston Mattoon March 30, 31 "April 1 I spent with Bro. J. T. Warren, near Tamaroa, and found him isolated from any Gospel church, but strong in the faith and is now planning to have a meeting in his neighborhood."

On this trip, notwithstanding bad roads, I visited forty-eight homes, preached eleven discourses publicly and many privately to more
than 100 people, traveled 250 miles, walking
thirty, and was kindly remembered by brethren
in a substantial way, and take up the work here
again with renewed strength and courage. The
O. R. has done me a wonderful sight of good,
and I am not ashamed to put it into the hands of
my friends. There are many who contribute to
make it a success that deserve the approbation
of all fair-minded people for their fearlessness
in maintaining a pure Gospel.

Word come to me from Missouri that I will be
compelled to meet a 'religious specialist' on the
'rebaptism' question. I have no fears whatever,
so far as I am concerned, but feel greatly griev-
ed that conditions make it necessary to enter
into any public contention regarding it…I now
am in my fifty-third year and earnestly desire to
spend the remainder of my life in the work of
the Lord. – W. E. Dudley."

OR 55.21 May 21 1912 p 8: "De Soto, Ill, May
15. - Held 2 nights in a school-house 5 miles
southwest of Tamaroa. House full, interest
good. Promised them a meeting in June.
Prospect favorable to establish congregation
there. Go to Knightsville, Ind., D. V., May 18,
for meeting. - W. E. Dudley."

OR 55.32 Aug 6 1912 p 8: "DeSoto, Ill., July
30. - Closed meeting near Dexter the 28th with
a congregation of 10 set in order. I want to
make a correction in report of assistance sent
for work at Tamaroa: credit of $1 for Liberty
church should have been to John Hoke. Go to
Tamaroa tomorrow for over Lord's day; to
Marengo, Ind., Aug. 10. - W. E. Dudley."

Haynes 353, 354 lists two congregations with Tamaroa: Friendship, three miles west, and the one in Tamaroa proper. The latter might be the one Dudley mentions. "Present membership, 50; value of property, $3,000; Bible-school enrollment, 57."

OR 55.43 Oct 22 1912 p 3: Dudley has returned to Charleston. Reports on his efforts in southern Illinois in a lengthy article; excerpts are: "Have just been in the region of Tamaroa where much hard work has been done, and, thank God, I succeeded in getting a few names to agree to meet each Lord's day, three of them from the Christian (?) church, one baptized who was a member also of the Christian church but who was not satisfied that she was properly qualified to be baptized when she was. Hearing the Gospel in its simplicity led her to reflect that when she joined the Christian church she did so in a banter with other girls and was not convinced of her own accord by the preaching of the Word...Then Bro. J. T. Warren [sic possibly "J. W. Warren" is meant, since J. T. Warren is not one of the Sand Creek signatories.] (who was once an Elder of the church at 'sand Creek' and who was responsible for the work done by me in his neighborhood) took a stand to keep house for the Lord. Bro. Warren life has been the means of doing much toward enlightening the people of that community, and he was very anxious to provide an arrangement by which he would be favored with opportunity to worship God as he was in his former days with the dear old battle-scarred and persecuted church at 'sand Creek.'"

"A favorable prospect seems now to confront this little band, as they have the confidence of unbiased minds in that locality, and one of the elders of the Christian church there says we have got the sure foundation to stand upon..."

Toledo	Cumberland	Corinth	OR 51.50, Dec 15 1908 p 8: O. A. Timmons reports, "Dix, Ill., - Since my last report I visited the church in Olney, and preached one sermon on 'Church Identity,' Friday night, before the fifth Lord's day in November. On Saturday following I went to Toledo, and preached three times for the Corinth Church…" Haynes 171: "Corinth (Toledo). Organized 1876; present membership, 45; value of property, $900. Two miles southwest of Toledo." [No hint of conservatism but so little detail to rule out a conservative bent. Timmons' presence there hints conservatism.]
Trimble	Crawford	Union or New Light building	Not in Haynes. OR 34.6 Feb 5 1891 p 3: "Trimble, Ill., Jan. 8th 1891. Am in a meeting here for this week only. There is but one church house here, and that is a 'union' house. The so-called New Lights have an organization here, the only one in the community. Several persons of the Church of Christ have gone into this organization for a home (?) but they say there is so little milk, and no meat at all, in the soup dealt out to them through the ministers of the church that they are hungry for the old Jerusalem gospel they used to hear; and so while the writer was at Hutsonville, in this county, three weeks ago, they made arrangements for him to come and sow the good seed, expecting to reap a harvest 'bye and bye.' We are having good audiences and good attention, but the 'rank and file' of the New Lights, so called, are scared for fear of their craft…If sufficient strength should be developed the brethren will organize here. It would be hard on the New Lights, so called."

*Villa Grove	Douglas		OR 51.25 June 23 1908 p 8: "Charleston, Ill., June 15 – Brothers Cuppy and Towles are in a tent meeting at Mattoon and are doing some good. One addition so far. Brother Cuppy and I are intending to hold a tent meeting at Bruce in July. A very favorable prospect is before us to do some good there. The people are eager to hear the plain preaching of the gospel. Nothing else will supply the real needs of sinful man. There is no Church of Christ there. Brothers Cuppy and D. A. Sommer expect to be at Villa Grove, with the tent, the first part of July, and the latter part of August in Sullivan. An inviting field is open for seed sowing, but the reapers are few. We pray much good may be done from this contemplated work. W. E. Dudley." Haynes 182: "Organized 1906, by Harold E. Monser; present membership, 110; value of property, $7,000; Bible school began 1906; present enrollment, 142. Mr. Monser was sent here by the mission board of the Sixth District, and conducted a four weeks' meeting in a tent. During the half-time service of R. L. Cartwright the house was built by the help of the Church Extension Society. The town depends for its life chiefly on railroad work, and the church has been pastorless part of the time, hence has not flourished. Dr. G. L. Kennedy is the clerk." https://www.findagrave.com/memorial/ 193397449/robert-lee-cartwright. Retrieved 1.19.2019. (1866 – 1945)
Westfield	Coles	Brick	Haynes 146: "This church is located about twelve miles southeast of Charleston. It is under the direction of the ultra-conservatives and has monthly preaching."

Appendix 4: Illinois Conservative Preachers/Congregations Mentioned in Haynes &
Conservative Papers

Westville	Vermil-ion		Haynes 414: "This church was first organized on the site of Westville. It grew to a membership of four hundred and exercised a wide influence for good in the surrounding community. Then a strong ultra-conservative preacher was engaged to serve the congregation. Under his teaching, in six years it sickened and died, and its members were scattered to the four winds."
Wilborn	Shelby	Wilborn Creek	"John [Roney] was an active member of Wilborn Creek Christian Church, serving on the committee to erect the church building 1867-1871. Several of John's children were baptized in Wilborn Creek and attended Wilborn Creek Church until its demise." http://carefree.com/genealogy/biographies/RoneyFamilyHistoryAndGenealogy_1690-1972.pdf. Retrieved 1.16.2019 OR 40.9 Mar 2 1897 p 6: "Sister Gaddis was baptized into Christ by Elder Bushrod Henry, about 55 years ago and was a charter member of the Church of Christ at Wilbern Creek, four miles north of here." OR 42.18 May 2 1899 p 6: "He [George Cavender] confessed faith in the Savior and was immersed by Bro. Haulman, Oct. 14, 1883, and has been a member of the Wilber Creek congregation since that date except while in Oregon, when he moved his membership by letter to that State...The funeral occurred Tuesday, April 18, 1899, and was held in Wilbern Creek meeting house where he loved so well to meet to worship God."

Windsor	Shelby	New Liberty	OR 42.52 Dec 26 1899: 8. Samuel Piety, writing from Duvall, mentions meeting at New Liberty.
			OR 42.6 Feb 7 1899: 5. Nance reports the congregation has a new chapel.
			Haynes 389, 390: "The resident members formed part of the Sand Creek Church till 1871, when a separate congregation, called Wolf Creek, was formed. The log house had then disappeared, for meetings were held in the Dodson and Baker Schoolhouses till 1874, when a chapel was built The name was then changed to New Liberty. It gave Jesse Baugher to the ministry. About 1880, under the lead of P. P. Warren, it became ultra-conservative."

| Windsor | Shelby | Sand Creek | OR 42.10 Mar 7 1899:6 J. V. Brady in "Reflections" "We are only preaching at one regular point this winter. This is at Sand Creek, Ill., where we have labored regularly for the past three years. This, with some transient work, is the amount of our preaching for the winter. For the past two years we have been doing what we could in preaching a great part of the time in destitute places, until, like Paul, we must give attention to temporal things for the welfare of our family."

Haynes 390, 391: "Peace and prosperity continued till 1889, when Min. Daniel Sommer came and began an aggressive opposition to the use of instrumental music in public worship and other "innovations." This church had never used an organ and had no thought of introducing one until the preaching of Mr. Sommer created a desire and a demand for its introduction. [391] This led to a division in 1904 and to a suit at law for the property. This was decided by the State Supreme Court at the October term, 1905, in favor of the conservatives, they being the majority. It was here that the pigmy and disloyal "Address and Declaration" was issued in 1889 (see Chap. VIII.). By that act this church wrote "Ichabod" in large letters upon its record.

Those members who protested against these puerile proceedings have since then conducted public worship and work in a near-by schoolhouse. They have been faithful and blessed of God." |
| Xenia | Clay | Xenia | Haynes 146: "The congregation prospered and did good service in its earlier years. Then a period of wars, led by ultra-conservatives, set in and crippled its usefulness for a long time. At present there are some signs of better days." [Organized in 1865. Wars would have been during Sommer's influence?]

OR 49.8 Feb 20 1906: 6: S. A. Walker writes from Xenia, Ill. |

Xenia	Clay	Old Union	OR 50.46 Nov 12 1907: 8: "Xenia, Nov.7 – Twenty-two added to the Old Union congregation. S. A. Walker"
			OR 50.47 Nov 19 1907 3: "Xenia, Ill.
			To the O. R. Family: Rejoice with us in the triumphs of the truth of Christ. In this part of the state of Illinois (Clay Co.), there was not one congregation that could truthfully be called the church of Christ. The Old Union congregation, being free from innovations, was the nearest New Testament congregation in the county; it, however, being divided by one of the elders being satisfied with what is written and the other one opposing with might and main the doctrine of Christ. Also a state of contention existed through 'preacherism.' [More details about a meeting held by O. M. Davis.] S. A. Walker."
Yale	Jasper		OR 54.16 April 18 1911 p 8: "Kemp, Ill., April 6. - Preached over Lord's day and till Tuesday night at Yale. A new congregation. We are getting several new ones in Illinois. I think there will be about 4 new houses built in this part of the State this summer. Am well pleased with outlook at Yale. Going to build up a good congregation. They, like Jewett, have men and women of influence. Brethren at Yale will build this summer. Restrictive Clause in their deed. Fine people. I promised to visit them again. Begin at Cowden the 15th. – *W. G. Roberts*."
			Yale is not in Haynes.
Zion (Todd's Point Township)	Shelby		Haynes 386: "Min. B. R. Gilbert organized the Zion congregation on the west side of Todd's Point Township in 1878 with thirty-two members. The same year a chapel costing $1,200 was built. The church met regularly for worship on the Lord's Days and maintained a mid-week prayer-meeting. It died of conservatism."

About the Authors

James L. McMillan grew up a preacher's kid in western Colorado. He attended Colorado State College and received degrees from Ozark Bible College and the University of Illinois Urbana-Champaign. From 1970 – 1995 he preached for non-denominational Christian Churches and taught at Ozark Bible College, Mid-South Christian College, and the University of Illinois Urbana-Champaign. From 1995 – 2019 he worked in Information Technology. As of April 2019 he is Archival Associate with the Disciples of Christ Historical Society, Bethany, WV.

Thomas H. Olbricht grew up in Southern Missouri. He attended Harding University and received degrees at Northern Illinois University, the University of Iowa, and Harvard Divinity School. Olbricht commenced preaching in 1948 in small congregations in Arkansas and Missouri. In 1948 he helped found a Church of Christ in DeKalb, Illinois, where he served as the full time minister in 1949-51. Olbricht has published books and essays on Biblical theology, rhetoric and church history, especially on the American Restoration Movement. He has taught at Harding, the University of Dubuque, Abilene Christian, and Pepperdine University.

About the Publisher

Sulis International Press publishes select fiction and nonfiction in a variety of genres under four imprints: Riversong Books, Sulis Academic Press, Sulis Press, and Keledei Publications.

For more, visit the website at
https://sulisinternational.com

Subscribe to the newsletter at
https://sulisinternational.com/subscribe/

Follow on social media
https://www.facebook.com/SulisInternational
https://twitter.com/Sulis_Intl
https://www.pinterest.com/Sulis_Intl/
https://www.instagram.com/sulis_international/

Index of People

Adams, Harold. 89, 94, 190, 192
Agassiz, Louis, 248
Akenson, Donald H., 247
Akers, Peter, 144
Alden, Edwin, 306
Aldridge, William, 15
Alkire, Adam, 91,
Alkire, Barton W., 83
Alkire, Catherine, 83
Alkire, Deborah, 83
Alkire, Dolly. 83
Alkire, Elizabeth
Alkire, George, 43-45, 69. 75. 76, 81. 90-98
Alkire, Harmonus II, 82
Alkire, Harmonus, 83, 84
Alkire, John. 83. 84, 87
Alkire, Maunis, 83
Alkire, Michael, 83. 85
Alkire, Sarah. 83. 85
Alkire, William. 83
Allen, C. Leonard, 203. 221, 225
Allen, Ethan. 269
Allen, J. M.., 261
Ames, Edward Scribner, 297-300
Ames, Van Meter, 298
Anderson, H. T., 218,
Arnold, Charley Harvey, 281-2
Arnold, Luther, 319
Arny, William Frederick Milton, 104-06 319-20, 344
Ashley, Harry, 90
Ashley, William, 78
Atkinson, Jonathan, 175, 191, 194, 197-8, 212
Axel, Larry E., 282

Babcock, Rufus, 181
Babcock-Hale, Clara Cesleste, 151
Bacon, Benjamin W., 276
Badger, Joseph, 3, 44-5, 85, 88, 90, 273, 337
Badgley, David, 20
Baker, Daniel, 311
Baker, Jesse, 311
Baker, W. K., 311
Bakewell, E. W., 213
Balch, Laura Dickey, 113
Baldwin, M. H., 113, 116, 394-5
Ballou, Hosea, 272
Baltzell, John, 181
Banta, Frances Irene, 151
Barney, William, 14-5
Barton, William Eleazar, 147
Bateman, Newton, 50, 351
Bates, Daniel, 53. 96, 205-6
Beckelhymer, Isaac, 152
Becker, Edwin L., 297
Beecher, Edward, 247
Beecher, Henry Ward, 247, 253
Beecher, Lyman, 254, 278
Belshe, E. P., 156-7, 160, 235-8
Benjamin, Robert L., 107, 109
Bennett, John Cook, 154
Bennett, Mary, 154
Berger, Abraham, 50
Berkowitz, Aaron, 315
Berry, T. V., 243
Biggers, Jeff, 318
Bittle, L. F., 232
Bizzle, Isaac., 181
Black, W. F., 31
Blackburn, Andrew Jackson. 323-4

Chamberlain, R. M., 324
Chance, Joseph, 20
Chandler, Riley, 109
Channing, William Ellery, 272-4
Charnock, Leonard W. H., 190
Chase, J. Richard, 254
Chatterton, Aaron, 167, 214, 216
Cherbury, Herbert, 269
Choate, J. E., 228, 231-2
Chrisman, B. H., 44, 86
Christensen, Ken, 104-5, 243, 320, 360
Christian, Persis L., 153
Churchill, Craig, 28
Clark, George Rogers, 19
Clark, Henrietta, 153
Clark, John, 18
Clark, Watson, 107-8
Claypool, Andrew, 109-10
Claypool, David, 109
Clough, Simon, 3
Coleman, Keith, 255
Coleridge, Samuel Taylor, 210
Coletta, Paolo Enrico, 270
Combs, Michael, 108
Conover, R., 189
Conover, Robert, 189
Cook, A. R., 325
Cooley, Lathrop. 113
Cooper. Anderson, 319
Cordery, Simon, 16
Corrington, Wesley, 148
Cory, David, 112
Cosat, J. J., 109-10, 386
Cotterill, Thomas, 90
Courson, Gussie, 153
Cousin, Victor, 210, 218-9, 213
Craig, E. L., 54, 158, 163, 166-9, 214, 218, 232, 238
Cramer, Mary Alkire, 82
Crank, J. R., 151

Crawford, S. J., 153
Creasy, William Charles, 155
Creath, Jacob, Jr., 28, 115
Creighton, Peden, 31, 279, 297
Crenshaw, T. A., 305
Crouch, Rachel Derrick, 151, 153
Cully, Workman, 38
Cummins, D. Duane, 172, 174-5, 188, 190, 194, 196, 198, 346
Curtiss, Zarah, 45, 89, 91
Dangerfield, Rachel, 151-2
Darby, John Nelson, 247
Darrow, Clarence, 269-71
Darst, John, Mrs., 153
Darwin, Charles, 248-9, 258-9
Daugherty, Nellie Burchart, 151
Davenport, William, 33, 69, 113, 184-5
Davidson, Annie E., 153
Davidson, Clara L., 153
Davie, Winstead P., 181-3
Dawson, N., 44, 86
Dawson, W. C., 219
De Hass. Dr., 18
Debs, Eugene V., 271
Deen, George, 326
DeGroot, A. T., 294, 296, 346
Dennis, Minnie, 153
Derrick, Neil, 151
Deweese, Nimrod, 191
Dewey, John, 298
Dickerson, Francis, 50
Dickinson, William, 45, 89
Dingman, Wesley, 202, 211-2, 217, 225
Dixon, Amzi Clarence, 245, 249, 252-3
Dorrien, Gary J., 276
Douglas, Stephen, 65
Doyle, D. H., 193-4. 211, 216. 222
Drollinger, William, 108

Scott, Lucy, 100, 147

Scott, Walter, 4, 7-8, 46, 174, 177, 179, 262, 290

Scott, William, 18

Seale, James M., 171

Seay, Scott D., 300

Secrest, John, 46

Seevers, Benjamin, 44

Shaw, Elijah, 59, 85, 87

Shaw, James, 192

Shelton, T. J., 152

Shepard, Emmons, 33, 69

Sherer, David, 108

Sherer, Elizabeth, 108

Sherer, John, 108

Shockley, W. S., 107-8

Shreve, Henry, 14

Sikes, Walter, 203, 214, 221

Simpson, James, 191

Sinks, P. W., 38

Skinner, Adolphos, Skinner

Small, Albion W., 282, 286

Smart, J. H., 152

Smedley, Hiram, 38

Smith, C. C., 314

Smith, Elias, 3, 6, 85, 89, 272-3, 336-7

Smith, Frank, 269

Smith, George Washington, 51, 181-2

Smith, Gerald Birney, 281-2

Smith, James, 19, 20, 91

Smith, John E., 282

Smith, Joseph, 25, 63, 345

Smith, Raccoon John, 62, 90

Smith, Samuel R., 185

Sommer, Daniel, 55, 118, 232, 245, 301-302, 305-307, 359, 380, 415. 425

Sommer, John, 304

Sommer, Magdalena Wyman, 304

Spencer, Claude, 10, 155, 198, 314

Spencer, Daniel, 181

Spicer, Eliza Martin, 108

Spinka, Matthew, 30

Spurgeon, Charles, 253

Staggs, Jan, 313, 319-20

Stark, Elizabeth, 57

Stark, Robert, 57

Stark. James, 57

Stark. John, 57

Stevens, Benedict, 33, 69

Stevens, William Arnold, 283-5

Stevenson, Dwight E., 172

Stewart, Clark E., 102

Stewart. Lyman, 353

Stewart. Milton, 253

Stipp, T. L., 109

Stone, Barton W., 1, 4, 35, 39, 44, 52. 58, 61, 71, 73, 75, 77, 85, 89, 90, 96, 101, 156, 161, 173-4, 178-9, 185, 187, 201, 211, 229, 235, 238, 264, 315,

Stone, John Timothy, 245

Storm, W. H., 151

Storm, William R., 311

Story, J. E., 152

Strictland, W. P., 78

Summerbell, J. J., 38, 54, 199

Summerbell, Nicholas, 38, 54

Sunday, Billy, 245, 256-7

Sweeney, John S., 17, 54, 116-7, 163, 167-8, 175, 194, 201, 212, 214-5, 217, 220-1, 225   390, 405

Sweeney, Z. T., 175, 198, 205, 212, 215, 217, 220-1, 225, 382

Sweet, Theophilus, 52

Taggart, Joseph J., 185

Tait, George, 212, 222

Tandy, H. P., 152

Index of Places

The place names in the alphabetized charts, for the most part, are not indexed here.

Made in the USA
Coppell, TX
13 January 2022

71535891R00267